RETAIL MANAGEMENT

Dr. A. Mustafa
Professor
Institute of Management Studies
RVS, College of Engineering and Technology
Dindigul - 624005

Himalaya Publishing House
ISO 9001:2015 CERTIFIED

First Edition : 2013
Edition : 2020

Published by : Mrs. Meena Pandey for **Himalaya Publishing House Pvt. Ltd.,**
"Ramdoot", Dr. Bhalerao Marg, Girgaon, Mumbai - 400 004.
Phone: 022-23860170, 23863863; **Fax:** 022-23877178
E-mail: himpub@bharatmail.co.in; **Website:** www.himpub.com

Branch Offices :

New Delhi : "Pooja Apartments", 4-B, Murari Lal Street, Ansari Road, Darya Ganj, New Delhi - 110 002.
Phone: 011-23270392, 23278631; Fax: 011-23256286

Nagpur : Kundanlal Chandak Industrial Estate, Ghat Road, Nagpur - 440 018.
Phone: 0712-2721215, 3296733; Telefax: 0712-2721216

Bengaluru : Plot No. 91-33, 2nd Main Road, Seshadripuram, Behind Nataraja Theatre,
Bengaluru - 560 020. Phone: 080-41138821; Mobile: 09379847017, 09379847005

Hyderabad : No. 3-4-184, Lingampally, Besides Raghavendra Swamy Matham, Kachiguda,
Hyderabad - 500 027. Phone: 040-27560041, 27550139

Chennai : New No. 48/2, Old No. 28/2, Ground Floor, Sarangapani Street, T. Nagar,
Chennai - 600 017. Mobile: 09380460419

Pune : "Laksha" Apartment, First Floor, No. 527, Mehunpura,
Shaniwarpeth (Near Prabhat Theatre), Pune - 411 030.
Phone: 020-24496323, 24496333; Mobile: 09370579333

Lucknow : House No. 731, Shekhupura Colony, Near B.D. Convent School, Aliganj,
Lucknow - 226 022. Phone: 0522-4012353; Mobile: 09307501549

Ahmedabad : 114, "SHAIL", 1st Floor, Opp. Madhu Sudan House, C.G. Road, Navrang Pura,
Ahmedabad - 380 009. Phone: 079-26560126; Mobile: 09377088847

Ernakulam : 39/176 (New No. 60/251), 1st Floor, Karikkamuri Road, Ernakulam,
Kochi - 682 011. Phone: 0484-2378012, 2378016; Mobile: 09387122121

Cuttack : New LIC Colony, Behind Kamala Mandap, Badambadi,
Cuttack - 753 012, Odisha. Mobile: 09338746007

Kolkata : 108/4, Beliaghata Main Road, Near ID Hospital, Opp. SBI Bank,
Kolkata - 700 010. Phone: 033-32449649; Mobile: 07439040301

DTP by : Page Designers, Bengaluru

Printed at : Trinity Academy, Mumbai. On behalf of HPH.

PREFACE

Retailing is the backbone of our economy. Big, medium and small business houses are very much involved in building their retail activities. I have referred to more than eighty sources including books, journals, articles and websites to write updated this book. Updated facts and figures are strenuously and tirelessly collected to fulfil the expectations of the readers. Global level and national level retailers and their strategies are presented in simple and lucid style for better understanding. I thank the publisher for having brought out this book attractively with aesthetic features.

Prof. Dr. A. Mustafa

CONTENTS

CHAPTER 1

Introduction

Marketing is an integrated communications-based process through which individuals and communities are informed or persuaded that existing and newly-identified needs and wants may be satisfied by the products and services of others. Marketing is a set of processes that are interconnected and interdependent with other functions, whose methods can be improved using a variety of relatively new approaches.

Marketing is used to create the customer, to keep the customer and to satisfy the customer. With the customer as the focus of its activities, it can be concluded that Marketing is one of the premier components of Business Management. The other being Operations (or Production). Other services and management activities such as Human Resources, Accounting, Law and Legal aspects can be "bought in" or "contracted out".

Marketing is defined by the American Marketing Association as the activity, set of institutions, and processes for creating, communicating, delivering, and exchanging offerings that have value for customers, clients, partners, and society at large. The term developed is from the original meaning which referred literally to going to a market to buy or sell goods or services.

The Chartered Institute of Marketing defines marketing as "The management process responsible for identifying, anticipating and satisfying customer requirements profitably".

Marketing practice is tended to be seen as a creative industry in the past, which included advertising, distribution and selling. However, because the academic study of marketing makes extensive use of social sciences, psychology, sociology, mathematics, economics, anthropology and neuroscience, the profession is now widely recognized as a science, allowing numerous universities to offer MBA programme. The overall process starts with marketing research and goes through market segmentation, business planning and execution, ending with pre and post-sales promotional activities. It is also related to many of the creative arts. The marketing literature is also adept at reinventing itself and its vocabulary according to the times and the culture.

The Marketing Concept

The term *marketing concept* pertains to the fundamental premise of modern marketing. This concept proposes that in order to satisfy its organizational objectives, an organization should anticipate the needs and wants of consumers and satisfy these more effectively than competitors.

Marketing Orientations

An orientation, in the marketing context, relates to a perception or attitude a firm holds towards its product or service, essentially concerning consumers and end-users. There exist several common orientations:

Product Orientation

A firm employing a product orientation is chiefly concerned with the quality of its own product. A firm would also assume that as long as its product was of a high standard, people would buy and consume the product.

This works most effectively when the firm has good insights about customers and their needs and desire as for example in the case of Sony Walkman or Apple iPod, whether these derive from intuitions or research.

Sales Orientation

A firm using a sales orientation focuses primarily on the selling/promotion of a particular product, and not determining new consumer desires as such. Consequently, this entails simply selling an already existing product, and using promotion techniques to attain the highest sales possible.

Such an orientation may suit scenarios in which a firm holds dead stock, or otherwise sells a product that is in high demand, with little likelihood of changes in consumer tastes diminishing demand.

Production Orientation

A firm focusing on a production orientation specializes in producing as much as possible of a given product or service. Thus, this signifies a firm exploiting economies of scale, until the minimum efficient scale is reached.

A production orientation may be deployed when a high demand for a product or service exists, coupled with a good certainty that consumer tastes do not rapidly alter (similar to the sales orientation).

Marketing Orientation

The marketing orientation is perhaps the most common orientation used in contemporary marketing. It involves a firm essentially basing its marketing plans around the marketing concept, and thus, supplying products to suit new consumer tastes.

As an example, a firm would employ market research to gauge consumer desires, use R&D to develop a product attuned to the revealed information, and then utilize promotion techniques to ensure persons know the product exists. The marketing orientation often has the following prime facets:

Organizational Orientation

In this sense, a firm's marketing department is often seen as of prime importance within the functional level of an organization.

Information from an organization's marketing department would be used to guide the actions of other departments within the firm. As an example, a marketing department could ascertain (via marketing research) that consumers desired a new type of product, or a new usage for an existing product. With this in mind, the marketing department would inform the R&D department to create a prototype of a product/service based on consumers' new desires.

The production department would then start to manufacture the product, while the marketing department would focus on the promotion, distribution, pricing, etc., of the product. Additionally, a firm's finance department would be consulted, with respect to securing appropriate funding for the development, production and promotion of the product.

Interdepartmental conflicts may occur, should a firm adhere to the marketing orientation? Production may oppose the installation, support and servicing of new capital stock, which may be needed to manufacture a new product. Finance may oppose the required capital expenditure, since it could undermine a healthy cash flow for the organization.

Mutually Beneficial Exchange

In a transaction in the market economy, the firms gain revenue, which leads to more profits/market share/sales. A consumer on the other hand gains the satisfaction of a need/want, utility, reliability and value for money from the purchase of a product or service. As no one has to buy goods from any one supplier in the market economy, firms must entice consumers to buy goods with contemporary marketing ideals.

The Four Ps

In the early 1960s, Professor Neil Borden at Harvard Business School identified a number of company performance actions that can influence the consumer decision to purchase goods or services. Borden suggested that all those actions of the company represented a "Marketing Mix". Professor E. Jerome McCarthy, at the Michigan State University in the early 1960s, suggested that the Marketing Mix contained four elements: product, price, place and promotion.

Product

The product aspects of marketing deal with the specifications of the actual goods or services, and how it relates to the end-user's needs and wants. The scope of a product generally includes supporting elements such as warranties, guarantees and support.

Pricing

This refers to the process of setting a price for a product, including discounts. The price need not be monetary; it can simply be what is exchanged for the product or services, e.g., time, energy or attention. Methods of setting prices optimally are in the domain of pricing science.

Placement (or Distribution)

This refers to how the product gets to the customer; for example, point-of-sale placement or retailing. This third 'P' has also sometimes been called *Place*, referring to the channel by which a product or service is sold (e.g., online vs. retail), which geographic region or industry, to which segment (young adults, families, business people), etc., also referring to how the environment in which the product is sold can affect the sales.

These four elements are often referred to as the marketing mix, which a marketer can use to craft a marketing plan.

The four Ps model is most useful when marketing low value consumer products. Industrial products, services, high value consumer products require adjustments to this model. Services marketing must account for the unique nature of services.

Industrial or B2B marketing must account for the long-term contractual agreements that are typical in supply chain transactions. Relationship marketing attempts to do this by looking at marketing from a long-term relationship perspective rather than individual transactions.

As a counter to this, Morgan, in *Riding the Waves of Change* (Jossey-Bass, 1988), suggests that one of the greatest limitations of the four Ps approach "is that it unconsciously emphasizes the inside-out view (looking from the company outwards), whereas the essence of marketing should be the outside-in approach".

Four Ps – Product, Price, Place, (Physical Distribution) and Promotion

In order to recognize the different aspects of selling **services**, as opposed to **Products**, a further. Three Ps were added to make a range of Seven Ps for service industries:

Process – the way in which orders are handled, customers are satisfied and the service is delivered.

Physical Evidence – is tangible evidence of the service, customers will receive (for example, a holiday brochure).

People – the people meeting and dealing with the customers.

As markets have become more satisfied, the seven Ps have become relevant to those companies selling products, as well as those solely involved with services: customers now differentiate between sellers of goods by the service they receive in the process from the people involved.

Some authors cite a further P – **Packaging** – this is thought by many to be part of **Product**, but in certain markets (Japan, China for example) and with certain products (perfume, cosmetics) the packaging of a product has a greater importance – may be even than the product itself.

According to one expert, there are Five Ps, namely: (1) People and perfection, (2) Professionalism and production, (3) Performance and production, (4) Perspective and personality, and (5) Peace and prosperity.

Marketing Research

Marketing research involves conducting research to support marketing activities, and the statistical interpretation of data into information. This information is then used by managers to plan marketing activities, gauge the nature of a firm's marketing environment, attain information from suppliers, etc.

A distinction should be made between ***marketing*** research and ***market*** research. Market research pertains to research in a given market. As an example, a firm may conduct research in a target market, after selecting a suitable market segment. In contrast, marketing research relates to all research conducted within marketing. Thus, market research is a subset of marketing research.

Marketing researchers use statistical methods (such as quantitative research, qualitative research, hypothesis tests, Chi-squared tests, linear regression, correlation coefficient, frequency distributions, Poisson and Binomial distributions, etc.), to interpret their findings and convert data into information.

A brand is a name, term, design, symbol, or other feature that distinguishes products and services from competitive offerings. A brand is more than a name, design or symbol. Brand reflects personality of the company which is organizational culture.

A brand has also been defined as an identifiable entity that makes a specific value, based on promises made and kept either actively or passively.

Branding means to create a reference of certain products in mind.

Co-branding involves marketing activity involving two or more products.

Marketing Communications

Marketing communications is defined by actions a firm takes to communicate with end-users, consumers and external parties. Marketing communications encompasses four distinct subsets, which are:

Personal Sales

Oral presentation is given by salespersons who approach individuals or a group of potential customers:

- Live, interactive relationship
- Personal interest
- Attention and response
- Interesting presentation
- Clear and thorough.

Public Relations

Public relations (or PR, as an acronym) is the use of media tools by a firm in order to promote goodwill from an organization to a target market segment, or other consumers of a firm's goods/services. PR stems from the fact that a firm cannot seek to antagonize or inflame its market base, due to incurring a lessened demand for its goods/services. Organizations undertake PR in order to assure consumers, and to forestall negative perceptions towards it.

PR can span:

- Interviews
- Speeches/Presentations
- Corporate literature, such as financial statements, brochures, etc.

Marketing Communications "mix"

Marketing communications is a "sub-mix" within the promotion aspect of the marketing mix, as the exact nature of how to apply marketing communications depends on the nature of the product in question.

Accordingly, a given product would require a unique communications mix, in order to convey successfully information to consumers. Some products may require a stronger emphasis on personal sales, while others may require more focus on advertising.

Marketing Planning

The area of marketing planning involves forging a plan for a firm's marketing activities. A marketing plan can also pertain to a specific product, as well as to an organization's overall marketing strategy.

Generally speaking, an organization's marketing planning process is derived from its overall business strategy. Thus, when top management are devising the firm's strategic direction/mission, the intended marketing activities are incorporated into this plan.

Promotional Mix

It is a combination of 'pull-push' strategy to motivate consumers, trade-people, and the sales force simultaneously in transacting sales.

"Pull" promotion – sampling, coupons, price-packs, rebates, contests, sweepstakes, tie-in-promotion, financing incentives, special events, premiums, bonus packs and exchange offer.

"Push" promotion – (Offered to traders) – discounts, display allowance, advertising allowance, free goods, contests, trade coupons, and quality discounts.

Offered by retailer: price-cuts, free goods, premiums, displays, feature advertising, quantity discounts and clearance sale.

Marketing Planning Process

Within the overall strategic marketing plan, the stages of the process are listed as thus:

- Mission Statement
- Corporate Objectives
- Marketing Audit
- SWOT analysis
- Assumptions arising from the Audit and SWOT analysis
- Marketing objectives derived from the assumptions
- An estimation of the expected results of the objectives
- Identification of alternative plans/mixes
- Budgeting for the marketing plan
- A first-year implementation programme

Levels of Marketing Objectives within an Organization

As stated previously, the senior management of a firm would formulate a general business strategy for a firm. However, this general business strategy would be interpreted and implemented in different contexts throughout the firm.

Corporate

Corporate marketing objectives are typically broad-based in nature, and pertain to the general. For an example, from one picture of a group of companies (or a conglomerate), top management may state that sales for the group should increase by 25 per cent over a ten-year period.

Strategic Business Unit

Strategic business unit (SBU), in this case, means strategic business unit. An SBU is a subsidiary within a firm, which participates within a given market/industry. The SBU would embrace the corporate strategy, and attune it to its own particular industry. For instance, an SBU may partake in the sports goods industry. It thus, would ascertain how it would attain additional sales of sports goods, in order to satisfy the overall business strategy.

Functional

The functional level relates to departments within the SBUs, such as marketing, finance, HR, production, etc. The functional level would adopt the SBU's strategy and determine how to accomplish the SBU's own objectives in its market.

To use the example of the sports goods industry again, the marketing department would draw up marketing plans, strategies and communications to help the SBU achieve its marketing aims.

Customer Focus

Many companies today have a customer focus (or market orientation). This implies that the company focuses its activities and products on consumer demands. Generally, there are three ways of doing this: the customer-driven approach, the sense of identifying market changes and the product innovation approach.

In the consumer-driven approach, consumer wants are the drivers of all strategic marketing decisions. No strategy is pursued until it passes the test of consumer research. Every aspect of a market offering, including the nature of the product itself, is driven by the needs of potential consumers. The starting point is always the consumer. The rationale for this approach is that there is no point spending R&D funds developing products that people will not buy. History attests to many products that were commercial failures in spite of being technological breakthroughs.

A formal approach to this customer-focused marketing is known as SIVA (Solution, Information, Value, Access). This system is basically the four Ps renamed and reworded to provide a customer focus.

The SIVA Model provides a demand/customer centric version alternative to the well known Four Ps supply side model (product, price, place, promotion) of marketing management.

Table 1 : SIVA Model

Product	→	**Solution**
Promotion	→	**Information**
Price	→	**Value**
Placement	→	**Access**

Product Focus

In a product innovation approach, the company pursues product innovation, then tries to develop a market for the product. Product innovation drives the process and marketing research is conducted primarily to ensure that profitable market segment(s) exist for the innovation. The rationale is that customers may not know what options will be available to them in the future so we should not expect them to tell us what they will buy in the future. However, marketers can aggressively over-pursue product innovation and try to overcapitalize on a niche. When pursuing a product innovation approach, marketers must ensure that they have a varied and multi-tiered approach to product innovation. It is claimed that if Thomas Edison depended on marketing research he would have produced larger candles rather than inventing light bulbs. Many firms, such as research and development focused companies, successfully focus on product innovation. Many purists doubt whether this is really a form of marketing orientation at all, because of the ex-post status of consumer research. Some even question whether it is marketing.

- An emerging area of study and practice concerns internal marketing, or how employees are trained and managed to deliver the brand in a way that positively impacts the acquisition and retention of customers (employer branding).
- Diffusion of innovations research explores how and why people adopt new products, services and ideas.
- A relatively new form of marketing uses the internet and is called internet marketing or more generally e-marketing, affiliate marketing, desktop advertising or online marketing. It tries to perfect the segmentation strategy used in traditional marketing. It targets its audience more precisely, and is sometimes called personalized marketing or one-to-one marketing.
- With consumers' eroding attention span and willingness to give time to advertising messages, marketers are turning to forms of permission marketing such as branded content, custom media and reality marketing.
- The use of herd behaviour in marketing.

The Economist reported a recent conference in Rome on the subject of the simulation of adaptive human behaviour. It shared mechanisms to increase impulse buying and get people "to buy more by playing on the herd instinct". The basic idea is that people will buy more of products that are seen to be popular, and several feedback mechanisms to get product popularity information to consumers are mentioned, including smart-card technology and the use of Radio Frequency Identification Tag technology. A "swarm-moves" model was introduced by a Florida Institute of Technology researcher, which is appealing to supermarkets because it can "increase sales without the need to give people discounts".

Marketing is also used to promote business' products and is a great way to promote the business.

Other recent studies on the "power of social influence" include an "artificial music market in which some 14,000 people downloaded previously unknown songs" (Columbia University, New York); a Japanese chain of convenience stores which orders its products based on "sales data from departmental stores and research companies"; a Massachusetts company exploiting knowledge of social networking to improve sales; and online retailers who are increasingly informing consumers about "which products are popular with like-minded consumers" (e.g., Amazon, eBay).

Areas of Marketing Specialization

- Agricultural marketing
- Advertising and branding
- Communications
- Customer relationship management (CRM)
- Database marketing
- Professional selling
- Direct marketing
- Ethical marketing
- Event organization
- Experiential marketing
- Global marketing
- Guerrilla marketing
- Integrated marketing
- International marketing
- Internet marketing
- Industrial marketing
- Market research
- Marketing strategy
- Marketing plan
- Political marketing
- Product marketing
- Promotional education
- Proximity marketing
- Public marketing
- Retailing
- Search engine marketing
- Segmentation
- Shopper marketing
- Social media marketing
- Sponsorship
- Strategic management
- Wholesale marketing

The Marketing Environment

The term "marketing environment" relates to all of the factors (whether internal, external, direct or indirect) that affect a firm's marketing decision making/planning. A firm's marketing environment consists of three main areas, which are:

- The macro-environment, over which a firm holds little control
- The micro-environment, over which a firm holds a greater amount (though not necessarily total) control

Retailing Environment

- A retailing environment consists of the actors and forces that affect a retailer's ability to build and maintain successful relationships with target customers.
- Micro-environment
- Macro-environment

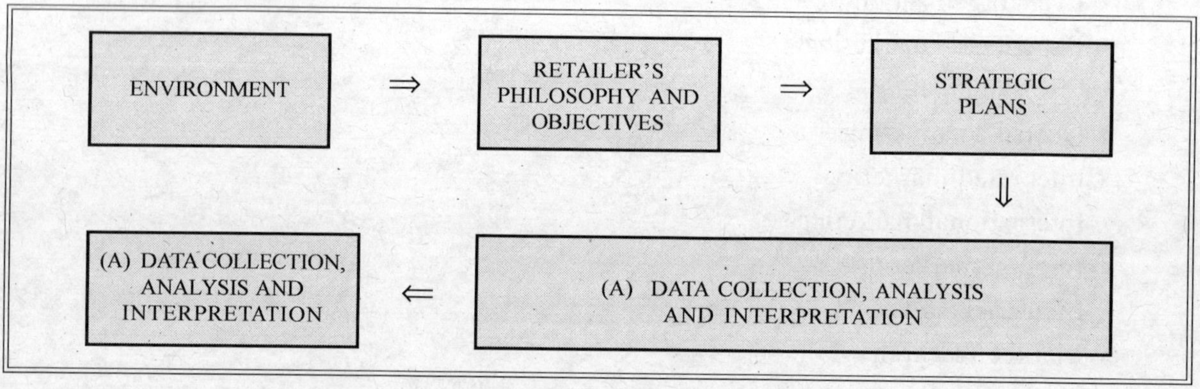

FIG. 1: RETAIL ENVIRONMENT

THE MICRO-ENVIRONMENT

A firm's micro-environment comprises factors pertinent to the firm itself, or stakeholders closely connected with the firm or company.

A firm's micro-environment typically spans:

- Customers/consumers
- Employees
- Suppliers

By contrast to the macro-environment, an organization holds a greater degree of control over these factors. All these factors a firm can handle/control by using the marketing tools.

COMPONENTS OF MICRO-ENVIRONMENT

- It consists of the actors close to the company that affect its ability to serve its customers
- The company
- Suppliers
- Marketing intermediaries

- Customers
- Competitors
- Public

Company

- Mission
- Objectives and top management
- Marketing dept
- Finance dept
- HR dept
- Admin dept (legal and time management, supervising security, record-keeping, communications
- Stores operations

Suppliers

- They provide the resources needed by the company.
- Supplier-related problems are:
  1. Supply shortages
  2. Supply delays
  3. Labour strikes
  4. Rising supply costs

Customers

They consist of individuals and households that buy goods and services for personal consumption.

Public

A public is any group that has an actual or potential interest in or impact on an organization's ability to achieve its objectives. There are seven types of public:

1. Financial public
2. Media public
3. Government public
4. Citizen action public
5. Local public
6. General public
7. Internal public

Marketing Intermediaries

- Resellers (wholesalers)
- Financial intermediaries (banks)

- Physical distribution firms (transportation, warehouses)
- Marketing services (research firms, advertising agencies, consultancies)

Competitors

- A firm that satisfies same need or want
- Type of competition
- No. of competitors
- Objectives of competitors
- Strategies of competitors
- Reaction pattern of competitors

The Macro-environment

A firm's marketing macro-environment consists of a variety of external factors that manifest on a large (or macro) scale. These are typically economic, social, political or technological phenomena. A common method of assessing a firm's macro-environment is via a PESTLE (Political, Economic, Social, Technological, Legal, and Ecological) analysis. Within a PESTLE analysis, a firm would analyze national political issues, culture and climate, key macro-economic conditions, health and indicators (such as economic growth, inflation, unemployment, etc.), social trends/attitudes, and the nature of technology's impact on its society and the business processes within the society.

(a) Data collection, analysis and information control centre

(b) Data storage and interpretation retrieval

(c) Updating of files

Elements of Macro-environment

- It consists of the larger societal forces that affect the micro-environment.
- Demographic.
- Economic.
- Natural.
- Technological.
- Political.
- Cultural.

Demographic Environment

- It involves people and people make-up markets and their vital statistics.
- Size, density, location, age, gender, race, occupation, etc.
- Population growth rate.
- Geographic shift in population.
- Population age mix and sex mix.
- Educational level.

- Household patterns.
- Ethnic and racial make-up.

Economic Environment

- It consists of factors that affect consumer purchasing power and spending patterns.
- Unemployment rate and national income concepts.
- Price level, average salaries, etc.
- Income distribution pattern, industrializing pattern.
- Saving rate, interest rate and credit availability.
- Inflation rate.
- Business cycle.
- Change in income rate and spending pattern of customers.

Technological Environment

- Technology is the application of science to convert an economy's resources into output
- Forces that create new technologies, creating new product and market opportunities
- Innovations, new retailing systems, electronic fund transfer, internet, distribution systems, stock handling mechanisms and control
- Technology affects Four Ps and shortens the length of product life cycle

Natural Environment

- It involves the natural resources that are needed as inputs by marketers or that are affected by marketing activities.
- Raw material availability.
- Increasing energy cost and fuel cost.
- Natural calamity.
- Climatic conditions and seasons.

Political Environment

- It consists of laws, government decisions, and principles of political parties.
- Taxation, duty, regulation, policies, statutory holidays, Sunday trading, opening times, planning permission for building.
- Acts – Consumer Protection Act, Sales of Goods Act, Drugs and Cosmetic Act, etc.

Socio-cultural Environment

- Institutions and other forces that affect society's basic values, perceptions, preferences, and behaviours.
- Culture means set of learned beliefs, values, habits and forms of behaviour and that are shared by the society and shared from generation-to-generation.
- Subculture (nationality, religion, geographic region).

- Social class.
- Changing role of women in the society.

Retailing: Retailing includes all the activities involved in selling goods or services directly to final consumers for personal, non-business use. Retailing is the set of business activities that adds value to the products and services sold to consumers for their personal or family use. A retailer or retail store in any business enterprise whose sales volume comes primarily from retailing. Any organization that sells goods to final consumers – whether a manufacturer, wholesaler, or retailer – is a retailer. It does, not matter how the goods or services are sold (by person, mail, telephone, vending machine or Internet) or where they are sold (in a store, on the street or in the consumer's home). Often people think of retailing only as the sale of products in stores, but retailing also involves the sale of services: overnight lodging in a motel, a doctor's exam, a haircut, a DVD rental, or a home-delivered pizza. Not all retailing is done in stores. One of the greatest things about the retail business is its immediacy. Inventory is bought and put on a certain shelf in a certain aisle at a certain price at a certain time of year. Soon after the store opens, the retailer has a pretty good sense of whether he or she has done all those things right or wrong. Retail executives don't have to wait years to learn whether they've won or lost. In retailing, fortunes are literally made and lost everyday based on thousands of seemingly insignificant contact points with customers.

- **Retail Myth 1: Retailers put customers first.**

  Reality: Retailers put their own interest way ahead of customers' interests.
- **Retail Myth 2: Retailers understand customer service.**

  Reality: Customers know better
- **Retail Myth 3: Retailers understand who their customers are.**

  Reality: Customers have changed dramatically over the past couple of decades, and many retailers have not changed with them.
- **Retail Myth 4: Retailers believe that customers love to shop at their stores.**

  Reality: Customers do not love shopping – most do not even like shopping.
- **Retail Myth 5: Retailers believe they can successfully control customers.**

  Reality: Customers have too many options and will go elsewhere if forced to do it the retailer's way.

Retailers are asserting greater control of their brands. Private label products are growing in the retail business, in all of its variations. This includes the traditional sense of private branding – offering less costly items and increasingly sophisticated brand programmes that replicate the role of a national brand. Retailers like Target (Target, an US discounter takes a significant share from its category- killer counterparts by offering selected assortments at lower prices) have brilliantly created captive or exclusive brands (Mossimo, Michael Graves, and Isaac Mizrahi). Large department store chains like Federal have developed their own brands successfully (e.g., INC) and are also leveraging their relationship with suppliers to launch exclusives (H by Tommy Hilfiger).

Global Retailing: The influence of Wal-Mart (USA) is like nothing retailing has ever seen. Wal-Mart will dominate retail headlines over the next decade because of its very big size, magnitude, and momentum. Wal-Mart's sales level is more than $ 250 billion per year. It controls nearly 10 per cent of every retail dollar spent in America. The undisputed leader in the retail world, namely, the Home Depot is the second-largest retailer (with sales almost three times as large as those of Carrefour), It has made significant sales gains over the last several years. Its fourth place ranking in 2004, was up from 24th in 1996. Food retailing continues to dominate among the largest retailers. Eight of the ten largest retailers sell food, and slightly over 50 per cent of the 200 largest retailers have supermarkets, warehouse, hypermarket, or cash-and-carry formats, or some combination of them. The dominance of food retailing would be even more pronounced if US drugstore chains, which place more emphasis on convenience food, were included as food retailers. Of the top 2004 global retailers, 42.5 per cent are headquartered in the US, 39 per cent in Europe, and 13 per cent in Japan. Largest retailers headquartered in the US tend to concentrate on the US and operate fewer formats than their global counterparts. American retailers in the top 50 list operate, on average, two formats in 35 countries, while top 50 retailers headquartered outside the US operate twice as many formats in three more countries. As powerful as Wal-Mart, establishment shows that there are a number of companies who compete quite successfully with the behemoth today and that there will be plenty of ways to compete in the future. Target has taken a hot-established positioning; Whole Foods sells more fashionable food; and others have more compelling services or product propositions.

An Overview of Global Retailing

Global retailing refers to any retailing activity that spans national boundaries. Today, there is a growing interest among successful retailers to expand globally, but this is not a new phenomenon. For instance, venturesome merchants have gone abroad both to obtain merchandise and ideas and to operate retail establishments. In 1929, itself there was foreign-owned jewellery shops in New York city. The development of trading company operations in Africa and Asia by British, French, Dutch, Belgian, and German retailing organizations progressed extensively during the nineteenth and early twentieth centuries. International trading and retail store operation were two of the economic pillars of the colonial system of that era. The big change taking place in international retailing today involves the gradual dissolution of the colonial retailing structure and, in its place, the creation of international retailing organizations operating in the industrialized countries. B2C becomes B2B2S (business to business retailer to shopper). This change in focus requires a whole new way of thinking.

Global retailing tends to have a chief information officer (CIO) overseeing their Retail Information System (RIS). A RIS anticipates the information needs of retail managers, collects, organizes and stores relevant data on a continuous basis; and direct the flow of information to the proper decision makers. Information systems departments often have formal, written annual plans. Computers are used by most companies that conduct information systems analysis, and many firms use the Web for some RIS functions. Growth in the use of retail information systems is expected.

Fifty years ago, most computerized retail systems were used only to reduce cashier errors and improve inventory control. Today, they often form the foundation for retail information systems and are used in surveys, ordering, merchandise transfer between stores, and other activities. These activities are conducted by both small and large retailers. Majority of small and medium retailers as well as large retailers have computerized financial management systems, analyze sales electronically, and use computerized inventory management systems. Retail Pro management information software to retailers is used at 24,000 stores around the world. Retail Pro software has an appeal among small retailers due to flexible pricing based on the number of users and stores, and the type of hardware. A small store pays 2 to 3 per cent of one year's sales to buy a complete Retail Pro System, including training and support. Retail Pro has the following features:

1. Online analytical processing (OLAP) processes, analyzes, and views data from different viewpoints on screen instantly without having to generate multiple reports.
2. The multidimensional data base can display values by stores, vendors and departments for up to 44 dimensions including store, region, day, month, vendor, department, style, size, colour, and season.
3. Drill down can instantly break out data into more detail. Pivoting is the ability to switch the hierarchy of how you view data.
4. Ranking can be done instantly by any value.
5. Forecast lets the user project performance along any dimension, using past history or other criteria, and track variances from projections.
6. Watches are minimum/maximum levels that can be set for any aspect of performance to activate an alert when exceptions occur.

Wilsons Leather sells men's and women's outerwear, apparel, and accessories at 800 stores in the US and Canada. Since 1997, it has spent $ 30 million to revamp its RIS.

Micro Strategy Desktop is the business intelligence software component that offers integrated query and reporting powerful analytics, and decision support workforce on the personal computing desktop. It provides an arsenal of features for online analysis of corporate data. Even complex reports are easy to create; they can be viewed in various presentation formats, published into production reports, distributed to other users, and extended through a host of features including data slicing. The interface itself is customizable to different users' skill levels and security profiles.

Micro strategy typically works with larger retailers including more than 60 per cent of the top 200 retailers in the world to prepare computerized information systems. Clients include Best Buy, Eddie Bauer, Lowe's, and Victoria's Secret. One of its leading software products is Micro Strategy Desktop, which is described at the firm's Website (www.microstrategy.com).

The Philippines is among the emerging markets in the world. Along with China, the Philippines attracts international enterprises seeking to establish a presence in Asia. This study examines small/medium enterprises (SMEs) management and employee perceptions of customer service on a number of dimensions. The results suggest that managers and employees in the Philippines behave in similar ways to those in Western countries, but there are differences, probably related to cultural characteristics. The Philippines market becomes more involved with global business.

Dillard's (NYSE: DDS), based in Little Rock, Arkansas, is an upscale departmental store chain in the United States, with 330 stores in 29 states. Its locations are concentrated in Texas and Florida; with a major presence in other states including Arizona, Iowa, Colorado, Kansas, Missouri, Alabama, Georgia, Tennessee, Oklahoma, Mississippi, Louisiana, Nebraska, Nevada, Utah, North Carolina, Idaho, South Carolina, Kentucky, Indiana, and Ohio. Wal-Mart stores, Microsoft, Hewlett-Packard, Philips Electronics, Home Depot and Toyota-owned luxury auto marquee Lexus have branded together to pilot a revolutionary new scheme that will buy TV airtime via a special auction facility on eBay. Its sponsors have committed $ 50 million to the embryo system, named eMedia Exchange, which was launched in 2007. Now the retailer has become the media controller.

Global Retailing Challenges

Retailers face numerous challenges. Many consumers are bored with shopping or do not have much time for it. Some local areas have too many stores, and retailers often spur one another into frequent price cutting (and low profit margins). Customer service expectations are high at a time when more retailers offer self-service and automated system. At the swarm-time, many retailers remain unsure what to do with the Web; they are still grappling with the emphasis to place on image enhancement, customer information and feedback and sales transactions. It is a challenge posed by an unfavourable trend or development that would lead, in the absence of defensive marketing action, to deterioration in sales or profit. Challenges may be classified according to seriousness and probability of occurrence. Some challenges may be major threats, because they can seriously hurt the retail business and have a high probability of occurrence. To deal with these major challenges (threats), the company needs to prepare contingency plans that spell out changes the retail-business unit can make before or during the threats. Challenges need to be monitored carefully in the event that they grow more serious. Very minor threats can be ignored.

These are the issues that retailers must resolve: "How can we best serve our customers while earning a fair profit? "How can we stand out in a highly competitive environment where consumers have so many choices?" "How can we grow our business while retaining a core of loyal customers?" Our point of view: Retail decision makers can best address these questions by fully understanding and applying the basic principles of retailing in a well-structured, systematic, and focused retail strategy. That is the philosophy behind retail strategy.

Retail Management: A Strategic Approach

Can retailers flourish in today's tough marketplace? You bet! Just look at your favourite restaurant, gift shop, and food store. Look at the growth of Costco, Kohl's, and Krispy Kreme Doughnuts. What do they have in common? To prosper in the long-term, they all need a strategic plan and a willingness to adapt to changing retail environment. The critical question for thc would be international retailer is, "What advantages do we have relative to local competition?". The answer will often be "Nothing", when local laws governing retailing practice are taken into account. In such cases there is no reason to expect highly profitable operations to develop from a venture into international retailing.

TUG OF WAR Challenge : Probability of getting a major sale			
Winning the Sale	+	–	**Losing the sale**
Superior	← Product		**Inferior**
None		Competition →	**Superior**
Lowest	← Shopper need	Price →	**Highest**
Real	← Shopper Knowledg		**Little or none**
High	← Shopper budget		**Low**
Able to buy			**Not able to buy**
Excellent		Sales presentation →	**Poor**
Able to overcome	← Answering objection		**Not able to overcome**
Liked by shopper		Shopper compatibility →	**Disliked by shopper**

FIG. 2: TUG OF WAR

Source and Inspiration: Thinkertoys

The Hot Zone: The key to realizing and developing a hot idea is to correctly assess three things: (i) the needs of customers, (ii) the competitive environment, and (iii) the retailer's own internal strengths and weaknesses. What we call the Hot Zone is where many of tomorrow's hot ideas germinate. It lies at the intersection of correctly responding to consumer trends, determining a retailer's capability of delivering on a strategy, and finding a market position defendable against the competition.

CHALLENGES FACING THE INDIAN ORGANISED RETAIL SECTOR are stopping the Indian retail industry from reaching its full potential. The behaviour pattern of the Indian consumer has undergone a major change. This has happened for the Indian consumer who is earning more now, due to Western influences. Women working force is increasing, and desire for luxury items and better quality is also increasing. He now wants to eat, shop, and get entertained under the same roof. All these have lead the Indian organized retail sector to give more in order to satisfy the Indian customer.

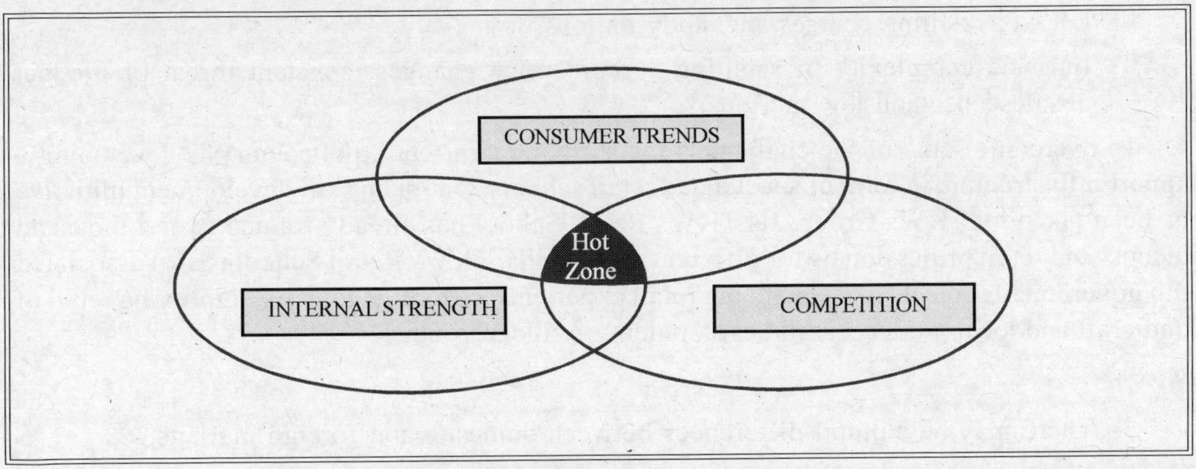

FIG. 3: RETAILING'S HOT ZONE

The biggest challenge facing the Indian organized retail sector is the lack of retail space. With real estate prices escalating due to increase in demand from the Indian organized retail sector, it is posing a challenge to its growth. With Indian retailers having to shell out more for retail space, is effecting there overall profitability in retail.

Trained manpower shortage is a challenge facing the organized retail sector in India. The Indian retailers have difficulties in finding trained person and also have to pay more in order to retain them. This again brings down the Indian retailers' profit levels.

The Indian government has allowed 51 per cent foreign direct investment (FDI) in the India retail sector to one brand shops only. This have made the entry of global retail giants to organized retail sector in India difficult. This is a challenge being faced by the Indian organized retail sector. But the global retail giants like Tesco, Wal-Mart, and Metro AG are entering the organized retail sector in India indirectly through franchisee agreement and cash and carry wholesale trading. Many Indian companies are also entering the Indian organized retail sector like Reliance Industries Limited, Pantaloons, and Bharti Telecoms. But they are facing stiff competition from these global retail giants. As a result discounting is becoming an accepted practice. This too brings down the profit of the Indian retailers. All these are posing as challenges facing the Indian organized retail sector.

The challenges facing the Indian organized retail sector are there but it will have to be dealt with and only then can this sector prosper.

To become a truly flourishing industry, retailing needs to cross the following hurdles:

- Automatic approval is not allowed for foreign investment in retail.
- Regulations restricting real estate purchases and cumbersome local laws.
- Taxation, which favours small retail businesses.
- Absence of developed supply chain and integrated IT management.

- Lack of trained work-force.
- Low skill level for retailing management.
- Lack of retailing courses and study options.
- Intrinsic complexity of retailing – rapid price changes, constant threat of product obsolescence and low margins.

To overcome some of the challenges faced by modern retail, the country is developing a support infrastructure in form of specialized retail schools. One such skill development initiative has been taken by TKWs Group. Its TKWs Retail School has already trained over a thousand students and retail professionals for different retail skills. TKWs Retail School is also associated with government projects like enhancing retail experience of foreign tourists, improving retail of handicraft and local produce, skill development of village youth.

Threats

- There may be cultural differences between domestic and foreign markets.
- Management styles may not be easily adaptable.
- Foreign governments may place restriction on some operations.
- Personal income may be poorly distributed among customers in foreign markets.
- Distribution systems and technology may be inadequate (for example, poor roads and lack of refrigeration). This may minimize the effectiveness of the Web as a selling tool.
- Institutional formats vary greatly among countries.
- Currencies are different. The countries in the European Union have sought to alleviate this problem by introducing the euro, a common currency, in most of their member nations.
- Rural retailing problem may arise due to:

1. Distribution logistics, storage, transport and handling;
2. Location and degree of concentration of demands;
3. Dealers attitude and motivation;
4. Consumer motivation and buying habits;
5. Mass communication media, their reach and influence; and
6. Organizational alternatives.

Obstacles are a part and parcel of every economy. It might be restrictions imposed by the government or any other public or private body due to which many times retailers are left with wrong part of the deal. For instance, interstate hikes that squeeze the market. In order to avoid putting the retailers in such a situation, help of financial instruments are suggested. They can make use of these institutions to seek advice on making appropriate investment at the right time in profitable sectors. Retail participation lends stability to the market which is very essential for an economy to develop. Thus, it is important to encourage retail investment.

Retailing Opportunities

A retailing opportunity is an area of buyer's need in which a retail-unit can perform profitably. There are lots of opportunities to start a new retail business or work for an existing one and to become a franchisee. Global retailing possibilities abound. A retailing-unit has to monitor key macro-environment forces (economic, demographic, political, technological, legal, cultural and social) and significant micro-environment actors (customers, competitors, distributors, suppliers) that affect its ability to market the product in the retail market. The retail-unit should set up a retailing intelligence system to track trends and important developments. For each trend or development, the shopper needs to identify the associated opportunities and threats. A major purpose of environmental scanning is to discern new retailing opportunities.

Opportunities can be classified according to their attractiveness and their success probability. The success probability of retailing depends on whether its business strengths not only match the key success requirements for operating in the target market but also exceed those of its competitors. Mere competence does not constitute a competitive advantage. The best-performing retail-business will be the one that can generate the greatest customer value and sustain it over time.

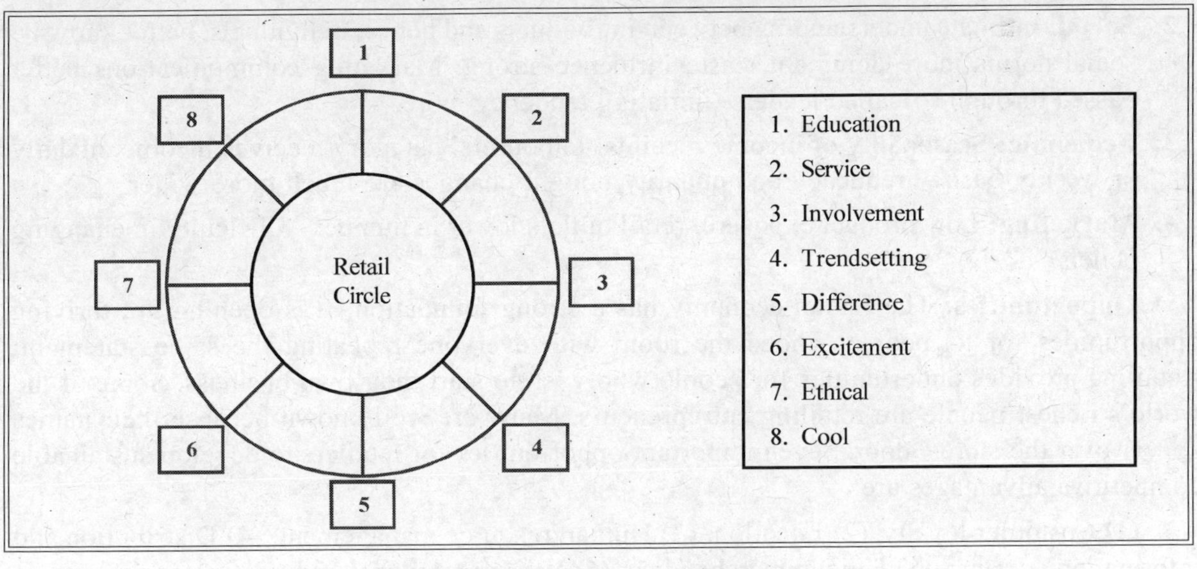

FIG. 4: RETAIL CIRCLE OPPORTUNITY

Once the retail-business has identified the major challenges and opportunities facing a specific retail business unit, it can characterize that business overall attractiveness. Four outcomes are possible:

(i) An ideal retail business is high in major opportunities and low in major threats.

(ii) A speculative retail business is high in both major opportunities and threats.

(iii) A mature retail-business is low in major opportunities and low in threats.

(iv) A troubled retail business is low in opportunities and high in threats.

Evolving consumer patterns offer retail banking new opportunities to thrive.

In the retail banking industry there are four emerging consumer patterns that will shape the future. First, customers want to feel comfortable dealing with a financial institution. Second, customers continue to thirst for financial knowledge presented in an easy to understand and personable way. Third, they want products and services delivered conveniently. Fourth, customers will reward useful relationships. The fascinating thing about each of these patterns is that they do not represent revolutionary thinking. Rather, the opportunity lies in the simple fact that no retail bank has adapted its marketing mix to address all of them adequately.

To adapt to emerging consumer patterns, banks must institute a marketing theory based on solid principles. They must build their business vision, objectives and strategies on achieving those principles. Where do you look for a retail marketing programme that will allow your bank to be successful? The answer lies in "Affinity Retail Marketing". The opportunities in rural markets in contrast to the urban markets are conditioned by the following factors:

1. **Spatial:** Low density of population, low mobility, low infrastructural level, low literacy level. But the market is contiguous.
2. **Social:** Intimate understanding between individuals and hence, individuals, better known – social norms more dominant, caste influence strong. Marketing communications better passed through so-called leaders' initiating tendency more.
3. **Economic:** Seasonality of income receipts: Labourers' category receives income on daily or weekly basis. Frequency and quantity bought changes are much more wider.
4. **Marketing:** Low product exposure, retail outlets lower in number – difficulty in changing beliefs.

Opportunities: The Indian economy has a strong foundation. It is opening up; thriving opportunities for its people echoed the room with everyone repeating the same statement. Retailing provides opportunities for people who wish to start their own business. Some of the world's richest people are retailing entrepreneurs. Many are well known because their names appear over the stores' door. Seven important opportunities for retailers to develop sustainable competitive advantages are:

(1) Customer loyalty, (2) Location, (3) Human resource management, (4) Distribution and information systems, (5) Unique merchandise, (6) Vendor relations, and (7) Customer service.

Kishore Biyani (CEO, Future Group), born in a middle-class Marwari trading family, started selling stonewash fabric to small shops in Mumbai. He ventured to redefine the retailing business in India with the launch of Pantaloons, Big Bazaar, and many more retail formats. Today, Kishore Biyani's Future Group, with ₹ 3,550 crore turnover, is one of the country's leading business groups present in retail, asset management, consumer finance, insurance, retail media, retail spaces and logistics. The group's flagship company, Pantaloon Retail (India) Limited operates over 7 million square feet of retail space, has over 1,000 stores across 53 cities in India and employs over 25,000 people. Some of its leading retail formats include, Pantaloons, Big Bazaar, Central, Food Bazaar, Home Town, eZone, Depot, Future Money and online retail format, future-bazaar.com. Kishore Biyani is the Indian doyen of retail. He conferred the Retail Leadership Award by the Reid & Taylor Awards for Retail Excellence, 2008.

Jeff Bezos (Amazon.com) started his first internet book retailer business. He is one of the few dot.com leaders. Amazon developed technologies to make shopping on the Internet faster, easier, and more personal than shopping in stores by offering personalized recommendations and home pages. Amazon.com has become more than a book-store. It now provides its website and fulfilment services for major retailers like Office Depot, Borders, and Toys "R" Us in addition to hosting storefronts for thousands of smaller retailers.

The systems used to control the flow of information to buyers and then on to vendors have become quite sophisticated. Retailers have developed data warehouses that provide them with intimate knowledge of who their customers are and what they like to buy. These data warehouses are being used to strengthen the relationships with their consumers and improve the productivity of their marketing and inventory management efforts.

Some retailers are using distribution centres for crossdocking instead of storing merchandise. Others have their vendors supply them with floor ready merchandise and adhere to strict delivery schedules. Still other retailers are having vendors deliver merchandise directly to their stores and use pull supply chains that base inventory policies on consumer demand. Retailers are outsourcing many of these logistics functions to third-party logistics companies.

Retailers and vendors are collaborating to improve supply chain efficiency. Electronic data interchange enables retailers to communicate electronically with their vendors. The internet has accelerated the adoption of EDI (Electronic Data Interchange), especially among smaller, less sophisticated vendors. Other more involving and effective collaborative approaches include information sharing. (VMI) Vendor Managed Inventory, and CPFR (Collaborative Planning, Forecasting and Replenishment). These approaches represent the nexus of information systems and logistics management. They reduce lead time, increase product availability, lower inventory investment, and reduce overall logistics expenses.

Finally, RFID (Radio Frequency Identification) has the potential of further streamlining the supply chain. These small devices are affixed to pallets, cartons, and individual items and can be used to track merchandise through the supply chain and store information such as, when an item was shipped to a distribution centre. Although still relatively expensive to be placed on all items. RFID technology can reduce labour, theft and inventory costs.

To Sum up the opportunities are:

- Foreign markets may be used to supplement domestic sales.
- Foreign markets may represent good growth opportunities when domestic markets are saturated or stagnant.
- A retailer may be able to offer goods, services, technology not yet available in foreign markets.
- Competition may be less in foreign markets.
- There may be tax or investment advantages in foreign markets.
- Due to government and economic shifts, many countries are more open to the entry of foreign firms.

- Communications are easier than before. The World Wide Web enables retailers to reach customers and suppliers well outside their domestic markets.

Opportunities in the Indian Organised Retail Sector

The opportunities in Indian organized retail sector are many because this sector is witnessing a boom. The retail industry in India amounted to US $ 200 billion in 2006, and out of this amount the Indian organized retail sector amounted to US $ 6.4 billion. The opportunities in Indian organized retail sector can be judged from the fact that by 2010, it is expected to rise to US $ 23 billion.

The various opportunities in the organized retail sector in India are mainly therefore the Indian consumers behaviour pattern has changed. Now the Indian consumer gets more hefty pay- packages, is younger, a large number of women are working, Western influences, and more disposable income have opened a lot of opportunities in Indian organized retail sector. The Indian consumer wants to shop, eat and get entertainment in one place and it has also given Indian organized retail sector an opportunity to grow.

The Indian government in 2005 allowed foreign direct investment (FDI) in single brand retail to 51 per cent. This has opened up a lot of opportunities in Indian organized retail sector. In fact 325 departmental stores, 300 new malls, and 1,500 supermarkets are being built which shows the tremendous opportunities in the organized retail sector in India.

Many Indian companies seeing the various opportunities in organized retail sector in India have entered it. Pantaloons have decided to increase its retail space to 30 million square feet with an investment of US $ 1 billion. Reliance Industries Limited is targeting for annual sales of US $ 25 billion by 2011. It is planning to invest US$ 6 billion in order to open 1,500 supermarkets and 1,000 hypermarkets. Bharti Telecoms is planning a joint venture with Tesco, a global retail giant worth £ 750 million.

The opportunities in the organized retail sector in India have also increased with the desire of many global retail giants to set up shop here. The global retail giants who are entering the Indian organized retail sector are: Tesco, Wal-Mart, Metro AG, Carrefour SA.

The opportunities in Indian organized retail sector are varied and it must be fully exploited by the Indian retailers.

Emerging Retail Trend : Store-as-medium Gaining Velocity

In 1964, communications theorist Marshall McLuhan forwarded the notion that the, "Medium is the message". His theory seems clearer today as we see in-store merchandising activity receiving more attention as a medium unto itself, rather than the recipient of benefits derived from other media. Two recent studies and one about to be released major study have made the idea of store-as-medium their major focus.

An article appeared in the *Cincinnati Business Courier*, on September 21, 2007, that reported on a major research investment being made by Procter & Gamble, Kroger and dozens of other major retailers. All-in-all, 40 companies have invested tens of millions of dollars in the project called PRISM, or Pioneering Research for an In-Store Metric. In the study, hundreds of infrared sensors were utilized over the last five months to count the number of people who walked down a particular aisle or specific product category, and purchases were tracked. This level of investment is clear evidence of the importance being placed on in-store as the emerging marketing medium of this century.

According to a report by Deloitte Consulting for the Grocery Manufacturers' of America, the overall marketing budgets of 19 CPG companies include an increase from 3 per cent to 6 per cent on in-store marketing this year. The companies think that amount will reach 8 per cent by 2010. That compounded annual growth rate is 21 per cent, greater than internet advertising at 15 per cent and traditional media (TV, print, radio) at 2 per cent. The report states that retailers are spending at an even faster rate of 26 per cent compound growth annually. According to Advertising Age, the previously mentioned P&G is spending $ 500 million of its $ 8 billion in global ad spending on in-store marketing.

In a recent *Times & Trends* report, Information Resources Inc. (IRI) seems to triangulate the notion of Store-as-medium. IRI says that manufacturers are indeed turning more and more to in-store marketing as traditional advertising seems to be on the decline. IRI suggests that, if the medium is the message, the message will have to be constantly tweaked and strategies sharpened as merchandising activity and effectiveness are already on the decline. As always, closer communication between the manufacturer and retailer is the prescription against any future slippage.

Insight on the retail industry from Mark Hunter, the "sales hunter'.

Table 2 : Retail Winners – who, why and how

Retail Brand Winner	**Winning Strategy**
Karmaloop	Turning shoppers into fanatics
Whole Foods Market	Ethics in action
Superquinn	Making customers a part of the family
Starbucks	Being in the people-first business
Guinness	Changing the shelf
Senseo	Brand co-creation
Courvoisier	Revitalization
H&M	Four seconds to get them!
Peroni	Challenging perceptions
ASSAABLOY	Solve a problem
Gillette	Constant innovation
Procter & Gamble	The moments of truth
Red Bull	Rewriting the rules
EasyJet	Creating choice where there's no choice
Apple	Merging buying with trying
Oliviers and Co.	Creating wants, not needs
Tchibo	Creating an unchallenged 'star'

Bose	Try, try and try again
Zara	React rather than predict
Dyson	Radical innovation
REI	Living the brand experience
Holland and Holland	Making more of more
Innocent	An innocent product from an innocent company
Gooh!	Reinventing the boring!
Yoyamart	A brand that understands the situation

Source: *How to Succeed at Retail*, Keith Lincoln and Lars Thomassen, 2010.

Emerging Retail Trends Blog

Emerging Retail Trend: In-store Media and CBS

There is growing importance of in-store media. As reported in the *Wall Street Journal*, Sept. 7, 2007, CBS paid $ 71.5 million for Sign Story, which had in-store video monitors in 1,400 supermarkets.

There is an equally increasing importance of in-store advertising. Mainstream news sources have been talking about how companies are running from traditional media such as network television, etc., and moving their spending to in-store activities. This is an understatement. The real problem is that there are not enough viable vehicles to absorb the movement of advertising dollars. In the next 5 years, we're going to see the emergence of a number of new "consumer-specific" advertising vehicles. In the words of the vintage broadcast networks, "Stay tuned. We'll be back shortly".

New, Bigger, Better Blog and Website.... It's coming, in just a few short weeks we'll be making the move from this blog site to a new website/blog.

Emerging Retail Trend: The Sell-off of Brands

Every couple of years, we go through the cycle of major companies selling off brands they deem no longer worthy of their focus. The cycle never ends. The amount of hedge money in the marketplace look for some interesting moves in the next couple of months. The announcement by Unilever is just the start. Kraft will sell-off some brands and SaraLee will sell even more. The end result is that it will create significant opportunities for some smaller companies to pick up some brands. The downside is that these brands will come with so much debt connected to them that it will be difficult for any of them to mount anything significant in terms of a long-term marketing push.

Consumer brands, CPG, Divestitures, Kraft, SaraLee, Unilever.

Emerging Retail Trend: The Pet Economy – Business Week Magazine

The headline read "The Pet Economy", with a picture of a pampered dog on the cover. The article talks about how the pet industry has been booming and is continuing to grow. The pet economy is showing no sign of slowing anytime soon.

Emerging Retail Trend: Secondary Sourcing

Companies need to have secondary suppliers and sources for goods and services. With all of the supply chain issues coming out of China, the need for companies to have alternative sourcing is more important than ever. The problem with China is only the tip of the iceberg. The ongoing issues with the transportation grid are only going to get worse. In the next 15 months, we will be facing potential strikes on the West Coast Ports and the implementation of new Homeland Security rules regarding the movement of containers. These factors are not to be taken lightly, and depending on how they all play out, could cause major disruptions even before we call into play the usual issues surrounding weather, currency valuations, energy, etc. Retailers and manufacturers alike need to be paying more than lip-service to this issue because if and when supply chain disruptions do occur, there will be those who cannot recover from them and will ultimately be forced out of business.

Emerging Retail Trend Update: Wal-Mart Discounting Strategy

Wal-Mart's announcement of price cuts on as many as 20,000 items in a back-to-school push really shouldn't surprise anybody. They are in a tough spot and the only way out is to dive deeper with their pricing.

Wal-Mart has to keep their real estate productive and the only proven method they have to build sales is through discounting. The vast majority of their other attempts to go upscale have backfired. For vendors, it means the ride is going to get rough. However, there is light at the end of the tunnel (although it is still probably 10 years away). Wal-Mart is now in a mature state of existence in the US. There are only a handful of things that will save them:

1. Spin-off Sam's
2. Build-up neighbourhood markets
3. Open a new, small deep-discount format
4. Begin to move away from the Super Centre concept

If you're in the real estate end of the retail business, you are going to see major shifts in space. Hang on! It's going to be a wild ride for the next few years and, as a result, it's a great time to be part of the retail industry.

Emerging Retail Trend: Decline of Television Shopping

HSN and other television-driven, shop-at-home formats are going to start rapidly declining in the next 3 years. They are already becoming very frayed around the edges on the following reasons:

1. There has always been a very high return rate on their products which have served as a damper on their profits.
2. When compared to the speed at which people can shop online for anything at anytime, the format moves too slow.
3. The ability to use the Internet to seek out a lower price for something that is being shown on the television shopping channel is quickly turning these programs into nothing more than a product showcase for the manufacturer.

4. Cable capacity/competition is forcing every cable operator to increase the fees they charge their content providers. The continued upward spike in these fees is another cost that must be passed along to the consumer.

A lot of money thrown at these formats in recent years from very smart investors like Barry Diller, but, in the end, they are going to lose out to the flexibility of the internet.

India retail industry is the largest industry in India, with an employment of around 8 per cent and contributing to over 10 per cent of the country's GDP. Retail industry in India is expected to rise 25 per cent yearly being driven by strong income growth, changing lifestyles, and favourable demographic patterns.

It is expected that by 2016, modern retail industry in India will be worth US $ 175-200 billion. Indian retail industry is one of the fastest growing industries with revenue expected in 2007, to amount US $ 320 billion and is increasing at a rate of 5 per cent yearly. A further increase of 7-8 per cent is expected in the industry of retail in India by growth in consumerism in urban areas, rising incomes, and a steep rise in rural consumption. It has further been predicted that the retailing industry in India will amount to US $ 21.5 billion by 2010, from the current size of US $ 7.5 billion.

Shopping in India witnessed a revolution with the change in the consumer buying behaviour and the whole format of shopping also altering. Industry of retail in India which has become modern can be seen from the fact that there are multistoried malls, huge shopping centres, and sprawling complexes which offer food, shopping, and entertainment all under the same roof.

Indian retail industry is expanding itself most aggressively as a result a great demand for real estate is being created. Indian retailers preferred means of expansion is to expand to other regions and to increase the number of their outlets in a city. It is expected that by 2010, India may have 600 new shopping centres.

In the Indian retailing industry, food is the most dominating sector and is growing at a rate of 9 per cent annually. The branded food industry is trying to enter the Indian retail industry and convert Indian consumers to branded food. Since at present 60 per cent of the Indian grocery basket consists of non-branded items.

An important aspect of the current economic scenario in India is the emergence of organized retail. There has been considerable growth in organized retailing business in recent years and it is poised for much faster growth in the future. Major industrial houses have entered this area and have announced very ambitious future expansion plans. Transnational corporations are also seeking to come to India and set up retail chains in collaboration with big Indian companies. However, opinions are divided on the impact of the growth of organized retail in the country. Concerns have been raised that the growth of organized retailing may have an adverse impact on retailers in the unorganized sector. It has also been argued that growth of organized retailing will yield efficiencies in the supply chain, enabling better access to markets to producers (including farmers and small producers) and enabling higher prices, on the one hand and, lower prices to consumers, on the other. In the context of divergent views on the impact of organized retail, it is essential that an in-depth analytical study on the possible effects of organized retailing in India is conducted. In order to assess the impact of growing organized retail on different aspects of the economy, the Indian Council for Research on International Economic Relations (ICRIER) was appointed by the Ministry of Commerce and Industry, Government of India to carry-out a study on organized retail focusing on the following issues:

- Effect on small retailers and vendors in the unorganized sector keeping in mind the likely growth in the overall market.
- Effect on employment.
- Impact on consumers.
- Impact on farmers and manufacturers.
- Impact on prices.
- Overall impact on economic growth. ICRIER has been asked by the Ministry to analyze the above issues in the context of a growth scenario of 7-10 per cent per annum in the next five years and in the light of practice in other fast-growing emerging market economies.

1.2 Partners in the Study

ICRIER sought and received assistance from three important groups:

(a) Development and Research Services Private Limited (DRS) for conducting all-India surveys;

(b) Technopak Advisers Pvt. Ltd., a leading management consultancy firm on retailing; and

(c) Dr. Thomas Reardon and Dr. Ashok Gulati as Co-directors of the International Food Policy Research Institute (IFPRI). Michigan State University (MSU) Joint Programme of Markets in Asia. After a study framework was prepared, it was discussed in a brainstorming session organized by ICRIER on April 9, 2007 in which industry representatives, government officials, and senior academics participated.

Indian retail industry is progressing well and for this to continue, retailers as well as the Indian government will have to make a combined effort. Though India allows 51 per cent FDI in single-brand retail, foreign funds were not permitted in multibrand retail. Companies are permitted to operate only wholesale or cash-and-carry outlets. But now the Government of India has come up with white paper on retail and has decided to permit 100 per cent FDI in the retail sector in India. Organized retail would bring operational efficiencies and effectiveness to the supply chain. Opening FDI is advantageous as it would bring supply chain efficiency and technological know-how. Shopping trends during the year 2010-11, indicate a stronger movement towards modern trade and faith in established brands. For instance, Aditya Birla Retail, which has seen a 25 per cent Spurt in Diwali sales over average growth during 2010 festival. Festival sales at apparel retail Megamart, owned by Arvind Mills, also grew 60 per cent from the year 2009. Future Group's central outlets have seen double-digit growth over the year 2009. Aided by promotional offers, retailers get new large crowds in the run-up to Diwali. Walk-ins at Megamart grew 30 per cent; ticket value also grew by 20 per cent. At Max, a landmark group retail, the average ticket value grew 15 per cent during the year 2010, across all its 20 stores. Gold sales in terms of volume of gold sold too picked 10 per cent in the year 2010. There was a 30 per cent growth in overall sales as well. C. Krishniah Chetty & Sons, Bengaluru, Dhanteras, Prince, Tanishq, Joy Alukkas and Jos Alukkas are popular jewellery shops In India.

- India Shopping Malls
- Scope of the Indian Retail Market

- Indian Organized Retail Market
- Growth Factors in Indian Organized Retail sector
- Opportunities in Indian Organized Retail sector
- Challenges facing the Indian Organized Retail sector
- Role of Supply Chain in Indian Organized Retail
- Employment Generation by Indian Organized Retail Sector
- Indian Organized Retail Sector's Impact on Lifestyles
- Emerging Trends in Indian Organized Retail Sector
- Growth of Retail Companies in India
- Evolution of Indian Retail
- FDI in Indian Organized Retail Sector
- Formats in Indian Organized Retail Sector
- Consumer Durables Retail

The country's largest financial daily, and *The Economic Times* is organizing Retail Awards 2010, to provide a platform to recognize and acknowledge excellence in the retail segment. This award is supported by Retailers Association of India. It is being presented in association with Fly Kingfisher. As on 24th March, 2012, Kingfisher has a debt of ₹ 7,057.08 crore. It is mainly due to labour strike. The financial crunch has hit its operations with dozens of flights being cancelled. The Event partners to the awards are the Ecoreco which focuses on the e-waste recycling business in an organized manner. Ernst and Young Private Limited are the process advisors and valuators for the Awards. The various categories for the awards include marketing, operation, innovation business model, popular-derive awards and jury-based awards. With rising consumer demand and greater disposable income, the $ 400 billion Indian retail sector is clocking an annual growth of 30 per cent. The organized retail sector, which accounts for around 5 per cent of the Indian retail market, is all set to witness maximum number of large format malls and branded retail stores in South India., followed by north, west and the east India in the years 2011 and 2012. With their huge growth potential, smaller cities such as Noida, Amritsar, Kochi and Gurgaon are emerging as hot destinations for the retail sector. The award will focus more on innovations rather than just formats.

Modern retail is changing the face of urban India. It is helping drive consumerism, creating demand for producers and suppliers. *The Times of India* Group is the largest job creator today. US-based premium sunglass brand OAKLEY Inc. is stepping up its distribution as part of its effort to garner market share in India. The company is also looking to add apparel, eyewear, accessories and footwear to its portfolio shortly in India. According to Mr. Scott Bowers, Senior Vice-president, Global Marketing and Brand development, Oakley Inc., "the sunglass market in India is highly underdeveloped". Oakley has a presence in India through Italian sunglass brand Luxottica with which it had merged. Luxottica owns nine brands, including Ray Ban, Prada and Versace. Oakley is being retailed through Sunglass, Hut stores, an eyewear chain of Luxottica besides some lifestyle retail outlets. Oakley's 2009, global turnover stood at nearly $ 1 billion. Oakley products are priced between ₹ 5,000 and ₹ 27,000. In India it will retail around 750 SKUs.

The ₹ 588 crore Gillette India Ltd., is shedding its premium image with a more than 50 per cent reduction in the price of its Mach 3 Turbo razors through a new variant under its franchise. It has introduced a new Mach 3 razor at a price point of ₹ 125 while its premium Mach 3 Turbo razor would continue to sell at ₹ 315. However, the price of single-blade cartridges was dropped 15 per cent (from ₹ 95 to ₹ 80) compare with the high-end razors where a new brand under Mach 3 would be sold without the 'turbo' rubberized effect at almost half the price of the Mach 3 Turbo razor.

The ₹ 1,750 crore blades and razors category is currently dominated by Gillette at the top-end of the market, while family-owned Indian companies such as the House of Malhotra and Vidyut comprise the mass-end of the market. Gillette India is now trying to capture the mass-end of the category and would also be focusing aggressively on the rural market in the future. These brands are also present in the rural market. Vector and Wilkinson Sword Gillette India Ltd., decided to penetrate its product in the rural India. With affordability being the key to reach out to the belly of the market, Gillette is now playing the price card to garner more consumers.

The Cadbury company introduced Eclairs in transparent jars and saw the brand fly. Replicating that experiment, the Managing Director of Britannia Industries Ltd., got the biscuits major to launch small packs of biscuits, priced ₹ 5, in similar jar. Introduced in 2008, Britannia's small-pack strategy is paying off big for the company and is tracking to be a ₹ 250-300 crore business for the year 2010. As Britannia found out, it wasn't just about the accessibility of a product such as Good-Day at a ₹ 5 price point but also about a consumer spending ₹ 5 for a few biscuits which is enough for him to have with a cup of tea and feel satisfied in terms of a healthy snack. In India there are more people at ₹ 5 price point than at ₹ 50. It's the frequency and velocity; a lot of people buying a little at a time, which adds up to a lot.

Now the company's biscuit brands such as Bourbon, Treat, Good Day and Tiger have ₹ 5 packs in different grammages ranging from 42 gms to 54 gms, placed in jars at all vantage points in bus or railway stations and where an impulse purchase could happen. A ₹ 5 pack of Good Day has six biscuits, while a Bourbon brand offers four for the same price. Britannia has also launched the four-biscuit pack of Bourbon for ₹ 5, which actually looks like chocolate bars in a jar.

Enthused by the growing tribe of consumers opting for gourmet food, RPG-promoted Spencer's Retail is in the process of setting up of a slew of gourmet stores. Spencer's Retail is looking to brand the gourmet stores individually to attract footfalls. Spencer's first outlets are, now, in Kolkata, Gurgaon, Bengaluru and Madurai. Gourmet stores are still a niche category. They may not attract enough traffic in the stand-alone format. However, positioning them adjacent to an existing food and grocery format will automatically attract the needed footfalls. The gourmet stores would typically be spread over 2,000 sq.ft. They will stock an assortment of breads, biscuits, beverages, chocolates, chilled and frozen food, cheese, cold cuts, convenience food, exotic and organic fresh fruits and vegetables, pasta, noodles, oils and vinegars. The stores will have at least 3,000 stock-keeping units from across all categories. Spencer plans to open 10 stores every year. The store would entail an outlay of ₹ 2,000 per sq.feet.

Riding on its growth in the emerging markets, Ranbaxy Laboratories Ltd., on 26th October, 2010, reported consolidated profits of ₹ 116.6 crore for the third quarter ended on September,

30, compared with a loss of ₹ 394 crore in the same period last year. Income from developed markets was down 30 per cent to ₹ 525 crore. But sales in emerging markets were at ₹ 1,067 crore, which was at similar levels in Q3 2008. Emerging markets account for 62 per cent of Ranbaxy's revenues. Due to marginal movement of the US dollar, there was no significant forex impact on the company's results for the quarter. Europe recorded sales of ₹ 326 crore, a 10 per cent decline from last year. Sales in India (excluding consumer health care business) grew by 2 per cent to ₹ 361.7 crore during the quarter. The global consumer health care business recorded sales of ₹ 56.3 crore during the quarter, a growth of 24 per cent.

Socio-economic and Technological Influence on Retail Management

Several persons have risen to the top information technology position in their retail companies. Norcen Iles is vice-president of retail systems at Sears (www.sears.com). She oversees Sears' consumer data warehouse and all of Sears' merchandise planning, assortment planning, and inventory replenishment systems. Iles manages an $ 85 million budget with a staff of 200, about 40 per cent of whom are women. According to Iles, women are even better represented in project management roles at Sears, where they comprise 50 per cent of the workforce.

Randy Allen is chief information officer, executive vice-president, and chief strategy officer at Kmart (www.kmart.com), where she directs a staff of 1,200 and oversees a $ 1.4 billion investment in IT. Although Allen admits to being detail-oriented, she says that it has not kept her from being viewed as an astute strategist.

Debbie Giotti, a data analysis specialist with an excellent knowledge of systems, was one of retailing's most visible chief information officers until she left Starbucks Coffee Co. (www.starbucks.com) to join a software company. Because Giotti joined Starbucks when it was young company, she had a lot of latitude in shaping the organizations of its information technology department.

A retailer, the last link in the distribution chain, plays an important role in making socio-economic changes in the society. Retailers can make or mark a product's life and viability by participating in the consumer's purchase decision. For many customers in India with very brand or quality recognition, retailer is a counsellor on fashions and durability of many products. Hence, manufacturers attach great deal of importance to the retailers in promoting a new product or design. Retail sales and employment are vital economic contributors, and retail trends often mirror trends in a nation's overall economy. The dress habit, the food habit, etc., are very much influenced by the entry of East India Company and MNCs in retail trade. The evils of caste system and joint family system are broken by the influencing role of retailers.

National Policy on Regulation of Organized Sector in Retail Trade: A Proposal by CPI (Marxist)

Background

Retail trade contributes around 10-11 per cent of India's GDP and currently employs over 4 crore people. Within this, unorganized retailing accounts for 97 per cent of the total retail trade. Traditional forms of low-cost retail trade, from the owner operated local shops and general stores to the handcart and pavement vendors together form the bulk of this sector. In the absence of any significant growth in organized sector employment in India in the manufacturing or services sector, millions are forced to seek their livelihood in the informal sector. Retail trade, which has been a relatively easy business to enter with low capital and infrastructure needs, acts as a refuge source of income for the unemployed.

Organized retailing has witnessed considerable growth in India in the last few years and is currently growing at a very fast pace. A recent KPMG survey report prepared for the FICCI states that organized retail, estimated as a $ 6.4 billion industry in 2006, is projected to reach $ 23 billion by 2010. The share of organized retail in overall retail sales is projected to jump from around 3 per cent currently to around 9-10 per cent in the next three years. A number of large domestic business groups have entered the retail trade sector and are expanding their operations aggressively. Several formats of organized retailing like hypermarkets, supermarkets and discount stores are being set up by big business groups besides the ongoing proliferation of shopping malls in the metros and other large cities. This has serious implications for the livelihood of millions of small and unorganized retailers across the country.

Need to Regulate Organized Retail

Large format retailing is controlled and regulated across the world. The experiences of Western European as well as South East Asian countries are particularly relevant in this regard. However, an appropriate regulatory framework for the organized retail sector in India has to be framed keeping in mind the Indian specificities. India has the highest shop density in the world with 11 shops per 1,000 persons, much higher than the European or Asian countries. The potential social costs of the growth and consolidation of organized retail, in terms of displacement of unorganized retailers and loss of livelihoods is enormous. Regulation in India therefore needs to be more stringent and restrictive. There are broadly three ways in which the adverse impact of the rapid and unbridled expansion of organized retail can be felt:

1. Around 95 per cent of the 12 million shops in India have a floor area of less than 500 square feet. The impact of the growing market share for organized retailers is being manifested in the falling sales for the unorganized retailers in several places. The NSSO surveys already indicate a significant decline of more than 12.5 lakh in the number of self-employed retailers in urban India (by current weekly status) between 1999-2000 and 2004-05. Further acceleration in the growth of organized retail would eventually result in making business enviable for a large number of unorganized retailers, particularly in the event of a slowdown in consumption growth and retail sales. In the backdrop of huge unemployment and underemployment persisting in India, small-scale retailing still provides livelihood security to around 20 million urban workers and 12 million rural workers. Their displacement would further worsen the unemployment scenario.
2. Giant organized retailers use their monopoly buying power to squeeze small producers of agricultural as well as manufactured products. The experience of the farmers of developing countries with the giant food retailers has been particularly bad. The farmers become dependent upon the inputs, credit and technology supplied by the food retailers and end up being at their mercy in terms of prices for their produce and quality standards. Contract farming, which is the preferred mode of operations as far as the agri-business corporations and food retailers are concerned, has led to agrarian distress in many places. Moreover, uncontrolled diversification in agriculture away from foodgrains can imperil food security. In the backdrop of the crisis being already faced in Indian agriculture, the entry of large retailers with monopolistic control can aggravate the situation.

3. The proliferation of large format retail outlets reshapes the urban landscape in myriad ways. Land use patterns change drastically, often in violation of city plans. Given the unplanned and chaotic path of urban development witnessed in India over the past decade and a half, and the pathetic state of urban infrastructure, the proliferation of large format retailers will only accelerate the undesirable trends of predatory real estate development and unsustainable pressures on urban infrastructure and the environment. Rather than enhancing choices for the consumers, especially the lower income groups, proliferation of large format retail stores would kill competition, lead to closure of neighbourhood markets and make consumers solely dependent upon the organized retailers. This would also increase the propensity to use private vehicles for shopping thus, leading to more pollution.

Regulation of the organized retail sector has to address all these areas of concern mentioned above. Organized retail cannot be allowed to grow in a way, which displaces existing unorganized retailers, jeopardizing livelihoods in the absence of other employment opportunities. The interests of the small producers, especially farmers, also have to be protected by preventing the emergence of local monopolies/monopsonies. It has to be ensured that competition is not stifled and potentially monopolistic practices in credit, input and output markets are not encouraged by the entry of large corporate retailers. Moreover, undue pressure on urban infrastructure and the environment arising out of the proliferation of large format retailers has to be prevented.

Framework for a National Policy on Regulating Organized Retail

Small retailers need protection and policy support in order to compete with organized retail. The Ministry of Housing and Urban Poverty Alleviation has formulated a National Policy for urban street vendors. The policy proposes several positive steps to provide security to street vendors considering it as an initiative towards urban poverty alleviation. However, what is required is a more comprehensive policy, which addresses the needs of small retailers, especially in terms of access to institutional credit and know-how to upgrade their businesses.

A regulatory framework for organized retail should also be framed. Since the operations of organized retailers impact upon various sectors of the economy, policy guidelines should be framed involving all the relevant departments, namely commerce, agriculture and urban development. Moreover, since regulation of the large format retailers would mainly be in the domain of the states and local bodies, State Governments have to be consulted and involved in the process of framing policy guidelines. A Central legislation or a Model legislation, which can be enacted by the State Governments, may also be considered for this purpose.

In addition, the UPA Government should also abandon the moves to permit FDI in retail trade through the back door, as in the case of the joint venture between Wal-Mart and Bharti whereby, the former proposes to operate in the cash-and-carry segment while the latter in the front-end. It is more than obvious that this proposed joint venture is nothing but a subterfuge, to circumvent the existing policy regime, which does not allow FDI in retail. The entry of giant MNCs like the Wal-Mart, TESCO, Carrefour, etc., besides accelerating manifold the already rapid growth of organized retail, would also sabotage any attempt by the Government to regulate the sector in order to protect the interests of the small retailers and farmers. The UPA Government should take a categorical position on this issue. Not allowing MNCs to operate in the retail sector should be the starting point of the national policy on retail.

The issues, which need to be addressed in the regulatory framework for organized retail, have already been discussed above. Some suggestions are made below which seek to address those issues:

A Licensing System for Organized Retail

1. A system of licensing should be introduced for organized retail. Any retail outlet with floor area over an appropriate minimum floor area should require prior licence from local authorities (city corporations or municipalities). Corporate entities should not be allowed to operate retail outlets below the specified minimum floor area.
2. The authority to grant licences should be the urban local bodies. A dedicated committee/board/department should be set up by the urban local bodies, with representation from street vendors and small retailer associations, which should be empowered to grant licences to organized retailers.
3. The system should be devised in a manner so that there is transparency in the process of granting licences in order to prevent corrupt practices. A process of open bids for granting licences may be considered.
4. Considering the multiplicity of formats of organized retail, there should be separate sets of regulations for each format, based on floor area. Slabs should be set for the different retail formats, like discount stores, supermarkets, hypermarkets, shopping malls, etc., based on floor area.
5. Licences for each format should be given on the basis of a population criterion, i.e., not more than X number of large format retail stores of Y format per Z population. The criteria may vary between states and cities depending upon the nature of the retail sector and needs of consumers. However, a commonality should exist in terms of assessing the employment impact by the local authorities in a scientific as well as democratic manner, before granting licence for a large format retail outlet.
6. There should be appropriate caps both on the total number of large format retail outlets that are being granted licences in particular areas as well as on the maximum floor area for a retail outlet.
7. Retail outlets above a certain floor area should not be allowed to operate within existing commercial zones/areas. In case a licence is granted for a large format retailer within an existing commercial area, it should only be on the basis of an agreement to share a substantial proportion of its floor area with small retailers at concessional rent. The allotment of space to small retailers in such cases should be done by the licence issuing authority.
8. Giant retail outlets like hypermarkets, which attract large numbers of customers should have adequate parking space and should ideally be located outside city limits. Environmental impact assessment should also be mandatory for giant retail outlets whose floor area exceeds a specified limit.
9. Penal provisions, including withdrawal of licences, should be laid down for violation of the terms and conditions of licences by organized retailers.

Government's Role in Preventing Private Monopolies

1. A single large format retailer should not be allowed to capture a large market share. For this it is important to restrict the number of retail outlets that has a single private entity can open in a city, state as well as region. Under no circumstances should a national level monopoly be allowed to develop in the retail sector.
2. There should be guidelines to prevent predatory pricing and below-cost sales by organized retailers. A mechanism should be set up where complaints against predatory pricing can be registered by small retailers. The Competition Commission in India is not suitably equipped to handle such issues. A dedicated mechanism is required for this purpose.
3. In order to prevent the development of big private monopolies in retail trade, it is also important for the Government to ensure its presence in the market. Several Government marketing agencies exist, both at the Central as well as State levels. With a few exceptions, these agencies have been experiencing decay, owing to various factors. These marketing agencies should be revived and encouraged to grow and compete with private large format retailers.
4. Consolidation of several Government marketing agencies in order to create a few big public sector retail chains should be seriously considered, which can also invest in developing modern supply chain infrastructure. Panchayati Raj Institutions (PRIs) should be involved in the administration of cold storages and procurement centres.
5. Encouragement should be provided to the existing retail chains in the cooperative sector. New retail cooperatives should also be promoted. Partnerships between existing Government marketing agencies and cooperatives can also be considered, especially in food retail where synergies exist.
6. The State Governments or urban local bodies should levy a cess on the VAT on all goods sold by large format retail outlets (including those in the public sector) in order to create a level-playing field between the organized and unorganized retailers. Revenues generated from the cess can be used to create a dedicated fund to provide infrastructure support, financial assistance or cheap credit for unorganized retailers to improve and upgrade their operations.
7. Tax incentives should not be provided, either by the Central or State Governments, for the setting up of procurement/distribution centres or "rural business hubs" by private players. Neither should tax breaks be provided to private players for contract farming.

Safeguarding Farmers' Interests

1. Handing over farmland to food retailers for contract farming should not be permitted. Rules for contract farming should ensure that there is no possibility of farmers being alienated from their land, even if there is a failure in meeting contract commitments.
2. Contract farming should be regulated and monitored by the Government to protect the interests of farmers. Farmers should be encouraged to form groups or cooperatives in order to enter into contracts collectively with corporates rather than entering into individual contracts.

3. The processes of credit provision linked to input supplies and subsequent purchase of the crop, all by one private player, need to be regulated carefully by State authorities and PRIs. Supply of inputs like seeds need to be monitored by the Government. It is also important to ensure that monoculture is avoided.
4. It should be ensured that the farmers are not denied the opportunity of selling their produce over and above the quantity specified in the contract to other agencies at a price higher than what is specified in the contract. Farmers also need to be protected from arbitrary refusal by the contracting parties to buy their produce on grounds of 'poor quality'. The Government should reserve the right to intervene in such contracts in situations when they are found to be operating to the detriment of farmers' interests.
5. Large procurement centres created by corporate retailers should compulsorily have separate space for Government agencies. The scope of activities of the Government agencies would depend on the scale of operations. They may range from a single information centre for Government services to various Government agencies supplying inputs, providing extension services, disbursing credit and undertaking procurement. Several State Governments have amended their APMC Acts in accordance with the Model. APMC Act framed by the Central Government. That model Act itself needs to be changed incorporating the suggestions made above. State Governments should also be persuaded to do the same.
6. It has to be ensured that a single corporate retailer does not monopolize procurement operations in a district or area. It is, therefore, absolutely critical that both public procurement agencies and cooperatives are given support, incentives and freedom to compete with the corporate retailers. This would require special initiatives from the State Governments to reinvigorate the Government agencies. The Central Government should also provide adequate funds required for the purpose.
7. Private procurement of foodgrains by large players who can manipulate the market should be discouraged. The experience of the last two years shows how the free hand given to corporate players has led to shortfalls in public procurement necessitating wheat imports. There is an urgent need to strengthen and expand the public procurement machinery into more areas and provide it with the required flexibility to ensure adequate procurement at remunerative prices. Private procurement of foodgrains, wherever it takes place, should be closely monitored by the PRIs and the Government.
8. Food retailers or other agri-business companies should not be allowed to corner and hoard foodgrains stocks under any circumstances. To prevent cornering of stocks by private players with the associated potential for speculation, there should be rules for public disclosure of stockholding levels. Public agencies should be empowered to purchase foodgrains from the private holders at pre-specified prices if their stocks exceed a specified level.

The Confederation of All India Traders (CAIT) has sought a speedy implementation of the Parliamentary Standing Committee report imposing a blanket ban on entry of multinationals and big corporate houses into retail trade.

"The recommendations of the Parliamentary Standing Committee headed by Dr. Murli Manohar Joshi laid down in Parliament few days back for imposing blanket ban on MNCs and big corporate houses in the retail trade should be adopted by the Government as it is a unanimous document of the Committee comprising members of all political parties", said Mr. Praveen Khandelwal, Secretary General, CAIT.

Noting that the report had vindicated the stand taken by traders in opposing entry of big corporate houses and MNCs in retail trade, he said the report will have far reaching consequences on retail trade in India. Mr. Khandelwal said that the report will be an instrumental document for protecting indigenous trade and employment of crores of people.

National Trade Policy

CAIT also said that the Government in its forthcoming budget should also announce a national trade policy for retail trade.

It also said that the Government should form a National Commission to study the intricacies and issues of the retail trade in which proper representation should be given to traders and other sections concerning retail trade.

These proposals are being made in a backdrop where private players are entering both in retail trade and agriculture in a big way. There is an urgent need to frame new rules in order to regulate the operations of corporates in these sectors, which employ the bulk of the Indian population. The UPA Government should consider the proposals seriously and take immediate initiatives to frame a national policy in this regard.

The Indian retail sector is eyeing rapid expansion. According to Mr. Kumar Rajagopalan, CEO, Retailers Association of India, Indian retail sector has grown 20 per cent over the year 2009. According to Mr. Kripesh Hariharan, HR Head, People Office, Central and Brand Factory, Future Group, his retail group is planning a six more central stores taking the total number to 20 by March 2011. Reliance Retail has added electronics retail format. Reliance Digital will add 75 stores to its existing 24 stores.

QUESTIONS

1. Present an overview of Global Retailing.
2. What are the challenges and opportunities in retailing?
3. Discuss about the retail trends in India and the micro and macro-environments in retailing.
4. Explain the Socio-economic and Technological influences in Retail Management.
5. Critically evaluate Govt. of India's Policy implications on retails.
6. Explain the concept of Seven Ps in marketing.
7. Explain terms marketing mix, marketing research and market research.
8. Discuss the significance of orientation in the marketing context.
9. Define strategic business unit. Also list the areas of marketing specialization.
10. Explain National Trade Policy.
11. What are the steps taken to safeguard farmer's interest?
12. Explain the recent role of Govt. in preventing Private Monopoly.
13. How far licensing system is applied in the organized retail sector?
14. Explain about retailing environment. What are the components of Micro-environment?

15. Define Retail Management.
16. What do you mean by marketing mix?
17. What do you mean by promotional mix?
18. Define Global Retailing.
19. What are functions of retailers?
20. Why is retailing important in our society?
21. What career and entrepreneurial opportunities does retailing offer?
22. What type of decisions do retail managers make?
23. How do retailers differ in terms of how they meet the needs of their customers?
24. How do service retailers differ from merchandise retailers?
25. What are the types of ownership for retail firms?
26. Who is your favourite retailer? Why do you like this retailer? What would a competitive retailer have to do to get your patronage?
27. From your perspective, what are the benefits and limitations of purchasing a garment directly from a garment-manufacturer rather than from a retailer?
28. What trends are shaping today's retailers?
29. What are the different types of retailers?
30. Explain the micro and macro-environments that influence retail management?
31. Choose any two retailers and explain how the companies started and how they have changed over time.
32. How can small, independent retailers compete against large national chains?
33. What do off-price retailers need to do to compete against other format in the future?
34. Compare and contrast the retail mixes of convenience stores, traditional supermarkets, supercentres and malls. Can all of these retail institutions survive over the long run? How? Why?
35. Which type of the store-based retail formats is most vulnerable to competition? Why? Which is least vulnerable? Why?
36. Many experts believe that customer service is one of retailing's most important issues. How can retailers that emphasize price (such as discount stores, category specialists, and off-price retailers) improve customer service without increasing costs and thus, prices?
37. What are the unique customer benefits offered by the retail stores?
38. How might technology affect the future shopping experience?
39. How do customers make decisions?
40. What social and personal factors affect customer purchase decisions?
41. How can retailers get customers to visit their stores frequently and buy more merchandise during each visit?
42. Does the customer buying process end when a customer buys some merchandise? Explain your answer.
43. Using the steps in the consumer buying process, describe how you used this process to select your college. When you were deciding on which college to attend, what objective and subjective criteria did you use in the alternative evaluation portion of the consumer buying process?

44. Why is geo-demographic segmentation used by retailers to locate stores?
45. Any retailer's goal is to get a customer in its store to stop searching and buy a product at its outlet. How can a garment retailer ensure that the customer buys garments at its outlet?
46. How would you expect the buying decision process to differ when shopping on the internet compared with shopping in a store?
47. Choose a retailer and describe how it has developed a competitive strategic advantage.
48. Identify a store or service provider that you believe has an effective loyalty programme. Explain why it is effective.
49. How is retail strategy reflected in retailers?
50. Why do retailers need to evaluate their performance?
51. What is the strategic profit model, and how is it used?
52. What measures do retailers use to assess their performance?
53. Buyers' performance is often measured by their gross margin percentage. Why is this measure more appropriate than net profit percentage?
54. How does the strategic profit model assist retailers in planning and evaluating their marketing and financial strategies?
55. Explain Dave Thomas (Wendy's) Retail Business.
56. Present an unique global analysis of the brands that are truly succeeding at retail.
57. "All retailers are destined to decline" – Do you agree?
58. Write a brief history of Wal-Mart retail store.
59. What do you mean by the concept of "Black Hole"?
59. Critically analyze India's Retail Policy.
60. What are the problems of Retail Management?
61. Explain current retail trends in India.
62. What are the technological influences on Retail Management?
63. Write an essay on challenges, opportunities and threats facing retailers today.
64. Define Branding.
65. What do you mean by "Marketing Communication Mix"?
66. Explain "Promotional Mix".
67. Explain Marketing Planning Process.
68. Expand SIVA.
69. What are the areas of marketing specialization?
70. Explain Retailing Environment.
71. What do you mean by Retailing Myth?
72. Discuss the winning strategies followed by leading business winners.

CHAPTER 2

Retail Formats

Retailing means buying and selling in small quantities. Retailers buy in small quantities from wholesalers and sell in still smaller quantities to the ultimate consumers. Retailing may be small-scale retailing and large-scale retailing. Small-scale retailing may be mobile or immobile retailing. Large-scale retailing may be stores or capitalist organizations. There is competition among them to capture the available demand. In spite of very severe competition from large-scale retailers, small-scale retailers still control more than 50 per cent of the total retail business in many countries. Retailers are widely scattered. They provide maximum local convenience to consumers. Retailing consists of the sale of goods or merchandise from a fixed location, such as a department store, boutique or kiosk, or by post. Retailing refers to selling of merchandise directly to the consumer. Retailing encompasses the business activities involved in selling goods and services to consumers for their personal, family, or household use. It includes every sale to the final consumer – ranging from cars to apparel to meals at restaurants to theatre tickets. Retailing is the last stage in the distribution process. Retailing began several thousand years ago with peddlers hawking their wares at the earliest marketplaces. It is extremely competitive, and the failure rate of retail establishments is relatively high. Price is the most important arena of competition, but other factors include convenience of location, selection and display of merchandise, attractiveness of the establishment, and reputation. The diversity of retailing is evident in many forms it now takes, including vending machines, door-to-door and telephone sales, direct-mail marketing, the Internet, discount houses, specialty stores, department stores, supermarkets, and consumer cooperatives.

The famed editor Maxwell Perkins (1884-1947), who helped make Ernest Hemingway famous, tested his hypothesis that no one really listens to what others say at most social events. To ensure we listen properly we need to separate our obsessions about creating brand fantasies from the realities of operating a brand in a pragmatic real retail environment (figure in the next page). Yes, the two are linked but they are not the same. Springwise has explained the concept of customer-made (i.e., Shopper Made). It is the phenomenon of corporations creating goods,

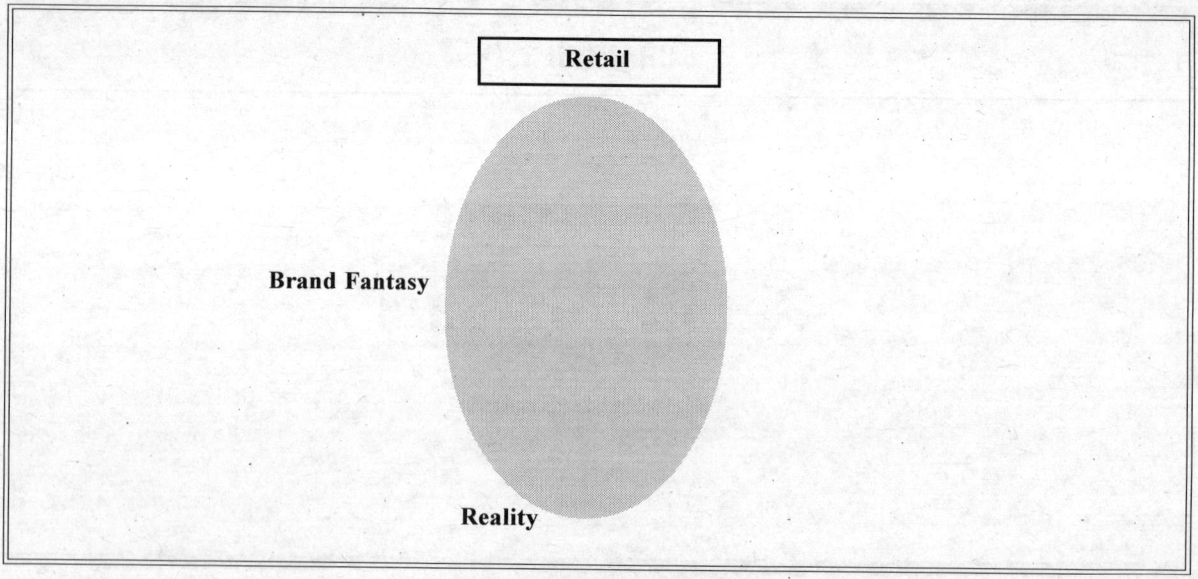

FIG. 5: REALITY VS. FANTASY

services and experiences in close cooperation with experienced and creative consumers, tapping into their intellectual capital, and in exchange giving them a direct say in (and rewarding them for) what actually gets produced, manufactured, developed, designed, serviced, or processed.

The festival seasons have erased memories of floods, flu and famine. Indians are shopping again and retailers, particularly in the organized segment, are back in high spirits thanks to sales figures that have exceeded expectations in the month of October, 2010. Consumer sentiment, which has been on a recovery path for sometime now, peaked in the month of October-November, 2010, in the large format stores. Retailing provides employment to the largest section of the population across most industrialized nations. It is an industry that promises a profitable road. The boom in the retail industry has brought with it many employment opportunities in this arena. People with varied skills and talents are required in this fast emerging industry. A career in retailing is considered a challenging option with growth potential.

The retail sector is expanding and modernizing rapidly in line with India's economic growth. It offers significant employment opportunities in all urban areas. This study, the second undertaken by ICRIER on the retail industry, attempts to rigorously analyze the impact of organized retailing on different segments of the economy. No distinction has been made between foreign and domestic players, in analyzing the impact of the increasing trend of large corporate companies entering into the retail trade in the country. The findings of this study are based on the largest ever survey of unorganized retailers (the so-called "mom- and pop-stores"), consumers, farmers, intermediaries, manufacturers and organized retailers. In addition, an extensive review of international experience, particularly of emerging countries of relevance to India, has also been carried out as part of the study. The study estimates that the total retail business in India will grow at 13 per cent annually from US $ 322 billion in 2006-07 to US $ 590 billion in 2011-12. The unorganized retail sector is expected to grow at approximately 10 per cent per annum with sales rising from US $ 309 billion in 2006-07 to US $ 496 billion. Organized retail, which constituted a low four per cent of total retail in 2006-07, is estimated to grow at 45-50 per cent per annum and attain a 16 per cent share of total retail by 2011-12. In short, both unorganized and organized retail are bound not only to coexist but also achieve rapid and sustained growth in the coming years. This is clearly not a case of a zero sum game as both organized and unorganized retail will see a massive scaling up of their activities. In fact, the retail sector, left entirely in the unorganized and informal segment of the economy, could well emerge as a major bottleneck to raising productivity in both agriculture and industry. One of the rather surprising findings of the study is that low-income consumers save more than others through shopping at organized retail outlets. This is a result of targeted discount shopping. It is also seen that farmers gain considerably from direct sales to organized retailers, with significant price and profit advantages as compared with selling either to intermediaries or to government regulated markets. Large manufacturers have also started feeling the competitive impact of organized retail through both price and payment pressures. Yet, they see the advantages from a more efficient supply chain and logistics that accompany the growth of organized retail. The extensive empirical evidence marshalled and analyzed by ICRIER researchers will hopefully provide a solid basis for policy in this sector. Based on the empirical evidence and analysis that have been extensively peer reviewed, the study makes a number of policy recommendations that have a bearing on both the unorganized and organized segments of the retail sector. The two most important recommendations in my view are: first, for the government to facilitate the emergence of a "private code of conduct" for organized retailers in their transaction with small suppliers; and, second, a simplification of the licencing and permit regime to promote the expansion of organized retail. The retail business in India, is estimated to grow at 13 per cent per annum from US $ 322 billion in 2006-07 to US $ 590 billion in 2011-12. The unorganized retail sector is expected to grow at about 10 per cent per annum from US $ 309 billion 2006-07 to US $ 496 billion in 2011-12. Organized retail which now constitutes a small four per cent of retail sector in 2006-07, is likely to grow at 45-50 per cent per annum and quadruple its share of total retail trade to 16 per cent by 2011-12.

Mass Market to Mass of Niches: The internet is displaying a key trend that backs up this movement to the 'me' culture for the future. Although we still obsess over the leading

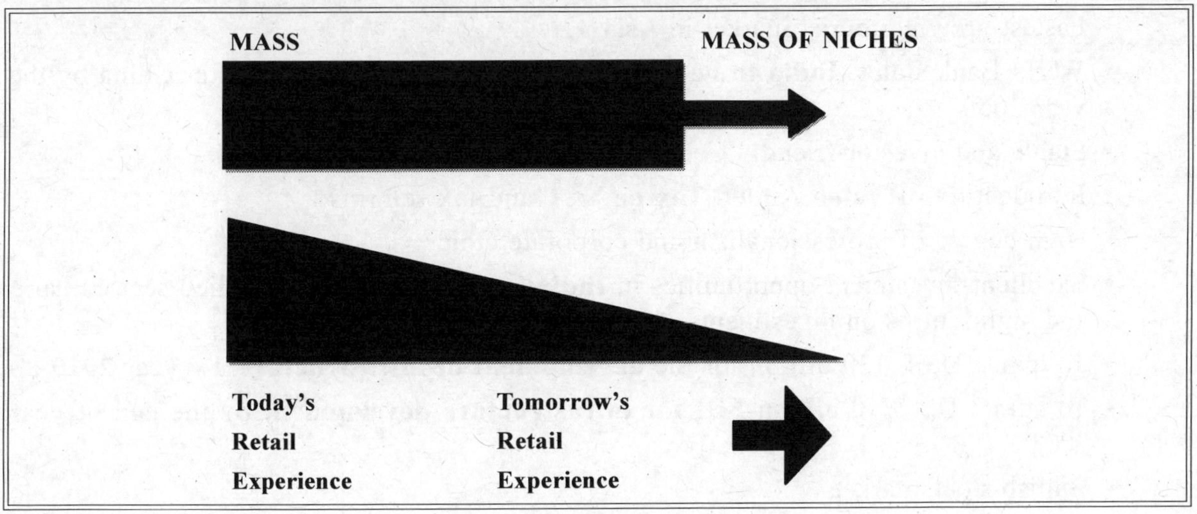

FIG. 6: THE LONG RETAIL-TAIL

brands, they are not the economic force they used to be. They are scattered to the winds as market fragments into countless niches as shown in the diagram. The mass market is turning into a mass of niches.

Retailing is one of the pillars of the economy in India and accounts for 35 per cent of GDP. The retail industry is divided into organized and unorganized sectors. Over 12 million outlets operate in the country and only 4 per cent of them being larger than 500 sq. ft. (46 m^2) in size. Organized retailing refers to trading activities undertaken by licenced retailers, that is, those who are registered for sales tax, income tax, etc. These include the corporate-backed hypermarkets and retail chains, and also the privately owned large retail businesses. Unorganized retailing, on the other hand, refers to the traditional formats of low-cost retailing, for example, the local kirana shops, owner manned general stores, paan/beedi shops, convenience stores, handcart and pavement vendors, etc. In India, a shopkeeper of such kind of shops is usually known as a dukandar.

Most Indian shopping takes place in open markets and millions of independent grocery shops called kirana. Organized retail such supermarkets accounts for just 4 per cent of the market as of 2008. Regulations prevent most foreign investment in retailing. Moreover, over thirty regulations such as "signboard licences" and "anti-hoarding measures" may have to be complied before a store can open doors. There are taxes for moving goods to states, from states, and even within states.

Formats in Indian Organized Retail Sector and its subsequent successful operation is credited to **India Economic System** reform in July, 1991. Formats in Indian Organized Retail Sector is at its nascent stage. The **Central Government** has ultimately realized the need to remove the insulation out of the Indian retail sector. Skeptics opine opening up Indian retail industry would jeopardize way of income for the poor small retailers. In fact, the actual story is quite heartening for the **small time retailer** and its vendors.

- It is the second fastest growing economy of the world
- Potential to be the third largest economy in terms of **GDP** in next few years
- It ranks high amongst the top 10 **FDI** destinations of the world
- Fastest growing tourist market in Asia
- World Bank states, **India to be world's second largest economy** after China by the year 2050
- Stable and investor-friendly Central Government at the helm of affairs
- Introduction of **Value Added Tax or VAT** and tax reforms
- High degree of professionalism and corporate ethics
- Excellent-investment opportunities in **Indian retail sector** and in allied sectors; sure and high returns on investments
- To invest US $ 130 billion for the **development of infrastructure**, by year 2010
- To attract US $ 10 billion **FDI for infrastructure development** by the end of year 2008
- Bullish stock markets
- Hordes of **foreign investors** are thronging into invest in Indian retail markets

- Highly educated English speaking young workforce
- Vibrant and multicultured cities
- Huge opportunity exists, especially in semi-rural and rural areas
- Till date the second largest employer after agriculture sector, for the huge **semi-skilled Indian population**
- Offers highest shop density in the whole world
- Having almost 1,20,000 shops, across the length and breadth of the country
- In a nascent stage of development as an organized industry

Formats in Indian Organized Retail Sector

- Supermarkets
- Hypermarkets
- Department Stores
- Modern Format Individual Retailers
- Shopping Malls
- Specialty Chains

Types of Retailers

Customers today can shop for goods and services in a wide variety of stores. The most important retail-store types are described below:

Specialty store concentrates on a limited number of complementary merchandise categories and provides a high level of service in relatively small stores.

Non-store retailing: 1. Direct selling, 2. Direct marketing, 3. Automatic vending and buying services

Examples of non-store retailing include internet sales of hot sauces, and the direct sales of cosmetics by Avon, and by L.L. Bean and Patagonia.

I. Mobile or Itinerant Retailers

(i) Hawkers and Peddlers
(ii) Street vendors (Traders)
(iii) Market Vendors
(iv) Cheap Jacks

II. Fixed Shop or Non-itinerant Retailers

Small-scale Fixed Shops

(i) Street Stalls
(ii) Second-hand Goods Dealers
(iii) General Stores
(iv) Single Line Stores

(v) Specialty Shops

(vi) Vending Machines

III. Shopping Centre

Large-scale Fixed Shops

(i) Department Stores

(ii) Multiple Shops of Chain Stores

(iii) Mail Order Houses

(iv) Hire Purchase Stores or Installment System

(v) Consumer's Cooperative Stores

(vi) One Price Shops

(vii) Super Markets

(viii) Shopping Centres

(ix) Tied Shops

Types of Shopping Facilities

- Big-box store
- Strip mall
- Plaza
- Market
- Main street
- High street
- Town square
- Power centre
- Lifestyle centre
- Outlet mall

Customers today can shop for goods and services in a wide variety of stores. The most important retail-store types are described below:

Specialty Store

It also includes Internet, and direct mail, direct selling, television home shopping and **vending machines**

- Examples of non-store retailing include internet sales of hot sauces, the direct sales of cosmetics by Avon, and catalogue sales by L.L. Bean and Patagonia.

While the rural retail business does not offer vast untapped potential, it should be recommended that it is not very easy to operate in this rural market because of several problems. The important problems faced by producers and marketers in rural areas are as follows:

Retail Management near Chennai, Tamil Nadu

Retail Consulting

Global Sales/Mgmt. Experts; est-1980

Free Friedman Enewsletter + Previews

www. thefriedmangroup.com

Euphoria Software Solutions

95/296, Paper Mills Road, Perambur, Chennai, Tamil Nadu 600011 044 4355 5117 5.6 km

Category: Retail Management Software

Euphoria Software Solutions

95/296, Paper Mills Road, Perambur, Chennai, Tamil Nadu 600011 044 4355 5117 – 097 90 144447 (Mobile)

euphoriass.com

Categories: Software Company, POS Software, Retail Software

Hours: 9 am – 8 pm (Expcept Sunday)

Euphoria Software Solutions is the Home of Retail Management Software Products. Its flagship product Kanakkar (TM) is a bilingual billing software and they have various other products. They have customers in 26 districts.

Public transport: Perambur Station (400 m)

Home of Retail Management Software Products. Our flagship product Kanakkar (TM) is a bilingual billing software and we have various other products. We have customers in 26 districts.

Email: umar@euphoriass.com

S Ibrahim & Co.

New no. 122, Anna Salai, Chennai, Tamil Nadu 600002 044 2852 1811

Category: Retail Stores - China & Glassware

New no. 122, Anna Salai, Chennai, Tamil Nadu 600002 044 2852 1811

s-ibrahim.com

Categories: Kitchen Appliances Stores, Laboratory Equipment Supplier, Office Equipment Supplier,..

Public Transport: Chitra Theatre Bus Stop (500 m)

This is a retail and Hotel supplies business, opp LIC on Anna Salai

"SRI MURUGAN TIMBER TRADERS 179, Sydenhams Road, Choolai, Chennai-600112...."

Vision Next India Private Limited

No. 25/11, Ramanujan Street, Off. Venkatnarayana Road, T.Nagar, Chennai, Tamil Nadu 600017

095 24 045801

Category: Retail Stores - Electronics

- 044 4354 6552 - 044 4354 6553 (Fax) - 09841776380 (Mobile)

visionnextindia.com

4 reviews

Categories: Audio Visual Equipment...., Audio Visual Store, Office Equipment Rental...,...

Public Transport: Panagal Park Bus Stop (800 m)

While the rural retail business does not offer vast untapped potential, it should be recommended that it is not very easy to operate in this rural market because of several problems. The important problems faced by producers and marketers in rural areas are as follows:

1. Multiple tiers of intermediaries and additional costs.
2. Underdeveloped markets.
3. Low level of literacy.
4. Large number of languages and dialects.
5. Seasonal demand
6. Low levels of logistics, storage, handling and transport facilities
7. Vast and uneven spread of villages
8. Lack of proper road and communication facilities
9. Low per capita incomes
10. Lack of media and communication facilities
11. Hierarchy of markets, etc.

Suggestion to Promote Indian Retail Business

1. Foreign companies are permitted to enter Indian retail market.
2. It poses threat to our retail manufacturers.
3. Hence, our domestic manufacturers must be protected.
4. Entry of foreign players must be gradual and with social safeguards so that the effects of the labour dislocation can be analysed and policy fine-tuned. Initially allow them to set up supermarkets only in metros. Make the costs of entry high and according to specific norms and regulations so that the retailer cannot immediately indulge in 'predatory' pricing.
5. In order to address the dislocation issue, it becomes imperative to develop and improve the manufacturing sector in India. There has been a substantial fall in employment by the manufacturing sector, to the extent of 4.06 lakh over the period 1998 to 2001, while its contribution to the GDP has grown at an average rate of only 3.7 per cent. If this sector is given due attention, and allowed to take wings, then it could be a source of great compensation to the displaced workforce from the retail industry.
6. The government must actively encourage setting up of cooperative stores to procure and stock their consumer goods and commodities from small producers. This will address the dual problem of limited promotion and marketing ability, as well as market penetration for the retailer. The government can also facilitate the setting up of warehousing units and cold chains, thereby lowering the capital costs for the small retailers.
7. According to Indialnfoline.com, agroproducts and food processing sector in India is responsible for $ 69.4 billion out of the total $ 180 billion retail sector (these are 2001 figures). This is more than just a sizeable portion of the pie. Returns are likely to be much higher for any retailer. Prices for perishable goods like vegetables, fruits, etc., are not fixed (as opposed to, say, branded textiles) and therefore, this is where economies of scale are likely to kick in and benefit the consumer.

Affinity: An Attractive Force Between Two Parties

The traditional definition of affinity is: "An attractive force between substances or particles that causes them to enter into and remain in chemical combination".

– **Webster's Collegiate Dictionary, Tenth Edition.**

The retail marketing definition of affinity is: "An attractive force between two parties that causes them to enter into and remain in combination". – **Gene Pranger.**

Retailing today is at an interesting cross-roads. On the one hand, retail sales are at their highest point of history. Wal-Mart is now the leading company in the world in terms of sales-ahead of ExxonMobil, General Motors, and other manufacturing giants. New technologies are improving retail productivity.

Features of Indian Rural Market

1. **Size of the Rural Market:** An analysis of National Sample Survey data shows that of the total expenditure on manufactured consumer goods, 75 per cent is spent in rural India. The per centage remained almost unchanged since 1950-61. Though per capita consumption and expenditure on manufactured consumer items is low in rural areas, the market is approximately three times larger. On the assumption that all persons or families above the poverty line form the market for some branded consumer goods, this market has a size of 42 million households. If we take Punjab, Rajasthan, Gujarat and Andhra Pradesh, the target market of 72 million people is largest numerically than France, UK or West Germany.
2. **Rural Target Population:** Wealth distribution in rural India is uneven and the top 12 per cent of the farmer's landholdings account for 37 per cent of cultivated area. Further, NSS data show that the top 10 per cent of the rural population accounts for above 37 per cent of the expenditure on consumer goods. Not surprisingly the potential market is at the top of the spectrum. However, with the increasing spread of the rural income, consumer goods are expected to make substantial penetration into the lower income strata by the normal percolation effect. Then there is an increasing cross flow of population between urban and project town centres which act as a conduct for cross flow of products and ideas thus supplementing the demand for such products.
3. **The Market for Agricultural Inputs:** There is a very rapidly expanding demand for agricultural inputs in rural market. This is borne out by the increased compound rate of growth in the offtake of agricultural inputs like pesticides, tractors, pumps and tubewells.

   A recent survey in Andhra Pradesh, Punjab and Haryana revealed that over 90 per cent of the farmers interviewed felt that they should use more and more new farm practices. The study established that in these areas the farmers are eager to use newer agricultural technology for improving profits and are prepared to take calculated risks.
4. **Rural Market in Value Terms:** For non-food consumption items the size and the value of the market has increased as estimated by NSSO and CSO. In real terms however, the growth has been very modest at 2.5 per cent per annum due to a number of factors such as:
   (a) Lack of concerted effort by the organized sector to perpetrate the rural market.
   (b) Averages are misleading in this type of analysis as peak opportunities which occur in certain pockets may not be fully realized.

(c) If the market for consumer products is considered as a whole it overshadows the opportunities that exist for selected products which may be growing at a much faster rate.

5. **Helpful in the Food Processing Industry:** India is a land of agricultural, horticulture, sericulture which produces a number of varieties of foodgrains, fruits, vegetables, commercial crops and flowers. The Government of India is making its efforts to develop the food processing industry while giving a number of benefits including tax benefits, incentives, subsidies, transportation and marketing facilities.

   Food manufacturers or processors are primarily engaged in adding form utility to raw farm products. Wheat is milled into flour, livestock is converted into meal products, fruits and vegetables are canned or frozen. These firms play a vital role in transforming bulky, raw perishable farm products into storable, concentrated, and more appealing good products. Food processors occupy a strategic position in the food industry. Through the purchase of farm commodities, their activities are closely linked to farmers, as the source of many food product innovations and as the major brand advertisers in the food industry, they are also in close contact with consumer markets. Punjab, Himachal Pradesh and Jammu and Kashmir are the main producers of fruits and vegetables, Gujarat, Kerala and Karnataka, Maharashtra are the producers of coconut, groundnut, bananas, cashewnuts and certain other products like tea and coffee. Government is developing food processing industries in these states, which is being responded as per the expectations. Fisheries, meat products and other eatables are also much appreciated and preferred.

6. **Sources of Rural Purchasing Capacity:** Following are the factors which contribute to purchasing capacity in rural areas:

   (a) **Marketable Agricultural Surplus and Rural/Urban Terms of Trade:** So far as manufactured consumer goods are concerned, regression analysis indicates that there is a 0.7 per cent rise in consumption for every one per cent increase in marketable surplus of foodgrains. As the surplus is increasing every year, there will be increasing purchasing capacity with farmers.

   (b) **Remittances:** The traditional remittances from within the country are now being supplemented in several states by remittances from overseas. The total inward remittances in the state of Kerala have increased significantly. This creates new consumption and purchasing patterns.

   (c) **Government Expenditure:** Investments in food control and irrigation facilities would be around ₹ 20,000 crore in 2007-2008 and central sector outlay for rural development and associated programmes would be ₹ 14,000 crore. These will generate income, and increased purchasing power of rural areas can be expected to support consumption of manufactured items. Further, these investments are expected to augment the income generation process from land in future years, which in turn, will accelerate the growth of rural markets. The investment proposed during the 11th Plan for developing village and khadi industries is of the order. These too will encourage the income generation process.

   (d) **Dispersal of Industry:** The investment in the development of backward areas will greatly speed up the income generation process in rural areas.

7. **Increase in Farm Income:** Efficient marketing system ensures higher levels of income for the farmers by reducing the number of middlemen or by restricting the commission on marketing services and the malpractices adopted by them in the marketing of farm products. An efficient system guarantees the farmers better prices for farm products and induces them to invest their surplus in the purchase of modern input so that productivity and production may increase. This again results in an increase in the marketed surplus and income of the farmers. If the producer does not have an easily accessible market-outlet where he can sell his surplus produce, he has little incentive to produce more. The need for providing adequate incentives for increased production is therefore very important, and this can be made possible only by streamlining the marketing system.
8. **Optimization of Resource Use and Output Management:** An efficient rural marketing system leads to the optimization of resource use and output management. An efficient marketing system can also contribute to an increase in the marketable surplus by scaling down the losses arising out of inefficient processing, storage and transportation. A well-designed system of marketing can effectively distribute the available stock of modern inputs, and thereby, sustain a faster rate of growth in the rural sector.
9. **Helpful in Economic Development:** Rural marketing plays an important role not only in stimulating production and consumption, but in accelerating the pace of economic development. Its dynamic functions are of primary importance in promoting economic development. For this reason, it has been described as the most important multiplier of rural development. The development of an efficient marketing system is important in ensuring that scarce and essential commodities reach different classes of consumers. Marketing is not only an economic link between the producers and the consumer; it maintains a balance between demand and supply. The objectives of price stability, rapid economic growth and equitable distribution of goods and services cannot be achieved without the support of an efficient marketing system.

   The rural marketing system plays a dual role in economic development in countries whose resources are primarily agricultural. Increasing demands for money with which to purchase other goods leads to increasing sensitivity to relative prices on the part of the producers, and specialization in the cultivation of those crops on which the returns are the greatest, subject to cultural, ecological and economic constraints. It is the marketing system that transmits the crucial price signals. In order to sustain non-agricultural development, resources have to be diverted from the agricultural sector – physical resources to guarantee supplies of food and raw materials for the agro-industry and financial resources for investment of non-farm economy as well as for reinvestment and financial resources for investment in agriculture.
10. **Employment:** The marketing system provides employment to millions of persons engaged in various activities, such as packaging, transportation and processing. Persons like commission agents, brokers, traders, retailers, weighmen, and regulating staff are employed in the marketing system. A number of employees are working in the marketing system which is a three tier system ranging from primary marketing society, central marketing committee and state marketing board. Side by side cooperative marketing system provides employments to a number of employees. Storages, warehousing, transportations and middlemen, provide employments to a number of prospects.

11. **Creation Utility:** Marketing is productive and is necessary for farm production. It is, in fact, a part of production itself, for production is completed only when the product reaches a place in the form and at the time required by the consumers. Marketing push up cost of the product; but, at the same time, it adds, utilities to the product. The following four types of utilities of the product are created by marketing:
    - (a) **Form Utility:** The processing function adds form utility to the product by changing the raw materials into a finished form. With this change, the product becomes more useful than it is in the form in which it is produced by the farmer. For example, through processing, oilseeds are converted into oil, sugarcane into sugar, cotton into cloth and wheat into flour and bread. The processed forms are more useful than the original raw materials.
    - (b) **Place Utility:** The transportation function adds place utility to products by shifting them to a place of need from the place of plenty. Products command higher prices at the place of need than at the place of products because of the increased utility of the product.
    - (c) **Time Utility:** The storage function adds time utility to the products by making them available at the time when they are needed.
    - (d) **Possession Utility:** The marketing function of buying and selling helps in the transfer of ownership from one person to another. Products are transferred through marketing to persons having a higher utility from persons having a low utility.
12. **Contribution to National Income:** Marketing activities add to the nation's gross national product and net national product. An estimate indicates that 14 per cent of the gross national product comes from the rural sector and 11 per cent is derived from rural industries. Moreover, there are number of activities which are called allied activities to rural sectors. They are also giving a reasonable contribution to the national net worth.
13. **Better Living:** The marketing system is essential for the success of the development programmes which are designed to uplift the population as a whole. Any plan of economic development that aims at diminishing the poverty of the agricultural population, reducing consumer food prices, earning more foreign exchange or eliminating economic waste has, therefore, to pay special attention to the development of an efficient marketing for food and agricultural products.
14. **Price Signals:** All efficient marketing system helps the farmers in planning their production in accordance with the needs of the economy. This work is carried out through price signals. The government is announcing the minimum support price of the agricultural produce every year and also emphasizing the importance of a particular farm products. For example, during the past five years the government is stimulating the farmers to produce more commercial crops like sugarcane, soyabean, sunbean, groundnut, tobacco and tobacco products, sericulture products, fruits and vegetables, cotton and oilseeds. To fetch a good price the farmers are directed to produce as per the requirements of the economy. This paves a way for the development of rural industrialization and hence, the development of rural market.
15. **Adoption and Spread of New Technology:** The marketing system helps the farmers in the adoption of new scientific and technical knowledge. Past experiences show that our rural areas were totally underdeveloped and underutilized because of the lack of mechanization

of agriculture. With the advancement of technology, mechanization, introduction of high yielding varieties, development of fertiliser and pesticides and proper government policy, the agriculture production has increased to a great extent which is the backbone of rural industries.

16. **Widening of Markets:** A well knit marketing system widens the market for the products by taking them to remote corners of the country, i.e., to areas far away from the production points. The widening of the market helps in increasing the demand on a continuous basis, and thereby, guarantees a higher income to the producer.
17. **Growth of Agro-based Industries:** An improved and efficient system of rural marketing helps in the growth of agro-based industries and stimulates the overall development process of the economy. Many industries depend on agriculture for the supply of raw materials. So, many producers have installed their industrial units near the village side and are also interested in installing the units in the rural areas so as to minimize the transportation cost, easy availability of raw materials and some benefits which are specially meant for rural producers. So the growth of agro-based industries constitutes one of the most important segments of rural marketing.

Rural Marketing Strategies

1. Product strategies: Small size packing.
2. Low-price package and products.
3. Rough, tough and loud: Village people believe that rugged looks tough or robust and bright colours last longer. They expect most of the products brought to serve them for a longer period.
4. Brand image.
5. Pricing strategies: Low pricing, cost saving packs and conversions (The standard pricing factors like costs, competition, premium product value, new product pricing, channel factor, promotion costs, etc., are not carefully thought out in the case of rural pricing as consumer goods are to be pushed in the rural sector).
6. Distribution strategies.
7. Promotion strategy.

Table 3 : Distribution of Villages in India

Distribution of Villages in India

Population	**No. of Villages**	**% of Total**
Less than 200	1,14,267	18.00%
200-499	1,55,123	24.20%
500-999	1,59,400	25.00%
1,000-1,999	1,25,758	19.70%
2,000-4,999	69,135	10.80%
5,000-9,999	11,618	1.80%
10,000 and above	3,064	0.50%
Total	6,38,365	100.00%

Table 4 : Location and Concentration of Rural Population

Sl. No.	Population Range (No. of Persons)	Number of Villages	Proportion
1	Less than 200	1,20,073	21.55
2	200 to 499	1,50,722	27.05
3	500 to 999	1,35,928	24.40
4	1,000 to 1,999	94,486	16.96
5	2,000 to 4,999	46,892	8.42
6	5,000 to 9,999	7,202	1.29
7	10,000 and above	1,834	0.33
	Total	**5,57,137**	**100.00**

Source : Census of India

Table 5 : Location and Concentration of Urban Population

Sl. No.	Population Range (No. of Persons)	Number of Towns
1	10,00,000 and above	8
2	5,00,000 to 9,99,999	9
3	1,00,000 to 4,99,999	134
4	50,000 to 99,999	219
5	20,000 to 49,999	652
6	10,000 to 19,999	987
7	5,000 to 9,999	820
8	Less than 5,000	290
	Total	**3119**

Income Generation

The occupation pattern dictates the pattern of income generation also. The proportion of income generated in rural areas, source-wise, is presented in a Tabular form.

Table 6 : Income Generation in Rural areas

Sl. No.	Source of Income	Proportion to Total
1	Agriculture	59
2	Agricultural Wages	16
3	Business and Craft	9
4	Non-agricultural Wages	7
5	Salaries	3
6	Current Transfers	2
7	Others	4
	Total	**100**

Seventy five per cent of income generation in rural areas is from agriculture and agriculture-related activities. This is logical, as the major occupation is agriculture. This further confirms the earlier statement that the prosperity of rural areas depends upon the status of agriculture and related activities. Therefore, the development of rural market, to a large extent, depends upon the progress of agriculture.

The following results are available from latest survey of the NCAER.

Urban income is growing at 3.2 per cent a year, rural incomes at 4.5 per cent a year.

- 1994-95: Rural income 55-58 per cent of Urban
- 2001-02: Rural income 63-64 per cent of Urban
- 2004 -05: Rural income 66 per cent of Urban income (estimated)

Rural middle class growing at 12 per cent, in Urban areas it is increasing at 13 per cent.

- 2001-02: 35 per cent of India's 60 million middle-class in villages.
- 2009 -10: 33 per cent of India's 154 million middle-class in villages (Middle-class: annual -household earning ₹ 2 lakh–10 lakh)

It would mean that the fruits of economic reforms are finally getting filtered down to rural areas.

The sources of income by occupation groups both in rural and urban sectors are summarized in Table 7 below:

Table 7 : Source of Income by Occupation Group

(Percentage distribution)

Occupation Group	Urban	Rural
Farming	1.72	35.37
Non-farming	20.74	11.16
Salary	54.07	17.42
Agricultural Wage	0.74	20.29
Non-agricultural wage	4.94	7.56
Others	17.78	8.20
All sources	100.00	100.00

Source: Basanta K. Pradhan *et al.*: "Rural Urban Disparities", *EPW,* Vol. XXXV, No. 29, July 21, 2000.

Share of the Organized and Unorganized Sectors

Another way to look at the structural change in the income is to look at the organizational pattern of the economy.

The NAS divides the economy into two sectors: Organized sector which is identified with a modern market economy and unorganized sector or traditional economy. The unorganized sector is defined to include all unincorporated enterprises and household industries, other than organized ones and which are not regulated by any of the Acts.

Expenditure Pattern

The expenditure pattern of the rural and urban areas are presented in the Table given below. The National Sample Survey Organization conducts consumer expenditure surveys in the country. The latest data available for 45th round conducted during July '89 to June '90 are presented in the table. Usually, the expenditure data is presented 'expenditure group-wise' for different items under two major headings – food items and non-food items. The figures are the value of consumption of different items per person per month.

From the Table certain interesting inference can be drawn. The total expenditure on food items is of the order of ₹ 9,07,505 million in rural areas as opposed to ₹ 4,26,887 million in urban areas. Approximately the expenditure incurred by rural areas is double that of urban areas. Similarly, the expenditure on non-food items in rural areas is about 1.5 times the expenditure in urban areas. For example, consider footwear, which is about 1.8 times the urban expenditure.

Table 8 : Value of Consumption per person per month

Sl.No.	Items	Rural (in ₹)	Urban (in ₹)
1	Cereals	45.38	42.34
2	Gram	0.40	0.59
3	Cereal Substitutes	0.24	0.22
4	Pulses	8.31	10.04
5	Milk and Milk Products	18.35	29.53
6	Edible Oils	9.10	14.60
7	Meat, Eggs and Fish	6.84	11.42
8	Vegetables	10.25	14.65
9	Fruits and Nuts	3.23	6.87
10	Sugar	6.34	7.78
11	Salt	0.33	0.38
12	Spices	4.88	6.00
13	Beverage and Others	8.13	21.04
14	Total Food Items	121.78	165.46
15	Paan, Tobacco and Intoxicants	6.69	7.57
16	Fuel and Light	14.44	19.26
17	Clothing	12.15	19.86
18	Footwear	1.63	2.61
19	Miscellaneous Goods and Services	27.80	55.89
20	Durable Goods	4.33	15.38
21	Rents	0.57	11.40
22	Taxes and Cess	0.03	0.57
23	Total Non-food Items	67.68	132.54
24	Total Consumer Expenditure	189.46	298.00

Source: National Sample Survey: 45th Round (July 89 to June 90), *Sarvekshana*, Vo.16, No.1, pp. S216–S217.

Very poor people do not spend any amount on footwear, while the families in higher expenditure classes spend as much as their urban counterparts. Similarly, the rural expenditure on durable goods is about ₹ 32,267 million, whereas the urbanites spend ₹ 39,680 million. Here again, the difference will be low per capita consumption in rural areas and higher per capita consumption in urban areas. In addition, the demand in urban areas may be for superior durable goods like automobiles, washing machines, quartz watches, televisions, etc., while in rural areas bicycles, mopeds, electrical goods, hand wound watches, etc., are in demand. The rural areas demand cheaper and long-lasting products.

From the above data it appears that the rural areas are not lagging far behind the urban areas in demand for food and non-food items.

- We may further look at the pattern of final consumption expenditure. Bulk of the income is still being spend on food items, as is natural in a UDC. The fact that the quality of food intake too has been poor leading to serious malnutrition among a large section of population can be established with the help of a number of indicators.
  - Heavy bias in favour of cereals and cereal substitutes.
  - A fall in the expenditure during the last five and a-half decades on such items as milk - and milk products, meat, egg and fish - the sources of animal-based proteins.
  - Consumption of fruits, vegetables and roots accounting for only an insignificant proportion of total expenditure.
- Per capita oil consumption which is generally accepted as a criterion for level of living is very low in India, a mere 0.6 barrels as against the world average of 4.5 barrels and 24 barrels in USA, 16.5 barrels in Japan and 14.4 barrels in South Korea. Per capita consumption of polymers in India is mere 3.6 kg. per annum against the world average of 24.6 kg. These are all manifestations of a low standard of living. No wonder, in a recent survey of 20 countries conducted by *The Economist*, India was the last country any foreigner would want to live in.

Coefficient of consumption expenditure has been around 40.40 in urban areas and somewhat lower in rural areas.

Population

India's population has been increasing at a very fast rate. During the four decades 1961-2001, India's population increased at an annual average rate of about 2.2 per cent and even currently is increasing at about 1.8 per cent. This is to be contrasted with zero per cent in Portugal, Germany and UK and between 0 and 1 per cent in all other industrialized countries. Apparently, the population growth rate is very high and it is on top of a very large population base that India has. As a consequence, the absolute annual increase in India's population is being estimated at about 17 million, i.e., India is adding daily about 50,000 new guests all through the year, 365 days of it.

The retail rural market has changed drastically in the past one decade. A decade ago, the retail rural market was more unstructured and was not a prioritized target location for corporates. Very few companies, mainly the agro-based ones, were concentrating in these markets. There were no innovative strategies and promotional campaigns. A distribution system did exist, but was feeble. Illiteracy and lack of technology were the other factors leading to the poor reach of products and lower level of awareness amongst villagers.

Gradually, corporates realized that there was saturation, stiff competition and clutter in the urban market, and a demand was building up in rural areas. Seeing the vast potential of 75 per cent Indians living in rural areas, they started focusing on these unexplored, high-potential areas.

Companies came up with special rural products, like Chic Shampoo sachets @ rupee one, Parle G Tikki Packs @ ₹ 2, customized TVs by LG, Shanti Amla oil by Marico. All these brought positive results for them.

Also, campaigns like Project Bharat by Hindlever, where trials were generated across India in 1999, saw 30 per cent of its total personal products growing to contribute 50 per cent five years down the line. In the first phase, they covered 11.5 million rural households and increased awareness by 41 per cent.

Project Jagruti in the second phase by Colgate Palmolive India was a village consumer contact programme in 2001. It increased penetration of Colgate Dental Cream by doubling the villages from 33,000 to 55,000, reaching to a million houses. Such projects lead to increased penetration of products in rural areas.

As a result, retail outlets have sprung up in practically all the villages that store products of various brands and categories. Also, high congregation areas, like fairs, haats, markets, etc., are proving to be an important marketing tool since clusters of target audience can be tapped at the same time and place.

Location plays a big role in marketing. Therefore, if a product is for kids, anganwadis and schools are good places to tap them and their mothers. Similarly, mandis and village influencers act as a catalyst in pushing a brand/product.

The various points that affect rural marketing are:

Reach

For a product to reach six lakh villages, one needs to know that 700 million villages are spread over 3.2 million sq. metres of area. The road conditions are usually poor. It is, therefore, important for the marketer to have a good distribution system.

The Indian retail market, which is the fifth largest retail destination globally, has been ranked as the most attractive emerging market for investment in the retail sector by AT Kearney's eighth annual Global Retail Development Index (GRDI), in 2009. The share of retail trade in the country's gross domestic product (GDP) was between 8-10 per cent in 2007. It is currently around 12 per cent, and is likely to reach 24 per cent by 2013.

A McKinsey report 'The rise of Indian Consumer Market', estimates that the Indian consumer market is likely to grow four times by 2025. Commercial real estate services company, CB Richard Ellis' findings state that India's retail market is currently valued at US $ 511 billion. Further, CB Richard Ellis states that India has moved up to the 39th most preferred retail destination in the world in 2009, up from 44 last year.

Banks, capital goods, engineering, fast moving consumer goods (FMCG), software services, oil marketing, power, two-wheelers and telecom companies are leading the sales and profit growth of India Inc., in the fourth quarter of 2008-09. India continues to be among the most attractive countries for global retailers. At US $ 511 billion in 2008, its retail market is larger than ever and drawing both global and local retailers. Foreign direct investment (FDI) inflows as on July 2009, in single-brand retail trading, stood at approx. US $ 46.60 million, according to the Department of Industrial Policy and Promotion (DIPP).

India's overall retail sector is expected to rise to US $ 833 billion by 2013 and to US $ 1.3 trillion by 2018, at a compound annual growth rate (CAGR) of 10 per cent. As a democratic country with high growth rates, consumer spending has risen sharply as the youth population (more than 33 per cent of the country is below the age of 15) has seen a significant increase in its disposable income. Consumer spending rose an impressive 75 per cent in the past four years alone. Also, organized retail, which is pegged at around US $ 8.14 billion, is expected to grow at a CAGR of 40 per cent to touch US $ 107 billion by 2013.

The organized retail sector, which currently accounts for around 5 per cent of the Indian retail market, is all set to witness maximum number of large format malls and branded retail stores in South India, followed by North, West and the East in the next two years.

According to the report 'Mall Realities India 2010' by leading property consultants, Jones Lang LaSalle Meghraj and Cushman and Wakefield India in association with Shopping Centres Association of India, over 100 malls of over 30 million sq. ft. of new shopping centre space are projected to open in India between 2009 and end-2010.

Further, this sector is expected to invest around US $ 503.2 million in retail technology service solutions in the current financial year. This could go further up to US $ 1.26 billion in the next four to five years, at a CAGR of 40 per cent.

India has emerged the third most attractive market destination for apparel retailers, according to a study by global management consulting firm AT Kearney. It further says that in India, apparel is the second largest retail category and is expected to grow by 12-15 per cent per year. Apparel, along with food and grocery, will lead the organized retailing in India.

India has one of the largest numbers of retail outlets in the world. The sector is witnessing exponential growth with retail developments taking place not only in major cities and metros but even in tier-II and tier-III cities in India.

- Marks and Spencer Reliance India is planning to open 35 more stores over the next five years, according to Mark Ashman, CEO of the company. The 51: 49 joint venture between UK's Marks and Spencer and Reliance Retail Ltd., already has 15 stores in India.
- Carrefour SA, Europe's largest retailer, may start wholesale operations in India by 2010 and plans to set up its first cash-and-carry outlet in the National Capital Region. Currently, Carrefour exports goods worth US $ 170 million from India to Europe, UAE, Indonesia, Europe, Thailand, Singapore and Malaysia.
- Jewellery manufacturer and retailer, Gitanjali Group and MMTC are jointly setting up a chain of exclusive retail outlets called Shuddi-Sampurna Vishwas. The joint venture, which plans to open around 60 stores across India by end of this year, will retail hallmarked gold and diamond jewellery.

- Mahindra Retail, a part of the US $ 6.7 billion Mahindra Group, plans to invest US $ 19.8 million by 2010, to step up its specialty retail concept 'Mom and Me'.
- Pantaloon Retail India (PRIL) plans to invest more than US $ 103.3 million to expand its seamless mall Central and the value fashion format Brand Factory over the next two years.
- Bharti Retail has introduced eight Wal-Mart private labels – including two of its largest, 'Great Value' and 'George'– in its supermarket chain Easyday, hoping to attract more consumers with their international design and packaging.
- Italian sportswear brand Lotto will launch two new footwear brands Sabots and Calcetto in the country in the next few weeks. The plan is to have at least 50 exclusive outlets by March 2010.
- Steel players such as JSW Steel and Essar Steel are increasing their focus on opening up more retail outlets in India. JSW Steel currently has 50 such steel retail outlets called JSW Shoppe and is targeting to increase it to 200 by March 2010. Similarly, Essar Steel also has such retail outlets called Essar hypermarts. With a total of 150 such outlets currently, this segment contributes to about 20-25 per cent to the Essar's total revenue.
- EBONY Homes, the home furniture retail arm of the US $ 3 billion DS Constructions, has plans to invest US $ 25.1 billion to set up a chain of 20-25 furniture stores styled Ebony Gautier across the country by March 2012.
- Gujarat Cooperative Milk Marketing Federation (GCMMF), which owns and markets Asia's largest dairy brand, Amul, plans to add 6,000 Amul retail parlours across the country in FY 2009.
- With rentals dropping sharply, large retailers such as Aditya Birla Retail, Reliance Retail and Shoppers Stop, and food chains such as McDonald's are also looking at metros and mini-metros for expansion.
- Many major international brands are also looking for a foothold in India. The brands planning to enter India include The Pizza Company and Spicchio Pizza (both pizza chains from Thailand), Coffee Club from Australia, Japanese brand Lolita Fashion, Revive Juice Bars from UK, Mrs. Fields Cookies and Jamba Juice from the US, and French fashion brand Jules.
- Retail brands such as United Colors of Benetton, Tommy Hilfiger and Puma are opening factory outlets to sell excess stock and woo the price-conscious buyers.

Policy Initiatives

- 100 per cent FDI is allowed in cash-and-carry wholesale formats. Franchisee arrangements are also permitted in retail trade.
- 51 per cent FDI is allowed in single-brand retailing.

Road Ahead

According to industry experts, the next phase of growth is expected to come from rural markets, with rural India accounting for almost half of the domestic retail market, valued over US $ 300 billion. Rural India is set to witness an economic boom, with per capita income having grown by 50 per cent over the last 10 years, mainly on account of rising commodity prices and improved productivity.

According to retail and consumer products division, E&Y India, basic infrastructure, generation of employment guarantee schemes, better information services and access to funding are also bringing prosperity to rural households. The rural market, product design will need to go beyond ideas like smaller sizes (such as single use sachets) to create genuinely new products, according to Ramesh Srinivas, national industry director (consumer markets), KPMG India.

According to a new market research report by RNCOS titled, 'Booming Retail Sector in India', organized retail market in India reached US $ 50 billion in 2011.

- Number of shopping malls is expected to increase at a CAGR of more than 18.9 per cent from 2007 to 2015.
- Rural market is projected to dominate the retail industry landscape in India by 2012, with total market share of above 50 per cent.
- Organized retailing of mobile handset and accessories reached close to US $ 990 million in 2010.
- Driven by the expanding retail market, third party logistic market is forecasted to reach US $ 20 billion in 2011.

Exchange rate used:

1 US $ = 47.9 INR (as on June 2009)

1 US $ = 48.41 INR (as on September 2009)

Retail Formats in India

Retail Formats

The following kinds of retail formats are found in India:

***Mom-and-pop Stores*:** These are generally family-owned businesses catering to small sections of society. They are small, individually run and handled retail outlets.

***Category Killers*:** Small specialty stores have expanded to offer a range of categories. They have widened their vision in terms of the number of categories. They are called category killers as they specialize in their fields, such as electronics (Best Buy) and sporting goods (Sport Authority).

***Department Stores*:** These are the general merchandise retailers offering various kinds of quality products and services.

These do not offer full service category products and some carry a selective product-line. K. Raheja's Shoppers' Stop is a good example of department store. Other examples are Lifestyle and Westside. These stores have further categorised, such as home and décor, clothing, groceries, toys, etc.

***Malls*:** These are the largest form of retail formats. They provide an ideal shopping experience by providing a mix of all kinds of products and services, food and entertainment under one roof. Examples are Sahara Mall, TDI Mall in Delhi.

***Specialty Stores*:** The retail chains, which deal in specific categories and provide deep assortment in them are specialty stores. Examples are RPG's Music World, Mumbai's bookstore Crossword, etc.

***Discount stores*:** These are the stores or factory outlets that provide discount on the MRP items. They focus on mass selling and reaching economies of scale or selling the stock left after the season is over.

***Hypermarkets/Supermarkets*:** These are generally large self-service outlets, offering a variety of categories with deep assortments. These stores contribute 30 per cent of all food and grocery organized retail sales. Example: Big Bazaar.

***Convenience Stores*:** They are comparatively smaller stores located near residential areas. They are open for an extended period of the day and have a limited variety of stock and convenience products. Prices are slightly higher due to the convenience given to the customers.

***E-tailers*:** These are retailers that provide online facility of buying and selling products and services via Internet. They provide a picture and description of the product. A lot of such retailers are booming in the industry, as this method provides convenience and a wide variety for customer. But it does not provide a feel of the product and is sometimes not authentic. Examples are Amazon.com, Ebay.com, etc. In recent years, online retail or the e-tail segment is growing. According to Kashyap Deorah, President, Futurabazaar.com, logistics cost in e-commerce is brought down to 5-6 per cent of sales. For an online retailer, logistics strategy dictates the kind of products that it offers to sell.

***Vending*:** This kind of retailing is making incursions into the industry. Smaller products such as beverages, snacks are some of the items that can be bought through vending machines. At present, it is not very common in India.

China Whole Sale Store DHgate.com

China Whole Sale Store is the international online trade platform providing world-class standards of China wholesale product sourcing, payment, tracking and delivery services to over 28,00,000 small businesses worldwide.

Chinese comprehensive product range, provided by their extensive China wholesale network of more than 6,00,000 manufacturers and wholesalers offer a unique opportunity to their buyer community of over 230 countries who depend on us to manage their growing international product sourcing programme and tap into new markets backed by our Payment Protection Service, English speaking customer care team and their understanding of today's wholesale business needs.

Clothing/Shoes/Handbags/MP4/DVDs/Cell Phones/Watches/Electronics.

World Class Product Created for India.

LG Life's Good

TV/Audio/Video

Computer Products

LCD TV

LED LCD TV

Plasma TV
Colour TV
Home Theatre System
Music System
V Player
All Types of Mobile Phones
LCD Monitor
LED Monitor
Projector
Optical Media
Digital Photo Frames
Home Appliances
Side by side Refrigerator
Single Door Refrigerator
Washer Dryer Combos
Front Loading Washing Machine
Semi Auto Washing Machine
Dish Washer
Microwave Oven
Vacuum Cleaner
Air Purifier
Air conditioning
Split AC
Window AC
Multi AC
Floor Standing AC
Cassette AC
Ducted AC
VRF
HRV
Network solutions
Support
Complaint Registration
Product Support
Mobile Support

Annual Maintenance Contract

Other Repair Option

Find a Repair Provider

Energy Consumption

Calculator

AC Tonnage Calculator

Reliance Retail Ltd., which runs at least 590 stores across 57 cities in India, has already managed to achieve a near break-even by posting a loss of less than ₹ 1 crore in its first full year of operations, just 17 months after opening its first store.

Closely held Reliance Retail posted a net loss of ₹ 0.82 crore on sales of ₹ 1,486 crore for the fiscal ended 31st March, 2010.

The results appear to underscore why Reliance Retail, owned by India's largest private company by sales, Reliance Industries Ltd., has eagerly embraced an early mover strategy despite bearing the brunt of protests, including vandalism, from small shopkeepers and wholesalers in some of the 13 states where it operates its stores.

The results for Reliance Retail, which is normally reticent about discussing its financial profile given the continuing backlash against organized retail in India, are tucked away on Page 149 of the 2007-08 annual shareholders report from Reliance Industries, which is controlled by Mukesh Ambani. Mukesh Ambani is the richest Indian as on 31st March 2012.

Organized retailers such as Reliance Retail were not expected to show a profit in their first several years of operations, partly because of high capital expenditure involved in setting up a chain of stores, especially with spiralling real estate costs of the past two years in India that have led to a doubling of lease rentals in some cities.

Reliance Retail's first-year results, while not necessarily an automatic indicator of how the still-rapidly expanding business will perform in year two, are nonetheless impressive given the state of profit margins in the retail business, where most Indian companies are still learning and experimenting with branded stores.

Retail Store Safety and Security Training

Retail safety and loss prevention teams require training in local laws, store policy and best practices, which filter down to a unique set of job training requirements. Unlike other security jobs in an industrial or residential building, retail security has to deal with an influx of thousands of customers and this requires special training. This training needs to be in line with the store's image and branding to allow for a functional team that does not discourage shoppers.

Health and Safety

Forklift safety image by Greg Pickens from Fotolia.com

All employees should have basic safety training

At a minimum, all employees are typically given formal workplace violence, workplace ergonomics, fire safety and blood borne pathogen seminars, sometimes via computer.

Uniformed Security

Several states have minimum standards for uniformed security guards. For instance, New York requires 24 hours of training, even for unarmed security personnel.

Store Detectives

Plain clothes store detectives are generally unarmed and are often skipped in minimum security training mandates. This is because they are unarmed and often serve only a surveillance role, identifying shoplifters and employee theft. To maintain a more professional team, many stores hire former police and military men for these jobs.

Greeters

Another element in the retail safety and security team is greeters stationed at exit and entry points. They are trained to check receipts and monitor both safety issues and potential shoplifters.

FIG. 7: SAFETY PERSONNEL

Paramedic image by JASON WINTER from Fotolia.com

Safety Personnel

Some large stores utilize a safety associate whose job is to maintain hazardous spills, check fire extinguishers and keep emergency exits and escape routes clear of obstructions. Specialized training is sometimes given on reading and understanding OSHA regulations and Material Safety Data Sheets.

Retail Store Management Tips

A retail store manager's job involves running retail outlets that range from small sized independent stores to large supermarkets. Here are a few retail management tips.

The job of a retail store manager is overseeing the everyday running of a retail store. Some of the key retail services performed by a retail store manager are: Meeting sales and personal targets as well as customer satisfaction via maximizing the shopping experience of customers; managing all aspects of the operations of the store in order to ensure maximum sales as well as profitability. Retail management also includes focusing on key initiatives in business, daily cost control in operations, risk management, payroll management, loss prevention, inventory management, marketing execution, and store presentation. Retail store managers should have organizational skills which includes the ability of paying attention to detail as well as following up matters. The job also involves the capability of managing multiple priorities along with management skills like communication, recruiting, training, and coaching. Here are some tips that can help you to become a successful retail store manager:

The Customer is Always Right: Yes, that age-old saying holds true even today. The customer is the most important facet of any business. Hence, as a retail store manager you need to ensure that the whole team comprehends that, and behaves as if they do.

Make the Customer Feel Special: Everybody likes feeling special. So, when you are with a customer, give him or her your exclusive attention, listening closely to whatever they may be saying to you. During that time don't let anything else interrupt you.

Please the Customer: Although this is touted often, it is seldom practised. As a retail store manager, see to it that the sales staff does that extra bit to make the customer feel pleased, especially as a measure of calming down their displeasure about something. For instance, some special store giveaways can be packed with their purchases.

Promise Less and Deliver More: You have heard of the old saying 'Don't promise what you cannot deliver'. Well, by giving more than whatever you may have promised, you can build a strong customer rapport, both inside as well as outside the retail store.

Appearances do Matter: Although you may dismiss it as a superficial aspect of a superficial consumerist society, however, there is no escaping the fact, that the first impressions of the store, including the staff – how they are dressed and how they behave – do matter. People do care about the ambience of where they shop.

Display Merchandise Attractively: A vital part of retail store management is seeing to it that the merchandise is displayed properly. If the items are not displayed or seen properly, they won't be sold in the numbers that they ought to be. Merchandise should look crisp and new at all times. If the items are shop-worn, they should be put in the bargain section. Items that are usually bought on impulse should be placed on display close to the cash out area. Also, appropriate sections should be made for merchandise, and the items should be placed in the correct sections. Items that are similar in nature should be placed in the same area.

Items Should be Shown to Advantage: Apart from displaying merchandise attractively, as a retail store manager, you should also make sure that the items are placed in such a way that they draw the customer's attention. Hiding or stacking merchandise will not attract the attention of the customer. When thinking about how to display items, try to imagine what the customers will view with the display. Placing merchandise at eye level, or a little lower than that, is the best way to display specials. Placards and signs are also another method of grabbing the eye of the customer.

Get Rid of Unsold Merchandise: The bottom 10 to 20 per cent of the product lines should be gotten rid of every year to be replaced by new products. The product-lines that are not selling well should be marked down to half their price in order to sell them off fast.

Clear up Shopping Areas: While making racks and other display areas full, clear up other areas. According to studies it has been shown that having easy shopping areas results in more sales rather than having more racks and tables cluttering up the store.

Timely Ordering of Inventory: This is another important aspect of a retail store manager's duties. The levels of inventory should be monitored and kept in adequate amounts at all times. If customers do not find what they are looking for, they will just go to another store. Hence, the store manager must keep track of the inventory constantly.

Hire the Right People: A retail manager's success is largely dependent on the kind of people he/she helps to hire. The staff that is hired has to have the ability of making a quantifiable and meaningful contribution to the store's performance. In order to be able to rise in the organization, the store manager has to draw the attention as well as the recognition of the top management. The correct people will help in showcasing their talents while they achieve their objectives. In order to get the best out of the rest of the team, the store manager has to be able to keep them motivated.

Training the Staff: However, hiring the right kind of people and keeping them motivated is just a part of a retail store manager's path to success. Part of a retail store manager's job is to train the staff so that they are aware of what is expected of them. This will ensure that all the people involved in the success of the store move in the same direction.

Incorporating Time Management Skills: After hiring the right people, training them fully, and getting them ready to achieve success, the next thing a retail store manager has to take care of is managing their time along with the changing priorities they have to deal with each day.

Long Range Planning: Therefore, a retail store management job involves long-range planning so that every hour of everyday in a week is managed effectively. The skill of long-range planning is what will be appreciated by the top management, for they look for people who have the ability of looking forward, and creating concrete plans, in order to increase the business. A retail manager who can accomplish this will rise in the organization.

Retail Software: These days, there are many retail software that are available which provide scalability, data integrity, stability, and speed offering a complete retail management solution, which can be adapted according to each type of doing business. From inventory management to Point of Sale (PoS) ticket entry to customer tracking, integrated purchasing, and monitoring the movement of merchandise, retail software provides all the capabilities required to run a retail store business more effectively and efficiently. Table: 9 Global Retail.

Table 9 : Global Retail

World's Top 15 Retailers Rank	Country of Origin	Name of the Company	Formats	Retail Sales in 2001 (US$ millions)	Countries of Operation
1	US	Wal-Mart	Discount, Hypermarket, Supermarket, Superstore, Warehouse	2,17,799	Argentina, Brazil, Canada, China, Germany, Mexico, Puerto Rico, S.Korea, UK, US
2	France	Carrefour	Cash&Carry, Convenience,	61,565	Argentina, Belgium,

			Discount, Hypermarket, Supermarket		Brazil, Chile,China, Columbia, Czech Rep, France, Dominican Repub, Greece, Indonesia, Italy, Japan, Madagascar, Malaysia, Mauritius, Mexico, Morocco, Oman, Poland, Portugal, Qatar Romania, Singapore, Slovakia, Spain, South Korea, Switzerland, Taiwan, Thailand, Turkey, UAE.
3	Netherlands	Royal Ahold	Cash & Carry, Discount, Drug,	57,976	Argentina, Brazil, Chile, Costa Rica, Czech
4	US	Home Depot	DIY, Speciality	53,553	Canada, Mexico, Puerto Rico, US
5	US	Kroger	Convenience, Discount, Specialty, Supermarket, Warehouse	50,098	US
6	Germany	Metro AG	Cash & Carry, Department, DIY, Hypermarket, Specialty, Superstore	43,357	Austria, Belgium, Bulgaria, China, Croatia, Czech Rep, Denmark, France, Germany, Greece, Hungary, India, Italy, Japan, Luxembourg, Morocco, Netherlands, Poland,

					Portugal, Romania, Russia, Slovakia, Spain, Switzerland, Turkey, UK, Ukraine, Vietnam
7	US	Target	Department, Discount	49,355	US
8	US	Albertson's	Drug, Supermarket, Warehouse	37,931	US
9	US	Kmart	Discount, Superstore	36,151	US
10	US	Sears	Department, Mail Order, Specialty	35,843	Canada, Puerto Rico, US
11	UK	Safeway	Supermarket	34,301	UK, US, Canada
12	US	Costco	Warehouse	34,137	Canada, Japan, Mexico, Puerto Rico, S.Korea, Taiwan, UK, US
13	UK	Tesco	Convenience, Department, Hypermarket, Supermarket, Superstore, Specialty	33,614	Czech Rep, Hungary, Malaysia, Poland, Rep. of. Ireland, Thailand, S. Korea, Slovakia, Taiwan, Thailand, UK, US
14	US	J C Penney	Department, Drug, Mail Order	32,004	Brazil, Mexico, Puerto Rico, US
15	Germany	Aldi Einkauf	Discount	3,13,100	Austria, Australia, Belgium, Denmark, France, Germany, Luxembourg, Netherlands, Rep. of Ireland, Spain, UK, US.

Source : 2003 Global Retail Report, Deloitte Touche Tohmatsu.

Retail Store Management

Approximately 85 per cent are single-unit, independent stores and account for approximately 55 per cent of all retail sales. Firms that operate more than one store amount to approximately 15 per cent of the total store population and they realize about 45 per cent of the total retail sales volume. Included in this 15 per cent are those that are termed non-store retailers, such as mail order firms, house-to-house companies and vending machine operators.

Retail Store Management as Purchasing Agent for the Customer

When a retailer opens a store the philosophy should be to serve the customer; this means that the retailer should be the purchasing agent for the customer rather than the distributing agent for the manufacturer. Therefore, from the opening day of the store, merchandise should be purchased that customers want rather than merchandise that the manufacturer wants the retailer to carry. When retailers act as purchasing agents for their customers, they assure themselves a greater probability of success. Customers like to do business with retailers who serve them and consider them their most valuable asset.

The Retail Business Manager (Retail Shop Management)

The sole owner/manager should like people. People are customers, and they represent "stock in trade". As a representative of customers in the market, the retailer should purchase for resale those items of merchandise that customers will buy. They should make certain they associate with manufacturers, wholesalers, manufacturers' representatives, or their middlemen, who are responsible, and who will stand behind their merchandise. The retailer should buy from vendors who believe in the adage, "No sale is final"! This means that the item purchased can be returned for credit if a customer is not completely satisfied.

Today's retail store business is vitally concerned with motivating customers, and attempting to learn why they purchase one product rather than another of equal price and quality. Customers today are better informed than ever before in our history. To do business with these customers requires the employment of well-educated and articulate individuals. The impact of poorly trained employees on the present and future image or reputation of the store can be very damaging.

Another important consideration in today's retailing business is the mobility of customers. Approximately 20 per cent of customers move each year. This does not mean that the customers move out of the city; they may move to another part of the city, and, in the future, another retail store will receive their business. This is important to the retailer because he or she should always be adding new customers. If retailers fail to replace this 20 per cent who move with new customers, they may soon find themselves without an adequate customer base, and this may cause them to fail.

Another aspect of mobility concerns new and attractive shopping plazas and malls. Customers often drive many miles to shop in them rather than doing business locally in an outdated, unprogressive retail store. This is an important consideration when store location or relocation is being planned.

Planning for the New Retail Store – Retail Shop Management

When a decision finally has been made to open a retail store operations, the retailer store management should make certain he or she possesses sufficient retail experience in the particular line of merchandise being sold. Far too many businesspersons believe that because they have sold a certain type of merchandise for another retailer, they are well qualified to go into business for themselves. This is a frequent cause of retail failure. There is much more to becoming a successful retailer than previous retail sales experience. The buying function for a new retail store requires knowledge of the raw materials, manufacturing costs, and an understanding of the retail value of the item. When purchasing merchandise for resale the retailer should be a keen judge of what the customer will pay for an item. The fact that another retailer's customers will pay a higher price for an item is no logical reason why the same method will be successful for someone else.

Financial Needs in Retailing Business

It is necessary to acquire capital to carry the retailer through a minimum of two to three years of operation. Many large retail firms believe that it requires three to four years before a new store will return a profit. The cash-flow position should be of concern because without sufficient cash coming into the business it is not possible to take advantage of "good buys" from vendors or to pay invoices in the cash discount period. Expenses continue, and should be cut when daily sales decline, or when the business is closed because of floods, strikes, or other unforeseen emergencies.

The retailer's largest item of expense is for personnel, and a close control on the productivity of each employee should be maintained. The small retailer cannot afford the luxury of specialists who are capable only of performing certain tasks; most small retailers employ those individuals who can be used in many different parts of the store. The motivation of employees rests on the retailer, and every attempt should be made to understand what makes employees productive and assist them in their desire to perform to the best of their abilities.

Tips for Retail Shop Management

One problem that creates difficulty for retailer store management is their reluctance to visit trade shows, or to visit the market occasionally in order to see what other retailers and manufacturers are doing. Retailers who do not attend trade shows are sincere in wanting to stay close to their business; however, they fail to realize their customers prefer to shop with those merchants who are progressive, not only in their merchandising offerings, but in their store layout, fixtures, and overall environment. The small retailer should pay periodic visits to other successful merchants in larger cities, visit the market centres occasionally to see what other vendors are offering, and visit "key" manufacturers with whom they do business.

In summary, store retailers should make stores exciting places to do business. Remember – if retailers want a captive audience, they must captivate the customer!

Other Topics of Interest

How to look for super cheap airline tickets? Go for scanning dozens of sources of cheap flights on the internet to find out super cheap flights airline tickets. Apply Ratio Analysis to Financial Statements to analyze the success, failure, and progress of business. A business plan can provide the owner-manager or prospective owner-manager of a small construction firm with a pathway to profit. Starting a new small business is the dream of many people starting that business converts business dream into reality. But there is a gap between dream and reality that can only be filled with careful planning. The quality of employees and their development through training and education are major factors in determining long-term profitability of a small business training and development process. Today, many researchers are concerned with the information sent by communication that is independent of and different from verbal information. Increasing profits through reduced costs and cost cutting must be based on the concept of an organized and planned programme.

New Ideas for Business: Getting business new ideas are essential to business progress. Top new idea invention for business is the secret of sucess.

Shopping behaviour analysis combines a unique set of research tools. We compare what shoppers actually do in-store with their conscious and subconscious motivations and opinions.

Shopping behaviour analysis brings the shopper into the very heart of retail marketing, merchandising and category management. We report what happens in-stores, why and what to do about it.

FIG. 8: RETAILING DECISIONS

DECISION MAKING with regard to retail outlet selection is very similar to consumer decision making on brands where the consumer goes through a process starting from identifying needs to post-purchase issues. There are a few interesting and important dimensions associated with consumer behaviour and retail outlet selection.

FIG. 9: SHOPPING

Marketeers need in-depth knowledge about the various dimensions which link retailing and consumer behaviour. Research is required to handle retail decisions in a competitive context. McDonald found that a major chunk of its consumers decide to eat a few minutes before they make the purchase decisions and hence, it is building small outlets in large supermarkets such as Wal-Mart and Home Depot. It is providing play areas to ensure a number of families visit its outlets with children. A few companies also operate through kiosks in airports, malls and high-traffic areas. Sunglass Hut is a brand which operates kiosks at various places which displays about 1,000 different models along with their prices. Consumers could place an order through these kiosks and the product is home-delivered.

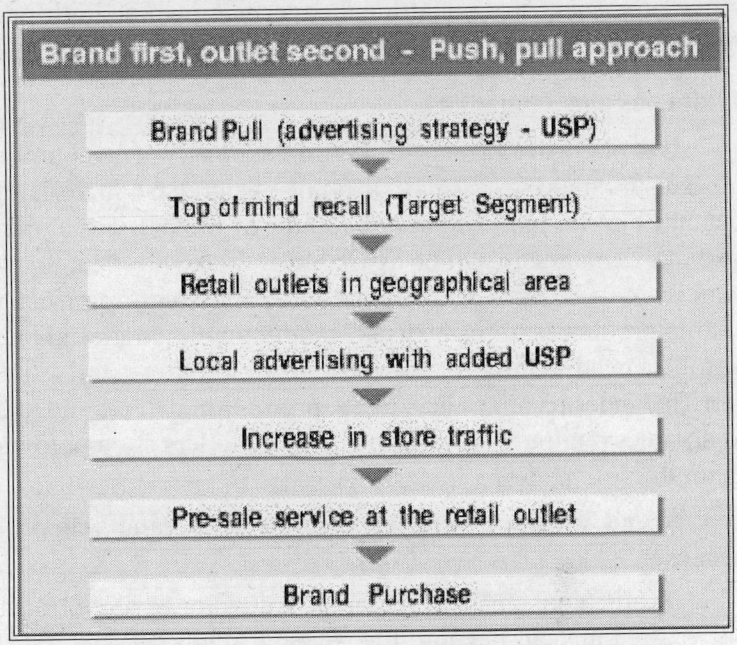

FIG. 10: RETAIL OUTLET SELECTION AND BRAND SELECTION

There are three fundamental patterns which a consumer can follow and they could be:

(i) Brand first, retail outlet second

(ii) Retail outlet first, brand second

(iii) Brand and retail outlet simultaneously.

A consumer wanting to buy a car may collect information on brands and purchase it from a retail outlet based on his perception of price offered or after-sales service provided by the outlet (typically, search for information on brands is followed by retail outlet selection in durables). In certain product categories, especially where 'category killers' exist, consumers may think of the retail outlet initially and then the brands (television, refrigerator and audio products retailed through outlets like Vivek and Co. in the South, could be an example).

One more dimension may be to compare brands in the evoked set at retail outlets which also exist in an evoked set of their own. This is highly possible, especially in the Indian context where dealers develop a social relationship with consumers, especially in semi-urban and rural areas. Primary research could be used to discover the specific sequence involved in a situation of this kind. A 'brand first' dimension may need feature-based advertising and a 'retail outlet first' dimension may require a set of point-of-purchase (PoP) materials and special training to sales personnel to recognize the needs of consumers.

Further, if it is known that a number of consumers may be oriented to visit their favourite retailer (before obtaining information on brands) in a geographical area, there would have to be more emphasis on regional/local advertising which highlights the retail shop rather than regular brand-based national advertising.

Strategies and Sequences

Retail Outlet First and Brand Second: When a number of consumers follow this sequence of decision making, display of point-of-purchase material and building the image of the outlet becomes important. The manufacturer of the brand may have to ensure that the brand (and the variants demanded) will be available at the key outlets in a locality. Point-of-purchase materials which are to be used at the retail outlet may require primary research – should visuals be used, should product features be used, should the PoP material be in the regional language. There may also be a need to monitor competition from other retail outlets to ensure that consumers are kept satisfied in terms of service, price, promotional deals and ambience. This is especially applicable to durables retailing in India (in cities). Retailers attempt to increase consumer traffic by providing a number of 'add-ons'.

Brand First and Outlet Second: The brand was probably thought of by the consumers because:

(i) The consumers may not have developed a relationship with any retailer which is strong enough to get into the 'evoked retail set' or

(ii) The brand has got into the evoked set because of advertising or positive word of mouth. Local advertising with the mention of brand names which have already got into the evoked set would enable consumers to be 'pulled' to the outlet.

Primary research may be required to identify the brands in the evoked set. This feedback may have to be provided by the manufacturers of a brand to retailers in various regions (especially if it is a brand with a major chunk of the market and one which is nationally advertised). Even multinational outlets could make use of this approach and mention the brands in the evoked set (in a given geographical area). This is likely to improve traffic to the outlet. Besides, the evoked set could also change from time-to-time depending on the strategies of brands.

About two decades ago, brands like Solidaire, Dyanora and Crown may have been top-of-the-mind (in a specific geographical area) but slowly gave way to other brands – these changes should be captured (how often this happens, why, and the differences between markets) to formulate retail strategies. The local advertising could be different from the national advertising for the brand. A brand may be advertised on features nationally but the retail outlet may prefer to highlight the effective after-sales service associated with the brand as this may be a priority of consumers. The interest generated in the brand would have to be backed by good pre-sale services at the outlet.

Brand and Retail Outlet Simultaneously: When consumers think of the brand and retail outlet together, it means that they have a certain preference for the outlet and would like to check the evoked set of brands there. The marketeer would have to carry-out primary research to find out specific markets where consumers have a very positive relationship with retailers. This is important because of the influence of retailers over the purchase behaviour of consumers in the Indian context.

It may also be worthwhile to check if the evoked brands are carried by the retailers who have a positive relationship with the target segments. This is to ensure that the retailers who have a favourable perception among the target segment carry the desired brands. Failing this, consumers may turn to a different retailer, which would be to the disadvantage of a retailer who has already won the confidence of consumers. Retail sales personnel also become important in this situation. The prospective consumers are "carried over" to the purchase stage by the store personnel and hence there should be incentive programmes for the store personnel.

If a company such as BPL or Videocon is dealing with a number of brands/subbrands, it has to ensure the availability of specific brands which may interest the consumers. If the retail outlet is a large one dealing with a number of brands (like Vivek), a shop-in-shop arrangement may be preferable. This model puts the brand in focus and reinforces the positive association a consumer may have about it. A considerable amount of pre-sale service would have to back-up the shop-in-shop concept.

The shop-in-shop concept creates an aura of exclusivity. Consumers tend to have higher expectations about the pre-sale service and the attention given to them. A large store also is likely to stock several brands and hence all brands in the evoked set would have to compete with each other to progress from the evoked set to choice set. Large outlets may also have a built-in provision for a lower price (because of volumes) and hence may be in a better position to clinch the deal with consumers who may simultaneously consider both the brand and the retail outlet. Green Retail Decisions launched to serve retailer information needs on sustainable business practices.

NEW YORK – In response to the growing Green Retail movement, Green Retail Decisions announced its debut as the first information resource exclusively devoted to Green Retail.

The mission of Green Retail Decisions (www.greenretaildecisions.com) is to advance best practices in sustainable retailing with a focus on program development, marketing and execution for retailers, including supermarkets, chain drug, mass merchandisers, dollar stores, warehouse club stores, department stores, as well as specialty and convenience stores.

Pic. 1: John Failla

Green Retail Decisions' content will focus on actionable insights and best practices in energy, facilities and construction, waste reduction, logistics and supply chain management, helping retailers demystify and execute green/sustainable initiatives as cost effectively as possible and in accordance with leading industry standards.

"As the world's first source of focused content on Green Retail sustainable business practices, Green Retail Decisions is committed to delivering information and analysis related to Green Retail news, trends and strategy", said John Failla, founder President and Editorial Director of Green Retail Decisions and Store Brands Decisions, a sister web publication launched more than a year ago. "We will serve as a catalyst for innovation in Green Retail program development, marketing and implementation, as well foster cross-industry collaboration and learning.

The $ 30 million Bergen Mall at Paramus, N.J., is expected to be the biggest US shopping centre. Puckett estimates that there are 1,588,000 customers within the 40-minute radius."

"10 Shopping Centres are Scheduled for Allied Stores within 3 years; Chain's Chairman gives details of biggest, 7 Miles From George Washington Span, where Stern will open branch by '57 Store chain plans opening up of more Retail Centres".

Identifying Trends

Shopping behaviour records are filtered and cross tabulated by as many as 50 different factors. The armoury of information subsequently obtained is phenomenal. Below are listed a small selection of the research factors that are filtered:

Consider the significance of quantifying and then being able to reduce the percentage of shoppers who actively browse your products but don't buy them. We have helped clients to improve conversion rate and subsequently raised sales by as much as 350 per cent.

Our clients are our priority and we endeavour to develop genuine partnerships with them. However, the shopper and the consumer are at the foundation of all that we do. "It is not about how big the market is, it is about how much value you can create".

SB-Excel a minority owned company partners with small to medium-sized business including start-ups that don't have access to the resources for sales optimization opportunity and business development strategy typically available to larger organizations. We work with your heads of Marketing and Sales to help create new programmes and optimize existing ones to achieve high performance among the sales force. Our solution offers methodology techniques that are tailored specific to the professional development of the sales force. This ensures the business meets or exceeds its quota month-after-month and maintains a healthy pipeline of qualified prospects.

Table 10 : Filtered List of Research Factors

Who shops	How they shop
Age groups of visitor	Products browsed
Gender	Products handled
With partners/children	Products selected
Buyers/non-buyers	Order of selection
Trolley or basket	Visitor to buyer conversion rates
With previously selected items	Products evaluated then rejected
Where they go	Media values
Stopping points (Category signposts)	Shopper sightlines
Traffic flow analysis	Time in view
Crowding areas and dead zones	Attention span
Shelf height analysis	Hot spot rating
Queuing details	Missed opportunities

SB-Excel – Categories

Hand Dryers

Hair Dryers

Baby Changing Stations

Swimsuit Water Extractor

Accessories

Parts

Made in America

World Dryer

Excel Dryer

Palmer Fixture

Columbia Vortex

Comac

Dyson Air blade

Suit Mate

TOTO

Mitsubishi

Dyson Air blade

Saniflow

SB-Excel also represents major equipment manufacturers and suppliers. As a result we are able to provide our customers with the certainty of products at competitive prices as business continues to grow.

Small to Mid-size businesses are the backbone of the US Economy employing the majority of the workforce.

"Our mission is to provide services that contribute to growth, stability and prosperity of businesses".

We strive to build a solid reputation as being the trusted business partner. Our commitment is to provide quality service to the business community. SB-Excel believes that honesty, reputation and consistent service is paramount. By being trustworthy, we believe that we will enjoy a long-term profitable company that serves the business community.

Shopping Behaviour Xplained Ltd., email: info@sbxl.com Telephone: (0044) 1827 56970 Fax: (0044) 1827 56560

Postal address: Shopping Behaviour Xplained Ltd., PO Box 8522, Tamworth, Staffordshire, B-78 3XG, Offices in UK, USA and France.

Category Research and Shopping Behaviour Research

Shopping behaviour research and analysis provides a vital but all too often forgotten human aspect to the overall science of category management. Here are just a few reasons why you should seriously consider incorporating shopping behaviour research into your category management process:

Compare the conversion rate (visitors to sales) for your brand with that of other brands in the same category.

Evaluate different category layouts such as merchandising by price or pack size and study the reactions of the shoppers.

Create more efficient category layouts by incorporating such factors as traffic flow and time needed to purchase.

During your next category review, negotiate more effectively by having access to an armoury of powerful shopping behaviour information.

Develop powerful arguments for specific space requirements and positions on shelf and in-store through better understanding shopping behaviour.

Quantify the true value of gondola ends and other promotional hot spots in category.

Fact: Younger shoppers don't like to shop next to the elderly (and *vice versa*) so the ages of visitors should be considered when designing the category layout.

Fact: The pack fronts of well known brands (category champions) are often more effective signposts to the category than expensive overhead aisle signage.

Shopping behaviour analysis doesnot only benefit those in retail. For information about how we can help numerous other types of client including hospitals and airports, click on the Public sector title.

Understanding retail shopper behaviour during final stages of purchase process.

The Research Challenge

Given consumers' increasingly globalised lives, how should mobile phone retail stores adapt to improve the customer experience and how does this impact on store layout to boost sales.

Quantitative research was used to provide robust data, in the form of exit interviews with shoppers intending to buy. Qualitative research was used to provide deep insight; this included observation of shoppers in stores, semiotic analysis of store environment and PoS, mini-discussions with selected shoppers and face to face depth interviews with store managers.

Retail stores offer significant room for impact and many shoppers entering stores with an intention to buy can still be influenced, even during final stages of the purchase process. Consistent patterns of the in-store journey were observed, which led to recommendations about how to design the store around key customer moments, as this would maximize impact. Importantly, we found that the priority of critical moments differed by market and the risk of failing to deliver on these critical moments caused the customer journey to break down. Our analysis identified a number of prominent shopper typologies illustrating how different shoppers engage with stores. We demonstrated how it was possible to redesign a retail store to accommodate all shopper types, encouraging both browser engagement and buyer sales transactions.

Outcome

By working in partnership with a number of retail outlets, the client was able to tailor the retail store environments of a national chain in line with customer needs. This collaboration was mutually beneficial to all parties, as boosted sales volumes were observed shortly after.

Retail and Shopper

TNS (USA) is the world's largest custom market research specialists. They provide quality marketing information delivered by global industry Sector expert consultants, innovative market research expertise across the product life cycle, in 75 countries.

TNS is the only custom market research company organized around the world liens industry sectors. TNS is leading the way in helping its retailer and manufacturer clients outsmart the competition by understanding and positively influencing shopper behaviour and decisions that result in improved performance of a brand, category or store. TNS delivers actionable insights to help clients make more effective business decisions.

TNS has over 30 years of shopper expertise with renowned industrial thought leaders at the forefront of the business. TNS delivers unrivaled shopper insights that help manufacturers and retailers understand in-store behaviour, motivations and decisions. TNS explores shopper behaviour around the key in-store touch points including store layout, category layout, packaging, promotions and in-store communications and provide competitive advantage in these areas. By converting the resulting shopper insights into action we enable our clients to build brand equity, stimulate purchase or trial, improve loyalty and customer retention and increase sales. TNS is the only custom market research company organized around our clients industry sectors – TNS 'speaks in their clients language. TNS delivers competitive advantage to clients through deeper and more relevant and actionable insights about the future marketplaces they're focusing on today. These "advance" insights are embodied in wholly-integrated research solutions. TNS is the world's largest provider of custom research and analysis with a global infrastructure that can reach people and businesses anywhere in the world. It has offices in more than 80 countries.

- Ranked world's largest provider of custom research and analysis
- Second largest global market intelligence company
- A leader in servicing over 50 of the world's largest multinational companies

Over 13,000 full-time employees worldwide.

Research conducted in more than 110 countries.

Specialist Retail and Shopper Solutions

Alongside traditional research techniques such as accompanied shops, quantitative observations and shopper interviews, we use advanced tools such as eye-tracking, using specialist glasses to record what shoppers actually see in-store, and Path-tracker to measure traffic flow and dwell time around a store.

The powerful combination of several specialist acquisitions in the retail and shopper arena – TNS Magasin and TNS Sorensen – in addition to our global custom services allows TNS to deliver unparalleled shopper insights and decision support to the clients.

TNS retail and shopper insights are used by many of the world's leading consumer goods companies.

Shopping behaviour analysis combines a unique set of research tools. TNS compares what shoppers actually do in-store with their conscious and subconscious motivations and opinions.

Shopping behaviour analysis brings the shopper into the very heart of retail marketing, merchandising and category management. TNS reports what happens in-store, why and what to do about it.

SF for instance, when a woman saunters into the supermarket and forgets to pick her basket, and is browsing through, you can know for sure that she is potentially a good customer. She doesn't have a list of items to buy and with gentle coaxing, can be made to buy much more than what she intends to.

Owing to the traffic rules we follow in the country, Indian shoppers prefer to stick to the left hand side of the store. They prefer to walk straight aisles and tend to turn right more than towards the left. While shopping with trolleys, they push the cart with the left hand and pick the merchandise with the right hand. Baskets are, however, carried in the right hand.

It is almost hilarious when popular brands try to get the rack closest to eye level, because unlike popular belief, shoppers prefer the rack that is just below their eye level. People read books holding it below eye level and the same principle holds true when they browse through products. So, the ideal rack is the one at shoulder level.

The next choice is the rack nearest to the elbow level followed by the level of the wrist. It is only after this that they look up. You will hardly ever come across shoppers bending down while browsing.

Shoppers are lured by premium/advanced personal care products, new product launches, imported products, promotional schemes, and snacks. However, it is necessary to keep in mind that shoppers walk in almost blind, which means they do not spend time in reading promotion posters placed at the entrance, or pick-up trolleys.

Bakery products, fruits, and vegetables impart a sense of freshness and completeness to the store but since these are products that are bought weekly, there is a tendency to grab and go, which the retailer needs to curb. This means that the most essential products that are bought weekly and the anchor products of the store need to be away from the billing counter so that the shopper moves through various aisles and may indulge in some impulse buying.

Processed food, basic personal care products, and fabric care products rank second in keeping the interest of Indian shoppers. Provisions and oils, and household cleaning products, although essential to their purchase, are seen to be "unimaginative" and "boring". Hence, there is ample possibility of cross-selling high margin imported products in these stores.

In supermarkets that have dairy and frozen products kept in refrigeration units with sliding doors, shoppers have to jostle other shoppers or wait for their turn to pick products. To induce more sales, stores have to provide more aisle space or switch to refrigeration units that do not have doors.

Shoppers seem to have an affinity for the billing counter, especially when they spy one that doesn't have a queue. It is ideal if you can create layout plans where the shopper is nudged to go through all the aisles and finally encounter the billing counter. The area demarcated for billing may be used not only for selling products that are bought on impulse, but also merchandise with promotions that the shopper may have missed out on.

A host of differences in shopping behaviour can be spotted once you consider the demographics of shoppers. For instance, women think of shopping as fun, exploration, and novelty; men think of their wallet and sticking to the "list". Women love to spend time browsing, which positively correlates to billing amounts, whereas men seek quiet efficiency. Women tend to shop more when they are with other women and are more willing to try out new products. This is greatly hampered when men "chauffer" them. Ideally there should be a sitting area where men can sip coffee, while women shop in peace.

When it comes to children as shoppers, it has been noticed that pester power works when the product is "known" or "endorsed" and is around ₹ 15. A good place to sell to children is near the billing counter, but the racks should not be too high for the children to reach. Men, more than women, are willing to indulge their children in a supermarket.

As final food for thought, now seems to be an apt time to test organic and health foods as a separate merchandise category altogether, since young shoppers today are more health-conscious and willing to spend more for all the things they may not really need in life.

An underperforming site has serious consequences to revenue – online and across channels.

Today's shoppers have high expectations when it comes to buying online. Websites which take too long to load can result in negative brand perception, diminished goodwill and a significant loss in overall sales. In our recent webinar Every Second Counts: How Website Performance Impacts Shopper Behaviour, we explored the findings of a new study by Forrester Research on behalf of Akamai which has identified two seconds as the new threshold for acceptable web page response times.

The Impact of Poor Performing Sites, Slow Rendering Websites Lead to Lost Online Sales

79 per cent of dissatisfied shoppers are less likely to buy from an online site again

This is up 17 per cent from those consumers surveyed in 2006

75 per cent would be less likely to return to the website again

In 2006, only 64 per cent stated they would not return

Consumers Who Make Purchases are particularly concerned about performance.

Those consumers who actually purchase at online stores are more likely to cite site performance as the reason they are unsatisfied with an online experience. Next to pricing and shipping issues, poor site performance is a major cause of dissatisfaction.

A Majority of Consumers Abandon Intended Purchases in the Checkout Process – Directly Impacting Sales.

More respondents are willing to, and do, abandon purchases than ever before. The percentage of consumers who intend to make a purchase but leave after the checkout process has begun is up 18 per cent from 2006.

Forrester asked "Thinking of the last time you visited an online store where you intended to buy a product but did not finish the online purchase, at what point did you leave the site?"

35 per cent of shoppers abandoned before beginning the checkout.

65 per cent of shoppers abandoned after initiating the checkout.

The Ripples of a Bad Experience Go Beyond Web Sales.

Customer loyalty is tied closely to how quickly a website loads (especially true for high-spending shoppers).

Overall, 52 per cent of online shoppers stated that quick page loading is important to their site loyalty.

61 per cent of online shoppers who spend more than $ 1,500 online per year insist on page loading quickly.

The Overall Brand or Image of the Company Will Also Suffer.

When faced with a dissatisfying shopping experience:

79 per cent are less likely to buy again

75 per cent would be less likely to visit the website again

64 per cent would purchase from another online store

46 per cent of online shoppers are more likely to develop a negative perception of the company

44 per cent would actively tell their friends and family about the bad experience

Site performance also impacts cross-channel shopping:

70 per cent of consumers research products online they buy offline

85 per cent of consumers are buying across channels

After a poor site experience, 27 per cent are less likely to buy from that retailer offline

A Poor Performing Site Opens the Doors for Competitors

Not only does an underperforming site lead to customer frustration, but 64 per cent of shoppers state they will simply purchase from another online store. This number is up 16 per cent from the 2006 study.

The Result

Consumer Expectations for Site Performance are Changing

47 per cent of consumers expect a web page to load in 2 seconds or less (perceived load time)

40 per cent would abandon if it takes more than 3 seconds

This represents a significant evolution in consumer expectation from the 2006 study, which showed the majority of customer expectations at less than four seconds. A major factor is the increase in broadband access. 3 years ago, only 54 per cent of consumers had broadband access at home. Today it's 91 per cent, and nearly half have it at work or school.

Conclusions from Forrester/Akamai Study

Perceived page load times should not be more than two seconds

Companies direct online sales suffer when not meeting those expectations

Companies will suffer indirectly across all channels and in the consumers' perceptions of their brand

Much of what we found in this survey is in the control of the online retail or travel company directly including some which are quick wins

Shoppers Demand Even Faster Sites

We know performance is a problem. With half of consumers expecting a page to load in less than 2 seconds, many online retailers are setting the bar even higher at sub-one second response time.

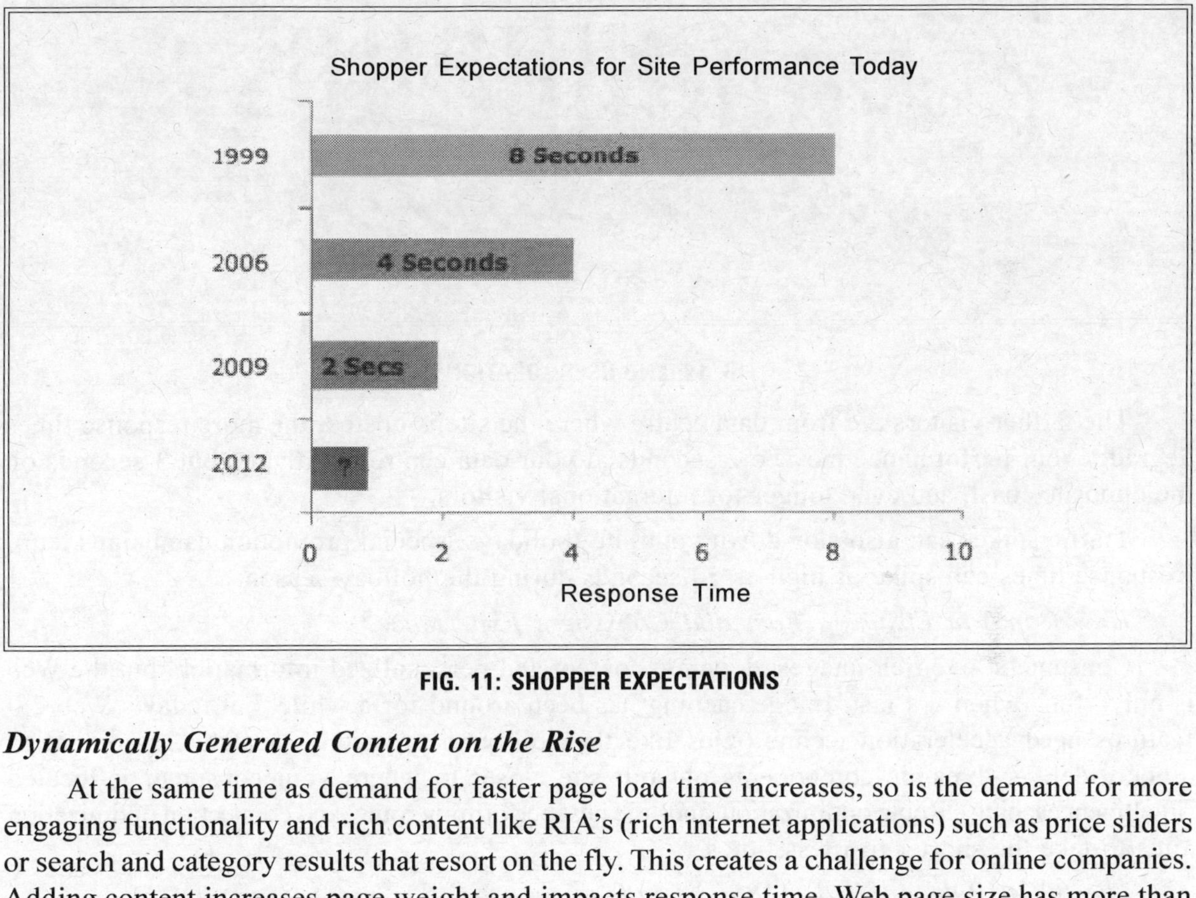

FIG. 11: SHOPPER EXPECTATIONS

Dynamically Generated Content on the Rise

At the same time as demand for faster page load time increases, so is the demand for more engaging functionality and rich content like RIA's (rich internet applications) such as price sliders or search and category results that resort on the fly. This creates a challenge for online companies. Adding content increases page weight and impacts response time. Web page size has more than tripled in the last 5 years.

Performance Issues Multiply with Distance

Often people try to fix performance issues by trying to "thin out" their site (decrease page weight). But many problems lie outside of your data centre.

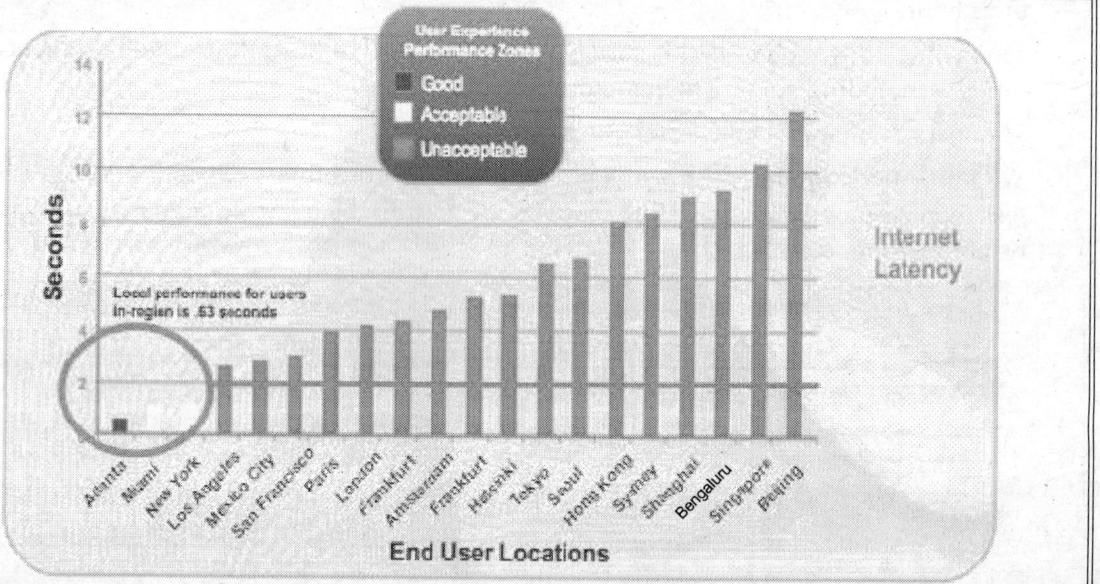

FIG. 12: END-USER LOCATION

The farther visitors are from data centre where the site is hosted, the more response times degrade. Your performance may be 2 seconds at your data centre in Atlanta, but 3 seconds on the opposite coast, and even longer for international visitors.

Traffic spikes can also slowdown your site (holidays, special promotion campaigns, etc). Response times can spike as high as 50 seconds during the holiday season.

How Can You Ensure a Fast and Consistent Experience?

Consumers love rich images, dynamic content and personalized information, but the Web is only "fun" when it's fast. Image caching has been around for a while, but today's Web 2.0 features need acceleration technologies like the ability to pre-fetch uncatchable content to quickly deliver dynamic components of your site closer to where your consumer is located (intelligent caching). Route optimization finds the best performing route, and connection optimization aims to take the shorter trip less times.

The 80/20 Rule Applied to Page Loads.

When optimizing a site for speed, there is an 80/20 rule applied to page loads — only 20 per cent of the time will be spent loading HTML. So, even if you have a superfast dual quad-core, 32GB of RAM application server serving the dynamic HTML content in 200ms, it doesn't matter, if the rest of your UI takes 5 seconds to download and render on the users browser.

In this example, the redirect and HTML took up 300ms, and the rest of the site took 3 seconds to load:

Minimize, Minimize, Minimize! We want to minimize connections and minimize data transfer (file size). We can do this by reducing object counts, compressing images and text, and caching properly.

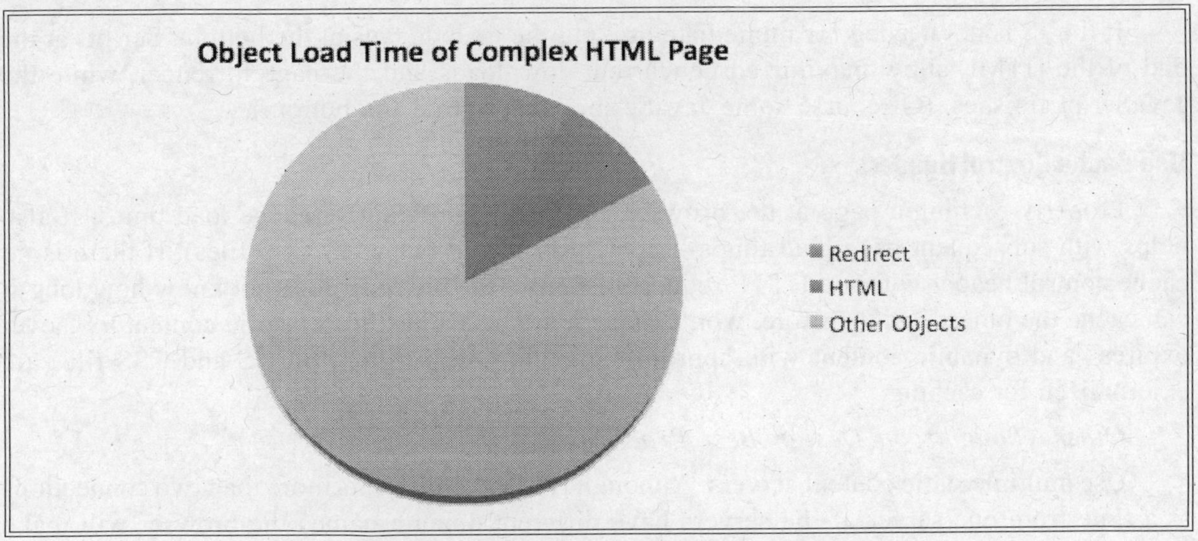

FIG. 13: DESIGNING WEB PAGES WITH PERFORMANCE IN MIND

Minimize HTTP Requests

Reducing connections as much as possible has shown the most performance improvement with the least changes. Combine your JS and CSS files and keep the image count to a minimum. If you need to load a lot of images for style, use a CSS image sprite. Image sprites require a bit extra effort in your style sheets but you can convert 10 images into 1 and take down the number of connections and potentially reduce file size.

Use HTTPS/SSL Only Where Necessary

Creating and tearing down HTTP connections is expensive, and adding SSL (secure sockets layer) to the mix makes it even worse due to the necessary handshaking and encryption/ decryption. Restrict SSL to data sensitive areas of your site such as the checkout only.

"Minify" Your JavaScript and Style Sheets

Compilers and browsers don't care about nicely spaced, human-readable JavaScript and style sheets as long as proper syntax is used. Javascript doesn't need extra spaces and a lot of the times doesn't need semicolons – these can be removed to create smaller JS/CSS files, which will reduce transfer time. Use a tool to compress JS/CSS for production pages — there are a number of simple, open source tools available.

Put JavaScript Includes at the Bottom

The HTTP 1.1 specification claims a "single-user client SHOULD NOT maintain more than 2 connections with any server at one time". This means you can "download in parallel" (two connections at once) but, when a browser hits a JavaScript include, it will not begin any other downloads until this script is transferred. If you have scripts at the start of your HTML, you will severely limit the browsers ability to retrieve in parallel.

If the JS is not needed for immediate use, put the include tags at the bottom. Scripts at the end of the HTML allow maximized concurrent downloads and the page to render, while the JavaScript finishes. (Of course some JavaScript cannot go at the bottom).

Use Cache Control Headers

Properly caching a page at the browser level can significantly reduce load times. It also helps with subsequent page load times if content is shared (same JS/CSS files). If there is no cache control header within a HTTP request response, the browser does not know how long it can cache the object and therefore, won't cache it at all. It's best to set static content to "never expires" and dynamic content with appropriate expiration. Ensure your JS and CSS files are externalized for caching.

Other Thoughts on Design Best Practices.

Use multiple static content servers. Although HTTP 1.1 prevents more than two connections at a time from one server, if the servers have different domain names the browser will make addition parallel connections to those servers and download more content concurrently. One good example of this is with Google Maps Street View. There is a lot of heavy image content, so they use multiple image servers and download a lot of data in parallel making the page load time quick.

Use Gzip compression for page responses. Gzip compresses the HTML response at the server and sends it back to the browser, which will then do the decompression. There is more CPU overhead but quicker transfer is typically a better trade-off.

Testing Your HTML

Manual Testing

The problem with manual testing is it's usually done with clients and servers on the same 1GB per second or hundred megabit network (or sub-network), so you're not really seeing the impact on page size or HTTP requests. Tools like YSlow and Firebug will show you relative load time comparisons. These Firefox plugins are excellent way to make sure your request response headers are properly setting browser caching and the browser is actually caching the objects.

The Throttle Control Linux tool simulates an Internet connection with varying throughputs and latency levels. Another way to test manually is to route your connection through the Internet to some degree, if possible, or use remote data centres. Even VPNs add a good degree of latency and can be used for testing.

Automated Testing

Testing of HTML efficiency usually doesn't come up during the load/performance test cycle. Load generators are typically on the sub-network and so page size and UI caching are not of major concern. Automated testing should be done at some point with only HTML and then with all objects being loaded for comparison. Testing can also be done through a Firewall/WAN simulation or with the Throttle Control tool to understand how latency and limited bandwidth affects you.

Load and performance testing typically focuses in on the application itself and is used to workout any slow performing components of the application. For example, if we're running a Java web application, we're going to do all the usual JVM tuning so that our application runs quickly and smoothly. We usually don't focus on the UI very much. Furthermore, load generators are typically on the same sub-network so the tests won't be affected by latency or bandwidth limitations. This means that large page sizes or invalid caching are not going to be noticed to a large degree.

How do Companies Typically Engage with Akamai?

There are different solutions for different sized businesses. It's a managed service with monthly billing which may be priced, based on various metrics such as secure transactions or account page views.

It needs to be something that's considered across all the business areas. We often see problems when the marketing people are not talking to the IT people (especially with outsourcing and platform-as-a-service). We always recommend that the great ideas be delivered in a way that creates a positive customer (site) experience, and design/feature performance should be brought to the table every time these discussions are happening.

Increasingly consumer shopping behaviour is being seen from the holistic perspective of the entire shopping experience. The experiential view of shopping takes a far more holistic approach to the consumption process, right from involvement to post – purchase usage, and incorporates the hedonistic perspective into the existing, primarily cognitive rational information processing view of consumption (Hirschman and Holbrook, 1982). Hedonic shopping value refers to the sense of enjoyment and pleasure that the consumer receives from the entire buying experience associated with shopping at a store (Griffin, Babin and Modianos, 2000) and this value perception could vary depending on individual shopping orientations, the cultural orientations as well as the economic and competitive environment in which the consumer shops (Woodruffe, Eccles and Elliott, 2002). This paper attempts to understand the impact of all three factors on the purchase behaviour of shoppers by examining hedonic value across different product categories signifying different shopping orientations; across culturally distinct countries; across developing and developed economies; and across different stages of retail evolution.

GLOBAL RETAILING INDUSTRY

The latter half of the 20th Century, in both Europe and North America, has seen the emergence of the supermarket as the dominant grocery retail form. The reasons why supermarkets have come to dominate food retailing are not hard to find. The search for convenience in food shopping and consumption, coupled to car ownership, led to the birth of the supermarket. As incomes rose and shoppers sought both convenience and new tastes and stimulation, supermarkets were able to expand the products offered. The invention of the bar code allowed a store to manage thousands of items and their prices and led to 'just-in-time' store replenishment and the ability to carry tens of thousands of individual items. Computer-operated depots and logistical systems integrated store replenishment with consumer demand in a single electronic system. The superstore was born.

On the Global Retail Stage, little has remained the same over the last decade. One of the few similarities with today is that Wal-Mart was ranked the top retailer in the world then and it still holds that distinction. Wal-Mart made a $ 3 billion bid for control of Massmart, giving a substantial presence in South Africa. Other than Wal-Mart's dominance, there's little about today's environment that looks like the mid-1990s. The global economy has changed, consumer demand has shifted, and retailers' operating systems today are infused with far more technology than was the case six years ago.

Saturated home markets, fierce competition and restrictive legislation have relentlessly pushed major food retailers into the globalization mode. Since the mid-1990s, numerous governments have opened up their economies as well, to the free markets and foreign investment that has been a plus for many a retailer. However, a more near-term concern, has been the global economic slowdown that has resulted from dramatic cutback in corporate IT and other types of capital spending. Consumers themselves have become much more price sensitive and conservative in their buying, particularly in the more advanced economies.

From an operational point of view, active practitioners have voiced their opinion that retailer concerns in 2003, have turned to deflation, lack of pricing power, global overcapacity, low interest rates, economic stagnation, slump in world tourism and declining consumer confidence. But, even before the global economic slowdown that forced retailers into monitoring costs more effectively, technological advances were a way of life in retail organizations. Technology has become the real enabler for retailers over the last six years. Supply chain innovations for retailers were particularly strong in the second half of the 1990s and have continued into today. With all the emphasis on technology and cost-cutting, a major thrust of retailers continues to be demand-based:

1. Vijay Anand, Assistant Vice President, Sathguru Management Consultants
2. Vikram Nambiar, Associate Consultant, Sathguru Management Consultants

Four years ago, more than half (53 per cent) of the top 200 retailers operated in only one country. Today, only 44 per cent remain single-country merchants. This globalization trend can only intensify in the years ahead. The benefits of increased sales and greater economies of scale are too large to be ignored.

The global retail industry has travelled a long way from a small beginning to an industry where the worldwide retail sales alone is valued at $ 7 trillion (*Source: 2003 Global Retail Report,* Deloitte Touche Tohmatsu). The top 200 retailers alone account for 30 per cent of worldwide demand. Retail sales being generally driven by people's ability (disposable income) and willingness (consumer confidence) to buy, compliments the fact that the money spent on household consumption worldwide increased 68 per cent between 1980 and 2003. The leader has indisputably been the USA where some two-thirds or $ 6.6 trillions out of the $ 10 trillions American economy is consumer spending. About 40 per cent of that ($ 3 trillions) is spending on discretionary products and services. Retail turnover in the EU is approximately Euros 2,000 billion and the sector average growth looks to be following an upward pattern. The Asian economies (excluding Japan) are expected to grow at 6 per cent consistently till 2005-06. Positive forces at work in retail consumer markets today include high rates of personal expenditures, low interest rates, low unemployment and very low inflation. Negative factors that hold retail sales back involve weakening consumer confidence.

The Far East Experience

The Food Retail Industry in the Far East has evolved into what could be called 'the breeding ground' for emerging models with countries like Singapore being the home to some of the big players in the industry in these parts of the world. The presence of all the major players of the retailing industry is found in Singapore. Singapore has 2 hypermarkets, one run by Carrefour and the other by Giant Hypermarket, part of Dairy Farm International. According to the government, there are slightly more than 11,000 market stalls operating in 150 markets located all across Singapore Island. The markets further spread to China, Thailand, and Malaysia thanks to the major support that the local governments provided in creating the necessary regulatory framework in establishing their presence. Singapore, Malaysia and Thailand not only fuelled the retail industry within the country, but also attracted hordes of tourists to experience the shopping "experiences" that they created in these islands. The markets are now saturated with no additional space for a new entrant and are expected to consolidate within the next few years.

Apart from Singapore, which is a more recent development, Japan enjoys an active spot on the retailers' map. The retail industry is as huge as US $ 1088 billion, with a split of US $ 594.8 billion in the non-food segment and US $ 493.2 billion in the food-retailing sector. The leaders in sales are Ito-Yokado, Aeon, Daiei, Takashimaya and Uny, in that order. Several retailers, however, have made recent improvements in their warehousing and distribution technologies to make their presence felt in the Japanese market. Convenience stores, which are small and suitable in a country where land is very expensive, continue to do well. Food, in fact, has been one of the few sectors that have experienced growth over the last several years. A period of shake up in the industry is likely now that Wal-Mart has entered Japan. Numerous smaller, less efficient retailers may become takeover targets. The entire Japanese retail sector will likely undergo some form of restructuring over the next decade as a result of overcapacity, dismal profits and the Wal-Mart factor. In Mainland China, the retail markets have mushroomed over the years of intense economic development to a very considerable size. The total volume of retail sales for consumer goods and food increased by 10.6 per cent in China over the last couple of years which shows tremendous growth. Consumer spending has held strong. A decade ago, the top five retail enterprises in China were all traditional merchandise companies, but now the top five are mainly supermarkets and chain stores. The world is enamoured with China's potential and opportunities. But in medium-sized and small cities and rural areas, traditional retailing methods, such as department stores and local retailing networks, will be sufficient, as consumption is lower. In Indonesia, wet markets and supermarkets remained the major distribution channels for food products. Although these retail subsectors also offered non-food products, such as household goods, food products remained dominant in terms of the number of items. Wet markets' distribution of food products tended to be much greater than non-food as these retail channels mainly provided fresh produce. Conversely, supermarkets had an almost equal distribution, with food taking up the greater proportion. On the other hand, the distribution of non-food products benefited from both food and non-food retailers. For example, some food retail formats offered non-food items, such as supermarkets, hypermarkets, and convenience stores. These retail outlets provided some basic non-food products, such as toothpaste, soap, or detergent. However, non-food retail outlets rarely provided food items, except certain department stores or druggists. In Malaysia, a majority of food retailer outlets offer food and non-food items with at least a 70 : 30 distribution. The traditional food distribution system in Thailand is through so-called 'wet markets' which sell fruits, vegetables, meat and fish, together with small 'mom-and-pop' food stores which distribute dry goods. However, the rapid growth of the economy, particularly during the decade before the financial crisis began, has led to dramatic changes in the structure of the food-retailing sector. Modern supermarkets, superstores, hypermarkets and convenience stores developed at breakneck pace to service the growing middle-class with their demand for more sophisticated food stores and a greater variety of products many of which were imported.

FOOD RETAIL IN INDIA

Though with a population of a billion and a middle-class population of over 300 millions organized retailing (in the form of food retail chains) is still in its infancy in the country. India has been rather slow in joining the Organized Retail Revolution that was rapidly transforming the economies in the other Asian Tigers. This was largely due to the excellent food retailing system that was established by the kirana (mom-and-pop) stores that continue meet with all the requirements of retail requirements albeit without the convenience of the shopping as provided by the retail chains; and also due to the highly fragmented food supply chain that is cloaked with several intermediaries (from farm-processor-distributor-retailer) resulting in huge value loss and high costs. This supplemented with lack of developed food processing industry kept the organized chains out of the marketplace. The correction process is underway and the systems are being established for effective Business-to-Business (farmer-processor, processor-retailer) solutions thereby, leveraging the core competence of each player in the supply chain.

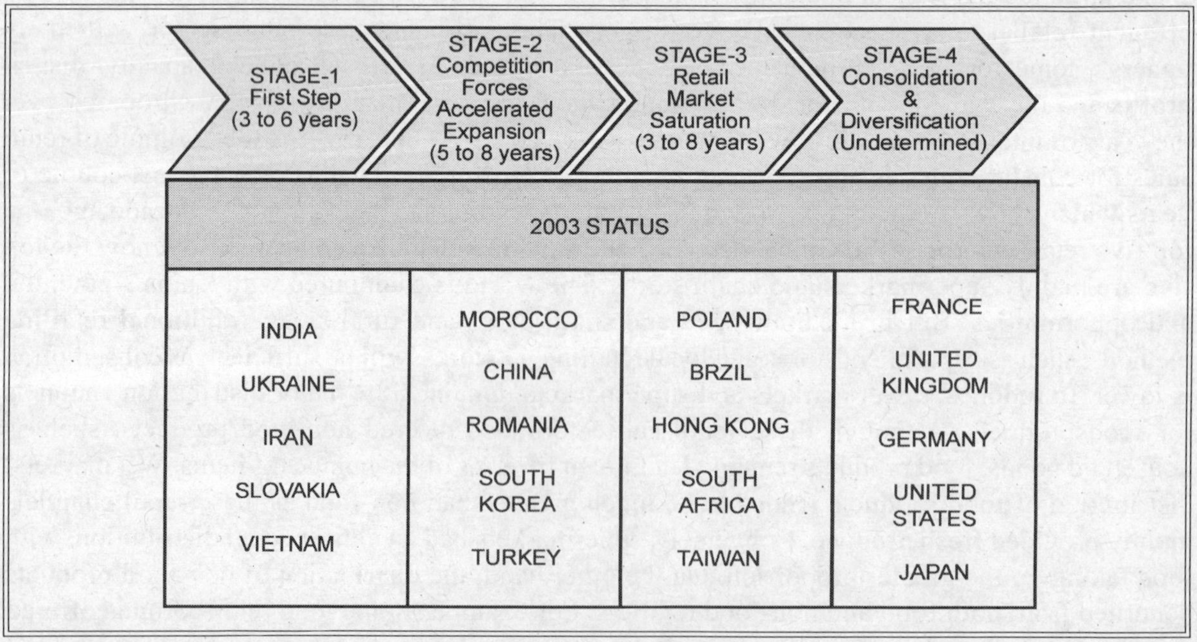

FIG. 14: STEPS IN SUPPLY CHAIN

Spread of Organized Retailing in India

Organized retailing is spreading and making its presence felt in different parts of the country. The trend in grocery retailing, however, has been slightly different with a growth concentration in the South. Though there were traditional family owned retail chains in South India such as Nilgiri's as early as 1904, the retail revolution happened with various major business houses foraying into the starting of chains of food retail outlets in South India with focus on Chennai, Hyderabad and Bengaluru markets, preliminarily. In the Indian context, a countrywide chain in food retailing is yet to be established as lots of supply chain issues need to be answered due to the vast expanse of the country and also diverse cultures that are present.

Retail Models in India: Current and Emerging

The Indian food retail market is characterized by several coexisting types and formats. These are:

1. The roadside hawkers and the mobile (pushcart variety) retailers.
2. The kirana stores (the Indian equivalent of the mom-and-pop stores of the US), within which are:
   (a) Open format more organized outlets
   (b) Small to medium food retail outlets.

Modern Trade – the Organized Retailers

Within modern trade, we have:

1. The discounter (Subhiksha, Apna Bazaar, Margin Free)
2. The value-for-money store (Nilgiris)
3. The experience shop (Foodworld, Trinethra)
4. The home delivery (Fabmart)

While the focus of this note is on modern organized retail trade, we hereunder present insights into the smaller, semi and unorganized retailers.

Hawkers – 'Mobile Supermarkets'

The unorganized sector is characterized by the lari-galla vendors (also known as "mobile supermarket") seen in every Indian bylane and is, therefore, difficult to track, measure and analyze. But they do know their business – these lowest cost retailers can be found wherever more than 10 Indians collect – a rural post office, a dusty roadside bus stop or a village square. As far as location is concerned, these retailers have succeeded beyond all doubt. They have neither village nor citywide ambitions or plans – their aim is simply a long walk down the end of the next lane. This mode of "mobile retailers" is neither scalable nor viable over the longer term, but is certainly replicable all over India. Most retailing of fresh foods in India occurs in Mandis and roadside hawker parks, which are usually illegal and entrenched. These are highly organized in their own way. Hawking of food products, cooked food and FMCG products is a very interesting model of retailing. Much has been written about these roadside "malls" – from social security issues to their nuisance value. However, if you put these hawkers together, they are akin to a large supermarket with little or no overheads and high degree of flexibility in merchandise, display, prices and turnover. While shopping ambience and the trust factor maybe missing, these hawkers sure have a system that works.

Kirana/Grocers/ Provision Stores/Mom-and-pop Stores

Semi-organized retailers like kirana (mom-and-pop stores), grocers and provision stores are characterized by the more systematic buying – from the mandis or the farmers and selling – from fixed structures. Economies of scale are not yet realized in this format, but the front end is already visibly changing with the times. These stores have presented Indian companies with the challenge of servicing them, giving rise to distribution and cash flow cycles as never seen elsewhere in Asia. The model is very antithesis of modern retail in terms of the buyer (retailer)-seller (FMCG) equations. It is not unknown for MNC leaders to link the supply of one line of products to another slower moving line of products. These retailers are not organized in the manner that they could challenge the power of the sellers, most protests have been in the form of boycotts, which really haven't hit any company permanently.

INTEGRATION OF FOOD INDUSTRY – THE KEY DRIVER OF FOOD RETAIL IN INDIA

India is world's second largest grower of fruits and vegetables after Brazil and China. While the agriculture sector has witnessed several leaps of innovation and technological advancements, the processing sector is still in its infancy. Even with less than 4 per cent processing of fruits and vegetables, the Food Processing Industry sector in India is one of the largest in terms of production, consumption within India, export and growth prospects. The government has accorded it a high priority, with a number of fiscal reliefs and incentives, to encourage commercialization and value addition to agricultural produce; for minimizing pre/post-harvest wastage, generating employment and export growth. As a result of several policy initiatives undertaken since liberalization in early 90s, the industry has witnessed fast growth in most of the segments. In the following few paragraphs, it can be noted that the processed food market for India is vast and the amount of scope that retail chains would be exposed to is phenomenal taking into consideration the demographics and raise in standards of living. Retailers could throng the market with all these processed and packaged foods with their private labels.

With the emergence of the big private corporates, NGOs (Non-government Organizations) and Government organizations into the food processing scene, India is making big in-roads into the Food Processing Industry. These corporates and NGOs have reached out to the farmers and provided them with timely advice and help in the upgradation of farm practices with valuable inputs on various areas of farming from sowing to harvesting which includes quality seed procurement, manures, fertilizers and pesticides etc. Some of the successful models are that of ITC's e-choupal a model that helps the soyabean farmers in contract producing for ITC for its commodity trading business. The PEPSI experimenting with Punjab farmers in growing the right quality tomato for its tomato purees and pastes. Some of the leading food retail chains working with farmers for contract growing greens for supply to their retail outlets, etc. These successful models are being replicated with required changes all over the country and the food industry is getting integrated more strongly.

India has also seen a flurry of food chain majors like McDonalds, Pizza Hut and Kentucky Fried Chicken finding their place among the Indian consumers. The trend still follows for food chains in India to spread to almost all cities and towns.

These advancements have revolutionized the integration of the Indian Food Industry and have played a vital role in solving, to a large extent, major supply chain issues that prevailed. The trend is that these successful institutional intervention models be replicated and spread in all segments of the food industry far and wide through the country that benefit all the incumbents of the chain evolve. This finally helps the retailer as his supply chain becomes much leaner and vertically integrated. He is in a position to offer a wide variety and highest degree of convenience to his customer.

ECONOMY

Economic growth at over 5.5 per centage over the last eight years, forex reserves of over $ 100 billion and a stable government has helped India to look more progressively towards future. The economic development was largely attributed to its dominance in the Information Technology Sector in the global marketplace and its large English speaking population that made it the ideal choice for back office operations for MNC's world over. The manufacturing sector also provided its mite to the economic development by going global hitherto restricting to export of raw materials or intermediaries that has not graduated to supply of end product be it pharmaceuticals or consumer vehicles. All this has translated in higher income levels and more surpluses for the middle class segment that is getting ploughed into the retail sector; again fuelling the economy to higher levels. The last five years have seen the PPP of average Indian middle-class (over 300 millions) go up several times unleashing the power of purchasing. The retail sector was the greatest beneficiary. The need for a shopping experience combined with the convenience of shopping for the upwardly mobile middle class has been on the major factors for retail boom in India. The Great Indian Jewellery Saga-Pg3 has introduced Gold Plus Nano I, Gold Plus Nano 2 and Gold Plus Nano 3 jewellery cars in the market. In commemoration with the celebration of 5,000 years of Indian Jewellery, TATA has introduced India's first jewellery car in the market on 20th November, 2010.

THE INFORMED CONSUMER

Over the years, the increasing literacy in the country and the exposure to developed nations via satellite television or by way of the overseas work experiences, the consumer awareness has increased on the quality and the price of the products/services that is expected. Today more and more consumers are vocal on the quality of the products/services that they expect from the market. This awareness has made the consumer seek more and more reliable sources for purchases and hence the logical shift to purchases from the organized retail chains that has a corporate background and where the accountability is more pronounced. The consumer also seeks to purchase from a place where his/her feedback is more valued.

EVOLUTION OF ORGANIZED RETAILING

Retailing, one of the largest sectors in the global economy, is going through a transitional phase in India. For a long time, the corner grocery store was the only choice available to the consumer, especially in the urban areas. This is slowly giving way to international formats of retailing. The traditional food and grocery segment has seen the emergence of supermarkets/ grocery chains, convenience stores and fast-food chains.

The traditional grocers, by introducing self-service formats as well as value-added services such as credit and home delivery, have tried to redefine themselves. However, the boom in retailing has been confined primarily to the urban markets in the country. Even there, large chunks are yet to feel the impact of organized retailing. There are two primary reasons for this. First, the modern retailer is yet to feel the saturation effect in the urban market and has, therefore, probably not looked at the other markets as seriously. Second, the modern retailing trend, despite its cost-effectiveness, has come to be identified with lifestyles.

In order to appeal to all classes of the society, retail stores would have to identify with different lifestyles. In a sense, this trend is already visible with the emergence of stores with an essentially 'value for money' image. The attractiveness of the other stores actually appeals to the existing affluent class as well as those who aspire to be part of this class. Hence, one can assume that the retailing revolution is emerging along the lines of the economic evolution of society.

It was only in the year 2000, that the economists put a figure to it: ₹ 4,00,000 crore (1 crore = 10 million) which is expected to develop to around ₹ 8,00,000 crore by the year 2005 – an annual increase of 20 per cent. Retailing in India is unorganized with poor supply chain management perspective. According to a recent survey by some of the retail consulting bodies, an overwhelming proportion of the ₹ 4,00,000 crore retail market is unorganised. In fact, only a ₹ 20,000 crore segment of the market is organized. As much as 96 per cent of the 5 million-plus outlets are smaller than 500 square feet area. This means that India per capita retailing space is about 2 square feet (compared to 16 square feet in the United States). India's per capita retailing space is thus the lowest in the world (*Source:* KSA Technopak (I) Pvt. Ltd., the India operation of the US-based Kurt Salmon Associates).

Currently, the retail landscape is filled with supermarket chains with over 1000 outlets all over the country to increase to around 5,000 by the 2005. The success of a couple of Hypermart's indicate the evolution of hypermarkets in the country prominent among them are Giant, Metro, Big Bazaar models. While the average bill value at a supermarket is in the range of ₹ 300 per bill, the average bill amount at a Hypermarket is in the range of ₹ 750-1,000, indicating that the model is in tune with the global models where the average spend is increasing with the shopping experience.

Impact of Organized Retail

Organized retailing is spreading and making its presence felt in different parts of the country. The trend in grocery retailing, however, has been slightly different with a growth concentration in the South. Though there were traditional family owned retail chains in South India such as Nilgiri's as early as 1905, the retail revolution happened with the RPG group starting the Foodworld chain of food retail outlets in South India with focus on Chennai, Hyderabad and Bengaluru markets, preliminarily. The experiment has reaped rich dividends and the group is now foraying into other territories as well. Owing to the success of Foodworld model of RPG group, several new models such as Trinethra, Subhiksha, Margin Free and others have made their foray into this sector albeit at regional levels. Today the food retail sector in India is about ₹ 10 lakh crore (US $ 200 billion) of which the organized food retail segment is about 1 per cent and increasing at a pace of over 20 per cent yr-on-yr.

To be successful in food retailing in India essentially means to draw away shoppers from, the roadside hawkers and kirana stores to supermarkets. This transition can be achieved to some extent through pricing, so the success of a food retailer depends on how best he understands and squeezes his supply chain. The other major factor is that of convenience shopping which the supermarket has the edge over the traditional kirana stores. On an average a supermarket stocks up to 5,000 SKU's against few hundreds stocked at an average kirana stores.

Though with excellent potential, India poses a complex situation for a retailer, as this is a country where each state is a mini-country by itself. The demography of a region vary quite distinctly from others. In order to appeal to all classes of the society, retail stores would have to identify with different lifestyles. Hence, we may find more regional players and it would take enormously long time before nation-wide successful retail chains emerge. This is the main reason as to why the successful retail chains in the country today operate at regional segments only and are not aiming at nation-wide presence, at least for the time-being.

In the organized retail industry, the gestation periods are long, institutional funding is difficult, and there is none or little government support. But the belief among top retailer chains in the country is that the industry will see large investments coming once the current ban on foreign direct investment is lifted. But that could be two-three years away. Food and grocery retailing is a tough business in India with margins being very low, and consumers not dissatisfied with existing shops where they buy. For example, the next-door grocery shopkeeper is smart and delivers good customer service, though not value.

As of now, while Chennai has about five organized food and grocery retail chains, other big cities such as Delhi, Bengaluru, and Mumbai average only two-three such chains. Almost all food retail players have been region-specific as far as geographical presence is concerned in the country. To illustrate with examples, the RPG Group's FoodWorld, Nilgiris, Margin Free, Giant, Venkey's and Subhiksha, all of which are more or less spread in the Southern region; Sabka Bazaar has a presence only in and around Delhi; names such as Haiko and Radhakrishna Foodland are Mumbai-centric; while Adani is Ahmedabad-centric. Industry topography in India is such that spreading presence across cities is a tough call. As pointed out by many experts, organized food and grocery retailing chains going national requires significant investments. Retailing within this sector is not just about the front-end, but involves complex supply chain and logistics issues as well.

The trend and mindset of the present retailer chains in India can be best understood by studying FoodWorld as an example, which came in first in the food and grocery retailing sector. The chain has no plans to venture beyond the Southern region just yet. Current plans are to focus on the Southern markets and achieve saturation. The intention is that by 2005, they could look at the other regions. Subhiksha, a Chennai-based discount chain, too wants to be the principal store of purchase for at least 40 per cent of all consumers living within 500-750 metres of the store, that is, within walking distance. This makes the point very clear that the strategy among most existing retail chains of various formats is to completely saturate the markets where they are already established players and then move on to virtually untouched areas where the challenge of sourcing resources and extending their supply chain model to best suit the size and expanse of the market would be a challenging task.

Meanwhile, the RPG group plans to take its new formats such as Giant Hypermarkets national over the next three years. Grocery is a large component of this format, but not the only one. To elaborate on the hurdles of going pan-Indian, fundamentally, the way a basic grocery retailing model works is that the high set-up costs in terms of setting up buying/distribution infrastructure is gradually amortized over a larger number of stores. The back-end costs without distribution centre costs, or what in retail jargon is called retail administration costs, should stabilize at around 2.5 per cent to 3 per cent of sales.

It can be explained that the obstacles of looking at a pan-India model for grocery are several. Given the federal nature of the country, the weak infrastructure and the major variances in eating habits in different parts of the country, one will have to replicate the retail administration costs for at least each region and therefore, the gestation period of the project becomes huge. However, if a model is in place where the upfront store revenues scale very rapidly, then it is possible. Therefore, if one is to attempt a pan-Indian grocery foray, it will have to be in the hypermarket format with its attendant investment numbers and risk profile.

If a close look is taken at the nature of the Indian Retail Markets, it can be seen that there is so much potential to extract from individual regions that players are in no tearing hurry to spread out. Based on a recent study by a renowned government institution in India, in the six major metros, Delhi has the highest per capita consumption of food and grocery, among supermarkets. Chennai, "the mecca of retailing", comes at fourth place. This shows the high potential the sector presents. Chennai has some five supermarket chains, and each of these are doing well for themselves. So there is enough scope to expand even in one single city in India.

Sabka Bazaar, a supermarket chain restricted to Delhi alone, is now generating sales of about ₹ 11 crore from its 19 stores which best illustrates the potential of each individual city. This explains the reason for delay in intentions of retailers to spread far and wide.

Pantaloon Retail (India) Ltd., which operates two types of retail formats, made its maiden foray in food and grocery retailing in North India in mid-2003. Big Bazaar, Pantaloon group's discount store chain, has taken off to a roaring start in Delhi. The Pantaloon Big Bazaar in Delhi is the sixth for the group, and the first in North India. It has been found that existing Big Bazaar stores in cities such as Hyderabad, Bengaluru and Mumbai attract average footfalls of 20,000 to 25,000 per day, more so during weekends. While Big Bazaar is essentially a discount store retailing product categories ranging from food and grocery to apparel to footwear to home and interior products, food and grocery retailing forms a significant part of the chain's business. Typically, while food and grocery retailing does well at the beginning of the month, the apparel sector sees maximum off-take during festivals.

It can be observed that the most popular retail format in India is the 'supermarket', beside the corner shop/grocery store/mom-and-pop' store. Hypermarkets have very recently come into being and are negligible in number though most retail chains do intend to expand their presence through this format as well very soon. 'Discount chains' are also substantial in number and are growing at a fast pace through the country, predominantly, in the southern region.

Given that organized retail has been registering growth rates of approximately 40 per cent over the last three years, it is expected to grow to about ₹ 35,000 crore in 2005 and close to ₹ 70,000 crore in 2010. If projections were to be made considering the current trends in food retailing in India, some years down the line, food and grocery stores will become dominating trade partners for the food industry, which, in turn, will be forced to offer special discounts and trade terms for them to get the shelf space in such stores. Also, once established, in-store label brands will become a real threat to the industry as manufacturers will have to compete with the store label brands that are generally very price-competitive. As for the spread geographically, strong chances stand that the major chains would spread to the next grade of cities in the country over the next five years or so and then progressively start covering every corner of the country. Most chains have already started developing their own unique supply chains that would suit their needs precisely. Replicating the success stories of the big names of the Western nations may still be a distant dream for Indian food and grocery retailers, but at least the winds are blowing in the direction of growth.

Decadal Analysis of the Food Retail Sector

Retailing is a sunrise industry in India with many challenges like exclusion of small farms, management of processing and distribution chains. Evolution of supermarkets and fast food chains is a recent phenomenon in India. Various demand and supply side factors have contributed towards this growth.

Supply Side

The liberalization of the economy in the 1990s, led to a boom in the "Consumer Goods" Industry with reductions in custom duties and shift from quota to tariff-based system. Entry barriers on multinationals were largely removed after which Food Industry majors like Kellogg's, Heinz, Tropicana, etc., entered the Indian food industry. This gave rise to tremendous development of sophisticated supply chain and logistics which eventually and gradually has led to the growth in the food processing and packaging industry.

Demand Side

The increase in the income levels of middle and higher income groups in the 1990s, coupled with the reduction in poverty levels was a major factor in contributing to the increase in demand for high quality food retailing services. Changing consumer lifestyles with the steep increase in time value, widespread change in the Indian family structure from vast Joint Hindu families to more manageable nuclear families and increasing level of quality awareness has also helped the cause of the Food Retailing industry considerably. Another major factor that has accelerated the growth of the Indian Food Retailing Sector has been the advent of cable television and the increasing instances of overseas travel by Indians for various reasons.

Government Policy on Food Retailing – India

100 per cent FDI in retailing in not allowed per say, foreign retailers can operate in India through joint ventures, where the Indian partner is an export house, franchising/local manufacturing/ sourcing from small-scale sector, cash and carry operations. The McKinsey report states FDI will help the retail businesses to grow from the present $ 200 billion to $ 460-470 billion by 2010.

Growth of supermarkets in most developing countries (Brazil, China,etc.), took-off in the 1990s, after FDI was allowed in this sector which is not the case in the Indian scenario. Retailing is not regarded as an industry very few banks are willing to invest in this sector. The shortage of warehousing facilities, cold storage and large-scale processing units has obstructed the growth of the Food Retailing Industry in India. As supply chain is fragmented and marked by existence of large number of intermediaries, organized retailing has been a very tough proposition. India is still in the second and third party logistic provider mode while fourth party logistic models have become global standards for logistic providers. Retailing is subject to a plethora of laws and regulations at Central, State and municipal/local levels, some of which have been listed below:

- Restrictive zoning legislation limits availability of land for retail/commercial purposes.
- Restrictions on inter-state movement of foodgrains deprive farmers from getting remunerative prices.
- Restrictive labour laws.
- Urban land ceiling regulations, restrictions on shop opening timings, requirements for shops to close once a week.
- There is no uniform tax structure. There are multiple layers of taxes.

EMERGING TRENDS

Likely Transformation of the Supply Chain

To counter the unbeatable advantages of convenience of a hop, skip and a jump access and home delivery, organized retailers seem to have just one option – offer attractive prices to the consumer. A successful retailer's winning edge will therefore come from sourcing – how best it can leverage its scale to drive merchandise costs down, increase stock turns and get better credit terms from its vendors. There are obvious and hidden areas where costs can be pruned and the benefits of this lower cost of retailing can be passed on to customers as lower prices, which in turn should fuel demand. One way of trimming costs is if the pressure points in the long, often unnecessary, supply chain for produce and staples can be identified and suitably dealt with. The food supply chain in India is full of inefficiencies – a result of inadequate infrastructure, too many middlemen, complicated laws and an indifferent attitude.

Corporate and NGO interventions at the farm end in the form of Farm Management Services are emerging to ensure quality and timely supply of produce for the operations. The farmer-corporate relationship has helped both the farmers and the corporates in bringing the high quality low cost product to the retail shelf. To ease the burden of the corporate in setting up farm management services, several leading NGO bodies have taken up this activity essentially due to the fact that their operations are mostly at the farm end.

We feel that these farmer-corporate models would be replicated and extended to all the farm end products. With the emergence of Private Label, we would soon find even the retail chains to work with the farm community in developing a efficient supply chain and to leverage on the cost advantage at both ends.

eBay has got real revolutionary development in e-commerce. eBay is mostly mom-and-pop merchant. It is making strides towards becoming the new Cheap-Est proponent. eBay competes against people selling products directly from their homes. It may truly usher in the next generation of Cheap-Est operations. The story of Costco, the US nation's largest chain of warehouse club stores, began in 1976, when a man named Sol Price founded the eponymous an appropriately named Price Club. With Price Club, Sol Price pioneered a new breed of retailers-warehouse clubs.

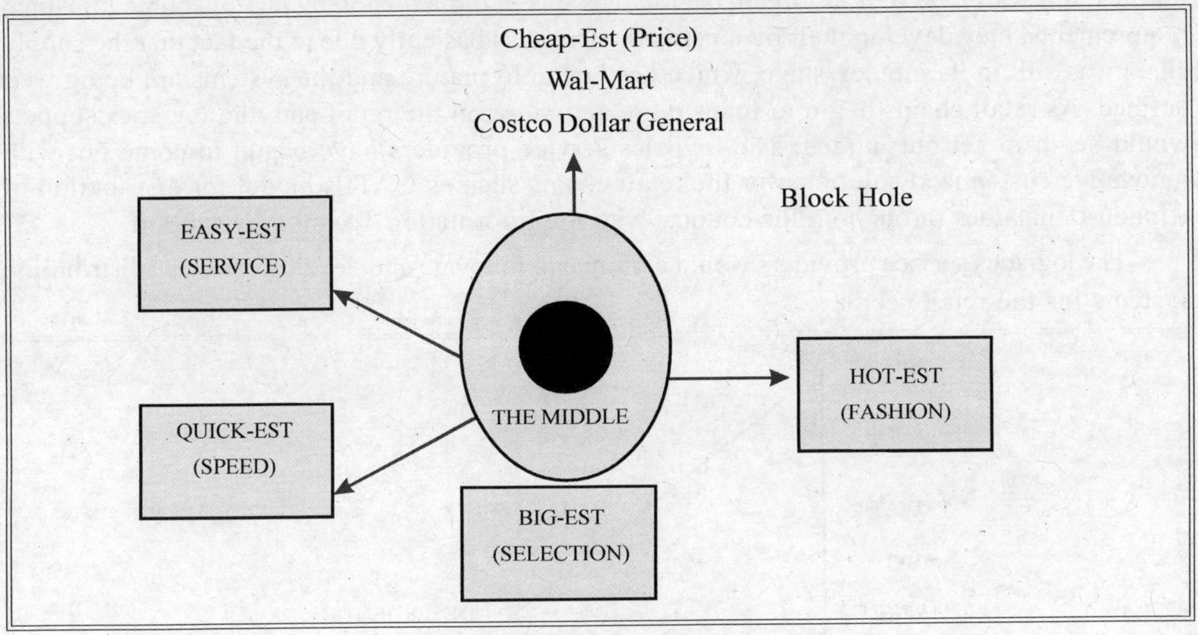

FIG. 15: CHEAP-EST RETAILER

Cheap-Est defined: It means consistently having lower prices than the competition on the products that a retailer sells. Wal-Mart, the quintessential Cheap-Est Retailer, is now the world's largest company – bigger than conglomerates like Exxon and General Electric.

Big-Est Retailers are stores that offer the most dominant assortment in specific categories of merchandise. They are the so-called category killers, like Home Depot in home improvement, PetsMart in pet food and supplies, Bed Bath and Beyond in housewares, Staples in office supplies, Best Buy in home electronics, Toys "R" Us in toys, and Amazon.com in books.

Supplier Retailer Relationships

Traditionally the supplier-retailer relation in India comprised several layers such as the national distributor, the regional wholesaler and the end retailer. However, this scenario is fast changing with the organized retail increasing its presence in the country where the relationship is directly with the manufacturer. However, this new model has been affecting the relationships that the manufacturer enjoys with the traditional system which is still the most dominant in the entire retail sector. The issue of differential pricing is being taken up at several forums and the growing dissatisfaction among the traditional retailers is being addressed by the manufacturers. However, we see that in the long-term, the role of a national distributor would slowly fade away or get restricted to the rural/upcountry regions.

The supplier-retailer relationship would come under severe pressure as each party would try to squeeze maximum margins out of the other.

Innovations in Transportation Logistics

The logistics service providers have been innovating several interesting formats and models for the retail sector. As of now, organized retail chains in India do not, by far, outsource logistical requirements, they develop their own network. This was basically due to the fact that the supply chain was still in its infancy stage, which has begun to mature and the systems are being well defined. As retail chains begin to focus more and more on the retail end, the logistics support would begin to get outsourced. The logistics service providers have begun to come out with innovative customized solutions for the retail chains such as GATI's model for distribution of Alphonso mangoes throughout the country with the Information Technology support.

The logistics service providers would continue to innovate and develop effective distribution systems for the retail sector.

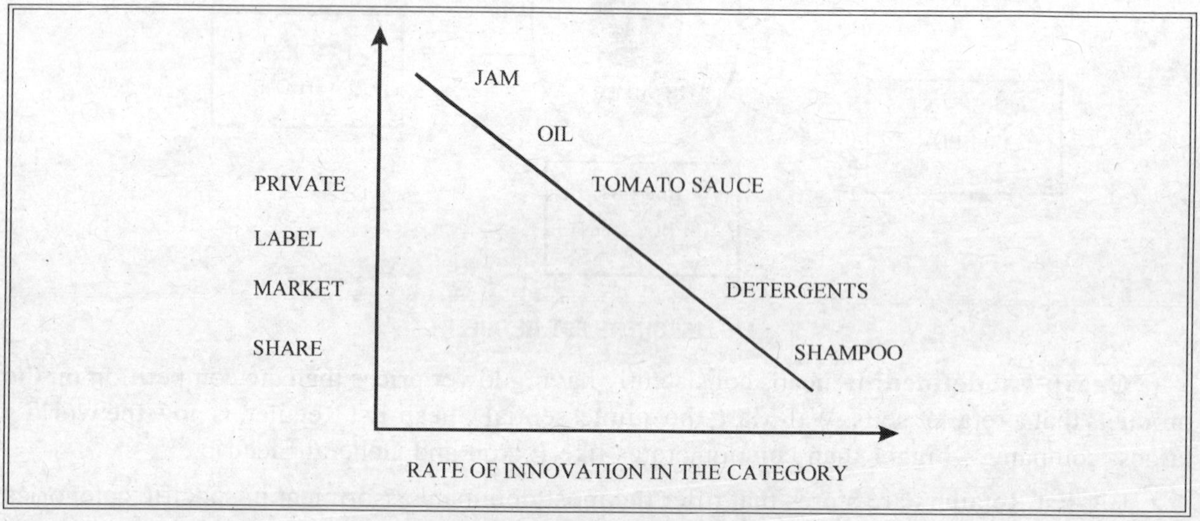

FIG. 16: INNOVATION IS THE BEST DEFENSE

Source: Jean-Noel Kapferer, HEC

Shopping for a brand is an important factor. There is no doubt that brands need retailers but retailers only need strong brands (as brands need strong retailers) – brands that understand the new retail world; brands that understand that the product is key; that they have to build their brands, not only from mass media, but also from the shelf. Innovation is and always has the key. One needs to make this innovation work for himself/herself as a cooperative tool with retailers. As global retailers grow ever bigger and more international they have more and more opportunities to source those innovations from anywhere and anyone. Logistics cost-wise, the world has never been smaller. It is as cheap to source from China and Eastern Europe these days as from Spain to France or Normandy to the Riviera. Anything can be copied, and copied very quickly these days – even and especially food. Being local would not save you. Being innovative just might. So, make sure your innovations are real and big and constantly reinvested.

Formats

Currently, the retail sector in India is populated with the traditional mom-and-pop stores and some 1,000 odd supermarkets under organized retail chains. A daring few ventured into the hypermarket segment with successful results and this format is being fast replicated by other players. This experience indicates that the Indian consumer has matured to the next level of shopping experience. Given the Indian conditions and the vast diversity a single format may not be possible for the national presence, but region specific formats may evolve.

An interesting observation is that of lack of presence of organized retail chains in the rural/semi-urban centres as over 60 per cent of Indian population is still in these parts. An ideal "no frills" model to start with, would be ideal for the rural markets, this would help to take them to the next level of supermarket experience.

Social Trends

Social trends of a country have impact on the scheme of growth of food retailing in a country. India is vast geographically and diverse culturally. This has taken its toll on food retailing with retailers having to adapt to the local cultures and palates of the area in which they have established or plan to establish. This is a major reason for many or most retailing chains restricting their operations to a certain part of the country. But the trends now are slowly moving towards cultural integration where people of all states and diametrically opposite cultures tend to try out foods and materials of other states and communities. This movement towards social integration would make it very feasible in the near future for retailing chains and erstwhile local chains to spread across the country.

Increased income levels and more women willing to make use of their education by joining work has increasingly affected the shopping pattern that is moving towards fulfilling the need of convenience shopping in the form of supermarkets (now graduating to hyper format), home deliveries. Indian consumer is quality and price conscious and this awareness would drive the retailers to rework their supply chain relationships.

A recent analysis shows that countries go through a distinct food consumption evolutionary pattern. In the first stage the focus is on obtaining basic dietary inputs, the second stage focuses on improving and building basic foods, before moving to the third stage of adding premium food to the diet. Most of urban India has already moved to the third stage and it is a great avenue for food retailers, if they could slowly introduce the rest of India to it. The future would witness creation of specific models/formats one for the upwardly mobile urbanite and the other for the rural markets.

Online Retailing

The single most important evolution that took place along with the retailing revolution was the rise and fall of the dotcom companies. A sudden concept of 'non-store' shopping emerged, which threatened to take away the potential of the store. More importantly, the very nature of the customer segment being addressed was almost the same. The computer-savvy individual was also a sub-segment of the 'store' frequenting traffic. Internationally, the concept of Net shopping is yet to be proven. And the poor financial performance of most of the companies offering virtual shopping has resulted in store-based retailing regaining the upper hand. Other forms of non-store shopping including various formats such as catalogue/mail order shopping, direct selling, and so on are growing rapidly. However, the size of the direct market industry is too limited to deter the retailers. For all the convenience that it offers, electronic retailing does not suit products where 'look and see' attributes are of importance, as in apparel, or where the value is very high, such as jewellery, or where the performance has to be tested, as of consumer durables. The most critical issue in electronic retailing, especially in a country such as ours, relates to payments and the various security issues involved.

However, using the internet to be able to source products and also check for availability of stock among stores of retail chains has been proven to be effective and cuts down on wastage by a vast amount. It makes logistical support very easy and efficient. The trend in India is such that usage of the electronic medium for business purposes and integrating it into the systems is increasing. This would slowly spread into the retailing sector as well. It has already started in the case of some large retail houses where the affects are here to see. This again would result in the supply chain getting leaner and vertically integrated. Though the initial costs to implement these systems are high, in the long run it results in cost reduction where this privilege can be passed on to the final consumer. The e-commerce generation doesn't need salespeople to help to make choices, and retailers are beginning to understand and adapt to the change. When Nadia Karim goes shopping, she doesn't wait around for salespeople. iPads, Apple, Nordstrom, etc., are examples for online retailing.

Impact of Technology

The other important aspect of retailing relates to technology. It is widely felt that the key differentiator between the successful and not so successful retailers is primarily in the area of technology. Simultaneously, it will be technology that will help the organized retailer score over the unorganized players, giving both cost and service advantages.

Retailing is a 'technology-intensive' industry. It is quoted that everyday at least 500 gigabytes of data are transmitted via satellite from the 1,200 point-of-sales counters of JC Penney to its corporate headquarters. Successful retailers today work closely with their vendors to predict consumer demand, shorten lead times, reduce inventory holding and thereby, save cost. Wal-Mart pioneered the concept of building a competitive advantage through distribution and information systems in the retailing industry. They introduced two innovative logistics techniques – cross-docking and electronic data interchange. Today, online systems link point-of-sales terminals to the main office where detailed analysis on sales by item, classification, stores or vendors are carried out online. Besides vendors, the focus of the retailing sector is to develop the link with the consumer. 'Data Warehousing' is an established concept in the advanced nations. With the help of 'database retailing', information on existing and potential customers is tracked. Besides knowing what was purchased and by whom, information on softer issues such as demographics and psychographics is captured.

Retailing, as discussed before, is at a nascent stage in India. Most organized players have managed to put the front ends in place, but these are relatively easy to copy. The relatively complicated information systems and underlying technologies are in the process of being established. Most grocery retailers such as Food World have started tracking consumer purchases through CRM. The lifestyle retailers through their 'affinity clubs' and 'reward clubs' are establishing their processes. The traditional retailers will always continue to exist but organized retailers are working towards revamping their business to obtain strategic advantages at various levels – market, cost, knowledge and customer. With differentiating strategies – value for money, shopping experience, variety, quality, discounts and advanced systems and technology in the back-end, change in the equilibrium with manufacturers and a thorough understanding of the consumer behaviour, the ground is all set for the organized retailers.

Food Safety Issues

As awareness grows about food safety issues, the need for countries to provide greater assurance about the safety and quality of food also grows. The increase in world food trade and the advent of the Sanitary and Physio-sanitary (SPS) Agreement under the World Trade Organization (WTO) have also raised interest in food safety requirements. To ensure a strong presence in global markets, India realizes the need to meet these challenges and keep pace with international developments.

In India, it has come to the notice of general public of late that very "popular" food companies could also go wayward as far as food-safety and public health is concerned. This has triggered off a drive by the public and the government to put more stringent food safety and public health measures in place while manufacturing, storing and packaging of foodstuffs takes place. Most foodstuffs pass through the organized retail channels on their way to the purchase baskets of consumers and therefore the retailers are beginning to realize the need for food safety and security. Grading and standardization measures are being taken at various stages of the manufacturing, processing, packaging and storing of all kinds of food materials.

To ensure food safety and maintain product integrity from the source to the customer (farm-to-plate) the Food Retailing Companies would have to establish a totally integrated infrastructure and services package. This connects and maintains the flow of food from the source (farmers/ food growers, farm service centres, market yards, processors, importers) to the customer (food service outlets, food processing units, food retailers and food exporters). This package will help eliminate or prevent identified hazards or reduces them to acceptable levels. This trend is slowly beginning to take shape with the efforts to integrate and consolidate the supply chain in Indian Food Retailing.

The Codex, HACCP (Hazard Analysis Critical Control Point) and food-hygiene standards have been adopted by the Bureau of Indian Standards, the national standards body in India. Food processing units are being encouraged to adopt these systems on a voluntary basis.

Organizations like VOICE (Voluntary Organization in the Interest of Consumer Education) have undertaken the responsibility to document the existing level of implementation of National Laws concerning labelling and packaging of imported food products, to analyze and compare with the Indian made food products and similar imported food products in terms of adherence of the National Laws, to prepare a well-documented campaign kit for the consumer groups in India on the study to sensitize and build awareness among consumers on seeking and demanding mandatory information on all packaged food products.

Food Labelling In India with Special Reference To Codex Guidelines

Food retailers have realized that they should have a fairly good understanding of the general concepts, role and functions of labelling of food products in view of the various kinds of foods available in the market. Consumers in Indian markets are now only buying products that are labelled and the labels should contain true information about the product, safety and its quality having the required standard that may not threaten the health or safety of any single individual. Knowledge of food standards for labelling as prepared by national (PFA) and international authorities (Codex) is essential for food retailers.

The Codex Alimentarius Commission body implements the joint FAO-WHO food standards programme, the purpose of which is to protect the health of consumers and to ensure fair practices in the food trade. In view of this, it is pertinent to follow its rules and regulations in matters of food safety and labelling. The decisions made by Codex have profound effects on economics and the health and well-beings of citizens around the world. The fact that 165 nations are members of Codex and this membership represents 98 per cent of the world's population further illustrates the great influence Codex has.

Most retailers in the organized food retailing industry in India have begun to insist on labelling that has to be standardized as awareness among consumers has increased considerably. Standards on labelling have become mandatory with a specific mention of the name of the food item, and date of manufacture and storage instructions. Where the scope of Codex Standard is not limited to pre-packaged foods, a provision for labelling of non-retail containers may be included. In such cases, the provision may specify that information on provisions shall be given either on the container or in the accompanying documents, except that the name of the product, lot identification, and the name and address of the manufacturer or packer shall appear on the container.

At the heart of retail marketing is the understanding of shopper behaviour, how people think, how they feel and how they act at any given time in any given situation – emotional branding, if you like.

This may seem to be an overwhelming subject to tackle, and one that has infinite permutations, but if you can grasp how your shoppers act and what influences them.

These include sensory effects such as colour and smells, priorities at different times of day or even external factors that affect people's choices. People are a step closer to understanding how to influence shoppers by their in-store marketing.

At Bezier, they use a model called 'Jane Brown'. An average working woman (who account for 80 per cent of retail spend), they use Jane to show her various shopping modes depending on shopping occasions and 'mission'.

Modes include 'fraught and functional', which relates to the weekly, possibly child hampered, grocery shop when Jane just wants to get in and out with what she needs.

Understanding this pattern can help with the development, for example, of clear navigational signage, clear category management and clear labelling to develop loyalty and ensure Jane has the smoothest shop possible.

Another very different mode is 'me me' mode, in which Jane requires something completely different from the retail environment.

In this shopping mode, Jane is out on her own, shopping for herself, looking for a luxury item or treat. In this situation, she wants to be inspired and drawn into her environment, so more complex messages, imagery and layouts can be used.

The beauty of using Jane as a shopper model is that she can be bestowed with different characteristics, acting in certain situations, and by thinking about her as a person, it becomes easier to see how important the retail environment is.

Along with helping clients understand shopper behaviour, they have recently completed several projects working with major retail organizations to audit their retail space – for example, how many gondola ends there are, the size of the foyer, or how much wall and floor space there actually is.

This valuable service has numerous benefits: making sure materials are fit for purpose, ensuring that compliance issues with PoP are reduced, saving money, and enabling large organizations to communicate on a store by store basis.

Both of these important issues, shopper behaviour and fully understanding your retail space, help greatly with that key measurement at the heart of marketing plans – the return on investment.

Demand for RoI is growing, and with increased pressure to justify expense, more detailed information and consumer insight just gives more power to your elbow. In-store marketing has an ever-growing part to play in consumer experience, make sure yours is as effective as it can be.

Food World

Food World has become India's largest and fastest growing supermarket chain. Today, over 89 stores offer customers a variety of brands at a very reasonable price. Food World in India, is an alliance between the RPG Group in India with Dairy Farm International of the Jardine Matheson Group. Food World aims at establishing 100 stores all over Tamil Nadu, Andhra Pradesh, Karnataka and Maharashtra by mid-2004 with a turnover of ₹ 500 crore.

Trinethra is a supermarket chain that has predominant presence in the southern state of Andhra Pradesh with 66 stores spread over 8 districts of the state. Their turnover was ₹ 78.8 crore for the year 2002-03. This figure is expected to touch the ₹ 100 crore mark by 2003-04. The Trinethra group came into being as a single store in the year 1986. They plan to saturate their presence throughout the state of Andhra Pradesh before venturing into two more southern states of the country. The group plans to venture into the lower level regions like smaller towns and mandals by using the franchisee-model. They are also very clear that they would be setting up three hypermarkets in the state soon.

Apna Bazaar, the ₹ 140 crore consumer cooperative society with a customer base of over 12 lakh, plans to cater to an upwardly mobile urban population – a first for the 55-year-old chain that has mostly been identified with the 'middle-class'. The plans include trimming and training the workforce, opening new outlets and focusing on the FMCG sector. Now, the cooperative has 80 outlets in Mumbai, Thane and the neighbouring Konkan region. It has recently opened its first shop outside the state in Goa. The revenue target for 2003-04 is ₹ 150 crore. The chain plans to remain open all days of the week and this itself is expected to fetch about ₹ 10 crore a year.

Big Bazaar – Pantaloons

After Bengaluru, Hyderabad and Kolkata, Big Bazaar, a division of Pantaloon Retail (India) Ltd., has stretched its brand to Mumbai by opening three hypermarkets in the city. Offering discounts ranging from 5 per cent to 60 per cent, discount store is still a nascent concept in India. Big Bazaar launched its stores in Bengaluru, Hyderabad and Kolkata in 2001. Marking an investment of ₹ 10 crore into this new division, Pantaloon is expected to record the highest turnover from its Mumbai stores to the tune of almost ₹ 80 crore from Mumbai alone within the first year of operations. But the turnover from its other Big Bazaar stores in Bengaluru, Hyderabad and Kolkata is ₹ 50 crore this year. Big Bazaar claims to be India's first chain of hypermarket discount stores.

Margin Free

The Kerala-based Margin Free discount stores, the 'pure retail' chain with arguably the largest presence in the country. The retail store chain is uniformly spread across the 240-odd Margin Free franchisees in Kerala, Tamil Nadu and Karnataka. Margin Free draws inspiration from the undying loyalty of its customers who have wholeheartedly welcomed all its growth plans in the past. Margin Free plans to open huge hypermarkets (50,000 sq.ft. each) in Ernakulam, Thiruvananthapuram and Kozhikode in the immediate future.

Subhiksha

The Chennai-based retail food and pharmacy chain Subhiksha supermarket and pharmacy is in expansion mode. It plans to go national and have 400 stores in the next two years. Currently, Subhiskha has a strong presence only in Tamil Nadu and Pondicherry with over 150 stores. The decision to expand outside Tamil Nadu, is because the city has reached saturation and also, the purchasing power is high in larger metros. Subhiksha stores sell household items and medicines at significant discount to normal prices. The retail chain earned a total revenue of ₹ 235 crore in 2002-03. The first Subhiksha store was opened in Tiruvanmiyur in Chennai in March 1997. Today, the chain has about 164 outlets in Tamil Nadu and Pondicherry. In 1997-98 Subhiksha was making a turnover of ₹ 12 crore and a profit of ₹ 10 lakh. In 2003, it has grown to ₹ 224 crore turnover and ₹ 3 crore profit. Major plans are on in Karnataka to open 40 stores in Bengaluru in the next nine months and another seven stores in Mysore in the same period. In all, it is intended to open at least 250 stores by 2005. The group is looking at extending operations in Karnataka and also venturing into the Maharashtra, Andhra Pradesh and Gujarat markets.

Subhiksha, a Chennai-based discount chain, too wants to be the principal store of purchase for at least 40 per cent of all consumers living within 500-750 metres of the store, that is, within walking distance. This makes the point very clear that the strategy among most existing retail chains of various formats is to completely saturate the markets where they are already established players and then move on to virtually untouched areas where the challenge of sourcing resources and extending their supply chain model to best suit the size and expanse of the market would be a challenging task.

R. Subramanian, Founder and Managing Director of Subhiksha Retail, India's largest retailer in terms of number of stores, feels that while global economic meltdown would cause some pain, it will in the long run help the industry lead a healthy life. Global meltdown has adversely affected growth of retail industry in India, says Subramanian.

"Everyone in retail industry are postponing their expansion plans and are adopting a wait and watch strategy", said Subramanian. He was speaking to PTI on retail industry in general and Subhiksha's business in particular.

On being asked about stock outs of mobile phones across his stores in Chennai, Subramanian attributed the same to mobile phone sales witnessing slow growth in the past few months.

There are several reports in the media about many of the fast moving consumer products not being available in many of Subhiksha's food and grocery as well as telecom stores. Subhiksha, as reported earlier, has already withdrawn from fresh foods (fruits and vegetables) business. Most of the Subhiksha store are also carrying limited stocks of many pharmaceutical products.

Subhiksha, as part of its expansion plans, is setting up consumer durable retail stores across the country. According to Subramanian, these stores would hold products like laptops, printers, computers apart from mobile phones.

Subhiksha has not paid salary to their employees since from last one year. There are no unidentified elements, their employee took control of few stores and were running the stores since last six months, just to recover their salary. They are just poor people and were forced to do so, at the fault of their management.

Recession is hitting the retail industry quite badly and Shubiksha has announced that it has closed 90 stores in the last one month.

Subhiksha was paying huge rent for these stores, which was a huge drain on the company's finances. This, coupled with less-than-expected footfalls, drove the operational costs to unsustainable levels. High rental rates have always been the bone of contention for organized retail owners. The retailers had taken up space on rentals as high as ₹ 250 per sq. ft. "At one point of time, the retailers were paying close to 40 per cent of their operational cost as rent, leaving hardly any room for profits".

Nilgiris

Muthusamy Mudaliar opened a small bunk shop in Ooty. That was in 1905 and the beginning of a long story in procurement and customer satisfaction. In 1936, the shop moved to Golden Enclave in Bangalore with its registered office on Brigade Road, a small shop exactly where the huge mother store is now located. The first expansion happened when Muthusamy Mudaliar's son Chenniappan also the chairman established Nilgiris as a modest store carrying Nilgiris own products, mostly dairy and bakery. Eventually, it evolved into a supermarket when Mr. Chenniappan visited the US and Europe and was influenced by the old supermarket concept in the West. This supermarket chain has now blossomed to cover a vast region in South India with 26 outlets and annual sales of about ₹ 2,300 Million. They plan to open an additional 30 outlets in their next phase of expansion. The retail chain Nilgiris has closed down 50 under-performing master franchise stores which were averaging revenues of just ₹ 250 per sq.ft. and added 65 individual franchise stores which on 28th September 2010 had average revenue of ₹ 1,100 per sq.ft. The Nilgiris had 92 stores in South India, all franchisees, and touched 100 stores in November 2010. It has 47 stores in Tamil Nadu (36 of them in Chennai) and 37 in Karnataka and a few in Kerala and Andhra Pradesh. Nilgiris is a food retailer.

MTR

The MTR Group of Companies promoted by the family of Maiyas took birth in the year 1924, with the commencement of a Restaurant in Bangalore. Later in 1976, MTR ventured into the business of retailing of groceries and other household general items by opening a department store. MTR first brought out a packaged, processed food product. Subsequently, efforts were made to extend the distribution of the above products to few other prominent Retail Stores in Bangalore, such as Nilgiris, Vijaya Bakery, Shivananda Stores, Home Needs, etc. The response was found to be very encouraging in terms of sales of the above products. Consequently, a major step with respect to marketing was taken by the Group in the year 1983. It was during 1983, that MTR appointed distributors in Bangalore, Madras, Hyderabad and Vijayawada with a view to capture business opportunities in the said markets.

Janatha Bazaars and HOPCOMS

Cooperative departmental stores were started with government patronage in the early 1960s, at a time when shortage of basic goods was the order of the day. Poor marketing strategies hindered their progress in the field. Total membership of 11,680 farmers, with 100 tonnes of horticultural produce being traded per day in eight districts. In 1998, each cooperative society was made independent, sixteen of which were subsequently federated at the state level, as members of the Karnataka Horticulture Federation.

Presence of MNC Chains

Metro AG

Opened its first Indian outlet in Yeshwanthpur, Bengaluru on a sprawling 6,500 square metres area. Also open one more centre in Bengaluru during November 2003. Capital expenditure for these two centres is ₹ 176 crore (35 million Euros). Employ 300 local people and headquarter will employ 750 local people.

Revival of Reliance: Reliance Fresh, however, sticks to its claim with fresh and packaged vegetables adorning its shelves. No wonder, they are being bought off the shelves like hot cakes.

"What I like about these private stores is that they have free home delivery service", said Pammi Arora, a resident of Paharganj that has one of the biggest Reliance Fresh stores in the city. "These days I mostly buy goods from here", she added.

Indeed, Reliance Retail's reported revenues are just around 1 per cent of Reliance Industries' total sales of ₹ 1.39 trillion for the fiscal year 2008.

Reliance Retail already has 3.5 million sq. ft. of trading space and has outlined a total investment of ₹ 25,000 crore over the next few years, even though protests from small retailers and wholesalers have slowed some of its expansion plans. So far, Reliance Industries has invested nearly ₹ 4,400 crore in Reliance Retail in the form of equity and preference shares. The equity investment amounts to ₹ 3,785 crore, giving Reliance Industries a 98.74 per cent stake in the retail venture, according to the annual report.

Not all the performance is rosy. Other retail subsidiaries of Reliance Industries such as Reliance Fresh Ltd., (formerly known as Ranger Farms Ltd.) and Reliance Dairy Foods Ltd., have reported losses for the year ended 31st March, 2009. Reliance Fresh has a loss of ₹ 20 crore on a revenue of ₹ 357 crore, while Reliance Dairy Foods incurred a loss of ₹ 3 crore on revenues of ₹ 66 crore.

The interlinkages between Reliance Retail results and these losses were unclear. Reliance Retail operates under 12 different store formats ranging from convenience store concept to consumer durables concept and automotive specialty formats. It has also entered into two joint ventures – Pearle Europe for optical retailing and Marks & Spencer for apparel retailing.

SCOPE OF THE INDIAN RETAIL MARKET

The scope of the Indian retail market is immense for this sector is poised for the highest growth in the next five years. The Indian retail industry contributes 10 per cent of the country's GDP and its current growth rate is 8.5 per cent. In the Indian retail market the scope for growth can be seen from the fact that it is expected to rise to US $ 608.9 billion in 2009, from US $ 394 billion in 2005.

The organized retailing sector in India is only 3 per cent and it increased to 25- 30 per cent by the year 2010. At present around 325 departmental stores, 300 new malls, and 1500 supermarkets are under construction. This proves that there is a tremendous scope for growth in the Indian retail market.

The growth of scope in the Indian retail market is mainly due to the change in the consumers' behaviour. The new generation have preference towards luxury commodities which have been due to the strong increase in income, changing lifestyle, and demographic patterns which are favourable.

The scope of the Indian retail market has been seen by many retail giants and that is the reason that many new players are entering the Indian retail industry. The major Indian retailers are:

Pantaloons Retail India Ltd., Shoppers' Stop, Bata India Ltd., Music World Entertainment Ltd. Judging the scope for growth in the Indian retail industry many global retail giants are also entering the Indian retail market. They are:

Tesco, Metro AG, Wal-Mart.

The scope for growth in the Indian retail market is seen mainly in the following cities:

Mumbai, Delhi, Pune, Ahmedabad, Bengaluru, Hyderabad, Kolkata, Chennai.

The scope of the Indian retail market is very vast. And reach to its full potential the government and the Indian retailers will have to make a determined effort.

Retailing in India is entirely different from Western countries including Asian counterparts. Studies show that upgraded kirana stores are growing at the same rate as organized retailers. It is also observed that in the changing retailing environment, understanding the psyche of customer is critical to success in retailing. Aggregate level picture may be misleading, as it averages the beats and the valleys. Hence, individual understanding is desirable. Though, some Indians are behaving as sophisticated shoppers, tens of millions are still novice but no less avid consumers are joining the fray every year. So, retailers have to acknowledge this change and also stay a step ahead of the evolution curve of the Indian market. Finally, it is not the format that gives business sustainability rather it is one of the vehicles to deliver the value to the customer. Indian consumers are still family-driven entities. Shopping, entertainment and eating out are family events. Since these decisions are normally group decisions, hence, a marketer has to address family sensibilities more rigorously to woo Indian customers. Indian customers have become more sensitive to quality, customer service and status. He/she is ready to pay, sometimes astronomical sums, provided their needs are satisfied. They are basically looking for an experience which is more of cognitive than physical. In brief, *Jo Dikhta Hai Wo Hi Bikta Hai*. In some cases, few Kirana store owners find no competition because they understand what their customer want. So ultimately it can be said that for a retailer understanding the customer is just like climbing the greased pole. Retailing encompasses the business activities involved in selling goods and services to consumers for their personal, family, or household use. It includes every sale to the final consumer – ranging from cars to apparel to meals at restaurants to theatre tickets. Retailing is the last stage in the distribution process.

In **niche retailing**, retailers identify specific customer segments and deploy unique strategies to address the desires of those segments rather than the mass market. Niching creates a high level of loyalty and shields retailers from more conventional competitors. Babies "R" Us (www.babiesrus.com) induces parents with very young children to buy their products. Catherine's Stores appeal to plus-size women. This approach will have a strong future because it lets retailers stress factors other than price and have a better focus.

Ramee Mall, a 15-storey-building that stands on Chennai's arterial road, Anna Salai opened its doors in the first quarter of 2011. Ramee Mall is promoted by the West Asia-based Ramee Guestline Hotels Group. Retail Shoppers' Stop will be the mall's anchor tenant. Shoppers' Stop has taken up 50,000 sq.ft. a third of the total space, on lease. According to Mr. Basill Mathew, General Manager, Marketing, Ramee Mall, a bookstore will take up 15,000 sq.ft. Besides large-format stores, there will be 30 vanilla stores-small shops each occupying less than 1,000 sq. ft. and a food court. Ramee has spent ₹ 120 crore on the property.

Direct Selling

It is a retail format in which salespeople, frequently independent business people, contact customers directly in a convenient location either at the customer's home or at work; demonstrate merchandise benefits and/or explain a service; take an order; and deliver the merchandise or perform in service. Direct selling is a highly interactive form of retailing in which considerable information is conveyed to customers through face to face discussion with salespeople.

Television Home Shopping

It is a retail format in which customers watch a TV programme that demonstrates merchandise and then place orders for the merchandise by telephone. The three forms of electronic home shopping retailing are: (1) Cable channels dedicated to television shopping, (2) Infomercials, and direct-response advertising.

Direct-response advertising includes advertisements on TV and radio that describe products and provide an opportunity for consumers to order them. Infomercials are TV programmes, typically 30 minutes long, that mix entertainment with product demonstration and then solicit orders placed by telephone.

Vending Machine Retailing

It is a non-store format in which merchandise or services are stored in a machine and dispensed to customers when they deposit cash or use a credit card. Vending machines are placed at convenient, high-traffic locations, such as in the workplace or on university campuses, and primarily contain snacks or drinks.

Services Retailing

Services retailers, firms selling primarily services rather than merchandise, are a large and growing part of the retail industry. There are several trends that suggest considerable future growth in services retailing. For example, the aging population will increase demand for health care services. Young people are also spending more time and money on health and fitness. Busy parents in two-income families are willing to pay to have their homes cleaned, lawns maintained, clothes washed and pressed and meals prepared so they can spend more time with their families. Many organizations such as banks, hospitals, health spas, legal clinics, entertainment firms, and universities that offer services to consumers traditionally have not considered themselves retailers. Due to increased competition, these organizations are adopting retailing principles to attract customers and satisfy their needs.

Interbank Mobile Payments (IMPs): IMPs has 7 banks including SBI. It has potential to change the retail payment landscape that boasts 600 million mobile subscribers and 300 million bank accounts. National Payments Corporation of India (NPCI) has been promoted by 10 banks and acts as the settlement agency between banks and delivers the back-end support for the system to be operated. A bank account-holder will have to get his Mobile Money ID (MMID) from the bank which will be his ID for mobile-commerce transactions. The bank account-holder can remit money to anyone. The banks will bear the cost of 25 paise a transaction. There is SMS-based remittance. RBI regulations cap the maximum amount to be remitted at ₹ 50,000 a day. The RBI is encouraging the bank-led model for m-commerce.

Differences between Services and Merchandise Retailers

Four important differences in the nature of the offering provided by services and merchandise retailers are:

1. Intangibility
2. Simultaneous production and consumption
3. Perishability, and
4. Inconsistency of the offering to customers.

Reasons for Studying Retailing

Retailing is an important field to study because of its impact on the economy, its functions in distribution, and its relationship with firms selling goods and services to retailers for their resale or use. A fourth factor for students of retailing is the broad range of career opportunities. Retailing includes all the activities involved in selling goods or services directly to final consumers for personal, non-business use. Retailing is the set of business activities that adds value to the products and services sold to consumers for their personal or family use. A retailer or retail store in any business enterprise whose sales volume comes primarily from retailing. Any organization selling to final consumers is doing retailing. It does not matter how the goods or services are sold (by person, mail, telephone, vending machine, or internet) or where they are sold (in a store, on the street, or in the consumer's home). Often people think of retailing only as the sale of products in stores, but retailing also involves the sale of services: overnight lodging in a motel, a doctor's exam, a haircut, a DVD rental, or a home-delivered pizza. Not all retailing is done in stores. FDI in retail and significant investments are required to transform the retail industry. The Indian Retail Forum (IRF) has listed out the advantages of FDI in retail. Besides, retailers such as Wal-Mart which have already tied up with Bharti Retails are looking forward to launching their own branded stores once FDI is allowed. Wal-Mart is already using India as a sourcing base. Bharti Wal-Mart is also in the process of launching new stores in West and South India in 2011. Because of this more money will be flowing into the retail industry in India. Retail is a long-haul business. The big players in the organized industry are mainly apparel and jewellery players.

Retailing is the interface between the producer and the individual consumer buying for personal consumption. This excludes direct interface between the manufacturer and institutional buyers such as the government and other bulk customers. A retailer is one who stocks the producer's goods and is involved in the act of selling it to the individual consumer, at a margin of profit. As such retailing is the last link that connects the individual consumer with the manfuacturing and distribution chain.

Definition of Retail Management: It is a distinct process consisting of planning, organizing, actuating, and controlling retail performance to determine and accomplish the objectives of retail management by the use of retail personnel and resources. It is concerned with seeing that the retail job gets done, its business tasks in all centres especially on planning and guiding the retail operations that are going on in the market. Retail management means to make the desired results to pass. It is simply the process of decision making and control over the retail actions of sales force for the express purpose of attaining predetermined retail sales goal. It consists of getting retail business done through others. Retail management concerns itself with the direction and control of various retail activities to attain the retail business objectives. It is the art of creating favourable environment so that retailers can perform as individuals, and as group and cooperate towards the attainment of Retail management goals. Retail management embraces all duties and functions that pertain to the initiation of an active retail enterprise, its financing, the establishment of policies, the provision of necessary credit facilities, the outlining of general form of organization under which the retail business is to operate and the group of officials in primary control of retail outlet. Retail management is concerned with profitability; this implies effectiveness and efficiency.

ORGANIZATIONAL STRUCTURE IN RETAIL MANAGEMENT

Meaning

The structure that an organization chooses to adopt is the key factor which affects the functioning of the various roles in the organization. Organizational structures are important as they define the hierarchy levels, the reporting relationships and the decision makers in any organization. In retail, as in any other business, defining the organizational structure is the starting point for managing a business.

Creating Organizational Structures

The first step in creating an organizational structure is to define the various tasks/activities that need to be performed. These can be broadly classified as:

- Top management
- Buying and merchandising
- Store operations
- Administration and human resources
- Support functions, like Advertising, Marketing, PR and Accounts.

The purpose of this classification is two-fold. It helps the various tasks to be identified and it also helps in understanding the roles to be played by people within the organization.

Once these tasks have been identified, the management needs to take into consideration, its own requirements and targets and how they can be achieved. It needs to consider the requirements of the target market and the needs of its own internal customers, i.e., the employees. An organizational structure or an organization chart is then developed, after taking all these factors into consideration.

Defining the organizational structure enables the activities and tasks to be performed and this aids for analyzing the need for specialists in various areas.

ORGANIZATIONAL STRUCTURE IN RETAIL

The manner in which a retailer is organized, contributes to its uniqueness. The organizational structure makes a definite impact on the various functions within the organization. Various factors which influence the creation of organizational structures, are:

- Scope and scale of operation, *viz.,* local, regional, national or international
- Types of products sold
- Types of departmentalization, i.e., and functional, product-wise or geographic
- Organized Retail Market in India
- Organized retail appeared in India in 1999, with the launch of the "first malls" – 'Ansal's Plaza' in Delhi and 'Crossroads' in Mumbai. They are hailed as the spark that led to the explosion of organized retail in the country and transformed the retail landscape.

The Indian market is currently witnessing a retail boom with organized retailers. It is characterized by large professionally managed format stores. It offers a whole assortment of goods and services to consumers under one roof with congenial shopping ambience. While providing shopping convenience through planned layout and attractive storage and display of goods based on consumer preference, organized retail offers good value for money as benefits. It is the next sunrise industry after IT and is gaining momentum with many global retail giants who are screening their interests to enter India. Even the traditional kirana stores have taken initiatives to organize and implement technologies into their stores. However, there is an apparent fear in the minds of millions of small retailers and hawkers that organized retail would endanger their livelihood.

The organized retailers are transforming a non-fun mundane shopping activity into an exciting activity where emerging technologies are being extensively used to synchronize the various activities across different operational verticals to enhance the business value. Shopping for apparel, home furnishings, cars, jewellery, grocery, fruits and vegetables, etc., are products that are bought with utmost involvement from the consumers. In recent times, several retail chains have gone about aggressively expanding their network of stores. The organized retail outlets have met with some initial success and also have faced various problems. They encountered several challenges before they could think of growing much further. Traditional buying habits of Indians, the conventional retail outlets and even the proliferation of retail chains have made the task of organized retailing quite difficult.

The book focuses on the gaining momentum of organized retailing in India. The 'Concept' discusses the conceptual part as to why we need organized retailing in India? why people buy from organized retailers?, the significance, the impact created, strategies adopted and role played by organized retailing in India, changing trends, promotional tools, role of technology and the strategies that a organized retailer is practicing to cope up with the changing scenarios. This book also discusses the experiences of the individual organized retailers in India. The transformational strategies adopted by the small retailers, the technologies deployed by the large players to enhance the services, the analysis and the alliances done by the foreign retailers to overcome the challenges for entering into the Indian market, and the success stories of the existing retailers of India are also explained.

The article **"Organized Retailing – An Insight"** authored by *Dr. Krishnabhushan E. Mahashabde,* discusses the advantages and disadvantages of the organized retail sector and the unorganized retail sector in India. Organized retailing which emerged post-liberalization has made a great impact on the minds of the consumers. Lot of importance is given to cleanliness, politeness and helping nature of the salesmen. Display of products helps the buyer in making a suitable decision. Organized retailing has also contributed towards employment generation in the country. The unorganized retail sector has certain disadvantages, as it is characterized by poor infrastructure, distorted real estate market, lack of skilled labour, etc. In order to overcome these weaknesses it is necessary to develop the organized retail sector in India. It is also a fact that the kirana stores are changing the way of doing business and are adapting with the changing times in order to survive in the market. Supply chain management, inventory management are the areas which are also touched upon in the article.

Matloob Hasan, Aneesh Issar and *Bhanu Pratap Singh,* the authors of the article **"The Indian Retail Bazaar"**, have briefly explained the Indian retail scenario and the gaining wider acceptance of the organized retailing in India. The article says that the Indian organized retail sector is set to become the new star on the commercial horizon with the improving infrastructure facilities and also with the government of relaxing rules for foreign brands. The article also says that the middle-class is the hope for large Indian retail players. The rising incomes, particularly in the lower and middle income households, are impacting retail growth in India as these groups tend to spend more on upgrading and diversifying their lifestyles, eating out and moving on to processed and convenience foods. The large and growing young working population is also a preferred customer segment for the retailers, because this segment is the early adopter of most of the modern product-line. Earlier the organized sector was limited to the big six key destinations, but, now the Tier II cities are also getting noticed because of the cheaper real estate options available which enables the retailers to break-even much faster as compared to larger areas. The article states that many foreign companies have also been exploring possible alternative entry routes such as brand licensing, franchising, cash and carry and wholesaling where hundred per cent FDI is allowed, apart from online retailing. The article also throws light on the future plans of new retail bazaars in India. The organized retail sector in India is expected to grow to $ 64 bn by 2015, from the current $ 10 bn enterprise.

In the next article **"Organized Retail Market Boom and the Indian Society"**, the authors *A. Sreejith and Jagathy Raj V. P.,* cite that India has the highest shop density in the world and the present retail market in India is estimated to be US $ 200 billion of which only 3 per cent is in the organized sector. IT and related services have played a major role in India's current GDP growth. India is ranked second in the global retail development index out of 30. The organized retail sector is poised for a take-off. The article gives a glimpse of the slow evolution of retail market over the years in India and its contribution to economic growth. The likely positive impact of this revolution in different sectors is also enumerated. The article addresses its ability to manipulate consumption pattern of society, increased customer satisfaction and likely change in the market shares of different types of sellers. The article discusses its-flip sides like increasing social tension among families below poverty line and greater loss of self-employment opportunities by this revolution. The article also elaborates the need for regulations in the retail sector in India, such as government intervention and the control over monopolizing by the foreign players. The illustrated FDI policies should be reformed from time-to-time, banking finance for the welfare of the unorganized sector for improving their efficiency should be enhanced and Agricultural Produce Marketing Committee (APMC) Act, etc., should be effectively implemented to make sure that small and local businesses are not adversely affected.

The article **"India's Changing Consumers"**, written by *Ranjan Biswas* discusses the growing consumerism in India. Nearly about 54 per cent of Indian population is below 25 years of age, who form a major part of the population demanding for organized retailing format. A significant factor for further development of the organized sector is the mindset of the people, which is now shifting from price consideration to design and quality of the product. There is also a willingness to experiment with mainstream fashion as greater emphasis is placed on looking and feeling good. The article describes the various retail segments present and the individual contribution of every segment in the retail sector. The author of the article explains the growing urbanization, the real estate revolution, the growing opportunity for FDI and the foreign retailers who are willing to enter into the Indian retail industry. The author also explains the risk associated with the new entries into the Indian retail sector and has written some guiding principles for risk management.

Sriram Rajann the author of the article **"Operational Efficiency Through InformationTechnology in Retail Decision Making and Marketing Management"**, discusses the significance of information technology in today's modern retailing. The article says modern organized retailing cannot survive without IT, which acts as a strong backbone. Modern retail operations have been revolutionized by the use of Information Technology (IT). It has now become an inevitable part of the process. The article says functions like store operations, merchandise management, planning and forecasting and inventory control are all smoothly carried out with the help of IT. It is also responsible for the efficient and effective supply chain management. It involves functions like Quick Response (QR), Efficient Customer Response (ECR) and Collaborative Planning and Forecasting (CPF). The article illustrates the significance of IT by explaining the example of Madura Garments Ltd., a chain of clothing shops. Madura Garments Ltd., makes use of information technology in all the activities in the store such as to maintain the company accounts, to calculate the wages and bonuses of employees, to store customer information in order to keep in touch with the best customers, to maintain the various day to day activities regarding sales and purchases of goods and so on. The article articulates that most of the retailers are of the opinion that proper use of information technology may cut costs, increase accuracy, reduce processing times, enable quicker decision 33making, and speed up customer service.

The article **"Visual Merchandising in Indian Organized Retail – An Overview"**, authored by *Kisholoy Roy,* gives a detailed description of Visual Merchandising and how it is helpful for the retailer to differentiate themselves from others. Visual merchandising is an art that involves the implementation of effective design and product presentation ideas to increase store traffic and sales volume. It puts the merchandise in focus, apart from educating customers and creating a desire in them to buy. With the rapid increase in the number of retail chains operating in various product categories and the proliferation of shopping malls, it has become extremely essential to differentiate oneself from the others in an appealing and striking manner. Effective visual merchandizing has become an important tool in this context for providing a distinct image and identity to one's retail outlet, thereby creating a unique image in the minds of consumers. The article states that the primary objective of visual merchandising is to turn a passerby into a browser, a browser into a spender, a spender into a big spender and a big spender into a loyal customer. Broadly speaking, visual merchandising includes exterior presentation, interior presentation and store layouts.

The author *Kisholoy Roy* in the article **"Background Music – A Tool to Boost Sales in Organized Retail"**, discusses the impact created by the background music in the retail stores and its consequence in generating revenue. Universally, music has been found to have a positive effect on people. It has often been instrumental in elevating moods by creating a soothing and pleasant ambience. Lately, it has been observed that various entities in India's organized retail industry are using music as a means to influence customer behaviour and boost their revenues. Through appropriate background music, stores, restaurants, cafés, gyms and salons are not just influencing customers' shopping attitudes and retaining them in their shops for a longer period of time but are also keeping the salespeople at the store entertained and active. The challenge, however, is that retailers need to understand the kind of music that will be right for a particular type of store and various other technicalities that will contribute to increased sales. It has been thus observed that playing the right kind of music at the stores helps the retailers to establish an emotional connect with the customers and positions the store distinctly in the customer's perceptual territory. The article states that research has established that background music is a critical tool to increase sales in the current Indian retail scenario. Retaining customers at a shop needs effective background music. Retailing is both an art as well as a science.

The article **"The Geography of Opportunity – The 'India 50'"**, written by the authors *Jeremy Kelly, Abhishek Kiran Gupta and Nikita Masih* review in brief the drivers of India's booming retail market. They also tell us how both retailers and the property sector are responding to the massive changes in the Indian retail environment. The authors have identified five types of cities – Maturing Cities, Transitional Cities, High Growth Cities, Emerging Cities and Nascent Cities. Each group is at a different stage in its market evolution and offers a different set of opportunities for organized retailers and the property sector. The article shows that the Indian retail market offers significant opportunities for domestic as well as international retailers, property developers and investors across a broad range of geographies. Rapidly changing consumer behaviour, new market entrants and changing government policy will further transform the sector and open up yet more opportunities. The article further articulates the future promises and the associated problems with the rapid expansion of organized retailing in India. The author says that in the rush to expand retail formats and build new malls, many retailers and developers have lacked strategic vision, and in a booming market they have often lost sight of the "end game". The reality will be that many planned retail schemes will not get built and of those that do eventually become operational will fall below international standards. As more choices become available for the Indian consumer, many malls and retail concepts will fail the test of time. The next stage in the evolution of the Indian organized retail market will be when international developers and financiers start to change the shape of Indian retailing, joining an elite group of visionary domestic developers, owners and retailers who have the scalability, the teams, the processes and the logistics required to flourish in this rapidly growing retail environment.

The author, *Meher Castelino,* of the case **"Kids Makeover their 'MOM-AND-POP' Stores"** talks about the success story of the 'Mom-and-Pop' stores run by 'Sheetal' and 'Roopam' in Mumbai, which are now transformed into mega brands. These are two stores located in middle-lass areas in Mumbai, that set the trend for other family-owned stores in the country turning into brands, both in India as well as abroad. 'Sheetal' which was started in 1979 by Babubhai Shah in the heart of Grant Road, was an 800 sq. ft. general store. Around the same time 'Roopam' was opened in Crawford Market in a 500 sq. ft. area selling assorted clothing. In 2005, 'Sheetal' was spread over 35,000 sq. ft., while 'Roopam' was an impressive 25,000 sq. ft. 'Sheetal' has grown into more outlets at Warden Road, Crawford Market, Santa Cruz, Inorbit Mall as well as in Singapore, New Jersey and Dubai. 'Roopam' has its flagship store in South Mumbai with franchisees in Mauritius, the US and Australia. The turnover of both the stores has grown by 30-35 per cent annually over the years. The case explains how these family stores have moved into the new millennium to meet the challenges thrown in by foreign brands, retailers and the mall culture and where they will go from here?

R. Subramnian, Managing Director, Subhiksha talks about his adventures, the success of his retail chain and also his future plans in an exclusive interview **"Success Story of Subhiksha, India's Largest Retail Chain",** with *Shobha Warrier*. The MD says that though he was an IIT-IIMA graduate he chose to stay back in India and start a company of his own. He was not fascinated with the opportunities available in the US. He explains how he started his journey at Citibank in India, how he generated money to start his own company and the factors which inspired him to open a low price retail chain, Subhiksha. He allocated ₹ 5 crore (₹ 50 million) corpus to Subhiksha and entered the retail business. There was a lot of thought process behind it and he wanted to attract not the top end customer but the *'aam aadmi'*. He faced many challenges but with corrective steps he overcame the same. Subhiksha was one of the early entrants, so it had the learning curve much to its advantage. On expansion plans, he decided to look at every part of India which is significantly literate and is a significant consumption market for the retail chain. He wanted Subhiksha to be everywhere and looked at the telecom companies as the role model and employed capable regional managers and expanded. On the entry of MNCs and Reliance in the retail market, the opinion of Subhiksha's MD is that, 'Subhiksha is not worried about anybody's entry. There is a huge potential for growth in India and there is potential for another ten people to come in.'

"It Happened in India: The Story of Pantaloons, Big Bazaar, Central and the Great Indian Consumer" is an autobiography that speaks about the journey of Kishore Biyani in the Indian retail sector. *Lopamudra Ghosh* has written the book review and *Kishore Biyani* with the help of *Dipayan Baishya* has scripted the book. They have shared the experiences of the company that started by venturing into garment manufacturing, later moving into franchising and direct marketing and finally forayed into retail. In this book, Biyani mentions an important chapter of his life when he, along with Sushil Sain and Krishna Jhunjhunwala set up a company named Dhruv Synthetics in 1986. It was a factory that produced fancy yarn. The focus of their business was to cater to the needs of ordinary people by providing them what only rich people could afford at reasonable prices. They always tried to offer 'strong value-for-proposition' to their customers. In the middle of 1996, it was decided that the company would set up retail stores, and in 1997, the Pantaloon Mega Store was launched in Gariahat, Kolkata. Big Bazaar was the next step to success and it was truly the inflection point for the organization helping it to reach a larger customer base. In May 2004, the first Central mall was set up in Bengaluru. Central turned out to be a unique offering for the masses, where no other retailer had ventured in that period. It proved to be a good showcase of the retailing skills of the organization. The biggest challenge they then faced was how to stimulate more consumption and make one's presence across the total consumption space. The answer was provided with the creation of Future Group in 2006 that encompassed an array of services which could be divided into several verticals namely – 'retail, capital brands, media, space and logistics'. The focus of the future group is to leave a lasting impression in the Indian consumption space.

In the case **"Growth Strategies of India's Leading Retail Group: Shoppers' Stop Limited"** the authors *Vandana Singh Dadhwal, K. Suresh, and Joel Sarosh Thadamalla*, state that Shoppers' Stop which has been successful in lifestyle and books retail formats, subsequently decided to branch out into the hypermarket formats. The case talks about the evolution, growth opportunities and the challenges that Shoppers' Stop Limited (SSL) has experienced. The store was air conditioned and special focus was given on interiors and amenities to create a lively shopping ambience. Today Shoppers' Stop has emerged as a lifestyle store chain with an extended product portfolio that includes a range of branded apparel, footwear, perfumes, cosmetics, jewellery, leather products, accessories, home products, electronics, books, music and toys. Besides its selection of premium brands, the in-store customer service played an important role in reinforcing SSL brand image as a premium retailer. The concept of HyperCity was a completely new retail format that the Shoppers' Stop group had started in order to diversify and capitalize the immense retail potential for hypermarkets. The initiative of starting the concept was challenging in itself because state-of-the-art technology was never used in the

Indian retailing segment before. The entire shopping experience at HyperCity for the customer is unique and highly satisfying; they don't have to face indefinite and long queues because of the highly technological environment.

Reena Poddar the author of the case **"Reliance's Foray into Organised Retailing",** states that Reliance Industries (RIL), controlled by billionaire Mukesh Ambani, unveiled an ambitious plan of foraying into India's retail market that would generate employment to at least 5,00,000 people across the nation. The case briefly discusses Reliance's venture into the Indian organized retail sector and also the factors which inspired the company to gamble the risk. The company has a goal to achieve annual sales of $ 25 billion by 2011, from the retail business enterprise. The company has planned to hire agricultural, veterinary and dairy experts in Punjab and is also expected to procure fresh produce, processed fruits, vegetables, grains, oilseeds, milk and poultry from Punjab farmers. The company is working on the supply chain infrastructure and logistics and aims to provide low priced goods to the consumers. The case talks about the challenges faced by the company while entering into the market in the journey of organized retailing and also talks about the constructive steps through which the company had overcome those challenges. It also illustrates the future plans of the company and says that the company eyes the franchisee route to ramp up the retail business.

The case **"Wal-Mart in India: A Success or Failure?",** is authored by *Jaya Halepete, K. V. Seshadri Iyer* and *Soo Chul Park*. It briefly discusses Wal-Mart's keenness for Indian market and the analysis and alliances which the company has made to enter into the Indian retail sector. Wal-Mart operates a total of 971 discount stores, 2,447 supercentres, 591 Sam's Clubs and 132 neighbourhood markets in the US and 3,020 retail stores internationally. Wal-Mart's business model is to provide lowest prices to its customers. Wal-Mart officials have indicated that India, where government reforms have lifted restrictions on foreign ownership of retail operations, is a major target market for the company. The case mentions that the Dunning's electic theory which was applied to international expansions is also used to analyze Wal-Mart's advantages and disadvantages in Germany and South Korea. The theory was then applied to India to understand the possible advantages and disadvantages for Wal-Mart in entering the Indian retail market. Wal-Mart's failures in Germany and South Korea are analyzed to identify learning that could be utilized in the Indian expansion. The main purpose of the case is to explore the challenges that Wal-Mart will face when it expands into the Indian retail market. These significant challenges need to be well-understood and suitably addressed for success in the Indian market. The joint venture between Wal-Mart and Bharti will manage the supply chain together while Bharti Enterprises will be franchised to run the retail portion. This operating model in India will expose Wal-Mart to potential challenges on the ownership and internationalization dimensions of the eclectic model. The case makes a contribution towards understanding the challenges in entering an international market. The case also helps to analyze the international experiences that can be leveraged in future plans of international expansion.

- Wal-Mart's President and CEO Mr. Michael T. Duke decided on opening up of 100 per cent for foreign direct investment in India's multi-brand retail sector. Wal-Mart currently has a 50:50 joint venture with the Bharti group and runs four cash-and-carry outlets in the country to supply to their retail stores. Wal-Mart Stores Inc. said it will match rivals' prices on "Black Friday" on 26-11-2010, upping the ante in the battle to win sales on what is considered to be the kick-off to the US holiday shopping season and a gauge of how overall holiday retail sales will shape up. Wal-Mart is one of the few retailers that will be open on Thanksgiving Day this year (2010), seeking to get an edge over rivals amid what forecasters say will only be modest sales growth in 2010.

- As India surges high with its growth story, the retail sector in the country is bound to come across opportunities like never before. Till a few years back, the retail sector in India was more of an unorganized one with petty vendors dominating the chunk of the industry but now the scenario has fast been changing. Finally, the sector is converting into what we call as organized retailing.
- Not only Indian corporate majors like Reliance, ITC and Pantaloon have entered into the segment but more and more foreign players are also showing interest in USD 350 billion Indian retail markets.
- Amazon.com Inc. on 22-11-2010 launched an application on Apple Inc.'s iPhone that it said allows shoppers to compare prices on a given items in brick-and-mortar stores with prices on its own website and gives them the option to instantly order the items through Amazon.
- Today, we turn around and find huge shopping malls and multiplexes all the way. Perhaps that's why the retail revolution is said to be spearheading the real estate boom in India.

The Retail Sector Boom

- While the Indian real estate markets boom with organized retailing, the segment ensures a fluffy growth pad for itself. According to the estimations of KSA-Technopark, a retail consulting and research firm, organized retailing in India will grow three-fold in the next three-years, achieving the size of USD 21.5 billion from the current one of USD 7.5 billion.
- Given the favourable growth patterns, expanding middle-class and easing economic-policies, India is ranked as the most attractive emerging markets for retail investment, even above Russia and China.

Growth Drivers

- The Indian middle-class.
- The growth story of Indian retail sector is based primarily on its huge middle-class. According to a study undertaken by the National Council for Applied Economic Research (NCAER) "The Growing Indian Middle-Class", the upper middle and high-income urban households in India will touch 3.8 crore by 2007 (from 1.46 crore in 2000).
- The sheer size of its upbeat middle-class market makes India a happening marketplace for retail players.
- Besides the number advantage, the purchasing power of Indian middle class is also growing substantially with a year-on-year growth rate of five-per cent in its household income.

- According to NCAER, the 9.2 crore strong Indian middle-class (whose annual income-ranges between ₹ 2 lakh and ₹ 10 lakh) is expected to cross ₹ 15.3 crore by 2009.
- Undoubtedly, such healthy trends corroborate that the retail sector boom is here to stay in India on sustained basis.

Policy Reforms

- The Indian government allows 51 per cent Foreign Direct Investment (FDI) in single brand retailing owing to which foreign multinationals like Reebok and Louis Vuitton can now operate directly in the Indian markets instead of going through franchise route as earlier. Some state government banned FDI in retail business in their states, e.g., Tamil Nadu.

The Road Ahead

- While Indian telecom major Bharti is all set to foray in the retail segment, a number of companies from the US, England and Australia have laid plans to sell their products directly at the retail outlets. As many as 12 Australian food producers have tied up with India-based distributor AB Mauri for the same. World's largest retailer Wal-Mart is also planning ambitiously to trade in India. With this there lies an exciting times ahead for the Indian retail markets.

ORGANISED RETAIL IN INDIA : THE NEXT GROWTH FRONTIER

Only player who can aggressively scale-up operations can target a ₹ 40,000 crore retail business in India by 2015, says Pankaj Gupta.

India like Britain, is also a nation of shopkeepers. With over 12 mn retail outlets, India has one of the highest densities of retail outlets in the world with one retail outlet for 90 persons. No wonder India is the ninth largest retail market in the world with annual retail sales of USD 215 bn in 2005. However, the share of organized trade in India is currently very low estimated at just ₹ 35,000 crore in 2005 (₹ 28,000 crore in 2004). This accounts for less than 4 per cent of the total retail trade in the country.

Organised Trade : India an Underdeveloped Market

Organised trade in India is highly underdeveloped as compared with other emerging markets in Asia, Latin America and Eastern Europe and developed markets like US. The retail industry in India is of late often being hailed as one of the sunrise sectors in the economy. At Kearney, the well known international management consultancy, recently identified India as the 'second most attractive retail destination' globally from among thirty emergent markets. It has made India the cause of a good deal of excitement and the cynosure of many foreign eyes. With a contribution of 14 per cent to the national GDP and employing 7 per cent of the total workforce (only agriculture employs more) in the country, the retail industry is definitely one of the pillars of the Indian economy. Table 11 below illustrates this:

Table 11 : Share of Retail Industry in GDP

Components	Share per cent in GDP (2002 - 03)	Growth during (2002 - 03)
Construction	5.3	7.3
Trade	14.0	4.5
Hotels and Restaurants	1.1	4.0
Railways	1.1	5.7
Other Transport	4.3	6.0
Storage	0.1	-7.8
Communications	3.5	22.0
Banking Insurance	6.9	11.6
Real Estate, Business / Legal Services	6.1	5.9
Defence	5.9	5.3
Other Community and Social Services	7.8	6.2
Total	**56.1**	**7.2**

Source: Presentation to FICCI by MBN Rao (Chairman, Indian Bank): *"Strategy for Financing Service Sector"* (Sept. 15, 2004).

The retail industry is divided into organised and unorganised sectors. Organised retailing refers to trading activities undertaken by licensed retailers, that is, those who are registered for sales tax, income tax, etc. These include the corporate-backed hypermarkets and retail chains, and also the privately owned large retail businesses. Unorganised retailing, on the other hand,, refers to the traditional formats of low-cost retailing, for example, the local *kirana* shops, owner manned general stores, *paan/beedi* shops, convenience stores, hand cart and pavement vendors, etc. (See Table 12)

Table 12 : Growth of Retail Outlets in India

Outlets	1996	1997	1998	1999	2000	2001
Food Retailers	2769.0	2943.9	3123.4	3300.2	3480.0	3682.9
Non-Food Retailers	5773.6	6040.0	6332.2	6666.3	7055.5	7482.1
Total Retailers	8542.6	8983.6	9455.6	9966.5	10534.4	11165.0

Source: P.G. Chengappa, Lalith Achoth, Arpita Mukherjee, B.M. Ramachandra Reddy and P.C. Ravi, *Evolution of Food Retail Chains: The Indian Context*, 5-6th Nov. 2003, www. ficci.com

Unorganized retailing is by far the prevalent form of trade in India – constituting 98 per cent of total trade, while organised trade accounts only for the remaining 2 per cent, estimates vary widely about the true size of the retail business in India. At Kearney estimated it to be ₹ 4,00,000 crore and poised to double in 2005. On the other hand, if one used the Government's figures the retail trade in 2002-03, amounted to ₹ 3,82,000 crore. One thing all consultants agreed upon was that the total size of the corporate owned retail business was ₹ 15,000 crore in 1999 and it grew to ₹ 35,000 crore by 2005 and keep growing at a rate of 40 per cent per annum. In a recent presentation, FICCI has estimated the total retail business to be ₹ 11,00,000 crore - or 44 per cent of GDP. According to this report dated Nov. 2003, sales now account for 44 per cent of the total GDP and food sales account for 63 per cent of the total retail sales, increasing to ₹ 100 billion from just ₹ 38.1 billion in 1996. Food retail trade is a very large segment of the total economic activity of our country and due to its vast employment potential, it deserves very special focused attention. Efficiency enhancements and increase in the food retail sales activity would have a cascading effect on employment and economic activity in the rural areas for the marginalized workers. Thus even without FDI driving it, the corporate owned sector is expanding at a furious rate. The question then that arises is that since there is obviously no dearth of indigenous capital, what is the need of FDI? It is not that retailing in India is in the need of any technology special to foreign chains.

Employment in Retailing

A simple glance at the employment numbers is enough to paint a good picture of the relative sizes of these two forms of trade in India. Organised trade employs roughly 5 lakh people (see Tables 11 and 12) whereas the unorganized retail trade employs nearly 3.95 crore. According to a GoI study the number of workers, in retail trade in 1998, was almost 175 lakh. Given the recent numbers indicated by other studies, this is only indicative of the magnitude of expansion the retail trade is experiencing, both due to economic expansion as well as the "jobless growth' that we have seen in the past decade. It must be noted that even within the organised sector, the number of individually-owned retail outlets far outnumber the corporate-backed institutions. Though these numbers translate to approximately 8 per cent of the workforce in the country (half the normal share in developed countries) there are far more retailers in India than other countries in absolute numbers, because of the. demographic profile and the preponderance of youth, India's workforce is proportionately much larger. That about 4 per cent of India's population is in the retail trade says a lot about how vital this business is to the socio-economic equilibrium in India.

Table 13 : Share of Retailing in Employment Across Different Countries

Country	Employment (%)	Country	Employment (%)
India	8	Brazil	15
USA	16	China	7
Poland	12		

Source : Presentation to FICCI by Alan Rosling (Chairman, Jardine Matheson Group): *"International Experience on Policy Issues.*

'Organised retail' is still in the stage of finding its feet in India even now. Though organised trade makes up over 70-80 per cent of total trade in developed economies, India's figure is low even in comparison with other Asian developing economies like China, Thailand, South Korea and Philippines, all of whom have figures hovering around the 20-25 per cent mark. These figures quite accurately reveal the relative underdevelopment of the retail industry in India. (Here development is used in the narrowest sense of the term, implying lean employment and high automation).

Table 14 : Retail Trade in India and South East Asia

Countries	Organised	Unorganised
India	2	98
China	20	80
South Korea	15	85
Indonesia	25	75
Philippines	35	65
Tailand	40	60
Malaysia	50	50

Source: CRISIL.

Retail as a 'Forced Employment' Sector

It is important to understand how retailing works in our economy, and what role it plays in the lives of its citizens, from a social as well as an economic perspective. India still predominantly houses the traditional formats of retailing, that is, the local kirana shop, *paan/beedi* shop, hardware stores, weekly haats, convenience stores, and bazaars, which together form the bulk. Most importantly, Indian retail is highly fragmented, with about 11 million outlets operating in the country and only 4 per cent of them being larger than 500 square feet in size. Compare this with the figure of just 0.9 million in the US, yet catering to more than 13 times of the Indian retail market size.

The Indian retail industry was, and continues to be highly fragmented. According to the global consultancy firms AC Neilsen and KSA Technopak, India has the highest shop density in the world. In 2001 they estimated there were 11 outlets for every 1,000 people. Further, a report prepared by McKinsey and Company and the, Confederation of Indian Industry (CII) predicted that global retail giants such as Tesco, Kingfisher, Carrefour and Ahold were waiting in the Tesco to enter the retail arena. This report also states that the Indian retail market holds the potential of becoming a $ 300 billion per year market by 2010, provided the sector is opened up significantly. It does not talk about creating additional jobs however, which should be the prime concern of the policy maker.

One of the principal reasons "behind the explosion of retail and its fragmented nature in the country is the fact that retailing is probably the primary form of disguised unemployment/ underemployment in the country. Given the already over-crowded agriculture sector, and the stagnating manufacturing sector, and the hard nature and relatively low wages of jobs in both, many million Indians are virtually forced into the services sector. Here, given the lack of opportunities, it is almost a natural decision for an individual to set up a small shop or store, depending on his or her means and capital. And thus, a retailer is born, seemingly out of circumstances rather than choice. This phenomenon quite aptly explains the millions of kirana shops and small stores. The explosion of retail outlets in the more busy streets of Indian villages and towns is a visible testimony of this.

The presence of more than one retailer for every hundred persons is indicative of the lack of economic opportunities that is forcing people into this form of self-employment, even though much of it is marginal. Because of this fragmentation, the Indian retail sector typically suffers from limited access to capital, labour and real estate options. The typical traditional retailer follows the low-cost-and-size format. Retailers are functioning at a small-scale level, rarely eligible for tax and following a cheap model of operations.

As on January 1st of this year 2011, there were 413.88 lakh job seekers registered at the Employment Exchange. They register at the exchange, to enjoy the benefits and security that a job in the organised sector provides – lifetime employment, pension, and union membership etc. But over the period 1992-93 to 2001-02, only a total of 30,000 jobs have been added in the organised sector in the whole country.

A vast majority is aware of what these figures signify – that they are most unlikely to get such jobs. Therefore, they find jobs in the informal sector, mostly in retail. Retailing is by-far the easiest business to enter, with low capital and infrastructure needs, and as such, performs a vital function in the economy as a social security net for the unemployed. India, being a free and democratic country, provides its people with this cushion of being able to make a living for oneself through self-employment, as opposed to an economy like China, where employment is regulated. Yet, even this does not annul the fact that a multitude of these so-called 'self-employed', retailers are simply trying to scrape together a living, in the face of limited opportunities for employment. In this light, one could brand this sector as one of "forced employment", where the retailer is pushed into it, purely because of the paucity of opportunities in other sectors.

The Waiting Foreign Juggernaut

The largest retailer in the world 'Wal-Mart' has a turnover of $ 256 bn. and is growing annually at an average of 12-13 per cent. In 2004, its net profit was $ 9,000 mn. It had 4,806 stores employing *IA* ran persons, Of these 1,355 were outside the USA. The average size of a Wal-Mart is 85,000 sq.ft and the average turnover of a store was about $ 51 mn. The turnover per employee averaged $ 1,75,000. In 2004, Wal-Mart had a 9 per cent return on assets and 21 per cent return on equity.

By contrast the average Indian retailer had a turnover of ₹ 1,86,075. Only 4 per cent of the 12 million retail outlets were larger than 500 sq.ft in size. The total turnover of the unorganized retail sector was ₹ 7,35,000 crore employing 39.5 mn persons.

Let alone the average Indian retailer in the unorganized sector, no Indian retailer in the organised sector will be able to meet the onslaught from a firm such as Wal-Mart – when it comes. With its incredibly deep pockets Wal-Mart will be able to sustain losses for many years till its immediate competition is wiped out. This is a normal predatory strategy used by large players to drive out small and dispersed competition. This entails job losses by the millions.

India has 35 towns each with a population over 1 million. If Wal-Mart were to open an average Wal-Mart store in each of these cities and they reached the average Wal-Mart performance per store – we are looking at a turnover of over ₹ 80,330 rnn with only 10,195 employees. Extrapolating this with the average trend in India, it would mean displacing about 4,32,000 persons. If large FDI driven retailers were to take 20 per cent of the retail trade, as the now somewhat hard-pressed Hindustan Lever Limited anxiously anticipates, this would mean a turnover of ₹ 800 billion on today's basis. This would mean an employment of just 43,540 persons displacing nearly eight million persons employed in the unorganized retail sector.

With possible implications of this magnitude, a great deal of prudence should go into policymaking, Rather we seem to moving towards a policy steam rolled obviously by vested interests acting in concert with the CII and FICCI. We need to take a deep hard look at FDI in the retail sector. In this context we must be concerned about the statement the Finance Minister, Mr. P. Chidambaram, made while making the mid-year review for 2004-05. "On retail, the review notes that creating an effective supply chain from the producer to the consumer is critical for development of many sectors, particularly processed and semi-processed agro-products. In this context, it says, the role that could be played by organised retail chains, including international ones merits careful attention".

The Question of Foreign Direct Investment (FDI) in Retail

Given this backdrop, the recent clamour about opening up the retail sector to Foreign Direct Investment (FDI) becomes a very sensitive issue, with arguments to support both sides of the debate. It is widely acknowledged that FDI can have some positive results on the economy, triggering a series of reactions that in the long run can lead to greater efficiency and improvement of living standards, apart from greater integration into the global economy. Supporters of FDI in retail trade talk of how ultimately the consumer is 'benefited by both price reductions and improved selection, brought about by the technology and know-how of foreign players in the market. This in turn can lead to greater output and domestic consumption.

But the most important factor against FDI driven "modern retailing" is that it is labour displacing to the extent that it can only expand by destroying the traditional retail sector. Till such time we are in a position to create jobs on a large-scale in manufacturing, it would make eminent sense that any policy that results in the elimination of jobs in the unorganised retail sector should be kept on hold.

Though most of the high decibel arguments in favour of FDI in the retail sector are not without some merit, it is not fully applicable to the retailing sector in India. or at least, not yet. This is because the primary task of Government of India is still, to provide livelihoods and not create so-called efficiencies of scale by creating redundancies. As per present regulations, no FDI is permitted in retail trade in India. Allowing 49 per cent or 26 per cent FDI (which have been the proposed figures till data) will have immediate and dire consequences. Entry of foreign players now will most definitely disrupt the current balance of the economy, will render millions of small retailers jobless by closing the small slit of opportunity available to them.

Imagine if Wal-Mart, the world's biggest retailer sets up operations in India at prime locations in the 35 large cities and towns that house more than million people. The supermarket will typically sell everything, from vegetables to the latest electronic gadgets, at extremely low prices that will most likely undercut those in nearby local stores selling similar goods. Wal- Mart would be more likely to 'source its raw materials from abroad, and procure goods like vegetables and fruits directly from farmers at preordained quantities and specifications. This means a foreign company will buy big from India and abroad and be able to sell low – severely undercutting the small retailers. Once a monopoly situation is created this will then turn into buying low and selling high.

Such reorientation of sourcing of materials will completely disintegrate the already established supply chain. In time, the neighbouring traditional outlets are also likely to fold and perish, given the "predatory" pricing power that a foreign player is able to exert. As Nick Robbins wrote in the context of the East India Company, "By controlling both ends of the chain, the company could buy cheap and sell dear". The producers and traders at the lowest level of operations will never find place in this sector, which would now have demand only for fluent English-speaking helpers. Having been uprooted from their traditional form of business, these persons are unlikely to be suitable for other areas of work either.

It is easy to visualise from the discussion above, how the entry of just one big retailer is capable of destroying a whole local economy and send it hurtling down a spiral. One must also not forget how countries like China, Malaysia and Thailand, who opened their retail sector to FDI in the recent past, have been forced to enact new laws to check the prolific expansion of the new foreign malls and hypermarkets.

Given their economies of scale and huge resources, a big domestic retailer or any new foreign player will be able to provide their merchandise at cheaper rates than a smaller retailer. But stopping an Indian retailer from growing bigger is something current public policy which cannot do, whereas the State does have the prerogative whether foreign entry in the retail sector should be stalled or not.

It is true that it is in the consumer's best interest to obtain his goods and services at the lowest possible price. But this is a privilege of the individual consumer and it cannot, in any circumstance, override the responsibility of any society to provide economic security to its population. Clearly collective well-being must take precedence over individual benefits.

Disturbing the Hornet's Nest

If you assume 40 mn adults in the retail sector, it would translate into around 160 million dependents using a 1: 4 dependency ratio. Opening the retailing sector to FDI means dislocating millions from their occupation, and pushing a lot of families under the poverty line. Plus, one must not forget that the Western concept of efficiency is maximizing output while minimizing the number of workers involved – which will only increase social tensions in a poor and yet developing country like India, where tens of millions are still seeking gainful employment.

This dislocated and unemployed horde has to be accommodated somewhere else. But if you look at the growth rates of labour in manufacturing and industry, you wonder where this new accommodation can be found? Agriculture already employs nearly 60 per cent of our total workforce, and is in dire need of shedding excess baggage. That leaves us with manufacturing as the only other alternative. With only 17 per cent of our total workforce already employed in industry, which contributes altogether only 21.7 per cent of our GDP, this sector can hardly absorb more without a major expansion. (See Table 15)

Table 15 : Share of Retailing in Employment Across Different Countries

Sectors	Share per cent in GDP	Employment	Cumulative Average Growth Rate during 1994-2004
Agriculture	22.1	60.5	2.70
Industry	21.7	16.8	6.53
Service	56.2	22.7	7.90

Source: FICCI (2004) and NSS 55th Round Employment Survey (1999-2000).

So far Indian economy has been heavily geared towards the service sector that contributes 56 per cent of our GDP. The service sector's contribution to the increase in GDP over the last five years has been 63.9 per cent, Having a high contribution from services is an attribute that is characteristic of developed economies. What is anomalous in the Indian case is the fact that in other fast developing economies, say China, manufacturing accounts for a significant share of GDP, whereas in India, manufacturing contributes a mere 23.1 per cent of the GDP (See Tables 15, 16 and 17).

Table 16 : Indian Economy: Sectoral Sources of Growth (per cent Contributions to GDP)

	1992-93 to 1996-97	1997-98 to 2003-04
Agriculture and Allied Sector	20.3	13
Manufacturing, Construction and Quarrying	30.9	23.1
Service	48.8	63.9

Source : Bhanoji Rao - "Industry, Ugly Duckling", (Dec. 1, 2004) *The Economic Times*.

The organized retail sector in the country that employs about 1.5 million people, is expected to add another two lakh employees by the end of the financial year 2011. Buoyed by the positive market sentiment and faster project handovers, Indian retail sector would achieve higher recruitment numbers; Brand Factory's expansion plans would require an addition of 6,000 people. Future Group employs about 36,000 people that would require an addition of 15,000 by the end of the year 2010. Reliance Retail would add 90,000 people in three years. Reliance Retail Group would hire 60,000 people for their stores. This is the figure given by Mr. Brian Bade, CEO, Reliance Digital. According to Mr.E.Balaji, CEO, Ma Foi Consulting, there was a 10-12 growth per cent job addition in the Retail sector compared to the year 2009. About 85 per cent of the jobs in the sector is for consumer goods. With both retail investors and domestic institutions in the 'sell' mode, foreign institutional investors have tightened their stranglehold on the Indian Retail market. The Commerce and Industry Minister Mr. Anand Sharma on 8th November, 2010, said that allowing foreign direct investment in multi-brand retail will require broad-based political and societal consensus as around 50 million jobs in the small and medium retail sector are at stake. The government has a 'positive mindset' on bringing such policy changes. India allows 100 per cent FDI in cash-and-carry operation and 51 per cent in single-brand retailing. Foreign investors are barred from investing in multi-brand retail. The objective of consultation with stakeholders on allowing FDI in retail and defence has been completed.

Retailing sector in India, though a late entrant, is emerging as a major industry and is also poised to bring another boom in job market. Pantaloon did the primary efforts in the retail industry. The Pantaloon chain at present retains the status of the largest retailing outlet in India. With entry of Reliance Industries Limited and others to follow suit, the industry is all set to make its mega march in the economy. It is estimated that the sector will emerge as the second largest industry in India within five years.

With retail sector to grow with its predictable potential in respect of quantity and stability, offers a respective boom in the employment market. It is estimated that by 2012, the sector will create about 13 million jobs in India.

It is also good to state that about 60 per cent of these job vacancies will be in the rural India. The trend will help a lot to check migration of educated manpower from rural areas to the metro cities. As major companies that are already operating in the sector, including Future Group, Reliance Industries and Retail Solution Group are targeting to multiply its workforce to ten-folds. About a dozen of world's renowned retail groups are preparing to take part in the march.

Table 17 : China: Sectoral Sources of Growth (Percentage Contributions to Increase in GDP)

	1990-96	**1997-2002**
Agriculture	9.3	6.4
Industry	62.2	58.5
Service	28.5	35.1

Source : Bhanoji Rao — "Industry, Ugly Duckling, (Dec. 1, 2004) *The Economic Times*.

It is evident that the manufacturing sector has been the engine for economic growth in China, which has been growing at 10.1 per cent since 1991, In India, the credit for its 5.9 per cent growth over the corresponding period goes mostly to the service sector. Ironically it would seem that the Indian economy is getting a post-industrial profile without having been industrialised.

Retailing is not an activity that can boost GDP by itself. It is only an intermediate value-adding process. If there aren't any goods being manufactured, then there will not be many goods to be retailed. This underlines the importance of manufacturing in a developing economy. One could argue that the alarmingly low contribution of industry is attributable to the structural adjustments going on in the sector, getting rid of the flab and getting ready to compete, but that still cannot undermine the seriousness of the issue at hand, in that only 6.215 million out of productive cohort of 600 million is employed in organised manufacturing.

Only until the tardy growth of the manufacturing sector is addressed properly and its productivity chart starts to look prettier, could one begin thinking of dislocating some of the retailing workforce into this space. Until that day, disturbing the hornet's nest would be one very painful experience for the economy.

Recommendations

1. The retail sector in India is severely constrained **by limited availability of bank finance.** The government and RBI need to evolve suitable lending policies that will enable retailers in the organised and unorganised sectors to expand and improve efficiencies. Policies that encourage unorganised sector retailers to migrate to the organised sector by investing in space and equipment should be encouraged.
2. A **National Commission** must be established to study the problems of the retail sector and to evolve policies that will enable it to cope with FDI – as and when it comes.
3. The proposed National Commission should evolve a clear set of **conditionalities on giant foreign retailers** on the procurement of farm produce, domestically manufactured merchandise and imported goods. These conditionalities must be aimed at encouraging the purchase of goods in the domestic market, state the minimum space, size and specify details like, construction and storage standards, the ratio of floor space to parking space, etc. Giant shopping centres must not add to our existing urban snarl.

4. Set up an **Agricultural Perishable Produce Commission (APPC),** to ensure that procurement prices for perishable commodities are fair to farmers and that they are not distorted with relation to market prices.

Recommendations for the Food Retail Sector

With 3.6 million shops retailing food and employing 4 per cent of total workforce and contributing 10.9 per cent to GDP, the food-retailing segment presents a focused opportunity to the government to catalyze growth and employment.

1. Provision of **training** in handling, storing,, transporting, grading, sorting, maintaining hygiene standards, upkeep of refrigeration equipment, packing, etc., is an area where ITPs and SISPs can play a proactive role.
2. Creation **of infrastructure** for retailing at *mandis,* community welfare centres, government and private colonies with a thrust on easier logistics and hygiene will enable greater employment and higher hygiene consciousness, and faster turnaround of transport and higher rollover of produce.
3. **Quality regulation,** certification and price administration bodies can be created at district and lower levels for upgrading the technical and human interface in the rural to urban supply chain.
4. **Credit availability** for retail traders must be encouraged with a view to enhance employment and higher utilization of fixed assets. This would lead to less wastage (India has currently the highest wastage in the world) of perishables, enhance nutritional status of producers and increase caloric availability.
5. Several successful models **of integrating** very **long food supply chains** in dairy, vegetable, fish and fruit have been evolved in India. *Cross integrations* of these unique food supply chains will provide new products in new markets increasing consumer choice, economic activity and employment.
6. Government intervention in food retail segment is necessitated by:
   (a) The lack of any other body at remote/grassroots level.
   (b) Need to provide market for casual and distant self-employed growers and gatherers.
   (c) Maintain regulatory standards in hygiene.
   (d) Seek markets in India and abroad (provide charter aircrafts, freeze frying, vacuuming, dehydrating, packing facilities for small producers at nodal points).
   (e) Provide scope and opportunity for productive self-employment (since Govt. cannot provide employment).

At a subsequent stage, these interventions can be integrated into the supply chains of the foreign retailers in India and abroad creating synergy between national priorities, market realities, globalization, and private-public cooperation.

In this fashion, the Government can try to ensure that the domestic and foreign players are approximately on an equal footing and that the domestic traders are not at a disadvantage, The small retailers must be given ample opportunity to be able to provide more personalized service, so that their higher costs are not duly nullified by the presence of big supermarkets and hypermarkets.

Table 18 : Employment in Organized Sector, 1992-97 (Nos. in lakh)

Public/Private Sector	1992-93	1993-94	1994-95	1995-96	1996-97
Wholesale and Retail Trade*	1.48	1.61	1.62	1.62	1.64

Table 19 : Employment in Organized Sector, 1997-2002 (Nos. in lakh)

Public/Private Sector	1997-98	1998-99	1999-00	2000-01	2001-02
Wholesale and Retail Trade*	1.64	1.63	1.63	1.63	1.56

Source : *Monthly Abstract Statistics*, Vol. 57, No. 7, July 2004, Central Statistical Organisation

* This is the figure only for Organised Retail Sector.

The retail management needs to reappraise their shoppers and get to grips with what is really driving them to consumption. Whether the retailer is truly near or far from his/her shopper can be understood from Figure 17.

INDIAN ORGANIZED RETAIL MARKET

Indian organized retail market is growing at a fast pace due to the boom in the Indian retail industry. In 2005, the retail industry in India amounted to ₹ 10,000 billion accounting for about 10 per cent to the country's GDP. The organized retail market in India out of the total market accounted for ₹ 350 billion which is about 3.5 per cent of the total revenues.

Retail market in the Indian organized sector is expected to cross ₹ 1,000 billion by 2010. Traditionally the retail industry in India was largely unorganized, comprising of drug stores, medium, and small grocery stores. Most of the organized retailing in India have started recently and is concentrating mainly in metropolitan cities.

The growth in the Indian organized retail market is mainly due to the change in the consumers behaviour. This change has come in the consumer due to increased income, changing lifestyles, and patterns of demography which are favourable. Now the consumer wants to shop at a place where he can get food, entertainment, and shopping all under one roof. This has given Indian organized retail market a major boost.

Retail market in the organized sector in India is growing can be seen from the fact that 1500 supermarkets, 325 departmental stores, and 300 new malls are being built. Many Indian companies are entering the Indian retail market which is giving Indian organized retail market a boost. One such company is the Reliance Industries Limited. It plans to invest US $ 6 billion in the Indian retail market by opening 1,000 hypermarkets and 1,500 supermarkets.

Pantaloons is another Indian company which plans to increase its retail space to 30 million square feet with an investment of US $ 1 billion. Bharti Telecoms an Indian company is in talks with Tesco a global giant for a £ 750 million joint venture. A number of global retail giants such as Wal-Mart, Carrefour, and Metro AG are also planning to set up shop in India. Indian organized retail market will definitely grow as a result of all this investments.

Table 20: State-wise Number of Workers Engaged in Retail Trade by Type of Enterprises in India (1998)

	Rural				Urban			
States/UT's	OAE	NDE	DE	ALL	OAE	NDE	DE	ALL
Andhra Pradesh	638358	42320	94699	780377	446500	217763	267496	931759
Arunachal Pradesh	5659	473	3518	9650	2933	706	3174	6813
Assam	218667	20583	57992	297242	82218	16768	68448	167434
Bihar	454703	19512	91591	565806	306323	61316	171381	539020
Goa	11719	2111	3158	16988	13117	5390	10167	28674
Gujarat	222208	17573	46004	285785	365753	73445	196940	636138
Haryana	91073	2951	12441	106465	124590	14999	67512	207101
Himachal Pradesh	51505	2275	10163	63942	17730	3706	10547	31983
Jammu & Kashmir	45465	2414	6945	54824	56870	12082	21327	90279
Karnataka	329875	36915	83415	450205	276345	130703	243345	650393
Kerala	302444	35376	165253	503073	71970	44521	125383	241875
Madhya Pradesh	418997	26141	58572	503710	437151	55169	166730	659050
Maharastra	493296	30361	109955	633612	635164	210386	519775	1365325
Manipur	15869	61	1098	17028	19372	1046	5604	26022
Meghalaya	9790	834	8204	18828	7333	1840	9156	18329
Mizoram	2877	151	743	3771	7154	898	1900	9952
Nagaland	5528	382	1999	7909	9730	2547	9647	21924
Orissa	420735	15367	59629	495731	136117	24826	80856	231799
Punjab	119219	7207	24517	150943	185621	33274	101943	320838
Rajasthan	224212	16027	39612	279851	256356	33960	113651	403967
Sikkim	3898	399	1434	5731	2142	528	2034	4759
Tamil Nadu	388859	83460	218380	690699	297470	248451	531755	1077670
Tripura	29028	653	6963	36644	14422	1106	8166	23694
Uttar Pradesh	705928	29957	81505	817390	753617	86449	401999	1242065
West Bengal	803718	29541	213391	1046350	416387	171080	556196	1143663
A&N Island	3111	296	1156	4593	1800	794	1902	4496
Chandigarh	866	142	525	1533	11226	7532	8404	27162
D&N Haveli	865	127	410	1402	260	97	545	902
Daman & Diu	730	289	375	1294	1518	181	762	2461
Delhi	12503	3872	8693	25068	174315	109134	227370	510819
Lakshadwep	257	43	53	353	273	63	138	474
Pondicherry	3505	994	2056	655	9136	7249	10672	27057
India	6035466	433507	1414479	7883452	5140913	1578064	3934925	10653902

Source: Economic Census 1998, MOSPI, GOI

OAE: Own Account Enterprises, DE: Directory Establishments, NDE: Non-Directory Establishments

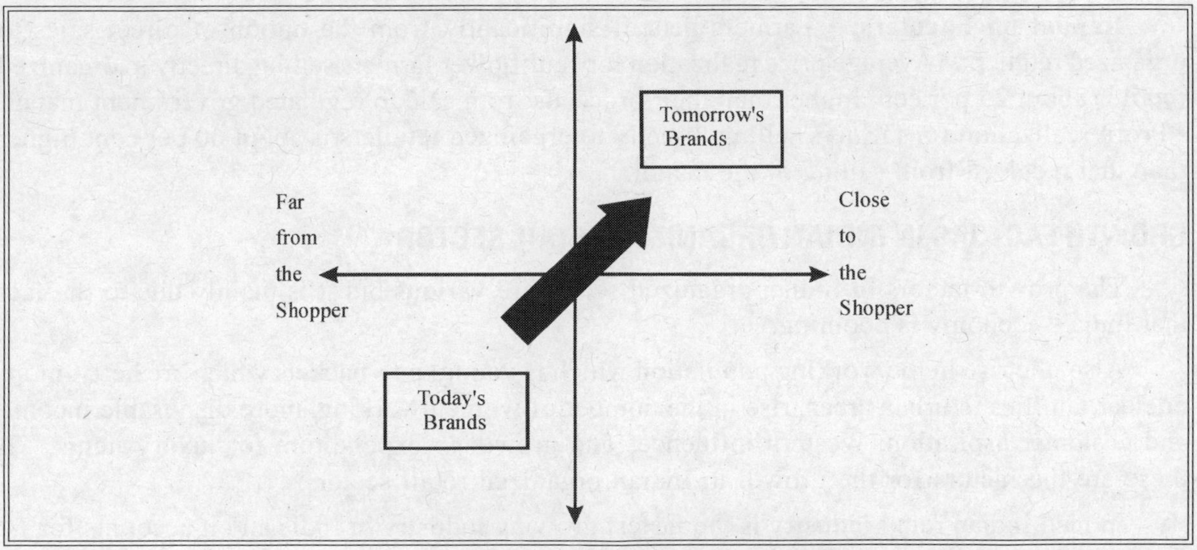

FIG. 17: NON-RETAIL ORIENTED COMPANIES

Indian organized retail market is increasing and for this growth to continue the Indian retailers as well as government must make a combined effort.

There is some decline in employment in the North and West regions which, however, also weakens over time. • The rate of closure of unorganized retail shops in gross terms is found to be 4.2 per cent per annum which is much lower than the international rate of closure of small businesses. • The rate of closure on account of competition from organized retail is lower still at 1.7 per cent per annum. • There is competitive response from traditional retailers through improved business practices and technology upgradation. • A majority of unorganized retailers is keen to stay in the business and compete, while also wanting the next generation to continue likewise. • Small retailers have been extending more credit to attract and retain customers. • However, only 12 per cent of unorganized retailers have access to institutional credit and 37 per cent felt the need for better access to commercial bank credit. • Most unorganized retailers are committed to remaining independent and barely 10 per cent preferred to become franchisees of organized retailers. Impact on consumers • Consumers have definitely gained from organized retail on multiple counts. • Overall consumer spending has increased with the entry of the organized retail. • While all income groups saved through organized retail purchases, the survey revealed that lower income consumers saved more. Thus, organized retail is relatively more beneficial to the less well-off consumers. • Proximity is a major comparative advantage of unorganized outlets. • Unorganized retailers have significant competitive strengths that include consumer goodwill, credit sales, amenability to bargaining, ability to sell loose items, convenient timings, and home delivery. Impact on intermediaries • The study did not find any evidence so far of adverse impact of organized retail on intermediaries. • There is, however, some adverse impact on turnover and profit of intermediaries dealing in products such as, fruit, vegetables, and apparel. • Over two-thirds of the intermediaries plan to expand their businesses in response to increased business opportunities opened by the expansion of retail. • Only 22 per cent do not want the next generation to enter the same business.

Impact on Farmers: • Farmers benefit significantly from the option of direct sales to organized retailers. • Average price realization for cauliflower farmers selling directly to organized retail is about 25 per cent higher than their proceeds from sale to regulated government mandi. • Profit realization for farmers selling directly to organized retailers is about 60 per cent higher than that received from selling in the mandi.

GROWTH FACTORS IN INDIAN ORGANIZED RETAIL SECTOR

The growth factors in Indian organized sector are various but it is mainly due to the fact that India's economy is booming.

Also, the rise in the working population which is young, pay-packets which are hefty, more nuclear families in urban areas, rise in the number of women working, more disposable income and customer aspiration, Western influences and growth in expenditure for luxury items. All these are the factors for the growth in Indian organized retail sector.

In fact, Indian retail industry is the fastest growing industry in India and it accounts for 10 per cent of the country's GDP. In 2006, the retail industry in India amounted to US $ 200 billion and out of this, the organized retail sector in India amounted to US $ 6.4 billion. By 2010, the Indian organized retail sector is expected to rise to US $ 23 billion. In 2003, the Indian organized retailing sector accounted for more than 4.5 million sq. ft. of space absorption by malls.

Many Indian companies have entered the retail industry in India and this is also a factor in the growth of Indian organized retail sector. Reliance Industries Limited is planning to invest US $ 6 billion in the organized retail sector in India by opening 1,500 supermarkets and 1,000 hypermarkets. Bharti Telecoms is planning a joint venture worth £ 750 million with Tesco a global retail giant. Pantaloons is planning to invest US $ 1 billion in order to increase its retail space to 30 million square feet. Such huge investments is also a factor in the growth of the organized retail sector in India.

Global retail giants are also entering the retail industry in India and this is also one of the factors in the growth of the organized retail sector in India. The global retail giants who are entering the organized retail sector in India are:

Wal-Mart

Tesco

Carrefour SA

Metro AG

The factors for growth in Indian organized retail sector are many and that is the reason behind its massive growth. But for this to continue both the Indian retailers and the government will have to work together.

Different Forms of Retail Organisations

- Functional
- Product
- Geographic
- Combination

PRODUCT ORGANISATION CHART

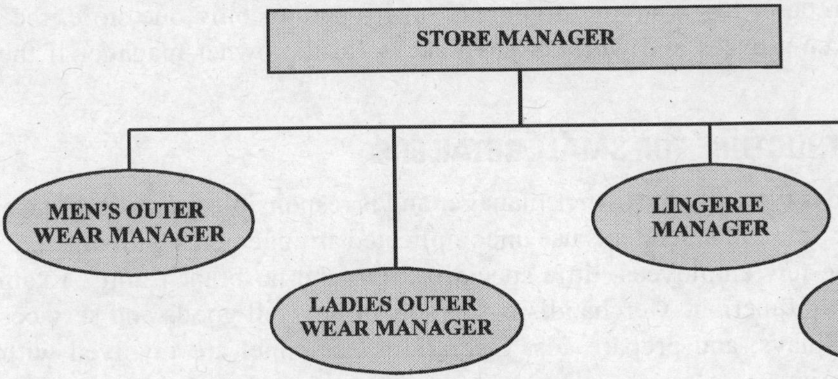

GEOGRAPHIC ORGANISATION CHART

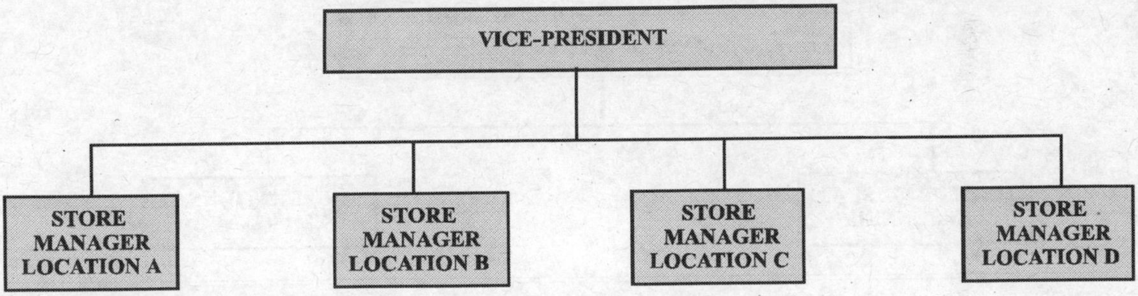

COMBINATION ORGANISATION CHART

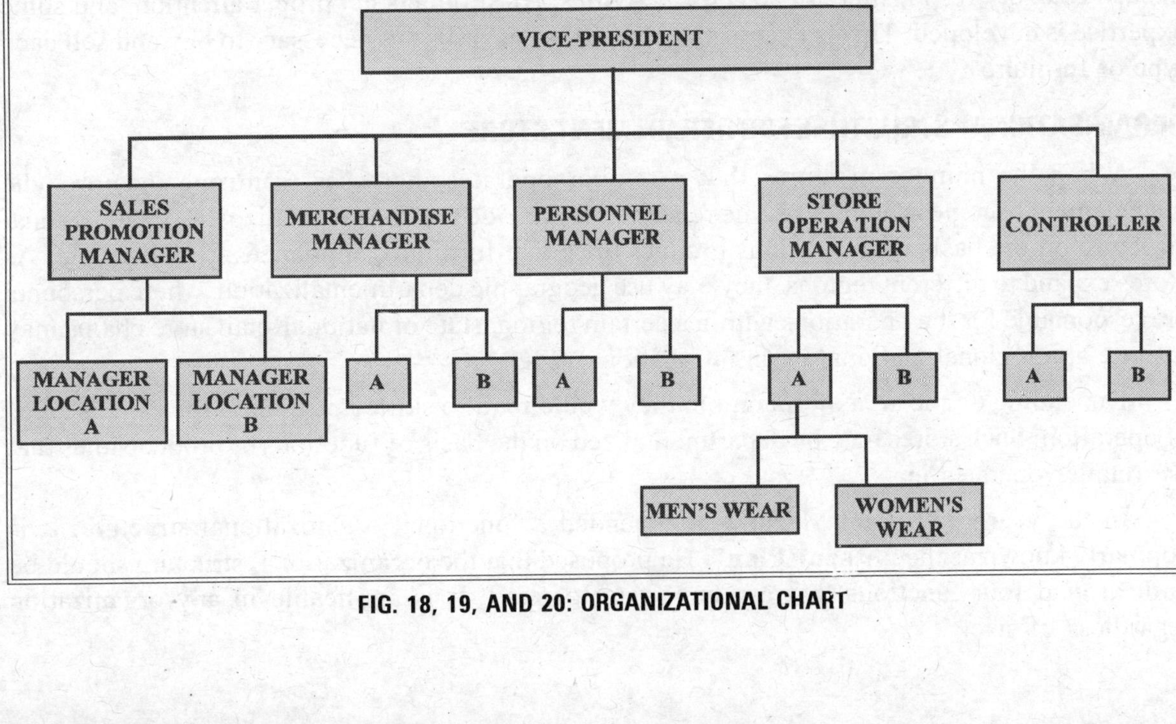

FIG. 18, 19, AND 20: ORGANIZATIONAL CHART

ORGANISATIONAL STRUCTURE FOR SMALL RETAILERS

An independent retailer has a simple organization. It operates only one store, the owner usually supervises all employees and workers have access to the owner-manager if there are problems.

ORGANISATIONAL STRUCTURE FOR SMALL RETAILERS

In this, one person is typically the owner/manager and is responsible for most of the aspects of the retail operations. Small independents use uncomplicated arrangements with only 2/3 levels of personnel. There are few employees, little specialization, and no branch units. Example, a boutique is organized by function. Merchandising personnel buy/sell goods and services, plan assortments, set up displays, and prepare ads. Operations personnel are involved with store maintenance and operations.

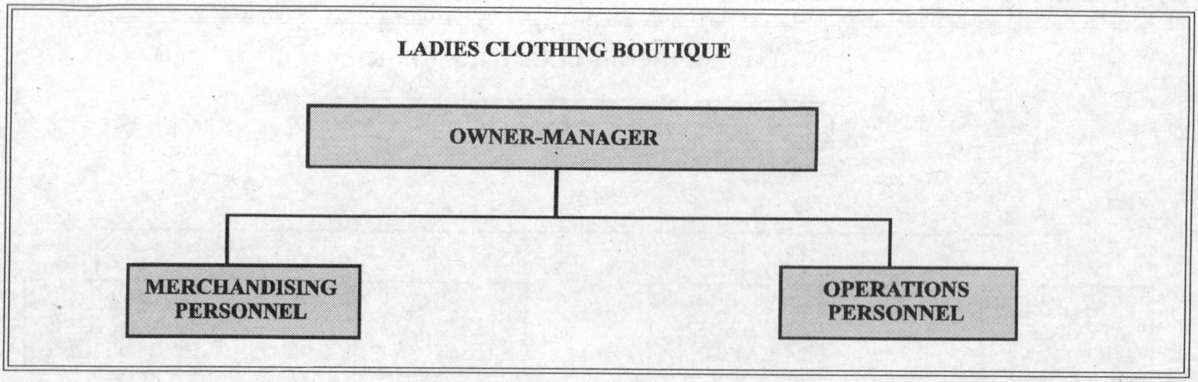

FIG. 21: LADIES CLOTHING BOUTIQUE

In case of a furniture store which is organized on a product- oriented basis, with personnel in each category responsible for selected activities. All products get proper attention, and some expertise is developed. This is necessary since different skills are necessary to buy and sell each type of furniture.

ORGANISATIONAL STRUCTURE FOR DEPARTMENT STORE

When the number of stores that a retailer operates increases from one to more, the management becomes complex. Some retailers may decide to departmentalize the organizational structure on the basis of the various product-lines like furniture, appliances, jewellery etc. As stores expand to different regions, they may use geographic departmentalization, where personnel are responsible for the operations within a certain region, state or nation. Retail store chains may operate at a regional, national or an international level.

Depending on the area of operation, they would require skilled personnel for various areas of operation. Such stores may be departmentalized on the basis of functions or product-lines that the retailer operates in.

In the year 1927, Paul Mazur recommended a functional organizational structure. It is popularly known as the **"Mazur Plan".** He proposed that the organizational structure should be built around four functions that are important to retail. It is applicable in any organization regardless of size.

The four functions are:

- **Merchandising:** Duties of this department would start with forecasting the merchandising required, procuring the merchandising, pricing it and making it available at the retail stores.
- **Publicity:** Responsibilities include advertising, sales promotions, public relations, publicity, etc.
- **Operations:** Include actual operations of store, including receiving goods, checking, maintaining records, and customer relations.
- **Control:** Responsible for credit and collections, expense budgeting and control, inventory planning and control, record-keeping.

A diversified retailer is one who operates more than one retail chain in more than one market, at the national or international level. The organizational arrangements are made by independent retailers, department stores, chain retailers, and diversified retailers. Many department stores continue to use organizational arrangements that are a modification of the **Mazur Plan,** which divides all retail activities into four functional areas – merchandising, publicity, store management, and accounting and control.

Merchandising – buying, selling, stock planning and control, promotion planning.

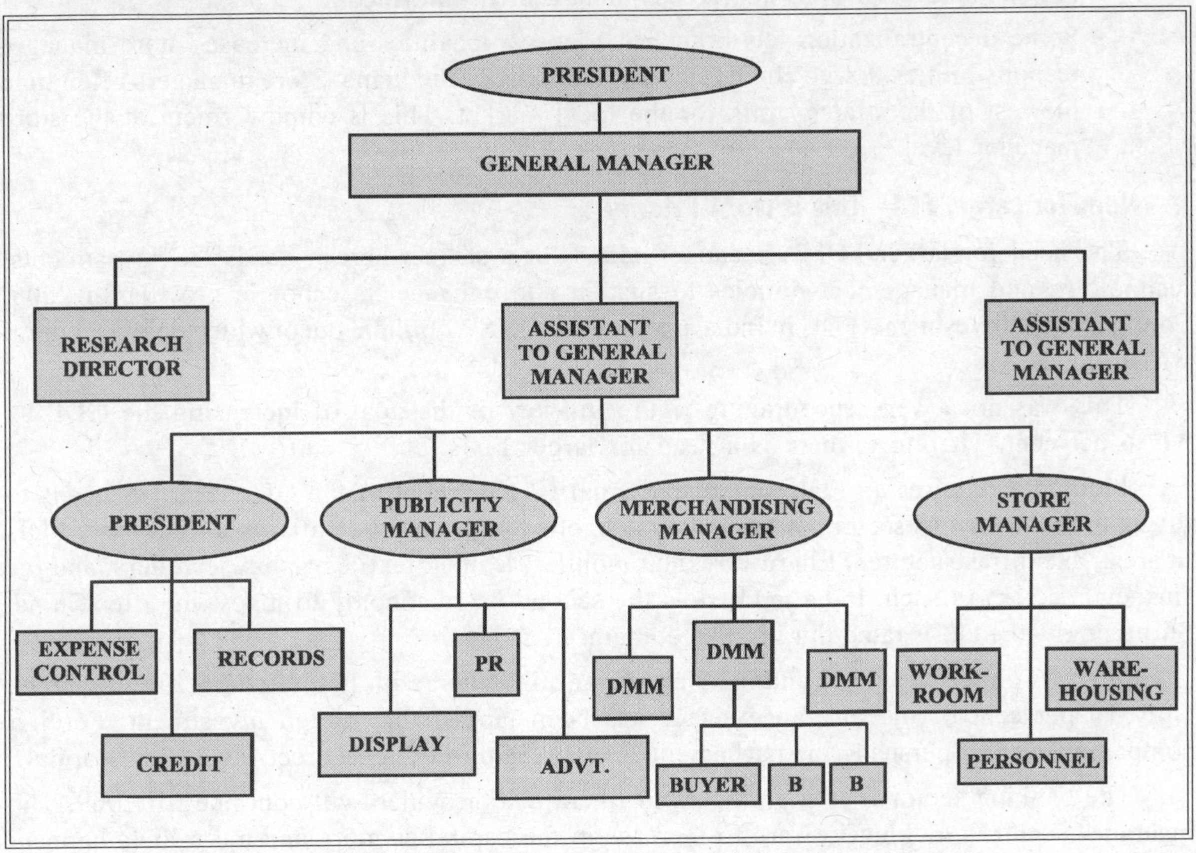

FIG. 22: ORGANISATIONAL STRUCTURE USED BY CHAIN RETAILERS

Publicity – Window and interior displays, advertising, planning and executing promotional events (along with merchandise managers), advertising research, public relations.

Store Management – Merchandise case, customer services, buying store supplies and equipment, maintenance, operating activities (such as receiving and delivering products), store and merchandise protection (insurance and security), employee training and compensation, workroom operations.

Accounting and Control – Credit and collection, expense budgeting and control, inventory planning and control, record-keeping.

These areas are organized by line (direct authority and responsibility) and staff (advisory and support) components.

Various chain retailers use a version of the equal store organization. They generally have the following attributes:

- There are many functional divisions, such as sales promotion, merchandise management, distribution, operations, real-estate, personnel and information systems.
- Overall authority is centralized. Store managers have selling responsibility.
- Many operations are standardized
- An elaborate control system keeps management informed
- Some decentralization lets branches adapt to localities and increases store manager responsibilities. Large chains standardize most of the items. Store managers often tune the rest of the strategy mix for the local market. This is empowerment at the store manager level.

I. Need for Larger FDI – This is No. 1 Priority

The need for larger FDI is because India is at a stage where it needs US investments, technology, and management policies to sustain and enhance its ecnomic growth. In 2006, Foreign Direct Investment (FDI) in India amounted to US $ 37 billion, out of which only $ 5 billion was from the US.

This was not a very encouraging figure in view of the goal of increasing the GDP by 34-36 per cent. Therefore, there is a need for larger FDIs.

India still requires an FDI component equal to 4 per cent of the GDP. The US needs to invest more in various sectors of the Indian economy. There is a potential to attract more FDIs in areas like infrastructure, IT hardware, automobiles, leather, textiles, gems, jewellery, and the financial sector. As such, India is rated as the second best economy to invest in, after China. Surprisingly, the US is rated third in this domain.

Focus is on the insurance and banking sector, in context with Foreign Direct Investments. Only 10 per cent of the insurance sector has been tapped for foreign investment. Foreign companies need to persuade the parliament for increasing Foreign Direct Investment capital.

The banking sector is in the process of liberalization which will continue till 2009. The insurance sector is looking forward to increase in the capital as more and more FDIs happen. So the insurance sector is also planning on liberalization, taking a cue from the banking sector.

Benefits of Larger FDI to the Retail Industry

The benefits of larger FDI can be tangibly felt in the domains pertaining to technological advancements, generation of export, production improvements, and hastening of manufacturing employment.

Capital inflow into India has increased and so have the exports from the country. Thanks to the economic boom India is experiencing, some Indian companies are doing better than even the multinational corporations.

The benefits of larger FDI have been briefly elaborated below:

Improved Human Capital: Indian industries are predominantly labor based but there is also a significant number of capital based companies. A capital intensive set up is indeed an expensive proposition but with the existing as well as potential labor intensive industries, India can look forward to more professional and sophisticated number of workers and employees at every level. Human capital, in terms of quantity was never a big problem in India, thanks to its huge population and quality and efficiency in work has been ushered in by the MNCs.

Competition Effect: The benefits of larger FDIs will include the launching and marketing of new products and brands in the Indian market. New products are used by the multinational corporations and then demonstrated in the Indian market. The processes followed by MNCs in India serve to have a demonstration effect on Indian companies which in turn improves market competition and the standard of products. This had started in the 1980s, due to Japanese firms and as a result, Indian firms started inculcating the practices of QC, JIT, and QA.

Manufacturing Employment: Larger FDIs definitely generate more and more employment opportunities. The opportunities are highly experienced in the manufacturing area. This not only includes the quality human resource but also provides for quick and efficient work and effective outcomes.

New Technology: Technological advancements take place as larger FDIs come in. In fact, three-fifths of the FDIs result in new and advanced technologies. The local industry is benefiting from this to a large extent. This as a result, would encourage more and more foreign firms for investment. The benefits of larger FDI are, however, very few in number but as India capitalizes on the above mentioned benefits, there will be more competition in the market at large and the rural sector of the country will be in the process of reformation, thus bringing about a socio-economic stability.

II. Supply Chain Management in the Indian Retail Industry – This is the Second Most Important Priority

The role of supply chain in Indian organized retail is very significant for on it depends the growth of this sector. The Indian Supply Chain Council have been formed to explore the challenges that a retailer faces and to find possible solutions for India.

The role of supply chain in the organized retail sector in India should be a shelf-centric partnership between the retailer and the manufacture for this will create supply chains that are loss free. This will also give rise to top and bottom line growth. In the organized retail sector in India the presence of fresh produce (vegetables and fruits) is very small. This is so for the nature of supply chain is very fragmented. This shows the important role of supply chain in the organized retail sector in India.

In the organized retail market in India the role of supply chain is very important for the Indian customer demands at affordable prices a variety of product mix. It is the supply chain that ensures to the customer in all the various offerings that a company decides for its customers, be it cost, service, or the quickness in responding to ever-changing tastes of the customer.

The infrastructure in India in terms of road, rail, and air links are not sufficient. And so warehousing plays a major role as an aspect of supply chain operations. To overcome these problems, the Indian retailer is trying to reduce transportation costs and is investing in logistics through partnership or directly. The Indian organized retail sector is growing so the role of supply chain becomes all the more important. It should become all the more responsive and adaptive to customers demand. There is also need for the supply chain to be more cost efficient and collaborative to win the immense competition in this sector.

The role of supply chain in Indian organized retail has expanded over the years with the boom in this industry. The growth of the Indian retail industry to a large extent depends on supply chain, so efforts must be made by the Indian retailers to maintain it properly.

III. The Third Priority in the Retail Industry

The Real Estate Support

- provides cheaper space for the retail.
- provides tax holidays for rural retail business.

IV. The Fourth Priority

The range/varieties of formats for the retail sector by providing tax benefits

Formats in Indian Organized Retail Sector

- Supermarkets
- Hypermarkets
- Department Stores
- Modern format individual retailers
- Shopping malls

V. The Fifth Priority for the Retail Industry

Incentives for training of retail managers

- category managers
- retail store managers
- retail marketing managers
- merchandising managers
- store warehouse managers
- supply chain managers
- procurement managers, etc.

VI. The Sixth Priority for the Retail Industry

- Incentives for training of the staff
- Sales Staff
- Customer Service
- Merchandisers

VII. The Seventh Priority To Focus

The Retail Business has two ends:

1. Front-end

- Retailing
- Merchandising
- Customer servicing
- Displays
- Sales promotions
- Consumer promotions
- Retail marketing, etc.

2. Back-end

- Buyers
- Supply chain
- Store supply
- Accounts
- Warehousing, etc.

In real life, it is the back-end which makes the real profit. Both ends are important from the business angle, but the profit churner is the back-end.

Critically, it is the

- Buyers
- Supply chain

which makes significant contribution to the business.

VIII. The Eighth Priority are Retail Issues in Future

Retail Industry will be afffected in future

- Globalization impact on demand/supply
- Supply base will be developing countries
- Multiple levels of brands [good • better • best]
- Population growth
- More demand in retails in developing countries
- Population shift means more retail outlets

- Increased income, means more retail demand
- Increased disposable income, means more retail demand
- Increased discretionary income, means more retail demand
- Lifestyle changes, affecting demand
- Demanding consumer needs/wants
- Technology impact on retailing
- Technology on customer servicing
- Shift in people's personal values
- Product packaging
- Diversity of population
- Demographical and structural change

IX. The Ninth Priority Area is the Major Factors to Consider in Evaluating Retail Trading Areas

- Population size and characteristics
- Total size and density
- Age distribution
- Average educational
- Per cent of residents owning home
- Total disposable income
- Per capita disposable income
- Occupation distribution
- Trends

Availability of Labour

- Sales staff
- Backroom staff
- Average wages in the area
- Average wages in the country

Closeness to Sources of Supply

- Delivery costs
- Timeliness
- Number of manufacturers and wholesalers
- Availability and reliability of product-lines

Promotion

- Availability and frequency of media
- Costs
- Waste

Economic Base

- Dominant industry
- Extent of diversification
- Growth projections
- Freedom from economic and seasonal fluctuations
- Availability of credit and financial facilities

Competitive Situation

- Number and size of existing competitors
- Evaluation of strengths and weaknesses for all competitors
- Short run and long run outlook
- Level of saturation

Availability of Store Locations

- Number and type of locations
- Access to transportation
- Owning versus leasing opportunities
- Zoning restrictions
- Costs

Regulations

- Taxes
- Licensing
- Operations
- Minimum wages
- Zoning

Tenth Priority is Conducting Regular Research

- Consumer research
- Market research
- Retail methods research
- Economic research of factors impacting retail sales.
- Social research of factors impacting retail sales.
- Technology research of factors impacting retail sales, etc.

SHOPPING MALL

A **shopping mall** or **shopping centre** is one or more buildings forming a complex of shops representing merchandisers, with interconnecting walkways, enabling visitors to easily walk from unit-to-unit, along with a convenient parking area – a modern, indoor version of the traditional marketplace.

Modern "car-friendly" strip malls developed from the 1920s, and shopping malls corresponded with the rise of suburban living in the United States after World War II.

In most of the world the term *'shopping centre'* is used, especially in Europe and Australia and Asia; however *shopping mall* is also used, predominantly in North America. *Shopping precinct* and *shopping arcade* are also used. In North America, the term *shopping mall* is usually applied to enclosed retail structures (and may be abbreviated to simply *mall*) while *shopping centre* usually refers to open-air retail complexes, both usually have large parking lots, face major traffic arterials and have few pedestrian connections to surrounding neighbourhoods.

Malls in Ireland are usually referred to as "shopping centres" and are typically very small and placed in the centre of town. They average about twenty years in age – the oldest, Stillorgan shopping centre, was built in 1966 – and include a mix of local shops and chain stores. These malls do not have shops found in the high street or modern shopping centres.

Shopping centres in the United Kingdom can be referred to as "shopping centres", "shopping precincts", or "town centres". The standard British pronunciation of the word "mall" is as in "The Mall, London" – the tree-lined avenue leading to Buckingham Palace, London and also like "pal" (friend).

In Hong Kong, the term "shopping centre" is most frequently used, and the name of a shopping centre in Hong Kong usually contains the word "centre" or "plaza".

Isfahan's Grand Bazaar, which is largely covered, dates from the 10th century. The ten kilometre long covered Tehran's Grand Bazaar also has a long history. The Grand Bazaar of Istanbul was built in the 15th century and is still one of the largest covered markets in the world, with more than 58 streets and 4,000 shops.

Gostiny Dvor in St. Petersburg, which opened in 1785, may be regarded as one of the first purposely-built shopping malls, as it consisted of more than 100 shops covering an area of over 53,000 m^2 (5,70,000 sq. ft.).

The Oxford Covered Market in Oxford, England opened in 1774 and still runs today.

The Burlington Arcade in London was opened in 1819. The Arcade in Providence, Rhode Island introduced the concept to the United States in 1828, making it the oldest mall in America. The Galleria Vittorio Emanuele II in Milan, Italy followed in the 1860s and is closer to large modern malls in spaciousness. Other large cities created arcades and shopping centres in the late 19th century and early 20th century, including the Cleveland Arcade and Moscow's GUM in 1890. Early shopping centres designed for the automobile include Market Square, Lake Forest, Illinois (1916) and Country Club Plaza, Kansas City, Missouri (1924).

An early indoor mall in the United States was the Lake View Store at Morgan Park, Duluth, Minnesota, which was built in 1915 and held its grand opening on July 20, 1916. The architect was Dean and Dean from Chicago and the building contractor was George H. Lounsberry from Duluth. The building is two-storeyed with a full basement and shops were originally located on all three levels. All of the stores were located within the interior of the mall with some shops being accessible from both inside and out. In the mid-20th century, with the rise of the suburb and automobile culture in the United States, a new style of shopping centre was created away from downtown. The first to go into operation will be the $ 30 million Bergen Mall at Paramus,

N.J., expected to be the biggest US shopping centre. Puckett estimates that there are 15,88,000 customers within the 40-minute radius. Wal-Mart remains are headquartered in the US, the undisputed leader in the retail world, with sales almost three times as large as those of Carrefour, the second-largest retailer. Home Depot also has made significant sales gains over the last several years. Its fourth-place ranking in 2004 was up from 24th in 1996. Wal-Mart is a single retail entity today that accounts for 35 per cent of the global sales of the world's top ten grocery retailers. As on 31 January, 2006, the company operated 1,209 discount stores, 1,980 super centers, 567 SAM'S clubs, and 100 neighbourhood markets in the USA and internationally. It operated 11 units in Argentina, 295 in Brazil, 278 in Canada, 88 in Germany, 398 in Japan, 774 in Mexico, 54 in Puerto Rico, 16 in South Korea and 315 in UK, as well as 56 stores through joint ventures in China. It employed 1.3 million people. Wal-Mart has worked hard to improve its image with new fashion brands, a trend-spotting office in Manhattan and fashion shows during New York's Fashion Week. The upgrading of its fashion is part of the company's larger campaign to expand into better quality, trendier merchandise. Wal-Mart, which has built its reputation on selling basics like socks and detergent, made a recent push into $ 2,000 flat-screen TVs and other trendy electronics, 600-thread-count sheets and organic foods. The goal is to pry more money from the hands of its wealthier customers, diversifying beyond its core low-income shoppers, who are more vulnerable to economic downturns. However, its main competitive advantage remains its sheer efficiency. It is a superbly lean machine. Wal-Mart now is one of China's biggest customers, buying at least $ 15 billion of goods from China every year, accounting for 80 per cent of its imports into the USA. If Wal-Mart were a country, it would rank as China's eighth biggest trading partner, ahead of Russia and Britain! That's a lot of clout in potentially the world's biggest retail market. Wal-Mart was forecast (*Fortune* magazine, July 2005) to reach $ 3.2 trillion in sales by 2020, and to employ eight million people and occupy the land space of Las Vegas! Wal-Mart and Tesco have discovered advantages online. Everything Wal-Mart does is focused on enhancing its position as the low-priced leader. With its Always Low Prices tagline and "Everyday Low Price" positioning, Wal-Mart wins with customers on price. Sam Walton founded what is now the world's largest company (period, not just in retail) on the simple belief that customers would like to pay less for the products they purchase and that ordinary folks should have the opportunity to buy that make their lives better. Every single action the company takes is measured against these fundamental principles.

- Wal-Mart Stores, Microsoft, Hewlett-Packard, Philips Electronics, Home Depot and Toyota-owned luxury auto marquee Lexus have banded together to pilot a revolutionary new scheme that will buy TV airtime via a special auction facility on eBay. Its sponsors have committed $ 50 million to the embroyo system, named eMedia Exchange, which launched in early 2007. Now the retailer has become the media controller. A new free website called mysupermarket.co.uk allows consumers to compare the price of their virtual shopping trolley at the major retailers and alerts them to cheaper alternative item and money-saving offers. They claim that the typical online shopper could save 20 per cent on their weekly bill and still get the same quality. Wal-Mart Store is a retailing giant that has seen better days, but, like MandS, it is not about to retire from the fight. It is effectively redefining its future. Once a proponent of the 'pile'em high, sell'em cheap' philosophy, Wal-Mart has decided to go upmarket to compete with Target and Kmart, both of which have enlisted name designers to spruce up their low-price offerings. In addition to a glitzy advertising campaign in luxury publications like *Vogue,* Wal-Mart has focused on improving the quality of its merchandise and presenting smaller sizes and brighter colours. The use of celebrities in advertisements may make Wal-Mart shareholders shudder – the advertising budget for 2009 was $ 1.4 billion, compared with $ 888 million at Target. Rising costs in China may ultimately cut into the profit margin of retailers like Wal-Mart, as well as companies that obtain their products in China, like Timberland or Nike. But the short-term impact on retail prices is likely to be negligible. Publix, Giant Eagle, Safeway and Wal-Mart are all trying to replicate the products and experiences Whole Foods delivers, but they can't replicate the people Whole Foods has delivering the products and experiences to customers. Products and programmes do not create brands, people create brands. People matter more in creating a brand than a product or programme.

- Food retailing continues to dominate among the largest retailers. Eight of the ten largest retailers sell food, and slightly over 50 per cent of the 200 largest retailers have supermarkets, warehouse, hypermarket, or cash-and-carry formats, or some combination of them. The dominance of food retailing would be even more pronounced if US drug store chains, which place more emphasis on convenience food, were included as food retailers. Of the top 2004 global retailers, 42.5 per cent are headquartered in the US, 39 per cent in Europe, and 13 per cent in Japan. Largest retailers headquartered in the US tend to concentrate on the US and operate fewer formats than their global counterparts. American retailers in the top 50 list operate, on average, two formats in 35 countries, while top 50 retailers headquartered outside the US operate twice as many formats in three more countries. P&G, the world's biggest branded company, keeps a permanent staff of 200 at Bentonville, the Wal-Mart HQ in Arkansas, the USA. According to *Fortune* magazine, the largest discount retailers are responsible for 80 per cent of the daily groceries sales in the USA. In UK four chains have 75 per cent of the grocery market. In Sweden the major grocery retailers have more than 80 per cent of the market. The extreme example is Finland, where three retailers control a staggering 91 per cent of the mass fast-moving consumer goods (FMCG) market.
- **Whole Foods Market (WFM)** is a company that has truly made ethics its mantra. WFM obtains its products locally and from all over the world, often from small, uniquely dedicate food artisans. WFM strives to offer the highest quality, least processed, most flavorful and naturally preserved foods. WFM recruits the best people and empowers them to make their own decisions, creating a respectful workplace where people are treated fairly and are highly motivated to succeed. It is simply the best merchandised anywhere. It was founded in 1980 as one small store in Austin, Texas. It is now the world's leading retailer of natural and organic foods, with 189 stores in North America and UK. To date, Whole Foods Market remains driven by a very single-minded Mission. They are highly selective about what they sell, dedicated to stringent quality standards, and committed to sustainable agriculture. It's hard to find fault with Whole Foods, the supermarket chain, that has made a fortune by transforming grocery shopping into a bright and shiny, progressive experience. Indeed, the road to wild profits and cultural cachet has been surprisingly smooth for the supermarket chain. It gets mostly sympathetic coverage in the local and national media and red-carpet treatment from the communities it enters. Under the umbrella creed of 'sustainability',

Whole Foods pays its workers a solid living wage – its lowest earners an average $ 13.15 an hour – with excellent benefits and health care. (Mackey's salary in 2006 was $ 342,000.) WFM seems to understand the power of a knowledgeable, caring and passionate workforce in creating highly satisfied customers. They've created a company culture that connects with their employees and they in turn pass that connection onto WFM shoppers (USA *Today*, 2006). WFM was recently voted the greatest food retailer in the world by the *Grocer* magazine's panel of experts in UK.

- **Tesco** from Britain may become the world's biggest retailer. With 23 per cent international growth per annum, it is possible to see it becoming as big as Wal-Mart. Tesco has, through the use of its loyalty card (14 million plus members) and scanning data information, divided its millions of customers into over 1,00,000 customer categories to better understand them, be they wine buyers or razor blade consumers. Tesco is so powerful that it can introduce any product or service and have an instant hit. When it launched its Tesco Mobile service, for example, it attracted 5,00,000 customers in less than 14 months. Tesco is knowledgeable and close to its customers. It pays 1 per cent in dividends to its customers over one billion pounds. It has 14 million Tesco cards in circulation. It sells the cheapest gasoline in UK to their customers. Many Tesco stores are kept open for 24 hours. Some specific changes being implemented by Tesco:
  - Cutting carrier bags by 25 per cent in two years. All bags to become biodegradable.
  - Will reduce deliveries to stores to cut congestion and make deliveries quicher.
  - Wants to introduce regional counters in stores to promote local produce.
  - Will host open days for regional producers to meet buyers.
- **Procter and Gamble:** It is the world's biggest branded company. It has a permanent staff of 200 at Bentonville, the Wal-Mart HQ in Arkansas, (USA). It is the maker of Tide, Crest and Pampers. According to A.G. Lafley, the head of PandG, there are only two moments of truth, 1. When people buy the product and 2. When people try the product. The 'first moment of truth' **(FMOT)** as P and G calls it, is the three to seven seconds when someone notices an item on a store shelf, when shoppers are about to buy the product. This instant is one of its most important marketing opportunities. It has over 16 brands exceeding sales of US $ 1 billion each, and is the global leader in four core product categories: fabric and home care, beauty care, baby and family care and health care. It is the most successful brands in the mass markets. It has built the biggest brand business in the world by understanding its competitive context better than anybody else. Its finest ability is to make continuous improvements to its brands through a constant series of innovations, adding small additional fighting features to its armoury, and sometimes creating entirely new product ideas and categories. It has used innovations to good effect when creating word-of-mouth marketing. Teenagers are the customers of P and G. It recently rebranded its Tremor Moms programme to a unique marketing bran "Vocal point". P and G is the champion of CUSTOMER-MADE, to the point of selling its co-creation expertise to others. One of P and G's most important belief is 'the shopper is boss'. For the launch of Kandoo wipes – flushable baby wipes for toilet-training toddlers- in the USA, P and G convinced retailers to place the packages low on shelves, so they would be at a toddler's eye-level. It also

created display shelves in the shape of the product's frog mascot to attract children's attention. P and G recently launched a major global review of its 60 million dollar point-of-sale budgets and Larry Light, who has been giving McDonald's makeover as its chief marketing officer, says bluntly: "The days of mass marketing are over". To keep in touch with their customers, consumer-goods companies are shifting their spending away from traditional media, such as network TV and print, to other types of promotion. Within P and G's $ 4 billion advertising budget, a growing proportion is shifting from mainstream media, such as television, radio and print, to new media and other forms of sales promotion, such as direct mail, public relations, promotions, sponsorship and product placement. This is called 'below-the-line' advertising, or marketing services. The two sorts of spending added up to more than $ 1 trillion in the year 2009, says WPP, a leading advertising group. Brands are increasingly refocusing on the real future – the retail future. One marketing firm has even hired an expert on the durability of corrugated cardboard. P and G has cut its commitments to advertise on cable channels for the current season by 25 per cent and its broadcast – TV allotment is down about 5 per cent. However, its overall ad spending rose slightly. Special shelf displays and packaging are very effective in the promotion of retail trade. P and G persuaded retailers to put fake doorknobs high up on restroom doors, to remind parents how much babies need to stretch.

Trying – the Second Moment of Truth: Tryvertising is coined by trendwatching.com. It is about encouraging loyalty from anyone by providing potential shoppers with a real product experience. Tryvertising is a new way of thinking about mass communications – a new way of getting trial. It is not about free shampoo samples in magazines, or a point-of-sale promotion stand in a supermarket. It is about the real world and integrating one's goods and services into daily life in a relevant way, so that shoppers can make up their mind based on their experience, not one's messages. Tremor of P and G is a marketing service that develops teen word-of-mouth marketing programmes by recruiting teens to help develop exciting and relevant product ideas and marketing programmes that teens want to talk about. Tremor works with companies in industries like entertainment, fashion, music, food and beauty and involves itself to build word-of-mouth among teenagers. P and G has launched **Connect + Develop** programme about six years ago with the goal of having at least 50 per cent of its new products derived from ideas generated by non-employee outside experts. P and G and the non-employee outside experts spend about 2 billion dollars a year on this activity and they have set themselves the ambitious goal of sourcing much of their idea input from outside the company. Besides its R & D employee base of 7,000, the company now has access to millions of potential innovators.

- **Karmaloop: Turning Shoppers into Fanatics:** Karmaloop was the first online retailer to carry the revered Ben Sherman line. Specializing in urban fashion, Karmaloop, the US's largest independent seller of cutting-edge urban fashion online, carries such well known brands as Kangol, Freshjive and Triple Five Soul, as well as lesser known such as Body Bag, House of Spy and Silent Revolution. It was started in 1999. It carried a scant four clothing lines (Snug, Kappa, Gat and Esdjco). Now, Karmaloop.com has successfully built the largest selection of boutique clothing online. It has become the spot online to go for cool, hip street-wear and offers eclectic styles and brands online. In addition, it also provides its brands with professional photo shoots, sales and demographic data, product testing, print and online co.op. advertising and various on- and offline promotions. Everyday a new CD is given away for free with every order. One CD for example is an Astralwerks sampler (Karmaloop.com).It has been able to weather the recent tough times for online retail with its blend of savvy marketing, tasteful buying, and extensive knowledge of its market. It is progressing in leaps and bounds. It has 3,50,000 visitors a month, 15 full-time employees and a smattering of part-time and intern employees. It has begun its creative reach, carrying Japanese toys.

- The priorities ranked in terms of the squeezes encountered by producers are:
  1. Retail power
  2. Shopper power
  3. Private label
  4. Media changes

Table 21 : Global Retailer

Global retailer	Per centage share of total $ 900 bn combined turnover
Wal-Mart	35
Carrefour (France)	9
Metro	8
Ahold	7
Tesco	7
Kroger	6.75
Costco	6
Rewe Gruppe	6
Aldi	5.75
Lidi and Schwarz	5.75

The table given below contains a small list of why brands and retailers should be helping each other.

Table 22 : Needs of Brands and Retailers

Brands need retailers	Retailers need brands
Distribution	Image
Selling power	Choice
Competitive context	Innovation
Promotion	Margin
Growth	Growth
Shopper knowledge	Consumer knowledge

THE WORLD'S LARGEST GROCERS - % SHARE IN 2006

The current revenue of Wal-Mart in 2006 was US $ 330 billion. The above table lists the global sales of the world's top ten grocery retailers.

Early Shopping Centres

The Arcade of Cleveland was the first indoor shopping mall in the US and an architectural triumph. When the building opened in 1890, two sides of the arcade were glazed with 1,600 panes of glass set in iron framing.

An early shopping centre in the United States was Country Club Plaza, which opened in 1924, in Kansas City, Missouri. Other important shopping centres built in the 1920s and early 1930s, are the Highland Park Village in Dallas, Texas; River Oaks in Houston, Texas; and Park and Shop in Washington, DC.

Southdale Center, in Edina, a suburb of Minneapolis in the US state of Minnesota, is the first modern fully enclosed under one roof shopping mall, it features a very wide central space, which its designer originally intended for communal gatherings.

However, the concept of the fully-enclosed shopping mall did not appear until the 1950s. The idea was pioneered by the Austrian-born architect and American immigrant Victor Gruen. This new generation, that were eventually called malls, included Northgate Mall, built in north Seattle, Washington, USA in 1950, Victor Gruen's Northland Shopping Centre built near Detroit, Michigan, USA in 1954, and Gulfgate Mall in Houston were all originally open-air pedestrian shopping centres that later were enclosed as malls. The first enclosed, post-war shopping centre (or mall) was the Gruen-designed Southdale Centre, which opened in the Twin Cities suburb of Edina, Minnesota, USA in 1956. These malls moved retailing away from the dense, commercial downtown into the largely residential suburbs. This formula (enclosed space with stores attached, away from downtown, and accessible only by automobile) became a popular way to build retail across the world. In UK, Chrisp Street Market was the first pedestrian shopping area built with a road at the shop fronts.

Ala Moana Centre in Honolulu, Hawaii is currently the largest open-air mall in the world and was the largest mall in the states when it was built in 1957. It is currently the sixteenth largest in the country. The Bergen Mall, the oldest enclosed mall in New Jersey, opened in Paramus on November 14, 1957, with Dave Garroway, host of The Today Show, serving as master of ceremonies. The mall, located just outside New York City, was planned in 1955 by Allied Stores to have 100 stores and 8,600 parking spaces in a 15,00,000 sq. ft. (139,000 m^2) mall that would include a 3,00,000 sq. ft. (28,000 m^2) Stern's store and two other 1,50,000 sq. ft. (14,000 m^2) department stores as part of the design. Allied's Chairman B. Earl Puckett confidently announced the Bergen Mall as the largest of ten proposed centers, stating that there were 25 cities that could support such centres and that no more than 50 malls of this type would ever be built nationwide.

Centre Commercial Al Qods in Algiers, the second largest shopping mall in Africa (behind Gateway Theatre of Shopping in Durban, South Africa).

Berjaya Times Square in Kuala Lumpur, Malaysia, is advertised at 7,00,000 m^2 (75,00,000 sq. ft.). Beijing's (Peking) Golden Resources Mall, which opened in October 2004, is the world's second largest mall, at 6,00,000 m^2 (65,00,000 sq. ft.). SM City North EDSA in the

Philippines, which opened in November 1985, is the world's third largest at 4,60,000 m^2 (50,00,000 sq. ft.) of gross floor area, and SM Mall of Asia in the Philippines, opened in May 2006, is the world's fourth largest at 3,86,000 m^2 (41,50,000 sq. ft.) of gross floor area.

Previously, the title of the largest enclosed shopping mall was with the West Edmonton Mall in Edmonton, Alberta, Canada from 1986–2004. It is now the fifth largest mall. Two of the largest malls are in China, South China Mall and Jin Yuan. Dubai Mall is the largest mall in Middle East and Europe, currently ranked seventh in the world. The current largest shopping centre in Europe is the Metro Centre near Newcastle upon Tyne in UK.

One of the world's largest shopping complexes in one location is the two-mall agglomeration of the Plaza at King of Prussia and the Court at King of Prussia in the Philadelphia suburb of King of Prussia, Pennsylvania, United States. The King of Prussia mall has the most shopping per square foot in the US.

The most visited shopping mall in the world and largest mall in the United States is the Mall of America, located near the Twin Cities in Bloomington, Minnesota. However, several Asian malls are advertised as having more visitors, including Mal Taman Anggrek, Kelapa Gading Mall and Pluit Village, all in Jakarta-Indonesia, Berjaya Times Square in Malaysia and SM Megamall in the Philippines. The largest mall in South Asia, and twelfth largest in the world, is Bashundhara City in Dhaka, Bangladesh.

British Usage

Mall can refer to either a shopping mall a place where a collection of shops all adjoin a pedestrian area or an exclusively pedestrianised street that allows shoppers to walk without interference from vehicle traffic. *Mall* is generally used in North America to refer to a large shopping area usually composed of a single building which contains multiple shops, usually "anchored" by one or more department stores surrounded by a parking lot, while the term *arcade* is more often used, especially in Britain, to refer to a narrow pedestrian only street, often covered or between closely spaced buildings. A larger, often partly covered and exclusively pedestrian shopping area is in Britain also termed a *shopping centre*, *shopping precinct*, or *pedestrian precinct*.

The majority of British shopping centres are in town centres, usually inserted into old shopping districts and surrounded by subsidiary open air shopping streets. A number of large out-of-town "regional malls" such as Meadowhall, Sheffield and the Trafford Centre, Manchester were built in the 1980s and 1990s, but planning regulations prohibit the construction of any more. Out-of-town shopping developments in UK are now focused on retail parks, which consist of groups of warehouse style shops with individual entrances from outdoors. Planning policy prioritizes the development of existing town centres, although with patchy success. The Metro Centre, in Gateshead (near Newcastle upon Tyne), is the largest shopping centre in Europe with over 330 shops, 50 restaurants and an 11 screen cinema, while the Westfield London is the largest inner-city shopping centre in Europe.

Classes of Malls

In many cases, regional and super-regional malls exist as parts of large superstructures which often also include office space, residential space, amusement parks and so forth. This trend can be seen in the construction and design of many modern supermalls such as Cevahir Mall in Turkey. The International Council of Shopping Centres' 1999 definitions were not restricted to shopping centres in any particular country, but later editions were made specific to the US with a separate set for Europe.

A **regional mall** is, as per the International Council of Shopping Centres, in the United States, a shopping mall which is designed to service a larger area than a conventional shopping mall. As such, it is typically larger with 4,00,000 sq. ft. (37,000 m^2) to 8,00,000 sq. ft. (74,000 m^2) gross leasable area with at least two anchors and offers a wider selection of stores. Given their wider service area, these malls tend to have higher-end stores that need a larger area in order for their services to be profitable. Regional malls are also found as tourist attractions in vacation areas.

Super Regional Malls

A **super regional mall** is, per the International Council of Shopping Centres, in the US. It is a shopping mall with over 8,00,000 sq. ft. (74,000 m^2) of gross leasable area, and which serves as the dominant shopping venue for the region in which it is located.

An outlet mall (or outlet centre) is a type of shopping mall in which manufacturers sell their products directly to the public through their own stores. Other stores in outlet malls are operated by retailers selling returned goods and discontinued products, often at heavily reduced prices. Outlet stores were found as early as 1936, but the first multi-store outlet mall, Vanity Fair, located in Reading, PA didn't open until 1974. Belz Enterprises opened the first enclosed factory outlet mall in 1979, in Lakeland, TN, a suburb of Memphis.

Components

A common feature of shopping malls is a food court, this typically consists of a number of fast food vendors of various types, surrounding a shared seating area.

When the shopping mall format was developed by Victor Gruen in the mid-1950s, signing larger department stores was necessary for the financial stability of the projects, and to draw retail traffic that would result in visits to the smaller stores in the mall as well. These larger stores are termed anchor store or draw tenant. Anchors generally have their rents heavily discounted, and may even receive cash inducements from the mall to remain open. In physical configuration, anchor stores are normally located as far from each other as possible to maximize the amount of traffic from one anchor to another.

In the US, as more modern facilities are built, many early malls have become abandoned, due to decreased traffic and tenancy. These "dead malls" have failed to attract new business and often sit unused for many years until restored or demolished. Interesting examples of architecture and urban design, these structures often attract people who explore and photograph them. This phenomenon of dead and dying malls is examined in detail by the website Deadmalls.com, which hosts many such photographs, as well as historical accounts. Until the mid-1990s, the trend was to build enclosed malls and to renovate older outdoor malls into enclosed ones. Such malls had advantages such as temperature control. Since then, the trend has turned and it is once again fashionable to build open-air malls. According to the International Council of Shopping Centres, only one enclosed mall has been built in the United States since 2006.

Some enclosed malls have been opened up, such as the Sherman Oaks Galleria. In addition, some malls, when replacing an empty anchor location, have replaced the former anchor store building with the more modern outdoor design, leaving the remainder of the indoor mall intact, such as the Del Amo Fashion Centre in Torrance, California.

In parts of Canada, it is now rare for new shopping malls to be built. The Vaughan Mills Shopping Centre, opened in 2004, and Crossiron Mills, opened in 2009, are the only malls built in Canada since 1992. Outdoor outlet malls or big box shopping areas known as power centres are now favoured, although the traditional enclosed shopping mall is still in demand by those seeking weather-protected, all-under-one-roof shopping. In addition the enclosed interconnections between downtown multistorey shopping malls continue to grow in the Underground city of Montreal (32 kilometres of passageway), the PATH system of Toronto (27 km (17 mi) of passageway) and the Plus15 system of Calgary (16 km (9.9 mi) of overhead passageway).

Vertical Malls

High land prices in populous cities have led to the concept of the "vertical mall", in which space allocated to retail is configured over a number of stories accessible by elevators and/or escalators linking the different levels of the mall. The challenge of this type of mall is to overcome the natural tendency of shoppers to move horizontally and encourage shoppers to move upwards and downwards. The concept of a vertical mall was originally conceived in the late 1960s by the Mafco Company, former shopping centre development division of Marshall Field and Co. The Water Tower Place Skyscraper, Chicago, Illinois, was built in 1975 by Urban Retail Properties. It contains a hotel, luxury condominiums, and office space and sits atop a block-long base containing an eight-level atrium-style retail mall that fronts on the Magnificent Mile.

Vertical malls are common in densely populated conurbations such as Hong Kong and Bangkok. Times Square in Hong Kong is a principal example.

A vertical mall may also be built where the geography prevents building outward or there are other restrictions on construction, such as historical buildings or significant archeology. The Darwin Shopping Centre and associated malls in Shrewsbury, UK, are built on the side of a steep hill, around the former outer walls of the nearby medieval castle; consequently the shopping centre is split over seven floors vertically – two locations horizontally – connected by elevators, escalators and bridge walkways. Some establishments incorporate such design into their layout, such as Shrewsbury's McDonalds restaurant, split into four stories with multiple mezzanines which feature medieval castle vaults – complete with arrowslits – in the basement dining rooms.

A shopping property management firm is a company that specializes in owning and managing shopping malls. Most shopping property management firms own at least 20 malls. Some firms use a similar naming scheme for most of their malls; for example, Mills Corporation puts "Mills" in most of their mall names and SM Prime Holdings of the Philippines puts "SM" in all of their malls, as well as anchor stores such as SM Department Store, SM Appliance Centre, SM Hypermarket, SM Cinema, and SM Supermarket. In UK, the Mall Fund changes the name of any centre they buy to *"The Mall (location)"*, using their pink-M logo; when they sell a mall it reverts to its own name and branding, such as the Ashley Centre in Epsom.

KINGDOM SHOPPING CENTRE, GLENROTHES

Many new towns in the United Kingdom – including Cumbernauld, Glenrothes, East Kilbride, Milton Keynes, Washington, Tyne and Wear, Newton Aycliffe and Telford – did not incorporate a traditional style town centre but instead developed a shopping centre. Unlike the shopping centres which were developing in established towns and cities, these also contained many civic functions and other community facilities such as libraries, pubs and community centres. As the towns grew, other facilities were usually developed around the centres, effectively enlarging the town centres.

Legal Issues

One controversial aspect of malls has been their effective displacement of traditional main streets. Many consumers prefer malls, with their spacious parking garages, entertaining environments, and private security guards, over downtown, which often suffers from limited parking, poor maintenance, and limited police coverage.

In response, a few jurisdictions, notably California, have expanded the right of freedom of speech to ensure that speakers will be able to reach consumers who prefer to shop, eat, and socialize within the boundaries of privately owned malls.

Planning concepts

- Public space
- Gruen transfer

QUESTIONS

1. What are the types of retailers?
2. Write a note on shopping facilities.
3. Suggest measures to promote Indian Retail Business
4. Define Affinity.
5. What are the characteristics of Indian Rural Retail Market?
6. What do you mean by organized rural sector?
7. Explain the scope of Indian retail market.
8. What do you mean by niche retailing?
9. Define direct selling.
10. What do you mean by Television Home Shopping?
11. Explain "Vending. Machine Retailing".
12. What do you mean by Services Retailing?
13. Differentiate between services and merchandise retail management.
14. List the reasons for studying retailing.
15. Define Retail Management.
16. What do you mean by organized structure in retail management?
17. Explain the steps to create organized structure.

18. Explain about organized retail market in India.
19. Present an overview of visual merchandising in Indian organized retail.
20. "Organized retail in India is in its growth frontiers" – Discuss.
21. "India is an underdeveloped market in organized trade" – Comment.
22. Trace the growth of retail outlets in India.
23. Write a note on employment in retailing.
24. "Retailing is a force employment sector", do you agree?
25. Which is the largest retailer in the world?
26. Explain about Wal-Mart.
27. FDI in India. Is it a Hornet's nest? Give your explanation.
28. Explain the role of China in Rural Market.
29. What are your recommendations for the growth and development of Food Retail Sector in India.
30. Explain the scope for employment in the organized sector in India.
31. What are the different organized retail market in India?
32. What are the characteristics of organized retail market in India?
33. Discuss the growth of organized retail market in India.
34. What are the different forms of retail organizations?
35. Explain suitable organizational structure for small retailers.
36. Explain the organizational structure of Departmental Store.
37. What do you mean by store management?
38. Who are the chain retailers?
39. What is the need for larger FDI?
40. Write a note on Shopping Mall/Centre.
41. Trace the early development of shopping centres.
42. Write a note on British usage of the concept of "Mall".
43. Classify Malls.
44. What are the components of Malls.
45. What do you mean by vertical mall?
46. What are the 7s in marketing.
47. What are the common features of Shopping Malls.
48. What are the benefits of larger FDI to retail marketing?
49. What do you mean by Regional (Retail) Malls?
50. Discuss the need for FDI in Retail Marketing.
51. Discuss the role of FDI in the growth of Retail Marketing in India.
52. What are the kinds of retail formats?
53. "Reliance is close to Break-even" – Discuss.
54. Write short notes on: (i) Hawkers, (ii) Mobile super-markets.
55. Write a note on HTML and Euphoria Software Solution.
56. What do you mean by retail store management and the concept of "Shopper Made" ?

57. What are your tips for retail store management?
58. Write notes on: (i) Mandi, (ii). Ankanwadi
59. What do you mean by Brand Fantasy and retail store management? What are the tips to RSM?
60. Explain shopper's experience in site performance.
61. Explain about Food Retail in India and the features of Indian rural market.
62. Write short notes on: (i) Kirana, (ii) Provision Store, (iii) Mom-and pop- store (iv) eBay, (v) Cheap-Est-proponent, (vi) Online retailing, (vii) Foodworld, (viii) Trinethra,(ix) Apna Bazaar, (x) Margin Free, (xi) MTR Group of companies, (xii) Subhiksha.
63. Explain the impact of organized retail market.
64. Explain Government's policy on food retailing in India.
65. "Innovation is the best defence in retailing"- Elucidate
66. What is the impact of technology on retailing.
67. Explain the nature and scope of retailing in India.
68. Write short notes on (i) niche retailing, (ii) Direct selling, (iii) Vending Machine Retailing (iv) Service Retailing and Cheap-Est Retailers.
69. Distinguish between Services and Merchandise Retailers.
70. Define Retail Management and Retail decision making.
71. What are the reasons to study about retail management.
72. Write short notes on (i) Karmaloop, (ii) P and G, (iii) Tesco, (iv)Shopping Mall/Centre and (v) World Foods Market.
73. What are the benefits of large FDI to retail industry? What are the priorities to focus on FDI?
74. State and explain the need for organized structure used by chain retailers.
75. Explain the characteristics of Organized Structure in Retail Management.
76. What are the functions of organizational structure in retailing?
77. Explain the different forms of retail organizational growth in India.
78. List the world's largest grocers and the experiences of Far East in Retailing.
79. Distinguish between Vertical Mall and Super Regional Mall.
80. "Brand needs Retailers and Retailer needs Brand" – Explain.

CHAPTER 3

Retailing Decision

STRATEGIC PLANNING

WHAT IS RETAIL STRATEGY?

A retail strategy is the overall plan or framework of action that guides a retailer. Without a defined and well integrated strategy, a firm can flounder and be unable to cope with the marketplace.

The process of strategic retail planning has several attractive features:

1. It provides a thorough analysis of the requirements for doing business for different types of retailers.
2. It outlines retailer goals.
3. A firm determines to differentiate itself from competitors and develop an offering that appeals to a group of customers.
4. The legal, economic, and competitive environment is studied.
5. A firm's total efforts are coordinated.
6. Crises are anticipated and often avoided.

STRATEGIC PLAN

Strategic planning can be done by the owner of a firm, professional management or a combination of the two. Even among family businesses, majority of high growth companies have strategic plans.

STEPS IN PLANNING

The steps in planning and enacting a retail strategy are independent; a firm often starts with a general plan that gets more specific as options and pay-offs become clearer.

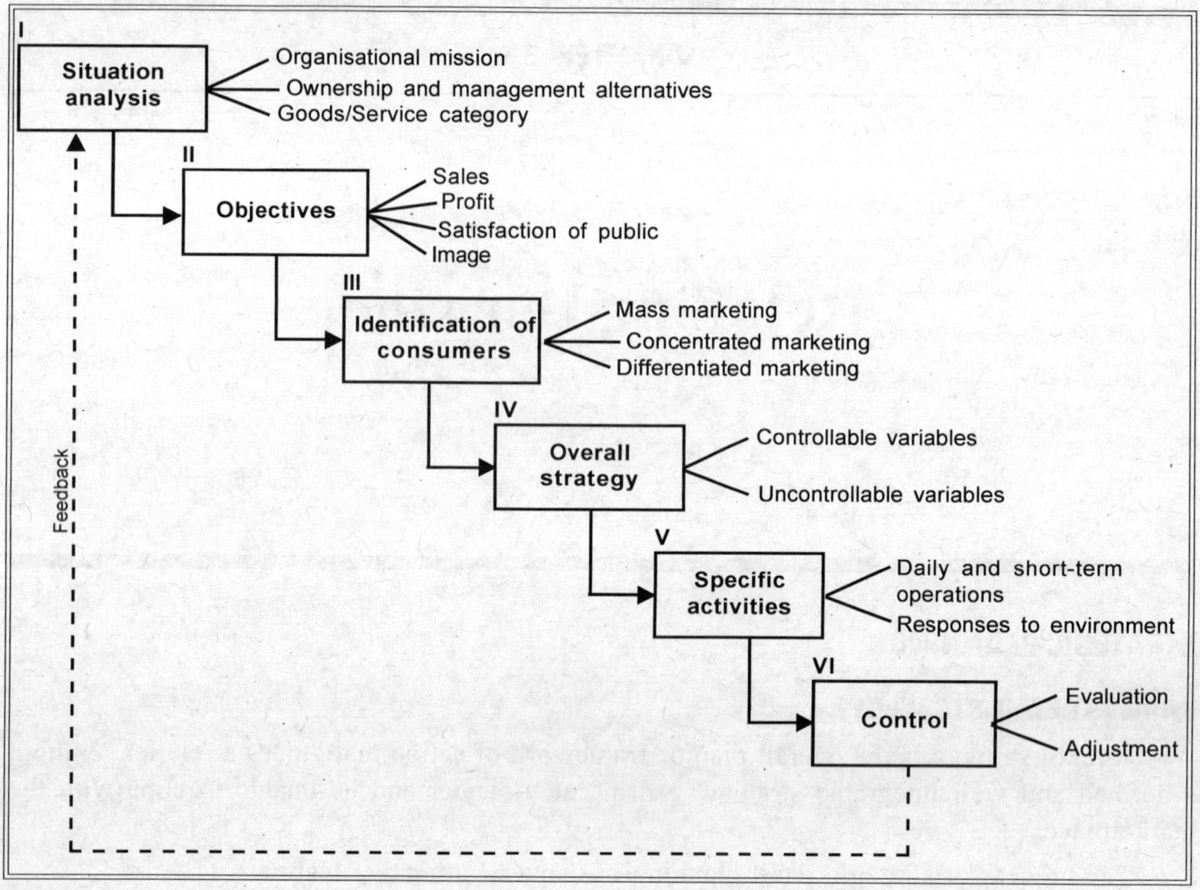

FIG. 23: HOW TO PLAN

SITUATION ANALYSIS

Situation analysis is a candid evaluation of the opportunities and threats facing a prospective or existing retailer. It seeks to answer two general questions:

1. What is the firm's current status?
2. In which direction should it be heading?

A. Organizational Mission

An organizational mission is a retailer's commitment to a type of business and to a distinctive role in the marketplace. It is reflected in the firm's attitude towards consumers, employees, suppliers, competitors, government and others. A clear mission lets a firm gain a customer following and distinguishes itself from competitors.

Although the development of an organizational mission is the first step in the planning process, the mission should be continually reviewed and adjusted to reflect changing company goals and a dynamic retail environment.

Some Retail Vision/Mission Statements

- **Wal-Mart:** "To give ordinary folk the chance to buy the same thing as rich people".
- **McDonald's:** "Quality, Service, Convenience and Value".
- **Café Coffee Day:** To be the best café chain in the country by offering world-class coffee experience at affordable price.
- **Shoppers' Stop:** "To be a global retailer in India, and to maintain the number one position in the Indian market in the department store category".
- **Pantaloon:** "We share the vision and belief that by improving our performance through innovative spirit and dedication, we shall serve our customers and stakeholders satisfactorily".

B. Ownership and Management Alternatives

An essential aspect of situational analysis is accessing ownership and management alternatives, including whether to form a sole proprietorship partnership, or corporation – and whether to start a new business, buy an existing business, or become a franchisee.

As two experts have noted "Customers may not notice if a firm is a sole proprietorship, a partnership or a corporation. The form chosen though can make a difference when its time to pay taxes, respond to law suit or split up the business".

Sole Proprietorship

- It is an unincorporated retail firm owned by a single person.
- All benefits, profits, risks, and costs accrue to that individual.
- It is simple to form, fully controlled by the owner, operationally flexible, easy to dissolve, and subject to single taxation by government.
- It makes the owner personally liable for legal claims from suppliers, creditors and others.
- It can lead to limited capital and expertise.

Partnership

- It is an unincorporated retail firm owned by two or more persons, each with a financial interest.
- Partners share benefits, profits, risks and costs.
- Responsibility and expertise are divided among multiple principles, there is a creative capability for raising funds than with a proprietorship, the format is simpler to form than a corporation, and it is subject to single taxation by the govt.
- Depending on the type of partnership it can make owners personally liable for legal claims, can be dissolved due to partner's death or disagreement, binds all partners to actions made by individual partner acting on behalf of the firm.
- It has less ability to raise funds than a corporation.

Corporation

- It is a retail firm formally incorporated under the state law.
- It is a legal entity apart from individual officers or stakeholders.
- Funds can be raised through sale of stock, legal claim against individual who are not usually allowed, ownership transfer is relatively easy, the firm is assured of long time existence (if the founder leaves, retires or dies).
- The use of professional manager is encouraged and unambiguous operating authority is outlined.
- Depending on the type of organisation it is subjected to double taxation.
- Faces more government rules, can require a complex process when established, may be viewed as impersonal and may separate ownership from management.
- A closed corporation is run by a limited number of persons who control ownership; stock is not available to the public. Open corporation stock is widely traded and available to the public.

Entrepreneurial – Starting a New Business

- It offers are (i) tailor flexibility in location, (ii) operating style, (iii) product-line, (iv) customer market, and other factors; and a strategy is fully tailored to the owners desire and strengths.
- There may be high construction cost, a time lag until the business is open and then until profits are earned beginning with an unknown name and having to form supplier relationships and amass inventory of goods.

Entrepreneurial – Buying an Existing Business

It allows a retailer to acquire an established company name, a customer following, a good location, trained personnel, and facilitates to operate immediately; to generate ongoing sales and profits; and to possibly get good lease terms or financing from the seller.

- Fixtures may be older there is a less flexibility in enacting a strategy tailored to the new owner's desires and strengths, and the growth potential of the business may be limited.

Franchisee

- By being a franchisee, a retailer can combine independent ownership with franchisor's support: strategic planning assistance; in known company name and loyal customer following; corporative advertising and buying; and a regional, national, global (rather than local) image.
- A franchisee-contract may specify rigid operating standards, limit the product-line sold, and restrict supplier's choice; the franchisor company is usually paid continuously (royalties); ad fees may be required; and there is a possibility of termination by the franchisor if the agreement is not followed satisfactorily.

Management Format

- It has a dramatic impact.

- With an owner manager, planning tends to be less formal and more intuitive, and many tasks are reserved for that person.
- With professional management planning tends to be more formal and systematic.

C. Goods/ Services Category

- Before a prospective retail firm can fully design a strategic plan, it selects a goods/ service category, i.e., the line of business.
- It is advisable to specify both a general goods/services category and a niche within that category.

A potential retail business owner should select a type of business that will allow him or her to match personal abilities, financial resources, and time availability with the requirements of that kind of business.

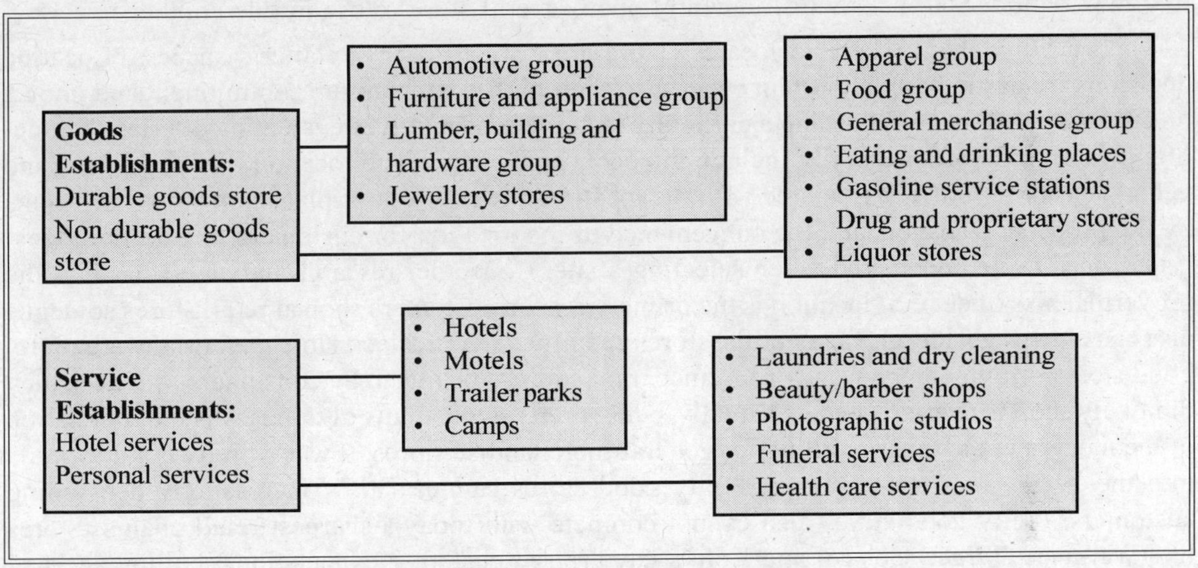

FIG. 24: GOODS AND SERVICES CATEGORY

Objectives

After situation analysis, retailer sets objectives, the long run and short run performance targets it hopes to attain. This helps mould a strategy and translates the organizational mission into action. A firm can pursue goals related to one or more of these areas:

1. **Sales:** Sales objectives are related to the volume of goods and services a retailer sells. Growth, stability, and market share are the sales goals more often sought.
2. **Profit:** With profitability objectives, retailers seek at least a minimum profit level during a designated period, usually a year. Profits may be expressed in dollars or as a percentage of sales.
3. **Satisfaction of Public:** Retailers typically strive to satisfy their public: stockholders, customers, suppliers, employees and government.

4. **Image:** An image represents how a given retailer is perceived by consumers and others. A firm may be seen as innovative or conservative, specialized or broad-based, discount-oriented or upscale.

LOCATION

The classical response to the question "What are the three most important things in retailing?" is "location, location, location". Location is the critical factor in consumers' selection of a store. For example, most people shop at the supermarket closest to where they live. For instance, once Walgreens has put a store at the best location at an intersection. Starbucks has developed a strong competitive advantage with its location selection. It conquers one area of the city at a time and then expands in the region, saturating a major market before entering a new market. For example, there were over 100 Starbucks outlets in the Scuttle area before the company expanded to a new region. Starbucks will frequently open several stores close to one another.

Decisions about where to locate a store are critical to any retailer's success. Location decisions are particularly important because of their high-cost, long run commitment and impact on customer patronage. Choosing a particular location type involves evaluating a series of trade-offs. These trade-offs generally include the occupancy cost of the location, the pedestrian and vehicle customer traffic associated with the location, the restrictions placed on store operations by the property managers and the convenience of the location for customers. In addition, legal issues need to be considered when selecting a site. Consumer research indicates that it is the proverbial kiss of death if location is the primary reason customers shop at retail stores someone else can always get closer. Many of the stores enshrined in our Black Hole memorial were pretty good stores. Montgomery War, for instance, ranked third or fourth by consumers as places they did likely shop for various items. Actually, being pretty good at lots of things was the foundation of the modern era of mass retailing for general-merchandise stores. It was a pretty good formula into the 1980s. It is not anymore. Pretty good stores cannot satisfy increasingly demanding customers. Pretty good stores also cannot compete with today's sharpest retail chains. Stores like Wal-mart, Target, Costco, and Kohl's have raised customer expectations. Falling short of expectations means not satisfying customers, and that is the most direct path to the Black Hole.

Types of Locations

Many types of locations are available for retail stores to retailers. What are the relative advantages of each with its own strengths and weaknesses? Retailers have three basic types of location type.

Companies select locations like freestanding, city or town business district, or shopping centre. Retailers can also locate in a non-traditional location like an airport or within another store, particularly well suited to specific retail strategies.

Freestanding sites are retail locations for an individual, isolated store unconnected to other retailers, however, they might be near other freestanding retailers, shopping centres, or, in the case of a kiosk, inside an office building or shopping centre. Advantage of freestanding location are their convenience for customers (easy access and parking); high vehicular traffic and visibility to attract customers driving by; modest occupancy costs; separation from direct composition; and fewer restrictions on signs, hours, or merchandise, as are typically imposed in shopping centres. For instance, Elizabeth Arden's kiosk at the Forum Shopping Mall at Bengaluru offers mall developers an opportunity for additional revenue from unused space.

Merchandise kiosks are small temporary selling spaces typically located in the walkways of enclosed malls, airports, railway stations, or office building lobbies. Kiosks in office lobbies often sell newspapers, flowers, or snacks.

City or Town Locations: Urban locations particularly cities have attractions for retailers. However, vehicular traffic is limited due to congestion in the inner city and parking problems reduce consumer convenience.

Central Business District: CBD is the traditional downtown business area in a city or town. Due to its daily activity, it draws many people and employees into the area during business hours. The CBD is also the hub for public transportation, and there is a high level of pedestrian traffic. The CBD has a large number of residents living in the area. But CBD locations are declining in the USA.

Main Street: Another city or town location alternative is Main Street, the traditional shopping area of smaller towns or a secondary business district in a suburb or within a larger city. Often streets in these areas have been converted into pedestrian walkways. They represent an effort by cities to draw people from the suburbs and revitalize the downtown area as a destination for shopping and recreation. They do not draw as many people as the primary CBD. They do not offer the range of entertainment and recreational activities available in the more successful primary CBDs. In UK, 80 per cent of retail sales are made by small retailers in Main Street (High Street) locations. High Street locations are threatened by large supermarkets and hypermarkets located in the suburbs or exurbs.

Inner City: Inner way in the USA is a high-density urban area consisting of apartment buildings populated primarily by lower-income consumers. There are about 8 million households in America's inner cities. Conservatively, inner-city consumers constitute $ 85 billion in annual retail buying power - far more than the entire country of Mexico.

A shopping centre is a group of retail and other commercial establishments that is planned, developed, owned and managed as a single property. By combining many stores at one location, disproportionately more consumers are attracted in the shopping centre than if the stores were at separate locations. Most shopping centres have at least one or two major retailers, referred to as anchors. These retailers are courted by the centre developer because they attract a significant number of consumers and consequently make the centre more appealing by other retailers.

Neighbourhood and community centres (strip shopping centres) are an attached row of store – managed as a unit, with onsite parking usually located in the front of the stores. Since the common areas are not enclosed, these centres are often referred to as 'open air centres'. The most common layouts are linear, L-shaped and inverted U-shaped. The term 'strip centre' has been applied to the linear configuration. The neighbourhood (small in size) centres are typically anchored by a supermarket or a drugstore; the community (larger) centres have additional anchors such as discount stores, and off-price stores.

Power centres are shopping centres that consist primarily of collections of big-box retail stores, such as discount stores, off-price stores, warehouse clubs and category specialists. Which types of locations are growing in popularity with retailers?

Why is store location such an important decision for retailers?

Pick your favourite store. Describe the merits and demerits of its current location.

Retailers are developing shopping centres and freestanding locations in central business districts that have suffered decay. Some people have questioned the ethical and social ramification of this process, which is known as gentrification.

The key to successful image is that the consumers view the retailer the manner the firm intends.

Trading Area Analysis and Site Selection

1. Location is an important decision for a retailer because once started, it is very difficult to change (loyal customers and employees lost, store fixtures cannot be easily removed)
2. 90 per cent of retail formats are store - based
3. A good retail location leads to success in businesses
4. The basic criteria of site selection are
   - Demographic data
   - Performance of other stores
   - Competition intensity
   - Transportation access
   - Parking availability
   - Property costs
   - Legal restrictions

Steps in Site Selection

- Market identification (which country to enter)
- Trading area analysis in terms of attractiveness (demography, household, competition etc.)
- Determine whether to locate as an isolated store, unplanned business district or in a planned shopping centre
- Select the above said option
- Analyze alternative sites in the specified retail location type

Step 1 – Market Identification

- Demography
- Economic factors
- Natural factors
- Technological progress

- Government, legal and political factors
- Socio-cultural factors

Step 2 – Trading Area Analysis

- A trading area is geographic area containing the customers of a particular firm. It is **the geographic area that generates the majority of the customers for the store.**
- Knowing the boundaries of the trade area helps the retailer estimate the number of potential customers that may patronize store.
- **Primary trading area** – covers between 50-80 per cent of the stores customers and the area closest to the store – 4 miles.
- **Secondary trading area** – 15-20 per cent of the stores customers – 5 miles.
- **The fringe of tertiary trade area** – covers the balance customers – 10 miles.

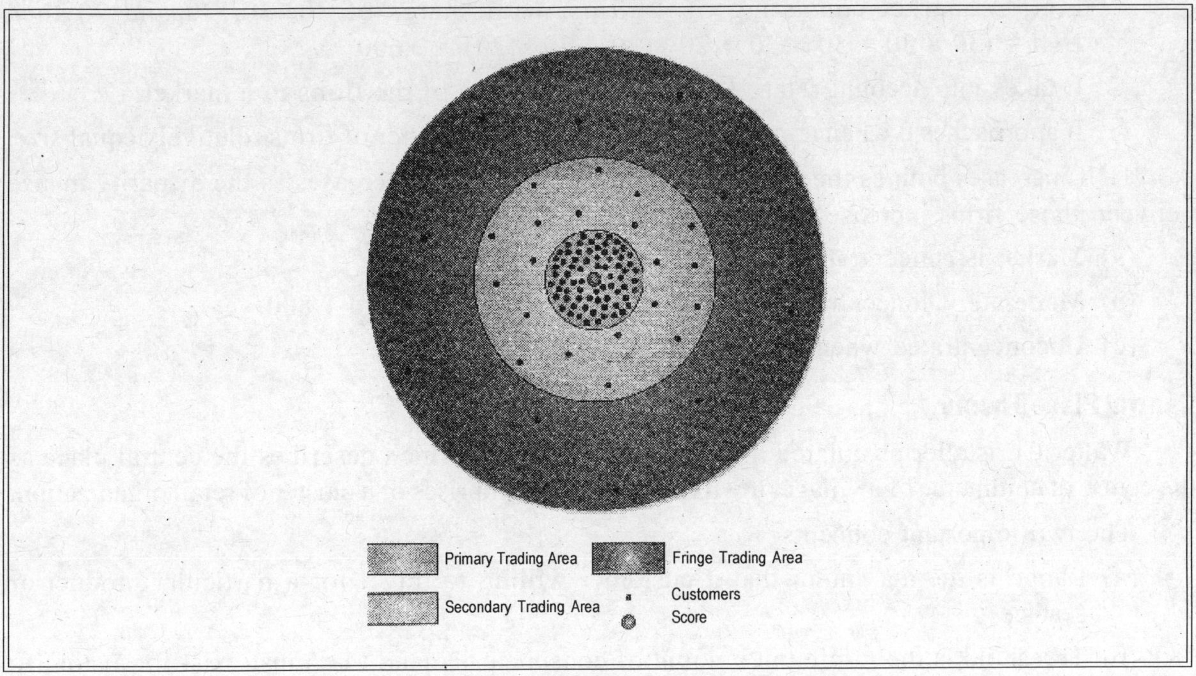

FIG. 25: THE SEGMENTS OF A TRADING AREA

Delineating the Trading Area of an Existing Store

- The size, shape and characteristics of the trading area for an existing store can usually be delineated by
- Store records (secondary data)
- Special study (primary data)

Delineating the Trading Area of a New Store

Trading areas with less defined shopping and traffic patterns – such area must normally be evaluated in terms of opportunity.

- **Trend analysis** – it helps to project the future based on the past – new households.
- **Consumer surveys** – time and distance people would be willing to travel to various possible retail location.
- **Analog model** – simplest and most popular method. on the basis of revenues for similar stores in existing area.
- **Regression model** – shows association between store sales and independent variables like – population size, average income, number of households, etc.

Herfindal – Herschman Index

It is a measure of market concentration

- It is determined by adding the squares of the market shares of each competitor within the relevant product category
- E.g., A market consisting of 4 firms, with shares of 30, 30, 20 and 20 then HHI = (30 × 30 + 30 × 30 + 20 × 20 + 20 × 20) = 2,600

It takes into account relative size and distribution of the firms in a market.

It approaches 0 when a market consists of a large number of firms relatively equal size.

HHI increases both as the number of firms in the market decreases as the disparity in size between those firms increase

(a) Market is concentrated when HHI is above 1,800

(b) Moderately concentrated when HHI is between 1,000 and 1,800

(c) Unconcentrated when HHI is below 1,000

Central Place Theory

Walter Christaller postulated the central place theory which describes the central place as the centre of commerce of a village, town or city which comprises of a cluster of retail organization.

The two important concepts

(a) Range is the maximum that a customer willing to travel for a particular product or service

(b) Threshold is the minimum amount of consumer demand that must exist for a store to survive

The Index of Retail Saturation

1. It measures the market attractiveness. The assumption is that if a market has a low level of retail saturation, the likelihood of success is higher
2. A higher IRS indicates lower level of saturation thereby increasing the likelihood of retail success
3. If the market has too few stores and is unable to satisfy the customer's demand satisfactorily then the market is understored
4. If the number of stores is too many it is overstored and it is unable to give a fair return on investment to retailer

5. $IRS = \frac{LH \times RE}{RF}$
6. IRS = index of retail saturation for a particular area
7. H = number of households in that area
8. RE = annual retail expenditure for a particular line of product of a household in that area
9. RF = square footage of that particular line of trade in that area including the proposed store
10. That is, it is the ratio of demand and supply
11. This theory implies that a retailer needs to clearly check the demand for a particular product or service that he wishes to retail and the number of stores offering the same, i.e., checking demand and supply is more important

REILLY'S LAW OF RETAIL GRAVITATION

1. It establishes a point of indifference between two cities so the trading area can be determined.
2. The point of indifference is the geographic breaking point between two cities at which consumers indifferent to shopping at either.
3. According to Reilly's law more customers go to the larger city because there are more stores and the assortment makes travel time worth.

Assumptions

1. Two competing areas are equally accessible from major road
2. Retailers are equally effective
3. Other factors are held constant

Dab = d/(1 + v(pb/pa)

- Dab = limit of city A's trading area measured in miles along the road to city B
- d = distance in miles along a major roadway between cities A and B
- pa = population of city A
- Pb = population of city B

Example

1. the cities with a population of 90,000(A) and (B) 10,000.
2. If the cities are 20 miles apart the point of indifference for the larger city is calculated as Dab = 20/(1 + v 10,000/90,000) = 15 miles

HUFF'S LAW OF SHOPPER ATTRACTION

It is a method of delineating trading area on the basis of:

1. the product assortment carried at various shopping location
2. travel time from the shoppers home to alternate location
3. the sensitivity of the kind of shopping to travel time

The assortment is rated by the total square foot of selling space a retailer expects all firms in a shopping area to allot to a product category.

Sensitivity to the kind of shopping entails the trips, purposes and the types of goods or services sold or bought.

Algebraic Expression of Huff's Law

- Pij = probability of a consumer's travelling from home i, to the shopping location j
- Sj = square footage of selling space in shopping location j expected to be devoted to a particular product category
- Tij = Travel time from consumer's home i to shopping location j
- λ = parameter used to estimate the effect of travel time on different kinds of shopping trips
- n = different shopping locations

(λ must be determine d through research or by a computer program)

$$P_{ij} = \frac{\dfrac{S_i}{(T_{ij})^{\lambda}}}{\sum_{j=1}^{n} \dfrac{S_i}{(T_{ij})^{\lambda}}}$$

Example

Assume a leased department operator studies three possible locations with 200,300,500 total square feet of store space allocated to men's jeans.

A group of potential customers lives 7 minutes from the first location, 10 minutes from the second and 15 minutes from the third and the operator estimates the effect of travel time to be 2.

- Pi1 = (200/7 × 7)/((200/7 × 7) + (300/10 × 10) + (500/15 × 15)) = 43.9 per cent
- Pi2 = (300/10 × 10)/((200/7 × 7) + (300/10 × 10) + (500/15 × 15)) = 32.2 per cent
- Pi3 = (500/15 × 15)/((200/7 × 7) + (300/10 × 10) + (500/15 × 15)) = 23.9 per cent
- To determine location 1's trading area a similar computation will be made for people living at a driving time of 10,15 ,20 minutes and so on.
- The probability of people shopping at a location depends upon the effect of travel time. If a product is important (TV, watch) consumers are less sensitive to travel. So, here λ of 1 leads to the location preferences like this
  - ∗ Location 1 - 31.1 per cent
  - ∗ Location 2 - 32.6 per cent
  - ∗ Location 3 - 36.3 per cent
  - ∗ Location 3 is more preferred

Benefits

- Reveals opportunities
- Gets idea about media coverage pattern

- The best number of stores for a chain to operate in a given area is calculated
- Anticipate whether competitors want to open nearby stores if the firm does not do so
- A retailer learns whether the location of a proposed branch store will service new customers or take business from its existing stores.

Table 23 : Chief Factors to consider in Evaluating Retail Trading Areas

Population Size and Characteristics	
Total size and density	Total disposable income
Age distribution	Per capita disposable income
Average educational level	Occupation distribution
Percentage of residents owning homes	Trends
Availability of Labour	
Management	
Management trainee	
Clerical	
Closeness to Sources of Supply	
Delivery costs	Number of manufacturers and wholesalers
Timeliness	Availability and reliability of product-lines
Promotion Facilities	
Availability and frequency of media	
Costs	
Waste	
Economic Base	
Dominant industry	Freedom from economic and seasonal fluctuations
Extent of diversification	Availability of credit and financial facilities
Growth projections	
Competitive Situation	
Number and size of existing competitors	Short run and long run outlook
Evaluation of competitor strengths/weaknesses	Level of saturation
Availability of Store Locations	
Number and type of locations	Zoning restrictions
Access to transportation	Costs
Owning versus leasing opportunities	
Regulations	
Taxes	Minimum wages
Licensing	Zoning
Operations	

STEP 3 and 4 - DETERMINING AND SELECTING TYPES OF LOCATION

1. THE ISOLATED STORE – is a free standing retail outlet located on either a highway or a street; there are no adjacent retailers.

Advantages

1. No competition
2. Rental costs are low
3. Larger space may be obtained
4. Better road and traffic visibility
5. More parking space

Disadvantages

1. Initial customers may be difficult to attract
2. Many people will not travel very far to get to one store on a continuous basis
3. Many people like variety in shopping
4. A store must often be built rather than rented
5. Costs such as outside lighting, security, etc., are not shared

2. The Unplanned Business District – is the place of commerce in a city, which developed historically as the centre of trade and commerce in the city or town.

Central Business District – is the main centre of commerce and trade in the city, example in Mumbai, Nariman Point and in Delhi, Connaught place.

Characteristics – peak land rates, intense development, vehicular and pedestrian traffics are very high shoppers drawn from the whole urban area and has at least one major department store and a number of specialty and convenience stores.

Advantages

1. Excellent goods/service assortment
2. Access to public transportation
3. Variety of store type
4. Wide range of prices and customer services
5. High level of traffic and nearness to social and entertainment facilities

Disadvantages

1. Inadequate parking
2. Traffic and delivery congestion
3. More travel time for those living in the suburbs
4. High rent and high cost for property
5. Discontinuity of offerings, such as four shoes store and no pharmacy

Secondary Business District – is one which has evolved over a period of time, with the spread of population within the city. A city may have more than one SBD.

Characteristics – stores are smaller than those in the CBD, smaller trading area and it includes traditional department stores and some specialty stores.

Advantages

1. Access to public transportation
2. Less crowding and personal service
3. Placement nearer to residential area

Disadvantages

1. Discontinuity of offering
2. High rent and parking difficulty
3. Fewer outlets

Neighbourhood Business District – is an unplanned shopping area that appeals to the convenience shopping and service needs of a single residential area. It contains several small stores, such as dry cleaner, stationary store, barber shop, liquor store and a restaurant. The leading retailer is a supermarket or a large drug store.

Advantages

1. Good location
2. Long store hours and a good parking
3. Less hectic atmosphere

Disadvantages

1. Limited selection of goods and services
2. Price is higher
3. Less competition

STRING – it is located along a street or highway. A string may start with an isolated store, success then breeding competitors.

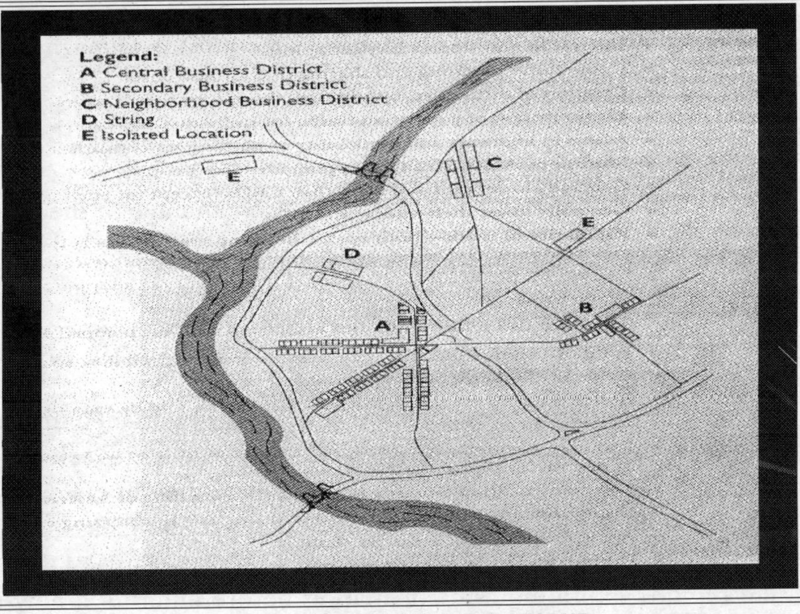

FIG. 26: SHOPPING LEGEND

3. Planned Shopping Centre – A group of retail and other commercial establishments that is planned, developed, owned and managed as a single property. Availability of parking is an important feature of a shopping centre.

Positive Attributes

- Family shopping
- Sharing of common costs
- Creation of distinctive, but unified shopping centre image
- Pedestrian traffic
- Parking space
- Access to highway
- Low theft rate

Limitations

- Reduce retailer's flexibility (working hours)
- Higher rate than isolated store
- Domination by large stores
- Competition
- Expansion is a problem

STEP 5 – LOCATION / SITE EVALUATION CRITERIA

Pedestrian traffic	Number of people, type of people
Vehicular traffic	Number of vehicles, type of vehicles, traffic congestion
Parking facilities	Number and quality of parking spots, distance to stores, availability of employee parking
Transportation	Availability of mass transport, access from major highways, ease of delivery
Store composition	Number and size of stores, retail balance and affinity
Specific site	Visibility ,placement in the location, size and shape of the lot, size and shape of the building, condition and age of the building
Terms of occupancy	Ownership or leasing terms, operations and maintenance cost, taxes and other restrictions
Overall rating	General location and specific store

The classical response to the question "What are the three most important things in retailing?" is "location, location, location". Location is the critical factor in consumers' selection of a store. For example, most people shop at the supermarket closest to where they live. For instance, once Walgreens has put a store at the best location at an intersection. Starbucks has developed a strong competitive advantage with its location selection. It conquers one area of the city at a time and then expands in the region, saturating a major market before entering a new market. For

Table 24 : Steps in Location

Type	Concept	Sq.Ft. (Incl. Anchors)	Number of Anchors	Types of Anchors	Anchor Ratio %	Primary Trade Area
Neighbourhood	Convenience	30,000 – 1,50,000	1 or more	Supermarket	30-50	3 miles
Community Centre	General Merchandise;	1,00,000 – 3,50,000	2 or more	Discount dept. store; supermarket; drug; home improvement discount apparel	40-60	3-7 miles
Regional	General merchandise; fashion (mall typically enclosed)	4,00,000 – 8,00,000	2 or more	Full line dept. store; mass merchant; discount dept. store; fashion apparel	50-70	5-25 miles
Super-regional	Similar to regional but has more variety	8,00,000 +	3 or more	Full line dept. store; merchant; discount debt. store; fashion apparel	50-70	5-25 miles
Fashion/ Specialty	Higher-end fashion-oriented	8,00,000 – 2,50,000	N/A	Fashion	N/A	5-15 miles
Power	Category-dominant anchors; few small tenants	2,50,000 – 6,00,000	3 or more	Category killer; home improvement; discount dept. store; warehouse club; off-price	75-90	5-10 miles
Theme/ Festival	Leisure; tourist-oriented	80,000 – 2,50,000	N/A	Restaurants; entertainment	N/A	N/A
Outlet	Manufacurer's outlet stores	50,000 – 2,50,000	N/A	Manufacturer's outlet stores	N/A	25-75 miles

example, there were over 100 Starbucks outlets in the Scuttle area before the company expanded to a new region. Starbucks will frequently open several stores close to one another.

Decisions about where to locate a store are critical to any retailer's success. Location decisions are particularly important because of their high-cost, long run commitment and impact on customer patronage. Choosing a particular location type involves evaluating a series of trade-offs. These trade-offs generally include the occupancy cost of the location, the pedestrian and vehicle customer traffic associated with the location, the restrictions placed on store operations by the property managers and the convenience of the location for customers. In addition, legal issues need to be considered when selecting a site.

Freestanding sites are retail locations for an individual, isolated store unconnected to other retailers, however, they might be near other freestanding retailers, a shopping centres, or, in the case of a kiosk, inside an office building or shopping centre. Advantage of freestanding location are their convenience for customers (easy access and parking); high vehicular traffic and visibility to attract customers driving by; modest occupancy costs; separation from direct composition; and fewer restrictions on signs, hours, or merchandise, as are typically imposed in shopping centres. For instance, Elizabeth Arden's kiosk at the Forum Shopping Mall at Bengaluru offers mall developers an opportunity for additional revenue from unused space.

Merchandise Kiosks are small temporary selling spaces typically located in the walkways of enclosed malls, airports, train stations, or office building lobbies. Kiosks in office lobbies often sell newspapers, flowers, or snacks.

City or Town Locations: Urban locations particularly cities have attractions for retailers. However, vehicular traffic is limited due to congestion in the inner city and parking problems reduce consumer convenience.

A Shopping Centre is a group of retail and other commercial establishments that is planned, developed, owned and managed as a single property. By combining many stores at one location, disproportionately more consumers are attracted in the shopping centre than if the stores were at separate locations. Most shopping centres have at least one or two major retailers, referred to as anchors. These retailers are courted by the centre developer because they attract a significant number of consumers and consequently make the centre more appealing by other retailers.

Neighbourhood and community centres (strip shopping centres) are an attached row of store – managed as a unit, with onsite parking usually located in the front of the stores. Since the common areas are not enclosed, these centres are often referred to as 'open air centres'. The most common layouts are linear, L-shaped and inverted U-shaped. The term 'strip centre' has been applied to the linear configuration. The neighbourhood (small in size) centres are typically anchored by a supermarket or a drugstore; the community (larger) centres have additional anchors such as discount stores, and off-price stores.

Internal External Atmospherics

Atmospherics refers to the design of an environment through visual communications, lighting, colour, music, and scent to stimulate customers' perceptual and emotional responses and ultimately to affect their purchase behaviour. Many retailers have discovered the subtle benefits of developing atmospherics that complement other aspects of the store design and the merchandise. Research has shown that it is important for these atmospheric elements to work together- for example, the right music with the right scent.

Lighting is used to highlight merchandise, sculpt space, and capture a mood or feeling that enhances the store's image. It has positive influence on shopping behaviour. A good lighting system helps create a sense of excitement in the store. Lighting must provide an accurate colour rendition of the merchandise. A green silk tie should look the same colour in the store as at the customer's office. A department store's cosmetics area, for example, requires more expensive lighting than the bare fluorescent lighting found in most grocery stores because it has to compliment the customer and make her skin look natural.

Highlighting Merchandise: Using lighting to focus on strategic pockets of merchandise trains shoppers' eyes on the merchandise and draws customers strategically through the store. Glass sculptures are highlighted with special lighting focusing spotlights on special items.

Mood Creation: Incandescent lighting sources are employed to promote a warm and cozy ambience. Overall lighting sources were reduced and accent lighting was pronounced to call attention to merchandise and displays. It was meant to feel like someone's home – dim lighting overall, with artwork and other areas of interest highlighted. European stores have long favoured high light levels, cool colours, and little contrast or accent lighting. European lighting design has been more bold, stark, and minimal than in the US, creating a very different mood and image than the softer incandescent lighting.

Display Features: Lighting can hide errors and outmoded store designs. At Sentry Foods in Madison, Wisconsin, product lighting is very high compared with that in the rest of the store. The ceiling was intentionally kept dark to downplay an unsightly concrete ceiling.

Colour: The creative use of colour can enhance a retailer's image and help create a mood. Warm colours (red and yellow) produce excitement, whereas cool colours (blue and green) have a calming effect.

Music: Retailers can also use music to affect customers' behaviour. Music can control the pace of store traffic, create an image, and attract or direct consumers' attention. Like colour and lighting, music can either add to or detract from a retailer's total atmospheric package. Unlike other atmospheric elements, however, music can be easily changed. For example, a retailer with 1,000 stores across the US wants to play jazzy music in the morning and adult contemporary in the afternoon, but just for stores on the East Coast. These selections are made because most of its morning shoppers are older, whereas the afternoon shoppers are more in the 35-40 year age range. For its West Coast stores, it wants modern rock in the morning and Caribbean beats in the afternoon. And in Texas, it's country music all day, everyday.

Scent: Many buying decisions are based on emotions, and smell has a large impact on our emotions, such as happiness, hunger, disgust, and nostalgia – the same feelings marketeers want to tap. Scent, in conjunction with music, has a positive impact on impulse buying behaviour and customer satisfaction. Scents that are neutral produce better perception of the store than no scent. Customers in scented stores think they spent less time in the store than subjects in unscented stores. Stores using scents may improve customers' subjective shopping experience by making them feel that they are spending less time examining merchandise or waiting for sales help or to check out.

Full-time discount stores are retailers that offer a broad variety of merchandise, limited service, and low prices. Discount stores offer both private labels and national brands, but these brands are typically less fashion oriented than the brands in department stores.

Drug stores are specialty stores that concentrate on health and personal grooming merchandise. In India, the highly fragmented drug retail market is worth around ₹ 32,000 crore apart from about ₹ 18,000 added by hospital pharmacies and exports. Organized pharmacy retail, which is only about 3-4 per cent, is expected to grow 25 per cent a year. Big corporate houses like Ranbaxy (Fortis), Reliance Retail, ADAG (Reliance Health Venture), together with other big multi-verticle, multi-formate retailers like Pantaloon (Tulsi) and Subhiksha and other regional health care players like Apollo Pharmacy (Apollo Hospitals Group and Guardian Pharmacy (Guardian Lifecare)), etc., have set up thousands of pharmacies and health care stores in 2010.

Category specialists are big box discount stores that offer a narrow but deep assortment of merchandise. The largest category specialists in India are: Pantation, Koutons, Ritu Wears, the Home Store, Nik Nish, Landmark and Computer Mart.

Extreme Value Retailers are small, full-line discount stores that offer a limited merchandise assortment at very low prices. The largest extreme value retailers are Dollar General and Family Dollar Stores.

Table 25 : Distinction between Mobile Retailers and Immobile Retailers

	Mobile retailers	**Immobile**
Meaning	Such retailers move from one place to another for selling goods since they have no fixed place of business.	Such retailers have a fixed place of business
Capital	They require limited capital	They may require limited or large amount of capital depending on the size of business
Management	They require limited managerial ability.	They require better managerial ability. In certain cases professional management is required.
	Generally, a limited variety of goods is sold.	
Types of goods	Generally, a limited variety of goods is sold.	They sell various types of goods.
Types of business	They do not remain in the same line of business.	They also sell expensive goods. They stick to the same line of business.
Suitability of goods	They are suitable for perishable goods.	They are suitable for all types of perishable and luxurious goods.

Strategic Profit Model

The Strategic Profit Model is a method for summarizing the factors that affects a firm's financial performance as measured by RoA. The model decomposes RoA into two components:

Net profit margin and Asset turnover.

The net profit margin is simply how much profit (after tax) a firm makes divided by its net sales. Thus, it reflects the profits generated from each rupee of sales. If a retailer's net profit margin is 5 per cent, it makes ₹ 05 for every rupee of merchandise or service it sells.

Asset turnover is the retailer's net sales divided by its assets. This financial measure assesses the productivity of a firm's investment in its assets and indicates how many sales rupees are generated by each rupee of assets.

The retailer's RoA is determined by multiplying the two components together:

Net profit margin × Asset turnover = Return on assets (RoA)

Net profit/Net sales × Net sales/Total assets = Net profits/Total assets.

Pull and Push Supply Chains

Information flow illustrates a pull supply chain – a supply chain in which orders for merchandise are generated at the store level on the basis of sales data captured by PoS (point of sales) terminals. Basically, in this type of supply chain, the demand for an item pulls it through the supply chain. An alternative and less sophisticated approach is a push supply chain, in which merchandise is allocated to stores on the basis of predicted demand. Once a forecast is developed, specified quantities of merchandise are shipped (pushed) to distribution centres and stores at predetermined time intervals.

Supply chain management and information systems have become important tools for achieving a sustainable competitive advantage. Developing more efficient methods of distributing merchandise creates an opportunity to realize expense and improve customer service levels.

Multiple Shop (Chain Stores): Stephenson defines multiple shops as 'a system of branch shops operated under a centralized management and dealing in similar line of goods'. They are started by big producers or manufacturers. Usually they deal in one type of product. Under a head office, there are large number of branches. The branches are located in different parts of the country. The head office controls the branches. Therefore, a multiple shop is a retail organization with a number of similar branches. There is a branch manager for each branch. The examples of multiple shops functioning in India are Delhi Cloth Mills, Bata Shoe Company, Carona, etc.

Features of Multiple Shops (Chain Stores)

1. Chain stores are under the same ownership and control
2. Same rules are applicable to all the branches
3. Chain stores are large-scale organization
4. Usually goods are sold on cash basis
5. Uniform prices are charged for similar goods sold in all branches

The multiple shops deal in one or limited varieties of goods. They are identical goods and are sold by all the branches.

Supermarkets: A supermarket is a self-service food store with grocery, meat, and produce departments and minimum annual sales of $ 2 million (in the USA). Included are conventional supermarkets, food-based superstores, combination stores, box (limited-line) stores, and warehouse stores.

A **conventional supermarket** is a departmentalized food store with a wide range of food and related products; sales of general merchandise are rather limited. This institution started 75 years ago when it was recognized that large-scale operations would let a retailer combine volume sales, self-service, and low prices. Self-service enabled supermarkets to both cut costs and increase volume. Personnel costs were reduced and impulse buying increased. The car and the refrigerator contributed to the supermarket's success by lowering travel costs and adding to the life span of perishables.

A **food-based superstore** is large and more diversified than a conventional supermarket but usually smaller and less diversified than a combination store. This format originated in the 1970s, as supermarkets sought to stem sales declines by expanding store size and the number of non-food items carried. Some supermarkets merged with drug stores or general merchandise stores but more grew into food-based superstores. There are more than 8,500 food-based US superstores, with sales of more than $ 170 billion.

A **combination store** unit refers to supermarkets (in the USA) and general merchandise in one facility, with general merchandise accounting for 25 to 40 per cent of sales. The format began in the late 1960s and early 1970s, a common checkout areas were set up for separately owned supermarkets and drugstores or supermarkets and general merchandise stores. The natural offshoot was integrating operations under one management. Meijer, Fred Meyer, and Albertson's are some of the combination stores in the USA.

A **super centre** is a combination store blending an economy supermarket with a discount department store. It is the US version of the even larger hypermarket (the European institution pioneered by firms such as Carrefour that did not succeed in the USA). As a rule, the majority of super centre sales are from non-food items. Stores usually range from 75,000 to 1,50,000 square feet in size and they stock up to 50,000 and more items, much more than the 30,000 or so items carried by other combination stores. Wal-Mart, Kmart, and Target all operate some super centres.

Box (Limited Line) Store is a food-based discounter that focuses on a small selection of items, moderate hours of operation (compared to other supermarkets), few services, limited manufacturer brands. It carries less than 2,000 items, few refrigerated perishables, and few sizes and brands per item. Prices are on shelves or overhead signs. Items are displayed in cut cases. Customers bag their purchases. Box stores rely on low-priced private-label brands. Their prices are 20 to 30 per cent below supermarkets. The box store originated in Europe and was exported to the USA in the mid-1970s. The leading box store operators are Save-A-Lot and Aldi.

Warehouse store is a food-based discounter offering a moderate number of food items in a no-frills setting. It appeals to one-stop food shoppers, concentrates on special purchase of popular brands, uses cut-case displays, offers little service, posts prices on shelves, and locates in secondary sites. The largest warehouse store is known as a super warehouse.

A **department store** is a large retail unit with an extensive assortment (width and depth) of goods and services that is organized into separate departments for purposes of buying, promotion, customer service, and control. It has the most selection of any general merchandise retailer, often serves as the anchor store in a shopping centre or district, has strong credit card penetration, and is usually part of a chain. To be classified as a department store, a retailer must sell a wide range of products – such as apparel, furniture, appliances and home furnishing; and selected other items, such as paint, hardware, toiletries, cosmetics, photo equipment, jewellery, toys, and sporting goods – with no one merchandise line predominating.

Department stores are among the retailers seeking multiple market segments. They cater to several customer groups, with unique goods and services for each. Apparel may be sold in a number of distinctive boutiques in the store.

At a traditional department store, merchandise quality ranges from average to quite good. Pricing is moderate to above average. Customer service ranges from medium levels of sales help, credit, delivery, and so forth to high levels of each. For example, Macy's targets middle-class shoppers interested in assortment and moderate prices, whereas Bloomingdale's aims at upscale consumers through more trendy merchandise and higher prices. **Department Stores** are retailers that carry a broad variety and deep assortment, offer customer services, and organize their stores into distinctly separate departments for displaying merchandise.

A **Full Line Discount Store** is a type of department store with these features:

1. It conveys the image of a high-volume, low-cost outlet selling a broad product assortment for less than conventional prices.
2. It is more apt to carry the range of product-lines once expected at department stores.
3. Shopping carts and centralized checkout service are provided.
4. Customer service is not usually provided within store departments.
5. Buildings, equipment, and fixtures are less expensive, and operating costs are lower than for traditional department stores and specialty stores.
6. Non-durable (soft) goods features private brands, whereas durable (hard) goods emphasize well known manufacturer brands.

A **Variety Store** handles an assortment of inexpensive and popularly priced goods and services, such as apparel and accessories, costume jewellery, notions and small wares, candy, toys, and other items in the price range. There are open displays and few salespeople. The stores do not carry full product-lines. The conventional variety store format (led by Woolworth and McCrory) disappeared from the US marketplace in the mid-1990s, because of heavy competition from specialty stores and discounters.

An **Off-price Chain** features brand-name (sometimes designer) apparel and accessories, footwear (primarily women's and family), linens, fabrics, cosmetics, and/or housewares and sells them at everyday low prices in an efficient, limited-service environment. It frequently has community dressing rooms, centralized checkout counter, no gift wrapping, and extra charges for alterations. The four biggest chains are T. J. Maxx and Marshalls (both owned by TJX), Ross Stores, and Burlington Coat Factory.

At a **flea market**, many retail vendors sell a range of products at discount prices in plain surroundings. It is rooted in the centuries-old tradition of street selling-shoppers touch and sample items, and haggle over prices.

Off-price retailers offer an inconsistent assortment of brand name merchandise at low prices. America's largest off-price retail chains are TJX Companies, Ross Stores and Burlington Coat Factory.

Closeout retailers are off-price retailers that sell a broad but inconsistent assortment of general merchandise as well as apparel and soft home goods (e.g., Big Lots).

Electronic Retailers (also called e-tailing, online retailing, and internet retailing) is a retail format in which the retailers communicate with customers and offer products and services for sale over the internet. Even though online retail sales continue to grow much faster than retail sales through stores and catalogue, we now realize the internet is not a revolutionary new retail format that will replace stores and catalogue. Some of the most well known internet-based companies associated with retailing, Amarzon.com and eBay, are not really retailers. They provide website development and fulfilment services for other retailers.

Catalogue Retailing is a non-store retail format in which the retail offering is communicated to a customer through a catalogue, whereas direct-mail retailers communicate with their customer using letters and brochures.

Retail Branding: A retail brand can create an emotional tie with customers that build their trust and loyalty. Retail brands also facilitate store loyalty because they stand for a predictable level of quality that customers feel comfortable with and often seek. A strong retail brand also becomes part of a retailer's positioning strategy.

PRODUCT

A product is any offering that can satisfy a need or want. Products that are marketed include physical goods, services, experiences, events, persons, places, properties, organizations, information, and ideas.

Product Positioning: Definitions

Although there are different definitions of positioning, probably the most common is: "A product's position is how potential buyers see the product", and is expressed relative to the position of competitors.

Positioning is a concept in marketing which was first popularized by Al Ries and Jack Trout in their bestseller book *"Positioning – a Battle for Your Mind"*.

This differs slightly from the context in which the term was first published in 1969 by Jack Trout in the paper *"Positioning" is a game people play in today's me-too marketplace"* in the publication *Industrial Marketing*, in which the case is made that the typical consumer is overwhelmed with unwanted advertising, and has a natural tendency to discard all information that does not immediately find a comfortable (and empty) slot in the consumers mind. It was then expanded into their ground-breaking first book, "*Positioning: The Battle for Your Mind*", in which they define positioning as "an organized system for finding a window in the mind. It is based on the concept that communication can only take place at the right time and under the right circumstances".

What most will agree on is that positioning is something (perception) that happens in the minds of the *target market*. It is the aggregate perception the market has of a particular company, product or service in relation to their perceptions of the competitors in the same category. It will happen whether or not a company's management is proactive, reactive or passive about the on-going process of evolving a position. But a company can positively influence the perceptions through enlightened strategic actions.

Retail Positioning is the act of designing the retailer's offering and image to occupy a distinctive place in the target market's mind. Positioning involves the design and implementation of retail mix to create an image of the retailer in the customer's mind relative to its competitors. Positioning involves the design and implementation of a retail mix to create an image of the retailer in the customer's mind relative to its competitors. Positioning emphasizes that the image in the customer's mind (not the retail manager's mind) is critical. The end result of positioning is the successful creation of a market-focused value proposition, a cogent reason why the target market should buy the product. The word positioning was popularized by two advertising executives.

Al Ries and Jack Trout: They see positioning as a creative exercise done with an existing product. Positioning starts with a product, a piece of merchandise, a service, a company, an institution, or even a person. Positioning is not what you do to a product but it is what you do to the mind of the prospect. That is, you position the product in the mind of the prospect. Ries and Trout favour one consistent positioning message. Each brand select an attribute and tout itself as 'number one' on that attribute. Number-one positioning include 'best quality', 'best service', 'lowest price', 'best value', 'safest', 'fastest', 'most customized', 'most convenient' and 'most advanced technology". If a company hammers away at one of these positioning and delivers on it, it will probably be best known and recalled for this strength. Home Depot (USA) has gained a reputation for 'best service' among home-improvement product retailers.

Double-benefit positioning may be necessary if two or more claim to be best on the same attribute. Steelcase, Inc., a leading office-furniture-systems company, claims two benefits: best on-time delivery and best installation support. Volvo positions its automobiles as 'safest' and 'most durable'. There are even cases of successful triple-benefit positioning. SmithKline Beecham promotes its Aquafresh toothpaste as offering three benefits: anticavity protection, better breath, and whiter teeth.

Retailers can Position Themselves as Offering One of Four Levels of Service

Self-service: It is the cornerstone of all discount operations. Many customers are willing to carry-out their own locate-compare-select process to save money.

Self-selection: Customers find their own goods, although they can ask for assistance. Customer complete their transactions by paying a salesperson for the item.

Limited Service: These retailers carry more shopping goods, and customers need more information and assistance. The stores also offer services (such as credit and merchandise-return privileges).

Full Service: Salespeople are ready to assist in every phase of the locate-compare-select process. Customers who like to be waited on prefer this type of store. The high staffing cost, along with the higher proportion of specialty goods and slower-moving items and the many services, results in high-cost retailing.

Four Broad Positioning Strategies

Bloomingdale's: Stores that features a broad product assortment and high value added. These types of stores pay close attention to store design, product quality, service, and image. Their profit margin is high, and if they are fortunate enough to have high volume, they will be very profitable.

Tiffany: Stores that features a narrow product assortment and high value added. Such stores cultivate an exclusive image and tend to operate on a high margin and low volume.

Sunglass Hut: Stores that features a narrow line and low value added. Such stores keep their costs and prices low by designing similar stores and centralizing buying, merchandising, advertising, and distribution.

Wal-Mart: Stores that features a broad line and low value added. They focus on keeping prices low so that they have an image of being a place for good buys. They make up for low margin by high volume. Wal-Mart CEO Mr. Mike Duke during his visit to India on 1st November, 2010 stated that Wal-Mart will have 100 per cent FDI in retail sector in India.

In marketing, **positioning** has come to mean the process by which marketeers try to create an image or identity in the minds of their target market for its **product, brand,** or **organization**. It is the 'relative competitive comparison' their product occupies in a given market as perceived by the target market.

Re-positioning involves changing the identity of a product, relative to the identity of competing products, in the collective minds of the target market.

De-positioning involves attempting to change the identity of competing products, relative to the identity of your own product, in the collective minds of the target market.

Positioning Errors

Underpositioning: When Pepsi introduced its clear Crystal Pepsi in 1993, customers were distinctly unimpressed. They didn't see 'clarity' as an important benefit in a soft drink.

Overpositioning: Buyers may have too narrow an image of the brand. Thus, a consumer might think that diamond rings at Tiffany start at $ 5,000 when in fact Tiffany now offers affordable diamond rings starting at $ 1,000.

Confused Positioning: Buyers might have a confused image of the brand resulting from the company's making too many claims or changing the brand's positioning too frequently. This was the case with Stephen Jobs's sleek and powerful Next desktop computer which was positioned first for students, then for engineers, and then for business people, all unsuccessfully.

Doubtful Positioning: Buyers may find it hard to believe the brand claims in view of the product's features, price, or manufacturer. When GM's Cadillac division introduced the Cimarron, it positioned the car as a luxury competitor with BMW, Mercedes, and Audi. Although the car featured leather seats, a luggage rack, lots of chrome, and a Cadillac logo stamped on the chassis, customers saw the car as merely a dolled-up version of Chevy's Cavalier and Oldmobile's Firenza. Although the car was positioned as 'more for more', the customers saw it as 'less for more'.

Different Positioning Strategies

Attribute positioning (Such as size or number of years in existence). Disneyland can advertise itself as the largest theme park in the world.

Benefit positioning (Leader in a certain benefit)

Use or application positioning (Product as best for some user group)

Competitor positioning (The product claims to be better in some way than a named competitor.)

Product category positioning (Leader in a certain product category)

Quality or price positioning (Offering the best value)

Product Category Positioning: The product is positioned as the leader in a certain product category. Marine land of the Pacific can position itself not as a 'recreational theme park' but as an 'educational institution'.

Price or Quality Positioning: The product is positioned as offering the best value. Busch Gardens can position itself as offering the 'best value' for the money.

Attribute Positioning: A company positions itself on an attribute, such as size or number of years in existence. Disneyland can advertise itself as the largest theme park in the world. Athisayam theme park near Paravai at Madurai, Black Thunder at Ooty road, Mettupalayam and VGP Golden Beach at Old Mamallapuram Road, Chennai, Kiskinta and MGP Park at Chennai are the theme parks in Tamil Nadu.

Benefit Positioning: The product is positioned as the leader in a certain benefit. Knott's Berry Farm may try to position itself as theme park that delivers a fantasy experience, such as living in the Old West.

Competitor Positioning: The product claims to be better in some way than a named competitor. For example, Lion Country Safari can advertise having a greater variety of animals than Japanese Deer Park.

User Positioning: Positioning the product as best for some user group. Magic Mountain can advertise itself as best for 'thrill seekers'.

Use or Application Positioning: Positioning the product as best for some use or application. Japanese Deer Park can position itself for the tourist who has only an hour to catch some quick entertainment.

Service Quality: A retailer may win by delivering consistently higher-quality service than competitors and exceeding customers' expectations. These expectations are formed by their past experiences, word of mouth, and advertising. After receiving the service, customers compare the perceived service with the expected service. If the perceived service falls below the expected service, customers lose interest in the provider. If the perceived service meets or exceeds their expectations, they are apt to use the provider again. The following gaps have to be eradicated to promote successful delivery:

Gap between consumer expectation and management perception.

Gap between management perception and service-quality specification.

Gap between service-quality specification and service delivery.

Gap between service delivery and external communications.

Gap between perceived service and expected service.

The following are the determinants of service quality:

Reliability: The ability to perform the promised service dependably and accurately.

Responsiveness: The willingness to help customers and to provide prompt service.

Assurance: The knowledge and courtesy of employees and their ability to convey trust and confidence.

Empathy: The provision of caring individualized attention to customers.

Tangibles: The appearance of physical facilities, equipment, personnel and communication materials.

Customer complaints: Studies of customer dissatisfaction show that customers are dissatisfied with their purchases about 25 per cent of the time but that only 5 per cent complain. The other 95 per cent either feel that complaining is not worth the effort, or that they don't know how or to whom to complain.

The retail management is expected to resolve customer complaints by means of:

Hiring criteria and training programmes that take into account retailers' service recovery role.

To develop guidelines for service recovery that focus on achieving fairness and customer satisfaction.

Removing barriers that make it difficult for customers to complain.

Maintaining customer and product databases that let the retail management analyze types and sources of complaints and adjust its policies.

Perceived Value Pricing: An increasing number of companies base price on the customer's perceived value. They see the buyers' perceptions of value, not the seller's cost, as the key to pricing. They use the other marketing-mix elements, such as advertising and sales force, to build up perceived value in buyers' minds.

Value Pricing: The retail management charges a fairly low price for a high-quality offering. Value pricing says that the price should represent a high-value offer to consumers.

Psychological Pricing: Many consumers use price as an indicator of quality. Higher-priced cars are perceived to possess high quality. Higher-quality cars are likewise perceived to be higher priced than they actually are.

The price must be consistent with retail management's pricing policy. Many retail companies set up a pricing department to develop policies and establish or approve decisions. The aim is to ensure that the salespeople quote prices that are reasonable to customers and profitable to the company. Retail management usually does not set a single price but rather a pricing structure that reflects variations in geographical demand and costs, market segment requirements, purchase variations in geographical demand and costs, market-segment requirements, purchase timing, order levels, delivery frequency, guarantees, service contracts, and other factors. As a result of discounts, allowances, and promotional support, a company rarely realizes the same profit from each unit of a product that it sells.

Positioning of Retail Shops

The original work on positioning was consumer marketing oriented, and was not as much focused on the question relative to competitive products as much as it was focused on cutting through the ambient "noise" and establishing a moment of real contact with the intended recipient. In the classic example of Avis claiming "No.2, We Try Harder", the point was to say something so shocking (it was by the standards of the day) that it cleared space in your brain and made you forget all about who was No. 1, and not to make some philosophical point about being "hungry" for business.

The growth of high-tech marketing may have had much to do with the shift in definition towards competitive positioning.

Product Positioning Process

Generally, the product positioning process involves:

1. Defining the market in which the product or brand will compete (who the relevant buyers are)
2. Identifying the attributes (also called dimensions) that define the product 'space'
3. Collecting information from a sample of customers about their perceptions of each product on the relevant attributes
4. Determine each product's share of mind
5. Determine each product's current location in the product space
6. Determine the target market's preferred combination of attributes (referred to as an *ideal vector*)
7. Examine the fit between:
    - The position of your product
    - The position of the ideal vector
8. Position.

The process is similar for positioning your company's services. Services, however, don't have the physical attributes of products – that is, we can't feel them or touch them or show nice product pictures. So you need to ask first your customers and then yourself, what value do clients get from my services? How are they better off from doing business with me? Also ask: Is there a characteristic that makes my services different?

Write out the value customers derive and the attributes your services offer to create the first draft of your positioning. Test it on people who don't really know what you do or what you sell, watch their facial expressions and listen for their response. When they want to know more because you've piqued their interest and started a conversation, you'll know you're on the right track.

Positioning Concepts

More generally, there are three types of positioning concepts:

1. Functional positions
    - Solve problems
    - Provide benefits to customers
    - Get favourable perception by investors (stock profile) and lenders
2. Symbolic positions
    - Self-image enhancement
    - Ego identification

- Belongingness and social meaningfulness
- Affective fulfilment

3. Experiential positions
    - Provide sensory stimulation
    - Provide cognitive stimulation

Measuring the Positioning

Positioning is facilitated by a graphical technique called perceptual mapping, various survey techniques, and statistical techniques like multidimensional scaling, factor analysis, conjoint analysis, and logic analysis.

Repositioning a Company

In volatile markets, it can be necessary – even urgent – to reposition an entire company, rather than just a product-line or brand. Take, for example, when Goldman Sachs and Morgan Stanley suddenly shifted from investment to commercial banks. The expectations of investors, employees, clients and regulators all need to shift, and each company will need to influence how these perceptions change. Doing so involves repositioning the entire firm.

This is especially true of small and medium-sized firms, many of which often lack strong brands for individual product-lines. In a prolonged recession, business approaches that were effective during healthy economies often become ineffective and it becomes necessary to change a firm's positioning. Upscale restaurants, for example, which previously flourished on expense account dinners and corporate events, may for the first time need to stress value as a sale tool.

Repositioning a company involves more than a marketing challenge. It involves making hard decisions about how a market is shifting and how a firm's competitors will react. Often these decisions must be made without the benefit of sufficient information, simply because the definition of "volatility" is that change becomes difficult or impossible to predict.

Positioning — how consumers perceive a brand or firm relative to its competitors — can ensure success. It can also contribute to failure. Unfortunately, positioning is one of the most misunderstood marketing concepts, Tony Adams explains. Four factors need to be considered when selecting the positioning for a brand or firm, Adams says. These are: 1) the positioning used by competitors; 2) the likely reaction to the chosen positioning strategy; 3) the compatibility of the desired positioning with consumer's needs, wants, and the current perception of the product's positioning versus its competition in the given product class; and 4) the firm's objectives and strategy. Three examples of positioning from mass merchandisers are:

- Wal-Mart — better value, low price;
- Target — more upscale, cheap, chic
- K-Mart — strong ethnic, blue collar, urban presence.

Yet K-Mart's use of Jacqueline Smith and Martha Stewart brands to appeal to blue collar urbanites is not in sync with how it positions itself, suggests Adams.

Adams has developed a model to assist marketers in developing the positioning for a brand. The following sentence can be used once: core user, brand name, competitive framework, brand benefit, and support for the brand are determined.

"To core user, brand name is the competitive framework that brand benefit because it supports and supports".

Market and Retail Brand Positioning

The ability to target shoppers through an understanding of their attitudes and buying behaviour is crucial to the correct positioning of any product or retail brand.

FSP uses an original form of Consumer Segmentation and Market Analysis to understand how markets work and the positions within them held by potential competitors, based on shopper attitudes, behaviours and life-stages. These techniques allow retailers and manufacturers to classify shoppers in order to identify exactly where their current offering is positioned, move existing products to new positions and target products effectively to the customer from the pre-launch onwards. The analysis includes the scale and nature of opportunities and the existing, or likely, competition.

Brand positioning is a complex science, but made even more complex by many consultants. FSP uses a system that combines depth of insight with simplicity. Unlike some cluster-based systems, each segment relates intuitively to one another and gives clients results that are easy to understand.

FSP's service extends to Brand Tracking, which provides a method of regularly verifying the market position of your brand.

Failure to position the brand correctly is one of the key reasons for failure of businesses.

Retailers must rethink positioning policies to differentiate themselves from competitors during slow-growth or no-growth periods. Market positioning helps customers identify differences between retailers. Customer loyalty must be attracted by emphasis either on price or services. The low-price, low-service approach is appealing for new, large-volume retailers, but small, new stores and existing traditional stores must adopt a high-price, high-service approach with service as the key to retail positioning strategies. Department stores and specialty shops must avoid the tendency to compete on the basis of price, because cost structure and other variables are only flexible in the long-term. Improved services must also be included in their positioning strategies, with sufficient profit margins to cover the costs of providing these services.

Image: It is the set of beliefs, ideas, and impressions a person holds regarding an object. People's attitudes and actions toward an object are highly conditioned by that object's image. The retailer should create an image and value for his product meant for sales. A retailer builds customer loyalty by developing a clear, distinctive image of its retail offering and consistently reinforcing that image through merchandise and service. The retailer needs to research what its image is and make sure that it is consistent with what customers in its target market want. A perceptual map is frequently used to represent the customer's held image and preferences for retailers. The product or offering will be successful if it delivers value and satisfaction to the target buyer. Perceptual maps may be developed to indicate how similar the retail stores appear to consumers. For example, the two primary characteristics, *viz.*, fashion/style and service may be marked (in the form of dots) on the map which will indicate the characteristics of an ideal retailer for consumers in different market segments. Retailers typically use TV for image advertising, to take advantage of the high reproduction quality and the opportunity to communicate through both visual images and sound. TV ads can also demonstrate product image.

The buyer chooses between different offerings on the basis of which is perceived to deliver the most value. We define value as a ratio between what the customer gets and what he gives.

Do you have a brand image that is good? Is the strength of that image reflected in what you achieve at retail? Surprisingly, it often is not. There are three major brands shown in the figure above. Only one-Apple can manage both. That is why it is such a success. That is why its sales, image and share price continue to grow, let alone its profits. Today, brands are squeezed by retailers, private labels, media and shoppers. Brands need to reconnect with their shoppers. Brands need to move from a focus on brand awareness to a focus on brand selection. Successful brands in the future will be those with relevant new actionable shopper insights. We need to spend our efforts re-obsessing about a company's prime objective – creating sales. The retail management can increase the value of the customer offering in several ways:

- Raise benefits
- Reduce costs
- Raise benefits and reduce costs
- Raise benefits by more than the raise in costs
- Lower benefits by less than the reduction in costs

The customer who is choosing between two value offerings, V1 and V2, will examine the ratio V1/V2. The customer will favour V1, if the ratio is larger than one, he will favour V2 if the ratio is smaller than one; and he will be indifferent if the ratio is equal to one.

Value is the ratio of what customers receive (the perceived benefit of the products and services offered by the retailer) to what they have to pay for it.

Value = Perceived Benefits/Price

In a retailing context, the name of the retailer is a brand that indicates to consumers the type of merchandise and services offered by that retailer. Retailers develop brand images and build customer loyalty. (The brand image is a set of associations that are usually organized around some meaningful themes). Some retailers develop private-label brands that are exclusively sold through their channel. This private-label merchandise bears the retailer's name, such as Walgreens aspirin. The value that a brand image offers retailers is referred to as brand equity. Strong brand names can affect the customer's decision making process, motivate repeat visits and purchases and build loyalty. In addition, strong brand names enable retailers to charge higher prices and lower their marketing costs. A strong brand image also enables retailers to increase their margins. When retailers have high customer loyalty, they can engage in premium pricing and reduce their reliance on price promotions to attract customers. Brands with weaker images are forced to offer low prices and frequent sales to maintain their market share. A retailer builds customer loyalty by developing a clear, distinctive image of its retail offering and consistently reinforcing that image through its merchandise and service.

BUILDING RETAIL STORE IMAGE

The opening up of the Indian retail sector has seen a proliferation of the corporate players through different retail formats and stores – the majority being in the food and groceries. This necessitates creating, building, and managing differentiated retail store brands, and image differentiation, to attract and retain shoppers. Indian shoppers have started identifying the dimensions of retail store image and are differentiating the various stores on the basis of functional attributes. Eventually, the stores would have to create differentiation based on psychological attributes.

Store's own brands can provide important opportunities for retail differentiation if they are considered by consumers to be uniquely associated with store image. A survey of shoppers measured attitudes toward individual stores' images and store brand perceptions, as well as general attitudes toward store brands. A regression analysis demonstrates a positive relationship between consumers' perceptions of individual store own brands and their associated store's image dimensions and attitudes toward store brands in general.

Corporate culture allows superstores with remarkable degree of managerial autonomy.

From giving associates the freedom to design their own name badges to the option of owning company stock (after two years of service), Borders' corporate culture consistently encourages individuality within the framework of a large corporate force.

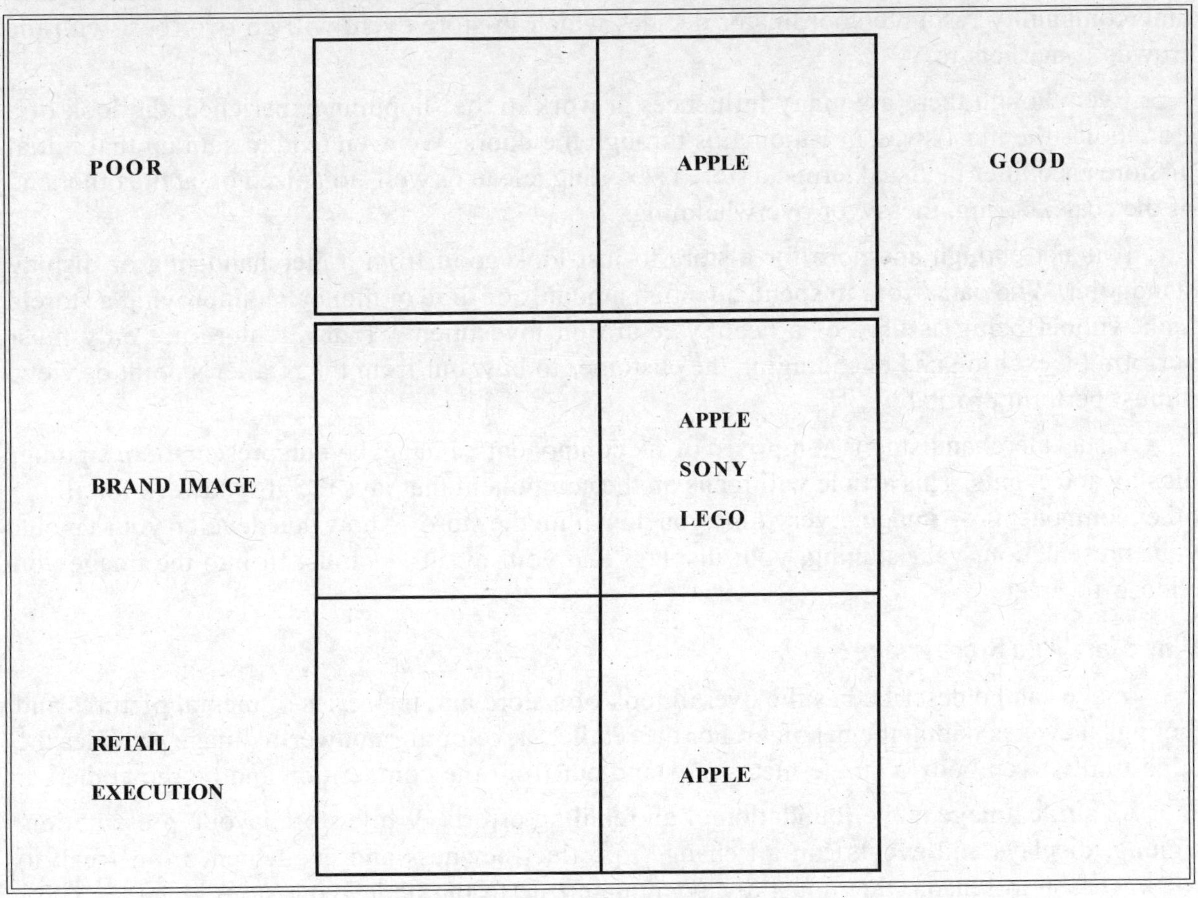

FIG. 27: IMAGE VS. EXECUTION GRID

"As a company, we're not about uniformity", said Vincent Altruda, senior VP retail operations for the 126-unit, dress-code-free chain, or "a collection of fine book stores" as it prefers to be called. The typical Borders store measures 30,000 sq. ft., and each unit is staffed with a full-time community resource coordinator (CRC) who plans 30 in-store events per month, including book signings, how to classes, live music performances, children-related activities or whatever matches the individual market.

But aside from stocking best-sellers and some of the fixtures, each superstore is empowered to find its own niche in the local marketplace.

The retailer has to figure out who is his customer, and then he has to find a way to express the personality of the people he wants to serve. Every store should look different.

For example, the recently debuted downtown Boston superstore opened inside a former three-level bank and has modified the vault from the old Boston Five Bank to serve as the spot for special-order processing.

Borders' proprietary information system, "The Expert System", which enables Borders to maintain its dominant position in title selection, is the base upon which the company's micromarketing strategy and operations rest.

Each store's merchandise manager decides the look of the end-caps, and each unit's full-time community resource coordinator decides which in-store event will go over best with the crowds it markets to.

Even though there are many influences at work in the shopping experience, the look of a store holds the most sway in enticing us through the doors. We even tend to sum up that initial in-store encounter in visual terms: a store is exciting, clean or well-organized or, at the other end of the scale, boring, messy, or overwhelming.

It is not enough anymore for a store to just look good from a merchandising or display standpoint. Who can afford to spend quantum amounts of time or money on improving a store's look without being assured of a healthy return on investment? Today, a store not only must perform by exciting and encouraging the customer to buy, but from the retailer's point of view, it must perform profitably.

Visual merchandising is comprised of six components: image, layout, presentation, signing, display and events. This article will focus on the component that lays the groundwork for all the other components — image. Everything you do within the store — how you develop your layout, your presentation, your signing, your displays and your events — must fit into the image you choose to create.

Why Start With Store Image?

Image can be described as the overall look of a store and the series of mental pictures and feelings it evokes within the beholder. For the retailer, developing a powerful image provides the opportunity to embody a single message, stand out from the competition and be remembered.

As a rule, image is the foundation of all retailing efforts. While store layout, presentation, signing, displays and events can all change to reflect newness and excitement from week to week, season to season, they must always remain true to the underlying store image.

Studies indicate that a retailer has roughly seven seconds to capture the attention of a passing customer. The following elements combine to form a distinctive image that not only reaches out and grabs the customer's attention, but makes a positive impression within those precious few seconds.

The Image-makers

1. An Identifiable Store Name
2. A Powerful Visual Trademark
3. An Unmistakable Storefront
4. An Inviting Entrance
5. A Consistent and Compelling Store Look and Hook

1. Identifiable Store Names, What's in a Name?

An effective store name sets the tone and provides a store's identification by conjuring up an image in the customer's mind.

A store name should be easy to say and remember, indicative of the images and feelings you want the customer to retain and unlikely to sound dated in a few years.

2. Powerful Visual Trademarks

On Your Mark An identifiable trademark adds a visual image to the memory recall of a store name, by combining words and pictures, colour, shape, typeface, texture and/or style to make it stand out. Identifiable even in the absence of the store name, a successful trademark should be unique to you, indicative of your products and services, consistent with the overall impression you want to leave on customers and be professional and well-designed.

3. Unmistakable Storefronts Traffic Stoppers

Customers simply don't have the time to "read" into the store, so just as your store name and trademark — the title of your "book" — must provide instant recognition and recall, your exterior storefront — the cover of your "book" — must project a welcoming, clear and concise image of what's in-store.

Traffic-stopping storefronts use a thoughtful combination of exterior architecture, signing and window displays to ensure a powerful first impression.

Exterior Architecture

A store's exterior look is often referred to as the architecture, and comprises aspects such as building materials, architectural style and detail, colours and textures. A store in a Victorian brownstone building, for example, will exude images associated with the building's architectural era, such as cozy, tastefully cluttered and comfortable.

If your exterior architecture is not projecting the right image, consider painting or refacing the storefront, adding or removing some architectural elements in keeping with your image, or consulting a designer to totally re-engineer the storefront.

The Store Sign

The store sign is a vital element of the storefront, identifying your store and beckoning the customer to take notice and stop. In realizing the value of a strong storefront sign, many retailers are employing new design techniques which include projecting or cantilevering the store sign beyond the lease line, adding motion, or using three-dimensional lettering and unique lighting applications to add depth to the sign.

If your storefront sign is losing the battle for visual dominance among neighbouring stores, consider repainting it or adding more colour, making it bigger and bolder, incorporating your trademark, using new, more contemporary materials to create your sign, and/or adding motion or lighting.

Store Windows

A store's exterior window or glass storefront provides an additional opportunity to reach out and grab the passing customer. Windows are integral in creating a positive impression since they offer an opportunity to begin telling your store's unique merchandise story immediately.

Many retailers underestimate the powerful pull of an effective window, treating the area more as additional stock space than the true image-maker and magnet it can be. This prime real estate should be approached as a showcase for the newest seasonal merchandise dramatized with props and themes in keeping with your store image.

Consider adding motion to your window with animated displays, turntables, fans, video-screens or motorized pulleys.

The Customer's Vantage Point

In planning your storefront, utmost consideration must be given to the customer's vantage point. Place yourself in the customer's shoes in considering their reverie — the speed at which they are travelling, their preoccupation-levels and the chances of getting them to stop. The more hurried and distracted a customer is, the less chance there is of getting their attention.

Often, plans that look good on paper fail miserably because they are developed from the retailer's vantage point, not the customer's. Many retailers plan their storefronts based on a "head-on" perspective, which entails a direct 90 degree-angle approach. But is that the customer's vantage? Not typically. Usually, the direction of customer traffic flow is influenced "by the location of a parking lot, a public transportation terminus or some other physical feature... displays canted or slanted to that dominant direction of traffic will get more serious attention".

To increase the chances of customers noticing your store, consider the following: What direction and angle is the customer coming from? Is your exterior sign visible and legible from a distance? Is the traffic predominantly drive by or walk by? Are there any discernible traffic patterns and at what speed are they moving at various times of the day? Are your store windows easy to read from the distance will the customer first notice them?

One brilliant pet retailer made sure that dog-walkers didn't pass by his store — he placed an antique fire hydrant right beside his entrance.

4. *The Store Entrance*

The entrance to the store is the division between the outside and inside environments. Mall retailers have an easier chance of luring customers into the store with a wide, open entrance, creating a seamless entry from the mall to the store. Retailers who depend largely on impulse traffic should try to create an open storefront, either by removing storefront barriers completely or by creating an unobstructed view into the store with a glass frontage.

Street retailers and some mall tenants who require portals due to climate control or a need for intimacy or security, have less opportunity to give customers a tantalizing taste of the interior, therefore have a greater challenge of persuading them through the door. For these retailer, an unobstructed and welcoming doorway combined with a great window display can provide the lure.

In all types of store entrances, customers need to get the impression that they (and their children) will be comfortable and welcome. Obstacle courses, visual clutter and "Do Not" signs on the doors are negative turn-offs that often result in a negative first impression and a lost customer.

Multiplying Positive Impressions

Creating a consistent positive impression is important — particularly so if you have more than one store. Customers should be able to recognize and identify with your store, whether it is in Victoria or Moncton. Even if your multiple locations differ in size, shape, design and even merchandise mix, you can create continuity of image by having common elements throughout the chain. Consider applying the same store trademark to all of your marketing, storefront and in-store applications, extending some common exterior elements to all of your stores and/or using similar props, treatments and themes in your store windows.

5. *By Look or by Hook Getting the Customer In*

Within the first few seconds of catching their interest, the customers' focus moves beyond the store's exterior for a visual scan of the interior while they mull over whether to enter or not. Getting a customer through the door is indeed a victory.

In most instances, customers are either on a mission to make a planned purchase (the Seekers), or are shopping for amusement, entertainment or ideas (the Browsers).

Seekers may plan a trip to your store to make a premeditated purchase or may decide to enter for something specific. For the seeker, a deeper look into the store must reinforce their confidence that the store will have what they are seeking and that they can get in and out easily and quickly.

Browsers are more inclined to enter a store impulsively, drawn by the overall impression that a store has something they should check out. For the browser, a further look into the store must plant a seed of interest and hook them in.

For both seekers and browsers, the deeper glance into the store and the resulting decision — to enter, or not — is often attributed to the overall store look and a compelling hook.

A Visual Look

An inviting entrance is crucial in stopping the customer and establishing a positive first impression, but if the inside store messages create feelings of inconsistency or confusion, all is lost. For example, a clear and well-articulated store entrance that is followed up with a barrage of inconsistent aisle patterns, sloppy merchandising and confusing signs signals to the customer that the exterior image will not be fulfilled on the inside. Truly impressive stores are consistent in all efforts from the storefront right through to the stockroom.

A Visual Hook

A visual hook is a call to action that diverts a customer's attention to your store with a "Stop! There's something here for you!" Powerful visual hooks are created by marrying other visual merchandising components for a more memorable first impression. An exciting entrance presentation, an effectively signed promotional offering, a powerful interior display, in-store animation or events all serve as magnets to draw the customer in. Successful hooks ensure that the impressions they project are consistent with the store's overall image.

Well-executed hooks hold tremendous appeal for the customer, particularly the browser. A fashion retailer, for example, recently created a compelling hook for one promotion using the sights, sounds and smells of the Orient. Sales associates posted at the entrance offered fortune cookies containing discount coupons to customers. Large colourful posters, banners and Oriental art and props throughout the store windows and interior carried the theme further. Even the air was filled with the subtle sounds of Oriental stringed instruments and lightest whiff of incense.

Just like the above example, many of today's retailers are extending their store hooks into the realm of sensory appeal for a total image package. But to ensure the result is appropriate, you need to understand the psychological effect of sight, sound and smell on the consumers.

Donna Geary is the founder and Executive Director of Impact Visual Merchandising. For the past 16 years, Donna has consulted with clients in the retail, tourism, museum, attraction, service, wholesale and banking sectors. Academically, Donna studied Fashion Design and Merchandising, Visual Merchandising, and has an MBA, with a Major in Marketing from Concordia University. She was formerly a senior executive in the Marketing departments of The Hudson's Bay Company and Woodward Department Stores. Donna is the author of Maximizing Store Impact: A Retailer's Guide to Profitable Visual Merchandising. She has instructed courses in Marketing, Visual Merchandising and Business Communications at Ryerson University, The International Academy of Merchandising and Design, CLDC in Brazil and Fleming College in Peterborough, Ontario, where she now resides. Donna is a sought-after keynote speaker, workshop leader and has developed customized merchandising training material for dozens of retail chains. For more information, visit: www.impactvisual.com

Retail Buildings: Information + Images

Customer Service in Your Retail Store

Develop customer-friendly policies, train your employees to provide excellent customer service skills, and learn how to personalize your shop's customer service. Browse our list of Mystery Shopper providers. We also have tips for creating customer loyalty, dealing with disgruntled customers and other customer relations advice.

Secret Shoppers and Mystery Shopper Services

Providers of secret shoppers, mystery shopper and other customer service programmes promote retail store image.

Retail Store Evaluations

An objective assessment of our stores can help us measure whether or not we are fulfilling our customers' expectations. Learn how and why retailers should conduct a retail store evaluation.

Retail Terms: Mystery Shopping.

What is a mystery shopping programme? Learn about this retailing term to effectively improve business.

Make 81 per cent in one Hour. Join our option trading platform. Successful Trading. Starts Here: OptionBit.com

Open Source CRM For FreePower Business with Open Source CRM Call — 056 1478772/ 04 2653202 www.networkgulf.com

About Face

About Face uses the frontline measurement tool secret or mystery shopping to help companies and teams reach their full potential. Their secret shopper programmes effectively allow clients to hold a mirror up to their business, urging them to look inward and discover all that is good and not so good about how they operate.

GfK Mystery Shopping

With more than 15 years of North American and international mystery shopping experience, this organization specializes in helping our clients increase revenues, grow brand equity, build positive customer experiences and drive operational improvement.

ICC Decision Services

Their mystery shopper services can help make your business better everyday. With a suite of programmes from which to choose, plus in-store audits, telephone and website options, they custom design the best solution for each client.

IntelliShop

No matter where marketers interact with their customers — stores, call centres, the web —IntelliShop can help the retailers evaluate and improve their customers' experience.

National Shopping Service

It provides of many customer service solutions. Audits and inspections are conducted with uniforms, badges, formal documentation, in-depth training, and advanced monitoring and quality control procedures to comprehensively scrutinize procedural, environmental, and aesthetic standards.

Secret Shopper

More than 15 years of experience providing mystery shopping. Utilizing their library of tested reporting forms and drawing on your individual needs, they craft a custom program that zeroes in on the areas that will be of most benefit to your business.

Shop'n Chek, Inc.

Provides clients with actionable information that helps them improve their operational performance and maximize sales. This company offers a full range of services including solutions for customer experience measurement, revealed audits, and customer feedback surveys.

No matter how wonderful your products are or how committed you are to provide the best customer service, problems do occur. When dealing with a dissatisfied customer, how do you stay cool and diffuse the situation? Share how you deal with the disgruntled shopper.

Retail Consulting Global Sales/Mgmt./Experts; est./1980 Free Friedman Enewsletter +Previews www.thefriedmangroup.com

Customer Service Over 2 Lakh Jobs on TimesJobs.com High paying Jobs from Top Employers TimesJobs.com/Customer+Service

Five Ways to Lose Customers

Without customers, we wouldn't be in business. That is why it is surprising how easily retail shops unintentionally drive customers away. Here are five simple ways to lose customers.

A positive tone and language are highly important when it comes to good customer service, but many retailers still use phrases that may give the wrong image and negative impact.

1. Appealing to Repeat (Loyal) Customers

Too many retailers concentrate on how to woo new customers and, thus, they do not pay enough attention to what they can do to gain the loyalty and increased patronage of their repeat customers. Unless you are actively engaged, you can't do a better job in this area.

2. Convert Returns into Sales

As retailers, our job is to satisfy our customers and returns and refunds are a reality of retailing. Here's how to turn those inconvenient returns into exchanges and avoid refunds by implementing these simple customer service skills.

3. Customer Comment Cards

A carefully planned and well-written customer comment card allows the customer to express their opinion and provide valuable feedback. This form of store evaluation not only helps measure customer satisfaction, but also shows the retailer what areas of operation may need additional resources.

4. Dealing with the Disgruntled

In retail, it's inevitable that there will be the occasional disgruntled customer. No matter how wonderful your products are or how committed you are to provide the best customer service, problems do occur. Armed with the following customer service tips, you can diffuse a situation and possibly even save the customer, as well as the sale.

5. *How to Build Customer Loyalty*

The Pareto Principle says that 80 per cent of your sales come from 20 per cent of your customers. To keep these customers coming back, you need to help them remain loyal to you. Here's how to build customer loyalty and keep customers coming back.

Positioning (image)

An image represents how a given retailer is perceived by consumers and others. A firm may be seen as innovative or conservative, specialized or broad-based, discount-oriented or upscale. The key to a successful image is that consumers view the retailer in the manner the firm intends. Positioning involves determining how shoppers perceive the retailer's product and also developing and implementing marketing strategies to achieve the desired position in the retail market. Product positioning is closely linked with market segmentation. A product's position is the place that it occupies relative to competitors in a given market as perceived by the relevant group of shoppers, that is, by the target-market segment. A brand is an offering from a known source. A brand name such as McDonald's carries many associations in the minds of people: hamburgers, fun, children, fast food, Golden Arches. These associations make up the brand image. All companies strive to build brand strength — that is, a strong, favourable brand image.

Through **positioning**, a retailer devises its strategy in a way that projects an image relative to its retail category and its competitors and that elicits a positive consumer response. A firm selling women's apparel could generally position itself as an upscale or mid-priced specially retailer, a department store, a discount department store, or a discount specialty retailer, and it could specifically position itself with regard to other retailers carrying women's apparel.

Two opposite positioning philosophies have gained popularity in recent years: mass merchandising and niche retailing. Mass merchandising is a positioning approach whereby retailers offer a discount or value-oriented image, a wide and/or deep merchandise selection, and large store facilities. Wal-Mart has a wide, deep merchandise mix, whereas Sports Authority has a narrow, deeper assortment. These firms appeal to broad customer market, attract a lot of customer traffic, and generate high stock turnover. Because mass merchants have relatively low operating costs, achieve economies in operations, and appeal to value-conscious shoppers, and their continuing popularity is forecast. Sometimes, exporting domestic image helps. For example, Levi's foreign ads have played up the company's American roots. An Indonesian television commercial shows Levi's-clad teens cruising around Dubuque, Iowa, in 1960s convertibles. In Japan, James Dean serves as the centrepiece for almost all the brand's ads. And in most foreign commercials for Levi's 501 button-fly jeans, the dialogue generally is in English.

Similarly, Coke has a 93 per cent share of the cola beverage market in Japan and has become the most powerful American brand in the country. Coke's universal message is 'Drink Coke and feel good'. In Japan good has become a near obsession. Thus, a recent 'I feel Coke' campaign struck a very responsive chord. Surprisingly Americanized TV commercials showed happy young Japanese enjoying the good life. Coke cans prominently in hand, at barbecues, picnics, and Christmas parties. Entire promotion campaigns may fail due to cultural barriers encountered, unless an adjustment is made. The following examples illustrate how two marketers were able to overcome the self-reference criterion.

Avon Products, Inc., had to reshape its personal selling programme for Hong Kong. In the United States, the Avon saleswoman was accustomed to being greeted at the door by the woman of the house and led into the living room where she could sell over a cup of coffee. In Hong Kong, however, it was likely to be a servant peering through a metal gate who met the visitor and announced that the mistress of the household wasn't at home. Because of this difference, Avon began recruiting special sales-women for Hong Kong. They tended to be well-to-do housewives or women at a certain professional level, such as travel consultants or executive secretaries, who were thought to be able to sell to their acquaintances or gain access to women in their neighbourhoods who would invite them to stop by.

DeBeers, the raw-diamond supplier, ran ads for years in Japan that depicted Western couples in evening dress, reflecting the standard mentality that equates diamonds with grandeur. After only small marketing gains, the company finally learned that Japanese women don't smile and kiss their husbands when they receive diamonds as presents. Instead they shed a few tears and pretend they're angry at their husbands for spending so much money. DeBeers' subsequent Christmas campaign showed a tired wage earner and his hard working wife in their tiny apartment. Upon receiving the sparkling present, she snaps at her extravagant spouse, 'Oh, you stupid'! The ad. was a marketing success, boosting the popularity of diamonds in Japan.

Strategies to Build Retail Store Image

Many ways exist for building retail store image. The following illustrate some of these strategies. It should be noted that combinations of these approaches are also possible.

Image on Product Features: Retail store image may be created on the basis of availability of varieties of products and exposure of their features to potential shoppers. For example, an advertisement may attempt to build retail store image by reference to its specific features.

Image on Benefits: This strategy is closely related to the previous method. Toothpaste advertising often features the benefit strategy, as the example of decay prevention. Close-Up (sex appeal through white teeth and fresh breath! And Aqua-fresh (a combination of these benefits) illustrate. The difference between this and the features method is illustrated by the adage. "Don't sell the steak, sell the sizzle".

Usage Image: This strategy is related to the previous method. Many products are sold in the retail shop on the basis of their consumer usage situation. The retail management has sometimes sought to broaden their brand's association with a particular usage or situation. Campbell's soup for many years was positioned for use at lunchtime and advertised extensively over noontime radio. It now stresses a variety of uses for soup (recipes are on labels) and a broader time for consumption, with the more general theme. "Soup is good food". Gatorade was originally a summer beverage for athletes who needed to replace body fluids, but it has also tried to develop a positioning strategy during the cold or flu season as the beverage to drink when the doctor recommends consuming plenty of fluids. Arm & Hammer very successfully added a position to its baking soda – as an odour-destroying agent in refrigerators – and sales jumped tremendously.

User Image: This strategy associates the product with a user or a class of users. Some cosmetics retailers seek a successful, highly visible model as their spokesperson (Christie Brinkley for Cover Girl) as the association for the brand. With its humorous sports personalities Miller Lite beer has been very successful in positioning itself as a beer for the heavy user who dislikes that filled-up feeling. A company may sometimes need to appeal to new users as it shifts markets. Johnson & Johnson baby shampoo now presents adult users as well as babies in its ads. Because users and sage situations are related, they may often be linked in an advertisement.

Self-image: Retail management has to develop brand images that match the target shoppers' self-image. **Retail** positioning identifying a highly attractive market segment and serving it through a strategy that distinguishes the retailer from others in the minds of people in that segment. In shopper behaviour, store image also plays an important part. The image or impression about a product depends upon the knowledge, information stored in the mind of a person and he/she selects, interprets and evaluates a product on the basis of such store image.

Image against Competition: Often success for building retail store image involves looking for weak points in the positions of its competitors and then launching marketing attacks against those weak points. In this strategy, the retailer may either directly or indirectly make comparisons with competing products. For example, the famous 'Uncola' campaign successfully positioned 7-Up as an alternative to Coke. Pepsi, and Colas (almost two-thirds of soft drinks consumed in the United States are Colas). For instance, it was originally thought of as a hangover cure, and it is still viewed as a special-occasion beverage, for an occasion other than a Cola time. Other classic examples of this positioning strategy include Burger King versus McDonald's (over broiling versus frying) and Hertz versus Avis. The retailer may use several techniques for determining the appropriate positioning.

Customer Relationship Management (CRM) is a method that companies use to interact with customers. The methods include employee training and special purpose CRM software. There is an emphasis on handling incoming customer phone calls and e-mail, although the information collected by CRM software may also be used for promotion, and surveys such as those polling customer satisfaction.

Initiatives often fail because implementation was limited to software installation, without providing the context, support and understanding for employees to learn. Tools for customer relationship management should be implemented "only after a well-devised strategy and operational plan are put in place".

- Other problems occur when failing to think of sales as the output of a process that itself needs to be studied and taken into account when planning automation.

OVERVIEW

From the outside, customers interacting with a company perceive the business as a single entity, despite often interacting with a number of employees in different roles and departments. CRM is the combination of policies, processes, and strategies implemented by an organization to unify its customer interactions and provide a means to track customer information. It involves the use of technology in attracting new and profitable customers, while forming tighter bonds with existing ones.

CRM includes many aspects which relate directly to one another:

1. Front office operations — Direct interaction with customers, e.g., face to face meetings, phone calls, e-mail, online services, etc.
2. Back office operations — Operations that ultimately affect the activities of the front office (e.g., billing, maintenance, planning, marketing, advertising, finance, manufacturing, etc.)
3. Business relationships — Interaction with other companies and partners, such as suppliers/vendors and retail outlets/distributors, industry networks (lobbying groups, trade associations). This external network supports front and back office activities.
4. Analysis — Key CRM data can be analyzed in order to plan target-marketing campaigns, conceive business strategies, and judge the success of CRM activities (e.g., market share, number and types of customers, revenue, profitability).

Proponents of CRM software claim that it not only allows customer relationships to be managed more efficiently, but also encourages a more customer-centric approach to conducting business. Executives often cite the lack of proper tools as a barrier to delivering the experience their customers expect. A 2009, study of over 860 corporate executives revealed only 39 per cent believe that their employees have the tools and authority to solve customer problems.

Types/Variations of CRM

There are **several** different approaches to CRM, with different software packages focusing on different aspects. In general, Customer Service, Campaign Management and Sales Force Automation (SFA) form the core of the system.

Operational CRM

Operational CRM provides support to "front office" business processes, e.g., to sales, marketing and service staff. Interactions with customers are generally stored in customers' contact histories, and staff can retrieve customer information as necessary.

The contact history provides staff members with immediate access to important information on the customer (products owned, prior support calls, etc.), eliminating the need to individually obtain this information directly from the customer. Reaching to the customer at right time at right place is preferable.

Operational CRM processes customer data for a variety of purposes:

- Managing campaigns
- Enterprise Marketing Automation
- Sales Force Automation
- Sales Management System

Analytical CRM

Analytical CRM analyzes customer data for a variety of purposes:

- Designing and executing targeted marketing campaigns
- Designing and executing campaigns, e.g., customer acquisition, cross-selling, up-selling, add on-selling

- Analyzing customer behaviour in order to make decisions relating to products and services (e.g., pricing, product development)
- Management information system (e.g., financial forecasting and customer profitability analysis)

Analytical CRM generally makes heavy use of data mining and other techniques to produce useful results for decision making. It is at the analytical stage that the importance of fully integrated CRM software becomes most apparent – the more information available to analytical software, the better its predictions and recommendations will be.

Sales Intelligence CRM

Sales intelligence CRM is similar to Analytical CRM, but is intended as a more direct sales tool. Features include alerts sent to sales staff regarding:

- Cross-selling/Up-selling/Switch-selling opportunities
- Customer drift
- Sales performance
- Customer trends
- Customer margins
- Customer alignment

Campaign Management

Campaign management combines elements of Operational and Analytical CRM. Campaign management functions include:

- Target groups formed from the client base according to selected criteria
- Sending campaign-related material (e.g., on special offers) to selected recipients using various channels (e.g., e-mail, telephone, SMS, post)
- Tracking, storing, and analyzing campaign statistics, including tracking responses and analyzing trends

Collaborative CRM

Collaborative CRM covers aspects of a company's dealings with customers that are handled by various departments within a company, such as sales, technical support and marketing. Staff members from different departments can share information collected when interacting with customers. For example, feedback received by customer support agents can provide other staff members with information on the services and features requested by customers. Collaborative CRM's ultimate goal is to use information collected by all departments to improve the quality of services provided by the company. Producers can use CRM information to develop products or find new market. CRM facilitates communication between customers, suppliers and partner.

Consumer Relationship CRM

Consumer Relationship System (CRS) covers aspects of a company's dealing with customers handled by the Consumer Affairs and Customer Relations contact centres within a company. Representatives handle in-bound contact from anonymous consumers and customers. Early warnings can be issued regarding product issues (e.g., item recalls) and current consumer sentiment can be tracked (voice of the customer).

Simple CRM

A relatively new spin-off of the traditional CRM model first appeared in 2006. At their core, CRM tools are designed to manage customer relationships. As described above there are countless supplemental features and capabilities. Simple CRM systems break-down the traditional CRM systems and focus on the core values, managing contacts and activities with customers and prospects. These systems are designed to create the most value for the immediate end-user rather than the organization as a whole. They often focus on satisfying the needs of a particular marketplace niche, organizational unit, or type of user rather than an entire organisation.

Social CRM

Beginning in 2007, the rapid growth in social media and social networking forced CRM product companies to integrate "social" features into their traditional CRM systems. Some of the first features added were social network monitoring feeds (e.g., Twitter timeline). Other emerging features include messaging, sentiment analysis, and other analytics. CRM experts agree that online social communities and conversations have significant consequences for companies, and must be monitored for real-time marketplace feedback and trends.

Strategy

Several CRM software packages are available, and they vary in their approach to CRM. However, as mentioned above, CRM is not just a technology but rather a comprehensive, customer-centric approach to an organization's philosophy of dealing with its customers. This includes policies and processes, front-of-house customer service, employee training, marketing, systems and information management. Hence, it is important that any CRM implementation considerations stretch beyond technology toward the broader organizational requirements.

The objectives of a CRM strategy must consider a company's specific situation and its customers' needs and expectations. Information gained through CRM initiatives can support the development of marketing strategy by developing the organization's knowledge in areas such as identifying customer segments, improving customer retention, improving product offerings (by better understanding customer needs), and by identifying the organization's most profitable customers.

CRM strategies can vary in size, complexity, and scope. Some companies consider a CRM strategy only to focus on the management of a team of salespeople. However, other CRM strategies can cover customer interaction across the entire organization. Many commercial CRM software packages provide features that serve the sales, marketing, event management, project management, and finance industries.

From this perspective, CRM has for some time been seen to play an important role in many sales process engineering efforts.

Implementation

Implementation Issues

Many CRM project "failures" are also related to data quality and availability. Data cleaning is a major issue. If a company's CRM strategy is to track life cycle revenues, costs, margins, and interactions between individual customers, this must be reflected in all business processes. Data must be extracted from multiple sources (e.g., departmental/divisional databases such as sales, manufacturing, supply chain, logistics, finance, service etc.), which requires an integrated, comprehensive system in place with well-defined structures and high data quality. Data from other systems can be transferred to CRM systems using appropriate interfaces.

Because of the company-wide size and scope of many CRM implementations, significant pre-planning is essential for smooth roll-out. This pre-planning involves a technical evaluation of the data available and the technology employed in existing systems. This evaluation is critical to determine the level of effort needed to integrate this data.

Equally critical is the human aspect of the implementation. A successful implementation requires an understanding of the expectations and needs of the stakeholders involved. An executive sponsor should also be obtained to provide high-level management representation of the CRM project.

An effective tool for identifying technical and human factors before beginning a CRM project is a pre-implementation check list. A check list can help ensure any potential problems are identified early in the process.

Privacy and Data Security System

One of the primary functions of CRM software is to collect information about customers. When gathering data as part of a CRM solution, a company must consider the desire for customer privacy and data security, as well as the legislative and cultural norms. Some customers prefer assurances that their data will not be shared with third parties without their prior consent and that safeguards are in place to prevent illegal access by third parties.

Market Structures

The following table lists the top CRM software vendors in 2006-2008 (figures in millions of US dollars) published in Gartner studies.

Table 26 : Top CRM

Vendor	(2008) Revenue	2008 Share (%)	Revenue 2007	2007 Share (%)	(2006) Revenue	2006 Share (%)
Oracle	1,475	16.1	1,319.8	16.3	1,016.8	15.5
SAP	2,055	22.5	2,050.8	25.3	1,681.7	26.6
Salesforce.com	965	10.6	676.5	8.3	451.7	6.9
Amdocs	451	4.9	421.0	5.2	365.9	5.6
Microsoft	581	6.4	332.1	4.1	176.1	2.7
Others	3,620	39.6	3,289.1	40.6	2,881.6	43.7
Total	**9,147**	**100**	**8,089.3**	**100**	**6,573.8**	**100**

The following table lists of the top software vendors for CRM projects completed in 2006 using external consultants and system integrators, according to a 2007 Gartner study.

Table 27 : Top Software Vendors

Vendor	% of Implementation	Vendor	% of Implementation
Siebel (Oracle)	41%	Amdocs	1%
SAP	8%	Chordiant	1%
Epiphany (Infor)	3%	Microsoft	1%
Oracle	3%	Metus Technology	1%
PeopleSoft (Oracle)	2%	SAS	1%
salesforce.com	2%	Others	15%
		None	22%

A 2007 Datamonitor report lists Oracle (including Siebel) and SAP as the top CRM vendors, with Chordiant, Infor, and SalesForce.com as significant, smaller vendors.

Retail Service Quality Management

In the field of computer networking and other packet-switched telecommunication networks, the traffic engineering term **quality of service** (QoS) refers to resource reservation control mechanisms rather than the achieved service quality. Quality of service is the ability to provide different priority to different applications, users, or data flows, or to guarantee a certain level of performance to a data flow. For example, a required bit rate, delay, jitter, packet dropping probability and/or bit error rate may be guaranteed. Quality of service guarantees are important if the network capacity is insufficient, especially for real-time streaming multimedia applications such as voice over IP, online games and IP-TV, since these often require fixed bit rate and are delay sensitive, and in networks where the capacity is a limited resource, for example, in cellular data communication. In the absence of network congestion, QoS mechanisms are not required.

A network or protocol that supports QoS may agree on a traffic contract with the application software and reserve capacity in the network nodes, for example, during a session establishment phase. During the session it may monitor the achieved level of performance, for example, the data rate and delay, and dynamically control scheduling priorities in the network nodes. It may release the reserved capacity during a tear down phase.

A best-effort network or service does not support quality of service. An alternative to complex QoS control mechanisms is to provide high quality communication over a best-effort network by over-provisioning the capacity so that it is sufficient for the expected peak traffic load.

In the field of telephony, **quality of service** was defined in the ITU standard X.902 as "A set of quality requirements on the collective behaviour of one or more objects". Quality of Service comprises requirements on all the aspects of a connection, such as service response time, loss, signal-to-noise ratio, cross-talk, echo, interrupts, frequency response, loudness levels, and so on. A subset of telephony QoS is Grade of Service (GoS) requirements, which comprises aspects of a connection relating to capacity and coverage of a network, for example guaranteed maximum blocking probability and outage probability.

QoS is sometimes used as a quality measure, with many alternative definitions, rather than referring to the ability to reserve resources. Quality of service sometimes refers to the level of quality of service, i.e., the guaranteed service quality. High QoS is often confused with a high level of performance or achieved service quality, for example high bit rate, low latency and low bit error probability. See also relation to subjective quality measures below.

An alternative and disputable definition of QoS, used especially in application layer services such as telephony and streaming video, is a metric that reflects or predicts the subjectively experienced quality. Other terms with similar meaning are the Quality of Experience (QoE) subjective business concept, the "user perceived performance", the "degree of satisfaction of the user", the "number of happy customers" or the Mean Opinion Score (MOS). In this context, QoS is the cumulative effect on subscriber satisfaction of all imperfections affecting the service.

Problems

When the Internet was first deployed many years ago, it lacked the ability to provide Quality of Service guarantees due to limits in router computing power. It therefore ran at default QoS level, or "best effort". There were four "Type of Service" bits and three "Precedence" bits provided in each message, but they were ignored. These bits were later redefined as DiffServ Code Points (DSCP) and are largely honoured in peered links on the modern Internet.

When looking at packet-switched networks, Quality of Service is affected by various factors, which can be divided into "human" and "technical" factors. Human factors include: stability of service, availability of service, delays, user information. Technical factors include: reliability, scalability, effectiveness, maintainability, Grade of Service, etc.

Many things can happen to packets as they travel from origin to destination, resulting in the following problems as seen from the point of view of the sender and receiver:

Dropped Packets

The routers might fail to deliver (*drop*) some packets if they arrive when their buffers are already full. Some, none, or all of the packets might be dropped, depending on the state of the network, and it is impossible to determine what will happen in advance. The receiving application may ask for this information to be retransmitted, possibly causing severe delays in the overall transmission.

Delay

It might take a long time for a packet to reach its destination, because it gets held up in long queues, or takes a less direct route to avoid congestion. In some cases, excessive delay can render an application such as VoIP or online gaming unusable.

Jitter

Packets from the source will reach the destination with different delays. A packet's delay varies with its position in the queues of the routers along the path between source and destination and this position can vary unpredictably. This variation in delay is known as jitter and can seriously affect the quality of streaming audio and/or video.

Out-of-order delivery

When a collection of related packets is routed through the internet, different packets may take different routes, each resulting in a different delay. The result is that the packets arrive in a different order than they were sent. This problem requires special additional protocols responsible for rearranging out-of-order packets to an isochronous state once they reach their destination. This is especially important for video and VoIP streams where quality is dramatically affected by both latency and lack of isochronicity.

Error

Sometimes packets are misdirected, or combined together, or corrupted, while *en route*. The receiver has to detect this and, just as if the packet was dropped, ask the sender to repeat **itself.**

Applications Requiring QoS

A defined Quality of Service may be required for certain types of network traffic, for example:

- streaming multimedia may require guaranteed throughput to ensure that a minimum level of quality is maintained
- IPTV offered as a service from a service provider such as AT&T's U-verse
- IP telephony or Voice over IP may require strict limits on jitter and delay
- Video Teleconferencing (VTC) requires low jitter and latency
- Alarm signalling (e.g., Burglar alarm)
- dedicated link emulation requires both guaranteed throughput and imposes limits on maximum delay and jitter
- a safety-critical application, such as remote surgery may require a guaranteed level of availability (this is also called *hard QoS*)
- a remote system administrator may want to prioritize variable, and usually small amounts of SSH traffic to ensure a responsive session even over a heavily-laden link

- online games, such as fast paced real time simulations with multiple players. Lack of QoS may produce 'lag'
- Industrial Ethernet protocols such as Ethernet/IP which are used for real-time control of machinery

These types of service are called *inelastic*, meaning that they require a certain minimum level of bandwidth and a certain maximum latency to function.

By contrast, *elastic* applications can take advantage of however much or little bandwidth is available. Bulk file transfer applications that rely on TCP are generally elastic.

Obtaining QoS

- Per call
- In call
- In advance: When the expense of mechanisms to provide QoS is justified, network customers and providers typically enter into a contractual agreement termed a service level agreement (SLA) which specifies guarantees for the ability of a network/protocol to give guaranteed performance/throughput/latency bounds based on mutually agreed measures, usually by prioritizing traffic.
- Reserving resources: Resources are reserved at each step on the network for the call as it is set up. An example is RSVP, Resource Reservation Protocol.

QoS Mechanisms

An alternative to complex QoS control mechanisms is to provide high quality communication by generously over-provisioning a network so that capacity is based on peak traffic load estimates. This approach is simple and economical for networks with predictable and light traffic loads. The performance is reasonable for many applications. This might include demanding applications that can compensate for variations in bandwidth and delay with large receive buffers, which is often possible for example in video streaming.

Commercial VoIP services are often competitive with traditional telephone service in terms of call quality even though QoS mechanisms are usually not in use on the user's connection to his ISP and the VoIP provider's connection to a different ISP. Under high load conditions, however, VoIP quality degrades to cell phone quality or worse. The mathematics of packet traffic indicate that a network with QoS can handle four times as many calls with tight jitter requirements as one without QoS. Yuksel *et al.*, have determined 60 per cent required extra capacity by simulating IP traffic under conservative assumptions.

The amount of over-provisioning in interior links required to replace QoS depends on the number of users and their traffic demands. As the internet now services close to a billion users, there is little possibility that over-provisioning can eliminate the need for QoS when VoIP becomes more commonplace.

For narrowband networks more typical of enterprises and local governments, however, the costs of bandwidth can be substantial and over provisioning is hard to justify. In these situations, two distinctly different philosophies were developed to engineer preferential treatment for packets which require it.

Early work used the "IntServ" philosophy of reserving network resources. In this model, applications used the Resource Reservation Protocol (RSVP) to request and reserve resources through a network. While IntServ mechanisms do work, it was realized that in a broadband network typical of a larger service provider, Core routers would be required to accept, maintain, and tear down thousands or possibly tens of thousands of reservations. It was believed that this approach would not scale with the growth of the internet, and in any event was antithetical to the notion of designing networks so that Core routers do little more than simply switch packets at the highest possible rates.

The second and currently accepted approach is "DiffServ" or differentiated services. In the DiffServ model, packets are marked according to the type of service they need. In response to these markings, routers and switches use various queuing strategies to tailor performance to requirements. (At the IP layer, Differentiated Services Code Point (DSCP) markings use the 6 bits in the IP packet header. At the MAC layer, VLAN IEEE 802.1Q and IEEE 802.1p can be used to carry essentially the same information).

Routers supporting DiffServ use multiple queues for packets awaiting transmission from bandwidth constrained (e.g., wide area) interfaces. Router vendors provide different capabilities for configuring this behaviour, to include the number of queues supported, the relative priorities of queues, and bandwidth reserved for each queue.

In practice, when a packet must be forwarded from an interface with queuing, packets requiring low jitter (e.g., VoIP or VTC) are given priority over packets in other queues. Typically, some bandwidth is allocated by default to network control packets (e.g., ICMP and routing protocols), while best effort traffic might simply be given whatever bandwidth is left over.

Additional bandwidth management mechanisms may be used to further engineer performance, to include:

1. Traffic shaping (rate limiting):
   - Token bucket
   - Leaky bucket
2. TCP rate control – artificially adjusting TCP window size as well as controlling the rate of ACKs being returned to the sender
3. Scheduling algorithms:
   - Weighted fair queuing (WFQ)
   - Class-based weighted fair queuing
   - Weighted round robin (WRR)
   - Deficit weighted round robin (DWRR)
   - Hierarchical Fair Service Curve (HFSC)
4. Congestion avoidance:
   - RED, WRED – Lessens the possibility of port queue buffer tail-drops and this lowers the likelihood of TCP global synchronization
   - Policing (marking/dropping the packet in excess of the committed traffic rate and burst size)

- Explicit congestion notification
- Buffer tuning

As mentioned, while DiffServ is used in many sophisticated enterprise networks, it has not been widely deployed in the internet. Internet peering arrangements are already complex, and there appears to be no enthusiasm among providers for supporting QoS across peering connections, or agreement about what policies should be supported in order to do so.

One compelling example of the need for QoS on the internet relates to this issue of congestion collapse. The Internet relies on congestion avoidance protocols, as built into TCP, to reduce traffic load under conditions that would otherwise lead to internet meltdown. QoS applications such as VoIP and IPTV, because they require largely constant bit rates and low latency cannot use TCP, and cannot otherwise reduce their traffic rate to help prevent meltdown either. QoS contracts limit traffic that can be offered to the internet and thereby enforce traffic shaping that can prevent it from becoming overloaded, hence, they're an indispensable part of the internet's ability to handle a mix of real-time and non-real-time traffic without meltdown.

Asynchronous Transfer Mode (ATM) network protocol has an elaborate framework to plug in QoS mechanisms of choice. Shorter data units and built-in QoS were some of the unique selling points of ATM in the telecommunications applications such as video on demand, voice over IP.

Table 28 : QoS Priority Levels

Priority Level	Traffic Type
0 (lowest)	Best Effort
1	Background
2	Standard (Spare)
3	Excellent Load (Business Critical)
4	Controlled Load (Streaming Multimedia)
5	Voice and Video (Interactive Media and Voice) [Less than 100ms latency and jitter]
6	Layer 3 Network Control Reserved Traffic [Less than 10ms latency and jitter]
7 (highest)	Layer 2 Network Control Reserved Traffic [Lowest latency and jitter]

QoS Problems

- Internet2 QoS Working Group concluded that increasing bandwidth is probably more practical than implementing QoS.
- Protocols that provide Quality of Service
- The Type of Service (ToS) field in the IP header (now superseded by DiffServ)
- IP Differentiated services (DiffServ)
- IP Integrated services (IntServ)

- Resource Reservation Protocol
- Multiprotocol Label Switching (MPLS) provides eight QoS classes
- RSVP-TE
- Frame relay
- X.25
- Some ADSL modems
- Asynchronous Transfer Mode (ATM)
- IEEE 802.1p
- IEEE 802.1Q
- IEEE 802.11e
- HomePNA Home networking over coax and phone wires
- The ITU-T G.hn standard provides QoS by means of "Contention Free Transmission Opportunities" (CFTXOPs) which are allocated to flows which require QoS and which have negotiated a "contract" with the network controller. G.hn also supports non-QoS operation by means of "Contention-based Time Slots".

QoS Solutions

The research project MUSE defined a QoS concept in Phase I which was further worked out in another research project PLANETS. The new idea of this solution is to agree on a discrete jitter value per QoS class which is imposed on network nodes. Including best effort, four QoS classes were defined, two elastic and two inelastic. The solution has several benefits:

- End to end delay and packet loss rate can be predicted
- It is easy to implement with simple scheduler and queue length given in PLANETS
- Nodes can be easily verified for compliance
- End-users do notice the difference in quality

The MUSE project finally elaborated its own QoS solution which is primarily based in:

- The usage of traffic classes
- Selective CAC concept
- Appropriate network dimensioning

Quality of Service Procedures

Unlike the Internet 2 Abilene Network, the Internet is actually a series of exchange points interconnecting private networks and not a network in its own right. Hence, the Internet's core is owned and managed by a number of different Network Service Providers, not a single entity. Its behaviour is much more stochastic or unpredictable. Therefore, research continues on QoS procedures that are deployable in large, diverse networks.

There are two principal approaches to QoS in modern packet-switched networks, a parameterized system based on an exchange of application requirements with the network, and a prioritized system where each packet identifies a desired service level to the network. On the

Internet, Integrated Services ("IntServ") implement the parameterized approach. In this model, applications use the Resource Reservation Protocol (RSVP) to request and reserve resources through a network.

Differentiated Services ("DiffServ") implement the prioritized model. DiffServ marks packets according to the type of service they need. In response to these markings, routers and switches use various queuing strategies to tailor performance to requirements. (At the IP layer, differentiated services code point (DSCP) markings use the first 6 bits in the TOS field of the IP packet header. At the MAC layer, VLAN IEEE 802.1q and IEEE 802.1p can be used to carry essentially the same information.)

Cisco IOS NetFlow and the Cisco Class Based QoS (CBQoS) Management Information Base (MIB) can both be leveraged within a Cisco network device to obtain visibility into QoS policies and their effectiveness on network traffic.

Non-IP protocols, specially those intended for voice transmission, such as ATM or GSM, have already implemented QoS in the core protocol and don't need additional procedures to achieve it.

Quality of Service Circumvention

Strong cryptography network protocols such as Secure Sockets Layer, I2P, and virtual private networks obscure the data transferred using them. As all electronic commerce on the internet requires the use of such strong cryptography protocols, unilaterally downgrading the performance of encrypted traffic creates an unacceptable hazard for customers. Yet, encrypted traffic is otherwise unable to undergo deep packet inspection for QoS.

Doubts about Quality of Service Over IP

Gary Bachula, Vice president for External Affairs for Internet 2, asserts that specific QoS protocols are unnecessary in the core network as long as the core network links are "over-provisioned" to the point that network traffic never encounters delay. In "quality of service" engineering, this formulation is guaranteed by the *admission control* feature.

The Internet 2 project found, in 2001, that the QoS protocols were probably not deployable inside its Abilene network with equipment available at that time. While newer routers are capable of following QoS protocols with no loss of performance, equipment available at the time relied on software to implement QoS. The Internet 2 Abilene network group also predicted that "logistical, financial, and organizational barriers will block the way toward any bandwidth guarantees" by protocol modifications aimed at QoS. In essence they believe that the economics would be likely to make the network providers deliberately erode the quality of best effort traffic as a way to push customers to higher priced QoS services.

The Abilene network study was the basis for the testimony of Gary Bachula to the Senate Commerce Committee's hearing on Network Neutrality in early 2006. He expressed the opinion that adding more bandwidth was more effective than any of the various schemes for accomplishing QoS they examined.

Bachula's testimony has been cited by proponents of a law banning quality of service as proof that no legitimate purpose is served by such an offering. Of course, this argument is dependent on the assumption that over-provisioning isn't a form of QoS and that it's always possible. Obviously, cost and other factors affect the ability of carriers to build and maintain permanently over-provisioned networks.

The following are the **determinants of service quality:**

Reliability: The ability to perform the promised service dependably and accurately.

Responsiveness: The willingness to help customers and to provide prompt service.

Assurance: The knowledge and courtesy of employees and their ability to convey trust and confidence.

Empathy: The provision of caring individualized attention to customers.

Tangibles: The appearance of physical facilities, equipment, personnel, and communication materials.

Supply Chain Management (SCM)

The supply chain describes a longer channel stretching from raw materials to components to final products that are carried to final buyers. The supply chain represents a value to delivery system. SCM is a set of business activities that manages the movements of products to retail distribution centres and stores and the exchange of information between retailers and vendors. It is the delivery of economic value to customers through the management of the flow of physical goods and associated information. Retailers are increasingly taking a leadership role in managing their respective supply chains. When retailers were predominantly small, family-owned businesses, larger manufacturers and distributors dictated when, where, and how merchandise was delivered. But with the consolidation and emergence of larger, national retail chains, retailers now play an active role in coordinating supply chain management activities. The size of these national retailers typically makes them more powerful than their vendors and thus better able to control their supply chains. In addition, retailers are more knowledgeable about their customers. They are in the unique position to collect purchase information customer by customer, transaction by transaction. This information is being shared with suppliers to plan production, promotion, deliveries, assortments, and inventory levels.

Efficient supply chain management provides two benefits to customers:

Reduced stockouts, and Tailored assortments

These benefits translate into greater sales, lower costs, higher inventory turnover, and lower markdowns for retailers. Apart from improving the efficiency and accuracy of data records, there has been tremendous savings on the time saved, about 80 per cent in inward warehouse processing and 12 per cent in outward. Real-time visibility of items during all stages of the supply chain improved to 98 per cent. Supply chain management has Dave Thomas (Wendy's).

Dave Thomas appeared in over 300 TV commercials and became the most well known restaurateur in the USA. His unassuming persona conveyed an image that the chain was owned by a caring grandfather rather than a faceless corporation, a lesson he learned from Colonel Sanders, founder of KFC. His personal appeal was so great that he continued to be used in commercials even after his death in 2002. Thomas never knew his parents, and his adoptive mother died when he was five. His involvement in the restaurant business began at the age of

12. After dropping out of high school and completing service in the army, he bought a run-down KFC franchise. Even with these challenges, at the age of 35, Thomas became a millionaire when he sold his KFC franchises. He soon decided to open some fast-food restaurants to pay for his children's college education. Wendy's success is attributed to his focusing on young adults and offering them sandwiches made to order with the condiments selected by the customer.

Retail Supply Chain Management (RSCM)

Retailing is one of the world's most challenging and competitive industry. In recent years retailers have made significant investments in supply chain management improvements to complement the continuous focus by traditional retailers on store operations. These investments have included latest generation warehouse management systems WMS, sophisticated **inventory management** and replenishment.

Supply Chain Management Solutions

Retailing comprises about 40 per cent of the US economy, and is a major economic engine of the world economy. While the retail sector has always been very competitive, in recent years, the competitive nature of the field has increased dramatically. Customers too have become more exacting, demanding ever-increasing levels of service. Retailers have responded by increasing the variety of their products, becoming more price competitive, striving towards higher service levels, and utilizing advances in computing capabilities and information technologies to improve

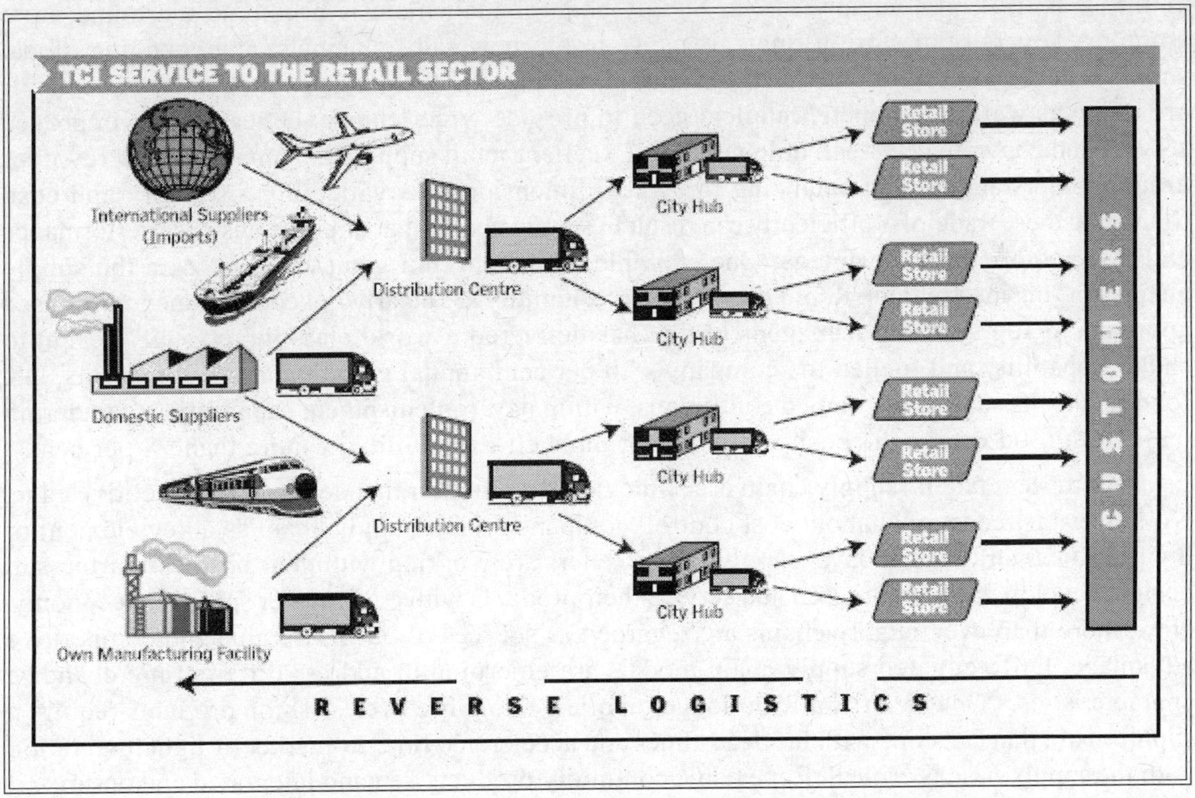

FIG. 28: SUPPLY CHAIN AND RETAIL: THE MEANS TO THE END

their supply chain efficiency. However, these developments have also greatly increased the complexity of managing the retail business environment. Consequently, most retailers have struggled to maintain profitability.

Rigorous analytical methods have emerged as the most promising solution to many of these complex problems. Indeed, the retail industry has emerged as a fascinating choice for researchers in the field of supply chain management. In **Retail Supply Chain Management**, leading researchers provide a detailed review of cutting-edge methodologies that address the complex array of these problems. A critical resource for researchers and practitioners in the field of retailing.

Why Accenture? Because we have deep knowledge of the retail industry coupled with leading supply chain skills in areas like: demand and supply planning, sourcing and procurement, fulfilment operations, inventory management, store operations and supplier management and collaboration. Industry analysts like IDC and Gartner Group rank Accenture number one in terms of pioneering supply chain applications, like radio frequency identification (RFID) and electronic product codes (EPC). Accenture's Supply Chain Centres of Excellence are located strategically around the world and support solution development, implementation and joint ventures that keep the clients on the cutting edge. Their client experience and ongoing research has shown them that high-performance businesses incorporate their supply chains into their business strategies. The supply chain can represent 40 to 70 per cent of a retailer's operating costs, and may comprise half of all company assets. Supply chain management is becoming more and more complex. Diversity of store formats, expansion into new sales channels, and changing global supply sources are driving the need for optimal supply chain management. Customer demands are rising as well: to compete, retailers need to provide wider choice, better quality, improved service and convenience — all at lower cost. Excellent retail supply chain management revolves around understanding and balancing three key dimensions of availability, inventory and cost. Managing these trade-offs efficiently can result in supply chains that improve business performance and drive competitive advantage. One example: Spanish retail giant Zara. At Zara the supply chain is the business model. Rapid growth and profitability are clearly linked to an uncompromised approach to supply chain management that has delivered a world class three week "design to shelf" capability and fuelled the company's 20 per cent annual growth and profit margins. UK food retailer Tesco has developed continuous, within day, replenishment capabilities to underpin their fresh food offer and consistently deliver on-shelf availability of more than 98 per cent.

For these retailers, supply chain is a strategic differentiator that delivers a competitive edge. No longer just concerned about cost control, companies view supply chain as a key element of their business strategy. Today's supply chain leaders are working with their business partners to design, develop, move, store, sell and service their products with ever greater speed and economy. Now, more than ever, supply chains are regarded as sources of business value and competitive advantage. Differentiated supply chain models are emerging to address different merchandise characteristics. "One size fits all" no longer applies. Short-life cycle fashion products require a supply chain that can cope with fast lead-times and accelerated time-to-market — tight integration with the supply base is critical. Repeatable continuity products demand integrated and optimized replenishment and forecasting. Regardless of type, all supply chains need to be supported by effective core processes and capabilities. Supply chain leaders develop robust basic processes

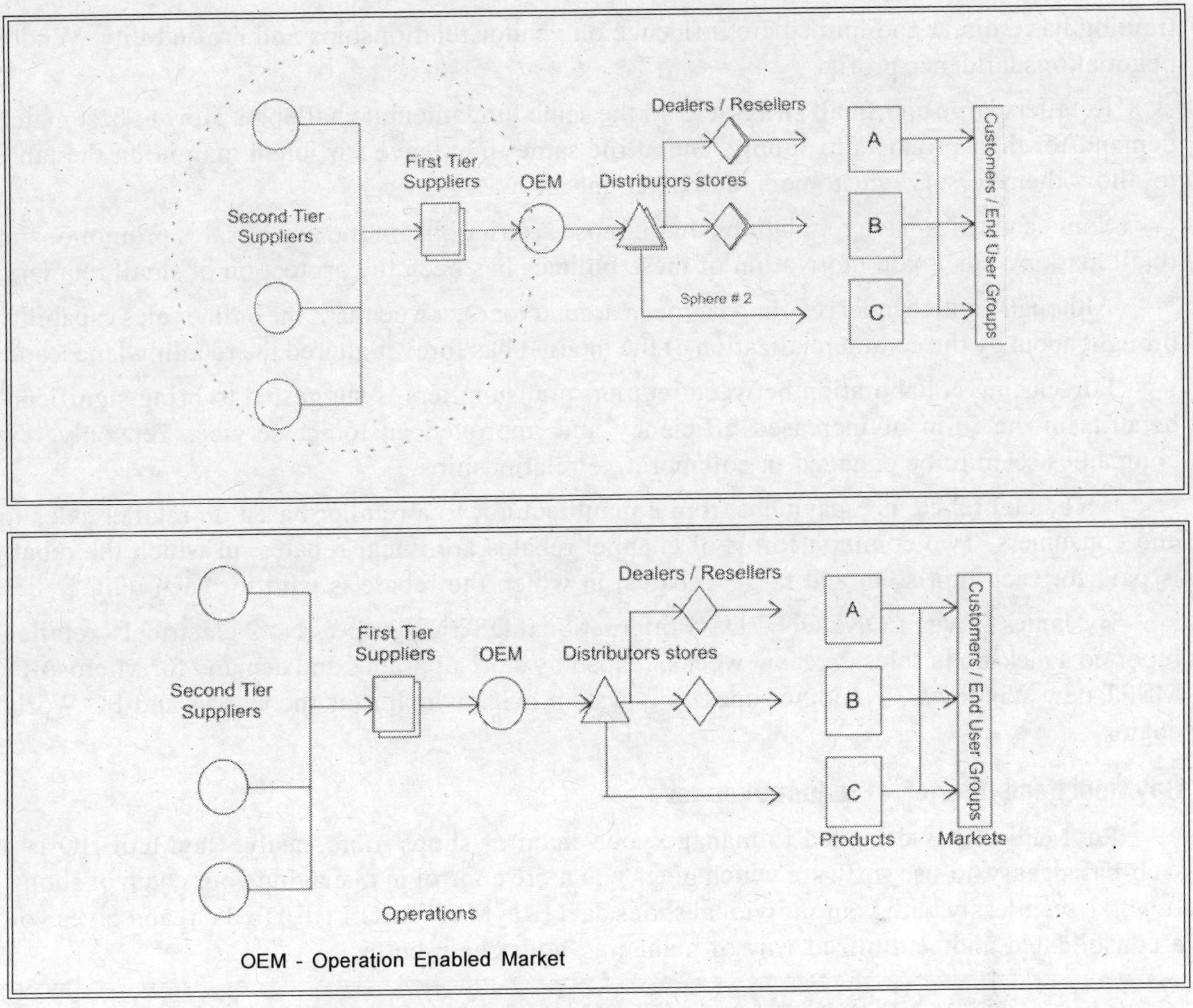

FIGS. 29 AND 30: SUPPLY CHAIN TRANSFORMATION

and disciplines, and then add new and differentiating capabilities that drive supply chain excellence. These new capabilities enable leading retailers to transform and differentiate their supply chains. Creating change in an existing supply chain can be daunting. Given the breadth and depth of impact, virtually all areas of a business are affected. Accenture can offer a range of services from providing advice on specific functional areas including case studies and insights into other retailers and your competition to helping to implement a complete supply chain transformation.

Retail Supply Force

For many retailers, the challenges faced by increasing competition, shrinking margins, and economic slowdowns are bringing about changes in thinking and the way they do business. Some retailers are beginning to take a much more serious look at managing the top line, and are showing the benefits.

Sales courses and sales training courses on negotiations, contracts and relationships are an important part of sales training for the retail store manager and the retail store owner. Sales training has a direct and immediate influence on vendor relationships and profitability. Vendor negotiations influence profit.

Retailers large and small struggle with the same fundamental challenge: How to best match demand for their products to supply, and at the same time leave sufficient margin on the table to allow them to serve customers, compete, and grow.

Some countries have regulations that impose restrictions on the use of sales promotions in retail markets. The main motivation of these policies has been the protection of small retailers.

Although multichannel retailing has been around for over a century, the online sales capability brought about by the commercialization of the internet has forever altered the retailing landscape.

Forecasting collaboration between retailers and suppliers is suggested to bring significant benefits in the form of increased efficiency and improved customer service. Yet, only few companies seem to be engaged in collaborative relationships.

A channel rebate is a payment from a manufacturer to a retailer based on retailer sales to end consumers. Two common forms of channel rebates are linear rebates, in which the rebate is paid for each unit sold, and target rebates, in which the rebate is paid for each unit.

By James Davey LONDON – DSG International DSGI, Europe's No.2 electricals' retailer, reported a pick-up in sales in recent weeks, helped by store upgrades and demand for Microsoft's MSFT new Windows 7 computer operating system.DSG, which runs the Currys and PC World chains.

RayMedi Head Quarter – Product Overview

RayMedi HQ is designed to manage your chain of shops more easily. RayMedi HQ is a web-based, easy-to-use software which gives you more control in managing your chain of shops. It works seamlessly with your individual shops data (RayMedi RPOS/RE/DE data) and gives you a consolidated and centralized way of managing your chain better.

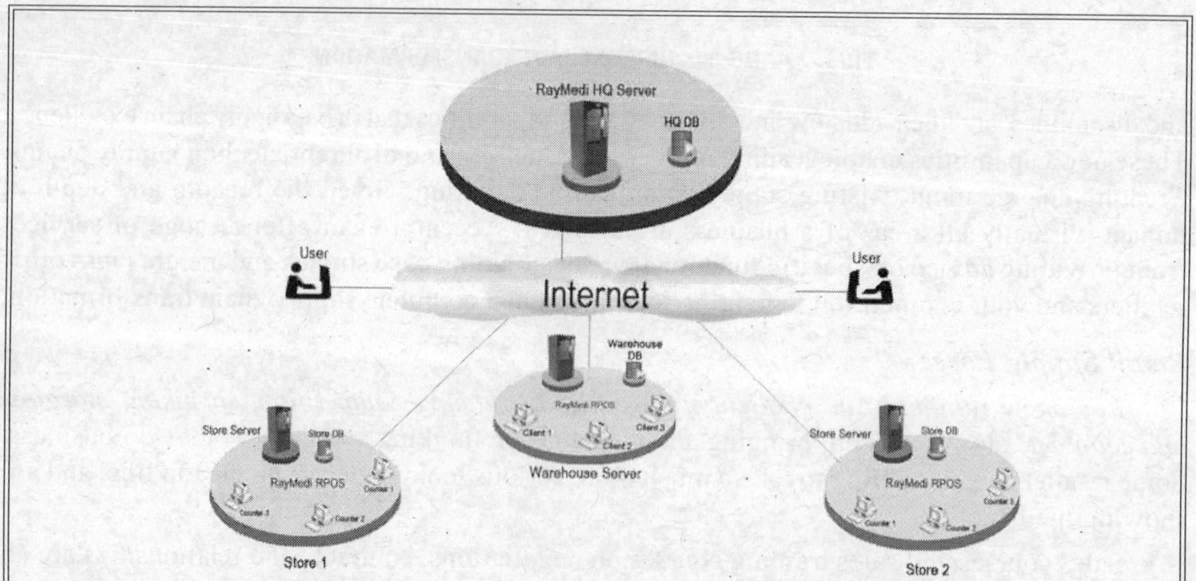

FIG. 31: RAYMEDI DEPLOYMENT ARCHITECTURE

RayMedi HQ gives you the Real-time business status at HQ from about every point of sale. From the head office, you can monitor sales and inventory position at each one of your store. The software helps you in consolidating the data from your various branches into one system and do an integrated analysis of sales, inventory and purchase. RayMedi HQ primarily focuses on managing your branch-wise sales, purchase, inventory, receivables and profits. It helps you in controlling expenses, decreasing costs and increasing your profits.

The key business benefits and the features of the product are detailed below:

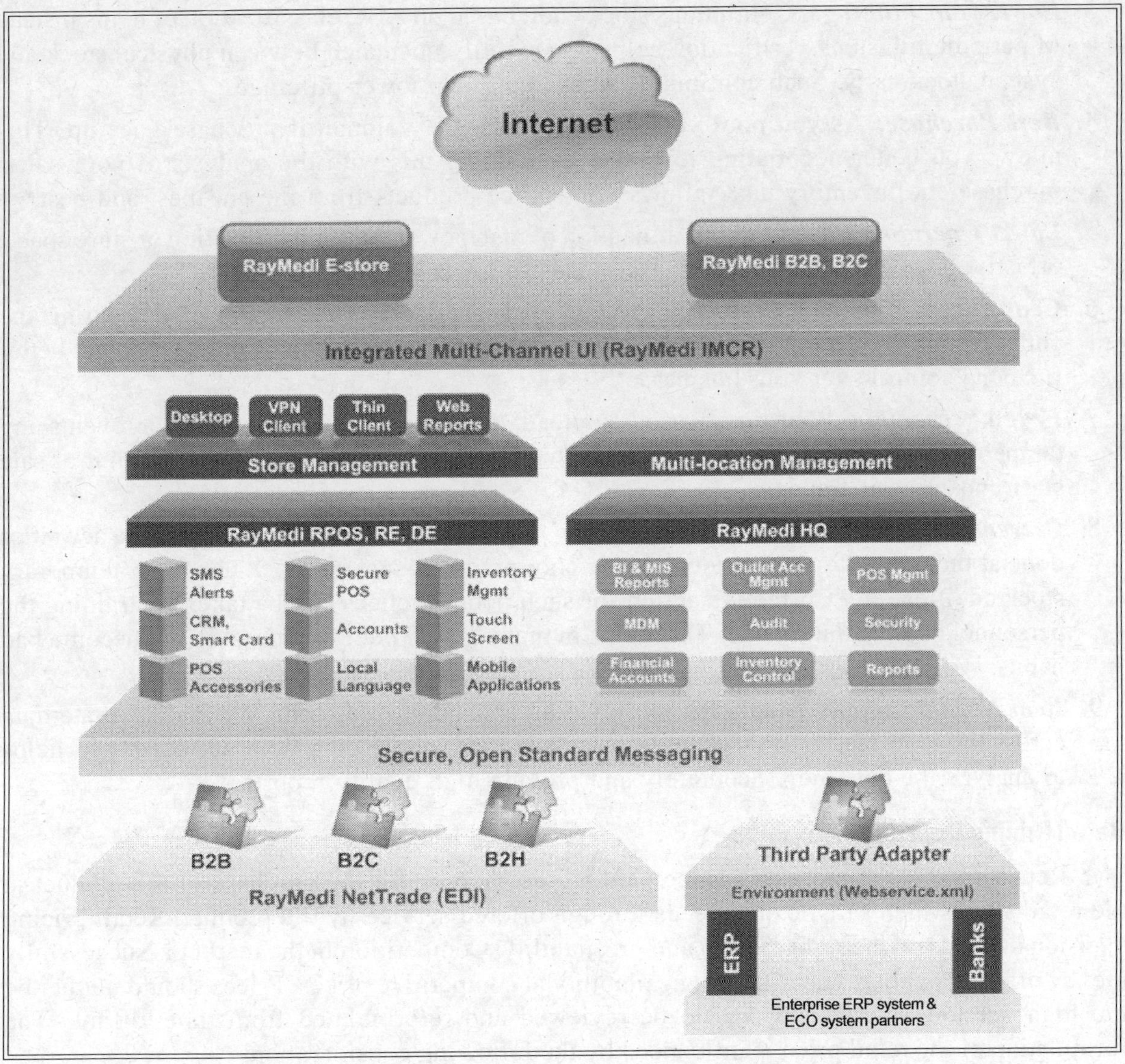

FIG. 32 : RAYMEDI SOLUTION ARCHITECTURE

Summary of Business Benefits

1. ***Lower your Inventory Investment:*** Consolidated view of inventory including the need at each point of sale facilitates optimum inventory at each point of sale. Also ensures that stock can be transferred to the point of sale at short notice. This lowers investment and increases the return.
2. ***Increase your ROI:*** Identify non-moving stock across the chain, transfer them to where they are selling and/or return them. Also, identify and return non-moving stock at purchase value to avoid any loss on non-moving stock return. Such effective stock transfers coupled with purchase returns increase the ROI.
3. ***Lower your Pilferage:*** Continuous stock audit based on ABC classification of items instead of periodic full stock verification helps you identify mismatch between physical stock and system stock early. Such continuous stock audit help lower pilferage.
4. ***Best Purchase:*** As you pool your requirements, the volume of purchase goes up. This allows you better negotiating leverage. Combining this with the analysis of your sales, purchase and inventory data, allows you source products from the cheapest and best.
5. ***Lower Operating Cost:*** Optimal utilization of man power, optimal utilization of store space, effective inventory management, etc., leads to lower operating costs.
6. ***Centralized Financial Control:*** As your business moves to a model of depositing the entire receipts/collections with the HQ and all payments are made from HQ, you get better financial control over your business.
7. ***Fraud Prevention:*** Real-time/Periodic upload of point of sale data to the HQ prevents any tampering with data at the point of sale. This builds better awareness among point of sale staff and prevent fraud.
8. ***Prevent poor practices from becoming bad habits***: Audit trail help HQ know the activities done at the point of sale and identify the poor practices such as stock updating, temporary stock addition, etc. Corrective action for such poor practices can be taken by training the personnel at the point of sale. This helps in making sure poor practices do not become bad habits.
9. ***Item Normalization:*** This helps in providing a standardized, complete and accurate data across the item master files of both the retailer and wholesaler. Item normalization helps to analyze the data more accurately and provide high quality reports.

Retail Pricing Decisions

Retail price is the monetary value paid by the shopper for the purchase of the product in the retail shop which satisfies his needs through offered service by the product. Retail pricing decision depends on the right margin and profitability. Competition in the market is successfully met by offering quality, selection and availability at competitive prices. Prices should neither be too high nor too low. Pricing has to be reviewed and reformulated from time-to-time. The formulation of the retail price is influenced by the following considerations:

1. Retail management's over all goals.
2. Degree of imperfection in the market.

3. Retail management's product and promotional policies.
4. Conflicting interests of manufacturers and middlemen.
5. Reutilization in pricing and active intervention of government.
6. Nature of price sensitivity and the product and importance of service sales, etc.,

The prices of the retail includes the store, the staff and the merchandise location, price level, merchandise, store layout, method of selling, brand name and service along with tangible products. Retail pricing is in line with overall objectives and business reputation and normally specified in terms of sales, profits and return on investment. Pricing being an integral part of marketing mix, it is consistent with the other elements of marketing mix. In the practical world, besides shoppers and retailers, rival retailers, potential rivals, middlemen and the government have got a say in the fixation of price. Pricing is a function of demand and supply. It is not perfectly inelastic. It is sensitive to many other factors such as market segments, target market, shopper behaviour, state of the market economy, demand curve which explains the reactions of the market to change in price. Demand process can be understood with price elasticity, which is a key element. The price sensitivity can be defined as the ratio of the per centage response in the quantity sold to per centage change in price.

$$\text{Price sensitivity} = \frac{\text{Percentage change in quantity demanded}}{\text{Percentage change in price}}$$

Factors Affecting Price Sensitivity

1. **Perceived Substitute Effect:** The local residents may avoid an area with higher priced shops because the shopper believes that the overall value is not accepted to them.
2. **Unique Value Effect:** If the retailer shop has unique value or attribute to offer to the shoppers, which offers competitive price or other retail shops do not offer under such circumstances, the shopper tends to be less sensitive to a product's price. For example, many shoppers are loyal to Hindustan Liver, Nestle, Surf Excel products.
3. **Utility Value:** If utility is very high, price will not be the most important. For example, purchase of emergency medicine.
4. **Difficulties in Comparison Effect:** When comparison between retail shops becomes difficult, then shoppers are less sensitive to price, which results into a demand for the more established brands, or greater store loyalty which reduces the risk of perception.

Price Quality Effect: A higher price may create an impression of superior quality of the product in the minds of shoppers. The market becomes less sensitive to price. **Expenditure effect**: If higher expenditure in absolute money amount or as a per centage of the income is required, then the shopper becomes more price sensitive. This is most prevalent in low income households and in recessional economies in which all expenditure is carefully controlled.

Fairness Expenditure: If the shoppers believe that the brand is out of his reach or the retailer charges exorbitantly high then, they become price sensitive and they switch to other economical products. Shoppers will perceive retailers, or the brands that stock to be 'ripping off' shoppers if they exploit situations of shortage by being greedy.

The Retail Trading Zone: Newspaper circulation figures are generally broken down into three categories: (1) The city zone, (2) The retail trading zone and all other areas. The retail trading zone is the market outside the city zone whose residents regularly trade with merchants within the city zone. The 'all other' category covers all circulation not included in the city or retail trade zone. Retail advertising rates apply to advertisers that conduct business to sell goods or services within the designated market area (DMA). The rates paid by general advertisers are on average, 75 per cent higher than those paid by retail advertisers. Newspaper publishers claim the rate differential is justified for several reasons . First, they argue it costs more to handle general advertising since ad agencies get a 15 per cent commission and commission must be paid to the independent sales reps. who solicit nonretail advertising. Second, they note that general advertising is less dependable than local advertising, general advertisers usually don't use newspapers on a continual basis like retail advertisers do. Finally, newspaper publishers contend that demand for general advertising is inelastic – it will not increase if rates are lowered or decrease if rates are raised.

Factors Affecting Retail Pricing Policy

1. The perishable nature of some products such as high fashion items or those with 'sell by dates' are influential.
2. Products which cannot be sold on future occasion lead retailers to engage in various forms of last minute tactical pricing of seasonal sales
3. The competitive nature of the industry places emphasis on setting price at competitive levels or retailers could face losing sales
4. The material is volatile in nature
5. Supply problem
6. Overall cost control
7. Psychological aspects of pricing

Types of Retail Pricing

1. ***Cost-oriented Pricing (cost-plus method/full-cost pricing):*** It is a popular method of pricing. It uses average costs. It is preferred in an uncertain market. It ignores demand. **According to this method, Price = AVC + AFC + Normal profit margin (or mark-up)**
2. ***Marginal Cost Pricing:*** It implies the practice of setting price just to cover the variable cost for marginal cost or incremental cost. Involved in the production. It is suitable for multi-product firm.
3. ***Target Rate of Return Pricing:*** It is based on cost of production incurred by the producer.
4. ***Going Rate Pricing:*** Retailer may fix price for his product on the basis of prices that prevail in the whole industry.
5. ***Peak Load Pricing:*** It implies the practice of raising the price above average variable cost during high demand periods and reducing it towards average variable cost during low demand.

6. ***Marginal cost pricing:*** It implies the practice of setting price just to cover the variable cost (or marginal cost or incremental cost) involved in the production of a commodity, ignoring its fixed costs. It permits adjustments in demand conditions.
7. ***The Target Rate of Return Pricing:*** The target rate of return considers the desired rate of return on initial investment made by the firm in setting the mark-up.
8. ***Going Rate Pricing:*** It refers to the prices which prevail in the whole industry; there is generally a price range which shows the magnitude of price variation from the lowest to the highest levels.
9. ***Peak Load Pricing:*** It implies the practice of raising the price above average variable cost during high demand periods and reducing it towards average variable cost during low demand periods.
10. ***Pricing a New Product:*** As soon as a new product is introduced in a retail market, it has to go through several problems as neither it has an established market, nor it commands a good demand for it. However, we can say that the pricing policy remains the same as for new and old products. It should cover the whole costs during the long run and direct costs in the short run. In addition, decisions have to be taken on market targets, design of the promotional strategy and the channels of distribution. Test marketing can be very useful in the solution of these problems. We can hope to have all the information necessary for better planning, pricing and full-scale production. Here also pricing mistakes that may come on the way can be avoided for the full-scale.
11. ***High Skimming Price:*** A high skimming price refers to the high initial price which would be charged when a new product is introduced in the market.
12. ***Low Penetration Price:*** It means charging a low price right from the beginning. The product quickly penetrates the market and consumers with low incomes are able to purchase it.
13. ***Price Discrimination:*** First Degree Discrimination: The retailer charges the same buyer a different price for each unit bought, e.g., quantity discounts.
14. ***Second Degree Discrimination:*** The retailer charges different prices for blocks of units instead of for individual units, e.g., different rates charged by an electricity undertaking for domestic power, and for industrial use.
15. ***Third Degree Discrimination:*** The retailer segregates buyers according to income, geographic location, individual tastes, kinds of uses for the product, or other criteria and charges different prices to each group or market despite equivalent costs in serving them. As long as the elasticity of demand among different buyers are unequal, it will be profitable for the seller to group the buyers into separate classes according to elasticity, and charge each class a separate price.
16. ***Value Pricing:*** The retail management charges a fairly low price for a high-quality offering. Value pricing says that the price should represent a high-value offer to consumers. Psychological pricing: Many consumers use price as an indicator of quality. Higher-priced cars are perceived to possess high quality. Higher-quality cars are likewise perceived to be higher priced than they actually are. The price must be consistent with retail management's

pricing policy. Many retail companies set up a pricing department to develop policies and establish or approve decisions. The aim is to ensure that the salespeople quote prices that are reasonable to customers and profitable to the company. Retail management usually does not set a single price but rather a pricing structure that reflects variations in geographical demand and costs, market segment requirements, purchase variations in geographical demand and costs, market-segment requirements, purchase timing, order levels, delivery frequency, guarantees, service contracts, and other factors. As a result of discounts, allowances, and promotional support, a company rarely realizes the same profit from each unit of a product that it sells.

RETAIL INVENTORY MANAGEMENT

Retail Industry

The business of retail is getting tougher every year. Shoppers have more choice than ever and are far more selective about where they shop. With more retailers and more stores chasing shoppers, it is no surprise that big names in retail have recently gone bust. In winning at retail, top retail consultants offer candid, straightforward, and passionate guidance for retailers who understand that winning at this game means setting themselves apart from the pack. Today's top retailers dedicate themselves to being the best at something and they defend that advantage at all costs.

Inventory is a detailed list of movable goods such as raw materials, work-in-progress, finished goods, spares, tools consumables and general supplies necessary to manufacture a product and to maintain plant and machinery. Inventory means storage of goods for productive purposes.

The Difficult Task of Retail Inventory Management

Retail inventory management is probably one of the most complex of all inventory management departments. In retail management, one will have a greater variety of products to store and a great deal more of each product. In fact, your warehouse may never be big enough to hold all the merchandise that one needs to keep in stock, and it can be difficult to maintain the right number of any particular item at any given time. How can one solve the problem, or at least address it, before it becomes too much to handle?

Retail inventory management should never be the job of a single individual but should be divided into departments and classified accordingly. For example, in a supermarket, there are two major departments – grocery and non-grocery – and each will have several subcategories. Under grocery, one can expect such departments as meat, dairy, frozen, canned, and more.

Delegation of Responsibility

Depending on the size of the store, the retail inventory management could be divided into the two main categories and delegated to two individuals who would be responsible for the management of the entire inventory, or it could be broken down further, having an employee in charge of each smaller division. This would allow the individual to gain an intimate knowledge of how quickly each product is sold and how often it needed to be reordered.

The important thing to remember in retail inventory management is that the shopkeeper most likely have a little storage space for an enormous array of products and have to determine what will and won't be important to maintain in quantity. Being efficient in carefully stocking the storage areas, as well as knowing what one's best sellers are, can help the retailer keep his retail inventory management process strong and in balance.

Quantity of inventory used in inventory management systems allow for deviations in demand or supply. Safety stock calculations take into account historic deviations and use a required service level multiplier to determine the optimal safety stock level. Marketers with more than a few stores.

Because merchandise flow and product placement are primary responsibility, retailers' proactive participation in inventory management functions will be vital to the success of the overall merchandising effort. In the course of completing the retailers visual merchandising tasks the retailers will also stock merchandise, take inventory, facilitate stock transfers, ticket and reticket, execute markdowns, and maintain awareness of potential loss prevention issues and activities. The retailers may also participate in the shipping and receiving process and ensure that merchandise is customer ready before it is placed on the sales floor.

RETAIL INVENTORY MANAGEMENT SYSTEM

At the heart of every good retail software package lies a powerful inventory management system. An inventory management system lets the retailers know what they have, what they need, and when they need it. Here are a few of the many ways your retail software and inventory management system can help you run a more efficient business.

More Accurate Inventory

With an inventory management system, the retailers can get up-to-the-minute reports on what they have in stock, on order, and in transit. No more "assuming" that there are enough of a particular item. No more "thinking" that they have placed the order to replenish their supply. Retail software with an inventory management system eliminates the guesswork from running their retail business.

Timelier Ordering

Some inventory management systems can be set up to automatically notify the retailer when it's time to order more inventory, such as when stock falls below a predetermined level. Retailers having hottest items in stock, they have to be sure not to miss sales due to out-of-stock items. Many retail software packages will even generate purchase orders, further streamlining your inventory management. In addition to increasing sales, retail software with an inventory management system can drastically reduce operating costs by reducing the time spent manually counting inventory and creating purchase orders.

Identify What's Hot (And What's Not)

An inventory management system tracks which items are selling and which aren't. This is a great way to identify hottest and coldest items. So, the retailers can make better business decisions. By identifying their slowest moving items, they can adjust their placement, pricing, or other issues sooner. They can also see which items are frequently purchased in pairs, so they can group them accordingly in the store. For example, the retailer can place batteries in the same aisle as their flashlights.

A retail revolution is happening in the country. For global giants looking at newer markets, India presents exciting opportunities on account of its vast middle-class and a virtually untapped retail industry.

The Indian retail sector has seen unprecedented growth in the last few years. The KPMG report, 'Consumer Markets in India: the next big thing?, has predicted that the organized retail sector is expected to grow at rate higher than GDP growth in the next five years. The AT Kearney's 2006 Global Retail Development Index positions India as a leading destination for retail investment.

The success in this competitive and dynamic sector depends on achieving an efficient logistics and supply chain, which can be provided by professionals, as they combine the best systems and expertise to manage a ready flow of goods and services.

i2 Supply Chain Management Solutions are geared toward solving customers' specific business objectives. Each one of i2's solutions is built upon industry's best practices and leverages the knowledge of years of experience with thousands of implementations. i2 solutions integrate with data, processes, and systems belonging to suppliers, customers, distributors, carriers, partners, and contract manufacturers.

But how do companies put these solutions into action in the unpredictable modern business landscape? The i2 Agile Business Platform, a unique service-oriented architecture, is designed specifically to meet the requirements of the new generation of supply chain management. The platform includes a technology layer of services such as XML data modelling, a business process workflow engine, and a business programming language.

In addition there is a layer of core business functionality that provides capabilities such as plan management, execution management, visibility, and collaboration. A company can simply "plug in" its existing i2 products into the platform to provide and extract critical data to make more informed decisions. The platform also accepts input from legacy and ERP applications.

Using workflows — easy-to-use programming capabilities based on i2's industry domain expertise — i2 customers are able to leverage the power of the i2 Agile Business Process Platform to automate solutions.

Supply Management

i2 Supply Management solutions allow you to manage the product costs through the overall product life cycle, with the capability to define target costs and compare them with actual costs.

Plan Management

i2 Plan Management enables companies to boost customer service levels due to increased product availability and improved responsiveness. Cash-to-cash cycles are lowered with synchronized planning and execution.

Inventory Management

i2 Inventory Management facilitates near real-time monitoring and event management throughout the inventory life cycle. It also enables companies to closely analyze point-of-sale data, profile buying behaviours and trends, and quantify risks and variability. A segmentation menu offers the ability to organize data by standard attributes such as volume, revenue, and margin, as well as any custom attributes. Inventory Management from i2 provides multiple optimization options to minimize cost, maximize performance, redistribute inventory, and analyze total landed cost. A performance manager dashboard in i2 Inventory Management enables continuous learning and improvement.

Transportation and Logistics Management

i2 Transportation and Logistics Management has been designed and proven to empower transportation as a strategic enterprise by enabling industry best practices in the areas of design, procurement, planning, execution, and visibility.

Manufacturing Management

i2 Manufacturing Management synchronizes material between the factory floor and multi-tiered supplier operations and optimizes capacity and labour while reducing inventory and order-to-delivery lead times. It provides intelligent material, capacity, and constraint management, along with the quick detection of problems, proactive exception-based management, and rapid "what-if" analysis, to streamline factory and supplier operations. Companies can consolidate planning and execution workflows, eliminating mismatches that create chaos and non-value added activities on the shop floor.

Multichannel Management

Through Point-of-Sale (PoS) Demand Sensing, Collaborative Customer Management, and Intelligent Selling, Multichannel Management serves as one of the most critical ways that a company can better serve its customers and establish competitive advantage.

GINNI SYSTEMS LIMITED (GSL)

Established in 1999, Ginni Systems Limited (GSL) today is a leading provider of specialized software solutions for the retail industries. The company's expertise in the retail domain makes it an ideal solution provider for an entire gamut of retail chains like Departmental Stores, Chain Stores, Hyper Markets, Discount Stores, Multibrand Outlets, Exclusive Stores, and Food and Grocery Stores etc.

GSL today, is recognized as one of the emerging IT solutions enterprises in India. During its initial years, GSL provided management consultancy and offered software solutions to corporate firms. The company gradually established itself as a leading software solutions expert catering to all kinds of process based manufacturing and retail stores through its state-of-the-art software GINESYS. GSL now offers management and financial consultancy to companies through its sister company Resurgent India Limited.

Equipped with GINESYS, GSL provides holistic solutions to retail chains, right from Point of Sale (Small stores requiring front end modules for billing) to a more complex retail structure (where intricate back office issues such as MIS, generating comprehensive reports, etc.) or a business model for manufacturing (requiring a manufacturing module) to enterprises which are multistores requiring management from a central server. In a word GINESYS is a one stop shop for any retailer who has started small with a one shop unit to the ones who have branched out as multi stores. GINESYS software helps retail and manufacturing businesses to run more profitably and achieve impressive results on their technology investments.

GSL have three world-class software solutions for the Retail Industry –

- GINESYS PoS for individual retailers or franchisee outlets
- GINESYS Retail for individual upscale retailers, multi-outlet retail chains, franchisee outlets
- GINESYS Business for small to medium-scale manufacturing operations, retail supply chain integrations

GSL also offers web-based ERP software solution GINESYS e-ERP for manufacturing companies on 3-tier architecture. This software is successfully running on large cement and automobile part companies. All GINESYS software solutions are based upon Oracle and have been implemented at more than 500 enterprises worldwide.

Corporate Chronology

- 1996 – Corporate inception as Ginni Management Private Limited as a management consultancy firm with a team of qualified professionals.
- 1999 – Started software operations with a team of four visionaries, Prashant Lohia, Arjun Roy, Soumyadip Bhattacharya and Harsh Nahata.
- 2000 – Changes name from Ginni Management Pvt. Ltd., to Ginni Systems Ltd. Partners with Oracle for building solutions on Oracle technology platforms.
- 2000 – Launches GINESYS for retail and manufacturing businesses.
- 2003 – Starts New Delhi operations.
- 2005 – Launches GINESYS e-ERP, successfully implements at cement and automobile sectors.
- 2006 – Starts West and South India operations
- 2007 – Surges ahead with 100+ customers; 500+ installations and 5,000 + users.

GSL proudly announces the release of GINESYS version 10.11 along with a new and completely revamped PoS (Point of Sales) system. GSL is the leading provider of software solutions for retail and manufacturing business. The software can be implemented at any type of retail and associated business and can be scaled from single to a chain of stores. GINESYS Retail has completed integrated retail ERP software covering PoS, Procurement, Store Management, Distribution, Merchandise Planning, Accounts and CRM.

At GSL, we believe in providing our customers complete solutions for their business needs. The GSL team is dedicated to provide efficient software and solutions for retailers and allied manufacturers. The retail division provides complete retail ERP solution along with Point of Sales (PoS) system to take care of Billing, Store Management, Inventory, Customer Loyalty CRM, Inventory, Purchasing, Chain Stores Distribution, Finance and Accounts.

The software can be used by all type of retail formats like Departmental stores, Super markets, Discount Stores, Hyper Markets, Multi-brand Outlets MBOs, Food and Grocery Stores, Exclusive Brand Outlets EBOs, Convenience Stores, Single Stores, Franchisee Stores, etc. It also provides software solutions for apparel, footwear, textiles and garments manufacturers and integrate with PoS to cover complete business from manufacturing to retailing. The software is available in different variants named as GINESYS PoS, GINESYS RETAIL and GINESYS BUSINESS software.

The enterprise division provides enterprise level integration for large retailers. The software provides Enterprise Reporting, Business Intelligence, Merchandise Planning, Replenishment Planning, Centralised Customer Loyalty, SMS and E-mail Notification System.

GSL ERP division provides ERP solutions specific to manufacturing industries like Apparel, Leather, Cement, Autoparts, Plastics, Real Estate, Packaging and Bottling. The ERP software take cares of Financial, Procurement, Sales and Distribution, Production, Planning, HR and Payroll.

The software is running successfully all over india, covering cities like Delhi (New Delhi), Gurgaon, Noida, Gaziabad (NCR), Kolkata, Mumbai, Chennai, Bhubhaneshwar, Hyderabad, Bengaluru, Indore, Jaipur, Jodhpur, Ludhiana, Chandigarh, Kanpur, Lucknow, Jaipur, Ahmedabad, Surat, Ludhiana, Pune, Siliguri, Guwahati, Cuttack, Behrampur, Patna, Jamshedpur, Raipur, Rourkela, Amritsar, Jalandhar, Coimbatore, etc.

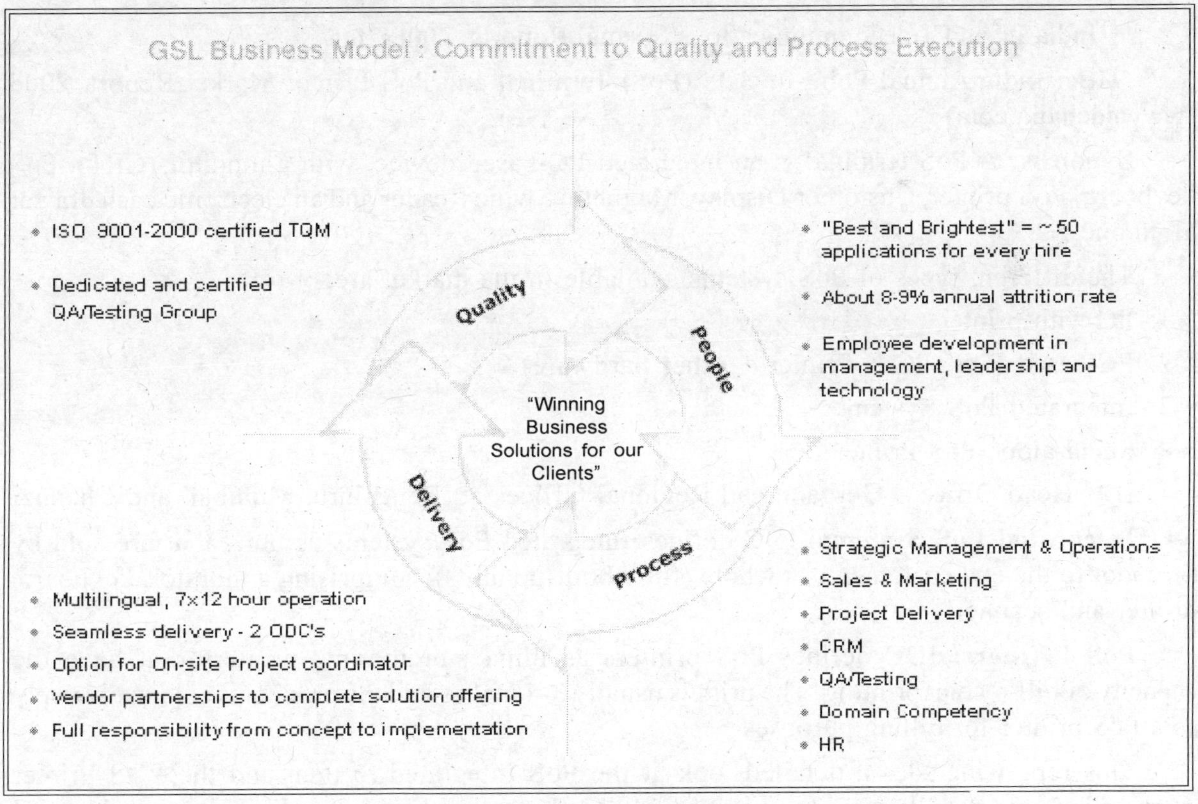

FIG. 33: GSL BUSINESS MODEL

Features

- Out-of-the-box, mature and ready to use retail automation software
- Efficient and error free data entry
- Real time reports with online filters and zoom in
- Customizable search for product, customer and supplier
- Fastest implementation
- Highly scalable and flexible
- Fully modular system
- Secure, reliable and robust database
- Manage chain stores (across cities and countries)
- Manage your sales staff
- Integrated financial accounting
- Integrated customer loyalty programs me
- Integration with tally accounting software
- Third party link for integrating with other systems
- Utilize a wide range of barcode and POS hardware
- Ongoing upgrades

India IT and Telecommunications Special Reports, 2006-2007

Title: India Annual Point of Sale (PoS) Terminal and PoS Printer Market Report, 2006 (www.idcindia.com)

Synopsis: A PoS terminal is an integrated PC-based device, with a monitor (CRT), PoS keyboard, PoS printer, Customer Display, Magnetic Swipe Reader and an electronic cash drawer all in one.

The different types of PoS systems available in the market are:

1. PC with printer
2. PC-based PoS (PC + Printer + other hardware)
3. Integrated PoS System
4. Stand-alone PoS Printer

IDC Head Office – Gurgaon and Regional Offices at: Bengaluru, Mumbai, and Chennai

Integrated PoS Systems: IDC defines Integrated PoS systems as units that are sold by a vendor to the end customer as a whole (fully built-up units), comprising a monitor, keyboard, printer and scanner.

PoS Printers: IDC defines PoS printers as impact or thermal printers that have the capacity of bill/receipt printing. The print is usually 3-4 inches and the product is sold exclusively as a PoS printer for billing purposes.

This report includes a detailed look at the PoS Integrated System and the POS Printer markets in India. It will provide vendors and distributors with a comprehensive overview and analysis, including recent trends, market statistics and forecast for the next five years.

Availability: 15-July, 2006

India Annual Point of Sale (PoS) Terminal and PoS Printer Market Report, 2006

Top Four Vendors

- **IBM**
- **Posiflex**
- **Extredge**
- **Wincor-Nixdorf**

Sales Force Automation Systems (SFA), typically a part of a company's customer relationship management system, is a system that automatically records all the stages in a sales process. SFA includes a contact management system which tracks all contact that has been made with a given customer, the purpose of the contact, and any follow-up that might be required. This ensures that sales efforts are not duplicated, reducing the risk of irritating customers. SFA also includes a sales lead tracking system, which lists potential customers through paid phone lists, or customers of related products. Other elements of an SFA system can include sales forecasting, order management and product knowledge. More developed SFA systems have features where customers can actually model the product to meet their required needs through online product building systems. This is becoming more and more popular in the automobile industry, where patrons can customize various features such as colour and interior features such as leather vs. upholstered seats.

An integral part of any SFA system is company-wide integration among different departments. If SFA systems aren't adopted and properly integrated to all departments, there might be a lack of communication which could result in different departments contacting the same customer for the same purpose. In order to mitigate this risk, SFA must be fully integrated in all departments that deal with customer service management.

Sales force automation systems can also affect sales management. Here are some examples:

1. The sales manager, rather than gathering all the call sheets from various salespeople and tabulating the results, will have the results automatically presented in easy to understand tables, charts, or graphs. This saves time for the manager.
2. Activity reports, information requests, orders booked, and other sales information will be sent to the sales manager more frequently, allowing him/her to respond more directly with advice, product in-stock verifications, and price discount authorizations. This gives management more hands-on control of the sales process if they wish to use it.
3. The sales manager can configure the system so as to automatically analyze the information using sophisticated statistical techniques, and present the results in a user-friendly way. This gives the sales manager information that is more useful in:
   - Providing current and useful sales support materials to their sales staff
   - Providing marketing research data: demographic, psychographic, behavioural, product acceptance, product problems, detecting trends
   - Providing market research data: industry dynamics, new competitors, new products from competitors, new promotional campaigns from competitors, macro-environmental scanning, detecting trends

- Coordinate with other parts of the firm, particularly marketing, production, and finance
- Identifying your most profitable customers, and your problem customers
- Tracking the productivity of their sales force by combining a number of performance measures such as: revenue per salesperson, revenue per territory, margin by customer segment, margin by customer, number of calls per day, time spent per contact, revenue per call, cost per call, entertainment cost per call, ratio of orders to calls, revenue as a per centage of sales quota, number of new customers per period, number of lost customers per period, cost of customer acquisition as a per centage of expected lifetime value of customer, per centage of goods returned, number of customer complaints, and number of overdue accounts. More complex models like the PAIRS model (by Parasuraman and Dey) and the Call Plan model (by Lodish) can also be used.

Advantages to the Marketing Manager

It is also claimed to be useful for the marketing manager. It gives the marketing manager information that is useful in :

- Understanding the economic structure of your industry
- Identifying segments within your market
- Identifying your target market
- Identifying your best customers in place
- Doing marketing research to develop profiles (demographic, psychographic, and behavioural) of your core customers
- Understanding your competitors and their products
- Developing new products
- Establishing environmental scanning mechanisms to detect opportunities and threats
- Understanding your company's strengths and weaknesses
- Auditing your customers' experience of your brand in full
- Developing marketing strategies for each of your products using the marketing mix variables of price, product, distribution, and promotion
- Coordinating the sales function with other parts of the promotional mix (such as advertising, sales promotion, public relations, and publicity)
- Creating a sustainable competitive advantage
- Understanding where you want your brands to be in the future, and providing an empirical basis for writing marketing plans on a regular basis to help you get there
- Providing input into feedback systems to help you monitor and adjust the process

Strategic Advantages

Sales force automation systems can also create competitive advantage. Here are some examples.

As mentioned above, productivity will increase. Sales staff will use their time more efficiently and more effectively. The sales manager will also become more efficient and more effective.

(See above). This increased productivity can create a competitive advantage in three ways: it can reduce costs, it can increase sales revenue, and it can increase market share.

- Field sales staff will send their information more frequently. Typically information will be sent to management after every sales call (rather than once a week). This provides management with current information, information that they will be able to use while it is still valuable. Management response time will be greatly reduced. The company will become more alert and more agile.
- These systems could increase customer satisfaction if they are used with wisdom. If the information obtained and analyzed with the system is used to create a product that matches or exceeds customer expectations, and the sales staff use the system to service customers more expertly and diligently, then customers should be satisfied with the company. This will provide a competitive advantage because customer satisfaction leads to increased customer loyalty, reduced customer acquisition costs, reduced price elasticity of demand, and increased profit margins.

Disadvantages

Detractors claim that sales force management systems are:

- difficult to work with
- require additional work inputting data
- dehumanize a process that should be personal
- require continuous maintenance, information updating, and system upgrading
- costly
- difficult to integrate with other management information systems

Encouraging Use

For all the reasons stated above many organizations have found it difficult to persuade sales-people to enter data into the system. For this reason many have questioned the value of the investment. Recent developments have embedded sales process systems that give something back to the seller within the CRM screens. Because these systems help the salesperson plan and structure their selling in the most effective way they give a reason to use the CRM.

BNET Daily Dispatch: Nestle, Vonage, Toyota, and Retail Sales

Nestle is buying Gerber from Novartis AG for $ 5.5 billion, making it the world's biggest baby food company. Nestle said today that the acquisition would give its nutrition division annual sales of about $ 8.21 billion, and it will boost its operating profit margin immediately.

Housing Activity Boosts Carpetright

By James DaveyLONDON (Reuters UK) – Carpetright CATVU, the country's biggest floor coverings retailer, grabbed market share from failing rivals and reported a boost from growing housing activity to post a second straight quarter of rising sales. Chairman and Chief Executive Philip Harris said the overall floor coverings market fell over.

Thorntons Sees Q1 Sales Rise

By James DaveyLONDON (Reuters UK) – Chocolate retailer Thorntons THT said it was well positioned for Christmas as it posted a 2.3 per cent rise in first-quarter sales (2011), sending its shares up nearly 5 per cent SalesKraft Foods Inc.Oukbs.

By James DaveyLONDON (Reuters UK) – Cycles and camping gear proved strong sellers for retailer Halfords Group in the first half, boosting profits above expectations and helping send its shares to a 12-month high. The car parts to bicycles retailer promised first-half profit would top market forecasts as it posted increased.

For many retailers, the challenges faced by increasing competition, shrinking margins, and economic slowdowns are bringing about changes in thinking and the way they do business. Some retailers are beginning to take a much more serious look at managing the top line, and are showing the benefits.

Retailers large and small struggle with the same fundamental challenge: How to best match demand for their products to supply, and at the same time leave sufficient margin on the table to allow them to serve customers, compete, and grow.

Some countries have regulations that impose restrictions on the use of sales promotions in retail markets. The main motivation of these policies has been the protection of small retailers. This paper studies empirically the welfare implications of this type of policies.

Although multichannel retailing has been around for over a century, the online sales capability brought about by the commercialization of the internet has forever altered the retailing landscape. The paper analyzes how can retailers position themselves to deliver a seamless customer shopping experience across channels.

Supply Chain Coordination Under Channel Rebates With Sales Effort Effects

A channel rebate is a payment from a manufacturer to a retailer based on retailer sales to end consumers. Two common forms of channel rebates are linear rebates, in which the rebate is paid for each unit sold, and target rebates, in which the rebate is paid for each unit.

Forecasting collaboration between retailers and suppliers is suggested to bring significant benefits in the form of increased efficiency and improved customer service. Yet, only few companies seem to be engaged in collaborative relationships.

This is a template for leading retailers in global food market sales.

Harvard's Anita Elberse: Forget the "Long Tail"

The Find: A Harvard Business School professor crunches the numbers and comes up with a startling conclusion for those in the media biz: forget the long tail, aim for the occasional and old fashioned blockbuster.

American Girl: The Shape of Retail to Come

American Girl stores aren't just about selling dolls. Instead, the dolls are part of a stage play that creates an experience for young girls and their mothers with dads in tow that is so compelling you happily plunk down hundreds of dollars to remember and memorialize it.

The Secret to Becoming an Industry Leader

What happens when a company straddles two industries, profiting in one arena and struggling in the other? That was Hewlett-Packard's story a couple years back — its printing business paid the bills while Dell took the lead in PC sales.

Wal-Mart Plans Higher-end Stores

Wal-Mart reported disappointing earnings for the second quarter of 2011 and predicted more troubles to come, blaming its poor clothing and home decor products as well as higher energy prices and problems in the housing market for the subdued earnings outlook. Shares in the company promptly fell 5 per cent.

Sara Lee Corp. saw a 7.1 per cent increase in sales for 2007 in all six of its divisions. Much of the company's success can be attributed to its new customer-centric sales strategy, which focuses on the vendor as customer. Lori DescheneFood and Beverage Retail Sales Strategy Mergers and Acquisitions Sara Lee Corp. Whole Foods Star bucks Corp. Midwest.

What's wrong in Bentonville? The world's largest retailer learns that being big is no guarantee of long-term success. 1. Domestic Saturation The Summary: After years of US expansion, Wal-Mart is running out of real estate. The Challenge: Opening new markets by overcoming opposition.

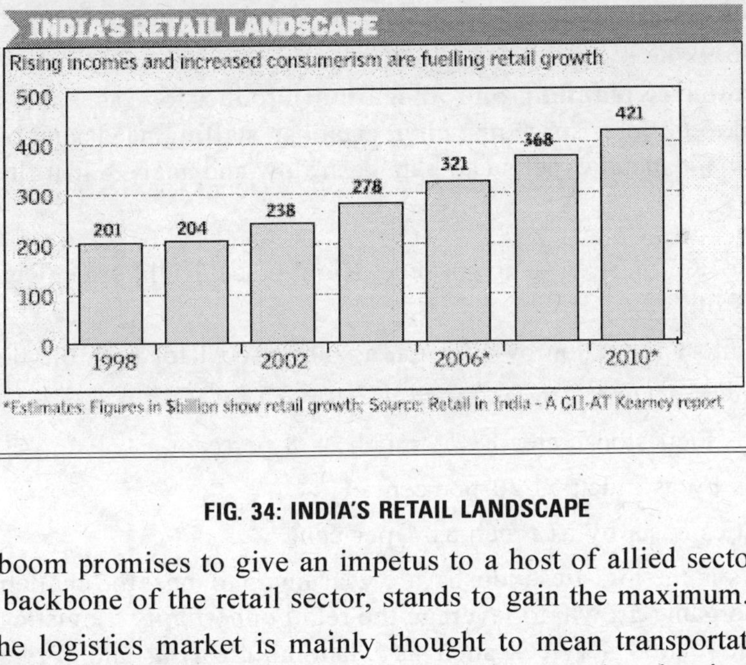

FIG. 34: INDIA'S RETAIL LANDSCAPE

The retail boom promises to give an impetus to a host of allied sectors and the logistics industry, as the backbone of the retail sector, stands to gain the maximum.

In India, the logistics market is mainly thought to mean transportation. But the major elements of logistics cost for industries include transportation, warehousing, inventory management, courier and other valued-added services such as packaging.

The logistics costs account for 13 per cent of GDP. The industry is currently on an upswing and is poised for a growth of 20 per cent in the coming years.

With the expansion of retail, supply chain will take on an increasingly important role. With the end consumer becoming more demanding and time conscious, the need for just-in-time services is increasing. In retail, where competition is intense and stakes are high, customer satisfaction is paramount.

Network Critical

Industry experts opine that in India too the large retail chains will follow the global model of outsourcing their logistics so as to better manage complex supply chains and focus on their core business.

For the retail chains in agri-produce, efficiency of logistics is critical and can indeed leverage the brand to a great extent.

The Main Asset

Retailers realize that knowing what is selling and what is not can improve the inventory processes. Inventory is the biggest cost factor, and if not managed well, it can also be the biggest drain. That's why retailers and their trading partners today set store by the inventory process and its impact. Effective SCM enables: inventory process and its impact. Effective SCM enables:

Realistic ordering lead-times: Suppliers are not surprised by the next order. Retailers respond better to demand spikes, minimize forced markdowns and avoid obsolete-inventory costs.

Averting problems: Stores easily identify potential stock-outs and request replenishment before the inventory drops to zero. Deciding to delist or replace a product is easier.

Facilitating resource planning and allocation: Product forecasts and supply schedules are easily converted to perform space planning, establish staffing needs and organize inbound/ outbound shipments. Financial experts can plan cash flow and analyze margins into the future.

Four 'Rs'

Follow the four 'Rs' of SCM — Right time, Right place, Right price, Right quantity — to reap the advantages of:

Sustained inventory reduction by as much as 60 per cent for both the buyer and seller.

Improved forecast accuracy by as much as 30 per cent.

Enhanced store shelf stock rates by as much as 8 per cent.

Increased sales by as much as 20 per cent.

Reduced logistics costs by as much as 4 per cent.

The key players in the logistics industry are gearing up to meet the challenges by initiating both organic and inorganic growth to leverage the retail opportunity. Logistics firms have also started focusing on related services such as Customs clearing and forwarding, inbound warehousing, labelling and packaging, fleet management, order picking and inventory management.

Cold Chain

The booming retail sector has set-off growth in the cold chain segment as well. It is a highly specialized service and caters to time sensitive and perishable items. The cold chain industry is growing at 20-25 per cent. However, there is an urgent need to establish the necessary infrastructure for an effective cold chain.

Retailing is one of the pillars of the economy in India and accounts for 35 per cent of GDP.

The retail industry is divided into organized and unorganized sectors. Over 12 million outlets operate in the country and only 4 per cent of them being larger than 500 sq ft (46 m^2) in size. Organized retailing refers to trading activities undertaken by licensed retailers, that is, those who are registered for sales tax, income tax, etc. These include the corporate-backed hypermarkets and retail chains, and also the privately owned large retail businesses. Unorganized retailing, on the other hand, refers to the traditional formats of low-cost retailing, for example, the local kirana shops, owner manned general stores, paan/beedi shops, convenience stores, hand cart and pavement vendors, etc. In India, a shopkeeper of such kind of shops is usually known as a dukandar.

Most Indian shopping takes place in open markets and millions of independent grocery shops called kirana. Organized retail such supermarkets accounts for just 4 per cent of the market as of 2008. Regulations prevent most foreign investment in retailing. Moreover, over thirty regulations such as "signboard licences" and "anti-hoarding measures" may have to be complied before a store can open doors. There are taxes for moving goods to states, from states, and even within states.

Growth

An increasing number of people in India are turning to the services sector for employment due to the relative low compensation offered by the traditional agriculture and manufacturing sectors. The organized retail market is growing at 35 per cent annually while growth of unorganized retail sector is pegged at 6 per cent. The retail business in India is currently at the point of inflection. Rapid change with investments to the tune of US \$ 25 billion is being planned by several Indian and multinational companies in the next five years. It is a huge industry in terms of size and according to management consulting firm Technopak Advisors Pvt. Ltd., it is valued at about US \$ 350 billion. Organized retail is expected to garner about 16-18 per cent of the total retail market (US \$ 65-75 billion) in the next five years.

India has topped the A.T. Kearney's annual Global Retail Development Index (GRDI) for the third consecutive year, maintaining its position as the most attractive market for retail investment. The Indian economy has registered a growth of 8 per cent for 2007. The predictions for 2008 is 7.9 per cent. The enormous growth of the retail industry has created a huge demand for real estate. Property developers are creating retail real estate at an aggressive pace and by 2010, 300 malls are estimated to be operational in the country. With over 1,000 hypermarkets and 3,000 supermarkets projected to come up by 2011, India will need additional retail space of 700,000,000 sq. ft. (65,000,000 m^2) as compared to today. Current projections on construction point to a supply of just 200,000,000 sq. ft. (19,000,000 m^2), leaving a gap of 500,000,000 sq. ft. (46,000,000 m^2) that needs to be filled, at a cost of US \$ 15-18 billion. According to the ICRIER report, the retail business in India is estimated to grow at 13 per cent from \$ 322 billion in 2006-07 to \$ 590 billion in 2011-12. The unorganized retail sector is expected to grow at about 10 per cent per annum with sales expected to rise from \$ 309 billion in 2006-07 to \$ 496 billion in 2011-12.

The Indian Retail Market

Indian market has high complexities in terms of a wide geographic spread and distinct consumer preferences varying by each region necessitating a need for localization even within the geographic zones. India has highest number of outlets per person (7 per thousand) Indian retail space per capita at 2 sq. ft. (0.19 m^2)/ person is lowest in the world Indian retail density of 6 per cent is highest in the world. 1.8 million households in India have an annual income of over ₹ 45 lakh (US $ 101, 250) .

Delving further into consumer buying habits, purchase decisions can be separated into two categories: status-oriented and indulgence-oriented. CTVs/LCDs, refrigerators, washing machines, dishwashers, microwave ovens and DVD players fall in the status category. Indulgence-oriented products include plasma TVs, state-of-the-art home theatre systems, iPods, high-end digital cameras, camcorders, and gaming consoles. Consumers in the status category buy because they need to maintain a position in their social group. Indulgence-oriented buying happens with those who want to enjoy life better with products that meet their requirements. When it comes to the festival shopping season, it is primarily the status-oriented segment that contributes largely to the retailer's cash register. While India presents a large market opportunity given the number and increasing purchasing power of consumers, there are significant challenges as well given that over 90 per cent of trade is conducted through independent local stores. Challenges include: Geographically dispersed population, small ticket sizes, complex distribution network, little use of IT systems, limitations of mass media and existence of counterfeit goods.

Major Indian Retailers

Indian apparel retailers are increasing their brand presence overseas, particularly in developed markets. While most have identified a gap in countries in West Asia and Africa, some majors are also looking at the US and Europe. Arvind Brands, Madura Garments, Spykar Lifestyle and Royal Classic Polo are busy chalking out foreign expansion plans through the distribution route and standalone stores as well. Another denim wear brand, Spykar, which is now moving towards becoming a casualwear lifestyle brand, has launched its store in Melbourne recently. It plans to open three stores in London by 2008-end. The low-intensity entry of the diversified Mahindra Group into retail is unique because it plans to focus on lifestyle products. The Mahindra Group is the fourth large Indian business group to enter the business of retail after Reliance Industries Ltd., the Aditya Birla Group, and Bharti Enterprises Ltd. The other three groups are focusing either on perishables and groceries, or a range of products, or both.

- Next retail India Ltd. (Consumer Electronics)(www.next.co.in)
- Vivek Limited Retail Formats: Viveks, Jainsons, Viveks Service Centre, Viveks Safe Deposit Lockers
- PGC Retail T-Mart India, Switcher, Respect India, Grand India Bazaar, etc.
- REI AGRO LTD Retail-Formats:6TEN Hyper and 6TEN Super
- RPG Retail Formats: Music World, Books and Beyond, Spencer's Hyper, Spencer's Super, Daily and Fresh
- Pantaloon Retail Formats: Big Bazaar, Food Bazaar, Pantaloons, Central, Fashion Station, Brand Factory, Depot, aLL, E-Zone, etc.

- The Tata Group Formats: Westside, Star India Bazaar, Steeljunction, Landmark, Titan Industries with World of Titans showrooms, Tanishq outlets, Chroma.
- K Raheja Corp Group Formats: Shoppers' Stop, Crossword, Hyper City, Inorbit Mall
- Lifestyle International Lifestyle, Home Centre, Max, Fun City and International Franchise brand stores.
- Pyramid Retail Formats: Pyramid Megastore, TruMart
- Nilgiris Formats: Nilgiris' supermarket chain
- Subhiksha Formats: Subhiksha supermarket pharmacy and telecom discount chain.
- Trinethra Formats: Fabmall supermarket chain and Fabcity hypermarket chain
- Vishal Retail Group Formats: Vishal Mega Mart
- BPCL Formats: In and Out
- Reliance Retail Formats: Reliance Fresh
- Reliance ADAG Retail Format: Reliance World
- German Metro Cash and Carry
- Shoprite Holdings-Formats: Shoprite Hyper
- Paritala Stores Bazar: Honey Shine Stores
- Aditya Birla Group – more Outlets
- Kapas – Cotton garment outlets

Trouble in Store: A Setback for India's Organized Retail Sector

Subhiksha is India's largest retail chain — or some would prefer to say "it was". Over the past few months, the network of neighbourhood discount shops has been coming apart at the seams. Most of the outlets are now closed. The company — Subhiksha Trading Services — has been unable to pay salaries and statutory dues for the past few months. With the unpaid security agency staff also not reporting for work, many of the stores have been vandalized. "The properties have become vulnerable targets", founder and managing director R. Subramanian told *The Financial Express*. The vandals, he said, could include "disgruntled vendors, employees, anti-social elements taking advantage of the situation, and even owners of the real estate" rented by the retail chain.

Subhiksha — which means "prosperity" in Sanskrit — is coming apart in other ways, too. In fast-moving developments, one of the investors — private equity company ICICI Ventures — has asked the government to step in and order an independent audit of the company's accounts. Another investor — the high-profile Wipro chairman Azim Premji's personal investment firm, PremjiInvest — has approached the Madras High Court to stop the proposed reverse merger between Subhiksha and Blue Green Constructions and Investments, a listed company Subramanian had acquired last year. Subramanian's objective was to get listed through the back door after the plan for an initial public offering fell through because of adverse market conditions. ICICI Ventures holds a 23 per cent stake in Subhiksha and PremjiInvest another 10 per cent, which was sold to it by ICICI Ventures last year for around US $ 50 million. In addition, the Employees Provident Fund Office recently said that Subramanian will be held personally responsible for non-payment of statutory dues to the staff.

Previously, Subramanian was the poster child of India's retail revolution. Others, like the Future Group's Kishore Biyani (who started Big Bazaar, Food Bazaar and Pantaloon) may have made a bigger splash. But Biyani had a business background; Subramanian's father was a Reserve Bank of India official and Subramanian was a first-generation entrepreneur, a product of liberalization and India's answer to Wal-Mart's Sam Walton. "Subhiksha was a value-focused retailer born at a time when organized retailing was only for the elite", said Subramanian in an e-mail to India Knowledge@Wharton. "From 150 stores in September 2006, all of which were in Tamil Nadu [a state in South India], the company grew rapidly to over 1,600 stores [across the country] by September 2008".

The big question: Is Subhiksha shutting down? "We are in pain but we are not shutting down", Subramanian wrote. "We had expanded rapidly; most of the growth was debt-led. The company had planned to raise equity during 2008 and was close to doing so in September when calamity hit the global markets. The company's lenders, while supportive, were also unable to extend further lines unless the equity was raised. The banks were not lending to each other, forget about lending to us.. It became a chicken-and-egg story with the company running out of cash by October. We were making money up to September, so the business is viable; it's just that the balance sheet was not. Money is like blood. If the blood flow stops, the entire brain stops working".

Subramanian acknowledges that employees, landlords and vendors have not been paid. "It's not because we do not want to pay; it's because we can't pay". Is the Indian retail story over for now? "In a market like this, there will be pain", Subramanian wrote. "However, people with long-term interest in retail and a sane cost structure will survive and thrive. Subhiksha will be there, too".

Lack of Demand

Subhiksha, of course, is not alone in facing a recent reverse. The woes of India's organized retail sector — or "modern trade", as it is called — have many causes and casualties. Even well-financed companies or those that have wealthy backers are feeling the heat.

"Lack of demand is the major problem", says Mathew Joseph, senior consultant with Delhi-based think-tank the Indian Council for Research on International Economic Relations (ICRIER). "Real estate prices are falling, and organized retail would like to wait until the bottom is reached. Finance is also difficult to come by in the context of falling demand and low profitability as banks are becoming risk averse". Gibson Vedamani, director of the Retailers Association of India (RAI), adds: "Like everyone else, the business groups in modern retail have been hit by the global recession by way of a credit squeeze [and a lack of] funding and working capital. The slump in real estate has been a big issue. Those who had big expansion plans had [acquired] real estate earlier at much higher prices. They are now relooking at their expansion plans and renegotiating the rates".

One example is Reliance Fresh, backed by Mukesh Ambani, the world's wealthiest Indian and chairman of Reliance Industries. Ambani considers retail the next big thing both for his group and the country. Reliance Retail, a subsidiary of Reliance Industries, launched its first store in November 2006 through its convenience store format, Reliance Fresh. At the end of the last fiscal year (March 2008), the group had 590 stores across 13 states. (It is close to 1,000 now.)

This includes other formats such as Reliance Digital, Reliance Mart (hypermarkets), Reliance Trends (apparel), Reliance Footprints (footwear), Reliance Jewels (jewellery), Reliance Timeout (books, music and other lifestyle products), Reliance Autozone (auto accessories and service) and Reliance Wellness (health and wellness).

There were problems from day one. Vegetable sellers stoned Reliance shops in Ranchi, Jharkhand, claiming their businesses would be killed. There was a dawn-to-dusk shutdown of all major markets in Bhubaneswar, Odisha. In West Bengal, Reliance Retail ceased operations after widespread protests. In Uttar Pradesh, the government ordered the closure of the chain following eruptions of violence and the ransacking of some outlets. In Mumbai, traders, farmers and shopkeepers moved into the streets, bringing the city to a near standstill. They were protesting not just against Reliance, but organized retail as a whole. "This is a do-or-die battle for us. Either they go, or the small traders and farmers perish", says Dharmendra Kumar, director of India FDI Watch, an organization that seeks to prevent Foreign Direct Investment (FDI) in the retail sector in India. Kumar says his mandate is to prevent multinationals like Wal-Mart, Tesco and Carrefour from entering the Indian market. As they are not yet in India — or are present in very restrictive formats — companies like Reliance Retail have become the substitute targets.

Much of this battle took place in 2007. Today, organized retail is downsizing by itself. Reliance has reassessed its plans and closed some stores; it is in consolidation mode. According to the Future Group's Biyani, growth has moderated. "While urban consumers have the ability to spend, we believe their confidence level has been low leading to disproportionate savings levels", says a report by equity research firm Enam Securities. "Weak same store sales have cast doubts on the retail consumption story". According to *The Economic Times*: "Almost all retailers, listed and unlisted, are putting off or curtailing large-scale expansion plans announced earlier".

Yet just a short while ago, the *kirana* (mom-and-pop) stores seemed to be fighting a losing battle. Groups like FDI Watch, along with the media and politicians, rose to the defense of the huge farmer-trader-shopkeeper segment.

The Future of *Kiranas*

But there are many who believe that both large and small retailers can thrive. According to Arvind K. Singhal, chairman of retail consulting firm Technopak Advisors: "The battle, if any, was being fought only by politicians and the media. In India, the *kiranas* will coexist with modern retail for many decades to come". Adds S. Ramesh Kumar, professor of marketing at the Indian Institute of Management Bengaluru (IIMB), who has recently done a study on the retailing sector: "*Kirana* shops, which number around 15 million to 20 million, are part of Indian shopping culture. They are spread throughout the length and breadth of the country and cannot be completely displaced by modern retail formats in the foreseeable future".

The future of the *kiranas* caused so much concern that the Union Commerce Ministry appointed ICRIER to do a special study to find out the impact of modern trade on these small outlets. The ICRIER report, released in the middle of last year, found that it was "a positive sum game in which both unorganized and organized retail [could] not only coexist but also grow substantially in size". The study found that:

- The total retail business in India would grow at 13 per cent annually, from US $ 322 billion in 2006-07 to US $ 590 billion in 2011-12.
- The unorganized retail sector would grow at about 10 per cent per year, with sales rising from US $ 309 billion in 2006-07 to US $ 496 billion in 2011-12.
- Organized retail, which now constitutes a small 4 per cent of the total retail sector, is likely to grow at a much faster pace of 45 per cent to 50 per cent per year and quadruple its share in total retail trade to 16 per cent by 2011-12.

Joseph, who led the ICRIER research team, says that some numbers have had to be whittled down since the report was published. "There is a general slowdown in the economy due to the global crisis and that is expected to affect the growth of organized retail in the country", he says". We had assumed a GDP growth of 8 per cent to 10 per cent during 2007-12 in the report. This is now impossible, at least for the current year 2008-09 and the coming year. Organized retail cannot therefore grow at 45 per cent to 50 per cent as we envisaged".

ICRIER was not alone in painting a rosy picture for organized retail. A November 2005 PricewaterhouseCoopers (PwC) study in tandem with the Confederation of Indian Industry (CII) said that one of the largest marketplaces for modern trade — India — was about to open up. "To reach its potential, the Indian retail sector requires significant capital, technology and best practices to bridge the existing productivity gap and achieve scale in operations, which are critical to the sector's success. One of the key steps towards facilitating the development of the retail sector and in accelerating its growth would be to allow foreign direct investment". Titled "The Rising Elephant", the report concluded that the organized sector share would account for 9 per cent to 10 per cent by 2010. Increased employment, efficiency in agriculture and increased exports through sourcing from India were the three most significant benefits of modern trade, the study said.

Another PwC-CII report, released in December 2008, said that the real beneficiaries of organized retail will be "the government, consumers, unorganized trade participants and producer-farmers". Mom-and-pop stores could become part of the system, benefiting everybody. Only about 100,000 "mid-category" stores would take a hit in the medium-term.

Yet another report in September 2008 was titled, "The Great Indian Bazaar: Organized Retail Comes of Age in India". The study, by consulting firm McKinsey, said that by 2015 India was likely to be a US $ 450 billion retail market. Organized retail would grow from 5 per cent to 14 per cent-18 per cent by 2015. The report made two other important points. First, "mom-and-pop stores will continue to remain relevant across large and small towns". Second, "retail in India can be profitable, but not with cut-and-paste global formats". The four mantras for success included innovative "local" formats; customer-backed merchandise platforms; an efficient supply chain; and an empowered front-end sales team, said McKinsey.

A Welcome Shift

Are these strategies and projections destined for the dustbin as India joins the global slowdown? The experts say no. "This is a passing phase but it could last for another year", Singhal of Technopak says. Adds Vedamani of RAI: "This is a temporary phase when many adverse forces are working together and organizations are therefore becoming very cautious. The boom in retail will surely return".

Many see this as a welcome shift to neutral gear, because Indian retail had been growing so quickly. "This calendar year will see companies consolidating their operations rather than looking at expansion", says Vedamani of RAI. "In the earlier retail rush, they were too busy to get their act together. They are now looking at putting their processes in place and getting their houses in order for when the market picks up".

Joseph of ICRIER notes that the slowdown has given the mom-and-pop shops some breathing space, too. "They now have more time to adjust and compete with organized retail", he says. "There are several cases of traditional retailers modernizing and successfully competing with organized retailing. We believe in the coexistence of both big and small retailers in the country, as each one has its own comparative advantages *vis-à-vis* consumers".

"The situation here is very different from the one in the US", says Kishan Bhat, engagement manager at Zinnov Consulting, a Bengaluru-based management consulting firm. "India is a market where everyone can coexist. The culture of *kirana* stores in a country like ours can never become obsolete. It is deeply rooted in the system and definitely has an edge over the organized sector in terms of convenience and personalized customer experience. The *kirana* stores today are also adapting to the growing competition from the organized sector. We do foresee them eventually organizing their way of business".

Bhat sees a mutual learning process which will benefit both eventually. "The organized retailers are also learning from the *kirana* stores and trying to provide a better customer connection", he says. "Besides this, both formats are implementing the best practices of each other. Hence, the two formats will definitely coexist as long as customers are the winners".

"Small retailers in India have inherent advantages", says the PwC-CII "Rising Elephant" report. "They are located next to the consumer, making it convenient for top-up purchase. They know them well, some even by name. They give credit too — which no large retailer does. Their fixed costs are so low that their break-even point is as low as 46 per cent of sales".

Finding a Model

Kumar of IIMB says there are opportunities now that may look more attractive for organized retailers. "Segmenting consumers on price sensitivity and lifestyles along with multiple retail formats holds the key for a retail chain in the Indian context", he says. "Organized retail, instead of competing with the unorganized sector using price cuts on branded offerings and short-term sales promotions, should get into private labels that provide good quality at relatively lower prices as compared to established brands. The economic slowdown is probably the ideal time for such retailers to launch these private labels. Private labels with limited merchandise will be an effective approach to target the middle-class consumers who shop almost every day as a part of their culture. Besides, since most residential areas have *kirana* shops, it is unlikely that consumers will drive long distances for their regular shopping cycles".

"Modern retail is a less-than-20-year-old phenomenon in India", says Singhal of Technopak. "It has attracted a diverse set of entrepreneurs and business organizations, and each one is trying to find out and develop its own unique business model. Some of these models are fundamentally flawed; in some cases the execution is flawed. However, overall, the growth of modern retail in India has been very steady and there is increasing width and depth [in terms of product categories, formats, etc.]. Modern retail trade in India is still in an evolutionary phase and will be in this phase for at least three-five more years before the winning formats and the winners stand out. Then, there will a consolidation and growth phase led by these winners".

Will the winners be Indian companies or MNC majors? There are no easy answers. "India's landscape is fundamentally unique", says Singhal of Technopak. One can't transport Western models and expect them to automatically succeed, he notes. For instance, infrastructure is in very bad shape. During the initial euphoria of the retail boom, several companies imported retail professionals from the West, who came armed with just-in-time and other cost-saving techniques. They realized, to their dismay, that none of this would work in a country where it could take days for a truck to traverse a few hundred miles, he adds.

"The large players usually try to gain on economies of scale and lure customers by reducing the margins", says Bhat of Zinnov. "This would [require] elimination of middlemen and brokers along with established logistics and infrastructure support. However, in the current scenario, lack of infrastructure and inefficient logistics services have dampened the growth of organized retail while providing continued shelter to the middlemen. As a result, organized retailers have not been able to provide higher value. On the contrary, unorganized retailers leverage the inefficiencies of the system and encourage consumers to drive a hard bargain, which enables a win-win situation for both".

One example of the potential pitfalls is the Piramal Group, which opened an up-market outlet in downtown Mumbai, the first of a planned chain. It proved to be a tourist attraction for visitors to a nearby religious shrine. Most visitors came to see, but not to buy. The company tried to insist that all who came to the mall should possess a mobile phone or a credit card to gain entry, but the idea was quickly withdrawn after a public outcry against discrimination. (The mall closed down shortly thereafter.)

These are problems that no amount of multinational expertise or FDI can likely address. "FDI is not so relevant in the current context, but technology can certainly help retailers understand their customers better", says Vedamani of RAI. Bhat of Zinnov disagrees. "The entry of foreign multinationals would make the market more competitive", he says. "Indian consumers will definitely benefit". But money or new technology will not help, he adds, "unless customers become the utmost priority".

"FDI in retail is extremely relevant", says Singhal of Technopak. "As India's consumption basket changes, new retail businesses have to be started to take care of emerging consumer needs. For this, both capital and know-how [in sourcing, distribution, etc.] is needed. From a consumers' perspective, they also need more choice in terms of retail options, and FDI can give them access to more choice of formats and value propositions". Adds Joseph of ICRIER: "Inexplicable restrictions on FDI investments in the sector are preventing even Indian retailers from raising global capital".

Early in February, the government announced major changes in its FDI policy through two "Press Notes". The ban on FDI in multibrand retailing such as supermarkets seems about to expire, but "the 10 pages of unintelligible official" leave many unanswered questions, according to *The Financial Times*. There have been no clarifications as political parties prepare themselves for the coming general elections. Subramanian of Subhiksha is certain he will be there when the

MNCs arrived. The problems for both organized Indian retail and his own venture will pass. "After all, challenges make boys into men", he says.

1. Indian Retail Problems

1. Since money was easily available in the form of debt, most Indian business houses resorted to reckless expansion. Thus most of them are overleveraged and unstable.
2. Indian retailers have opted to have multiple formats. Reliance, Pantaloon, *et al.*, individually have at least 10 categories of stores serving different customers. However, instead of setting up a supply chain backbone and then expanding they opted to put the cart before the horse.
3. There is overall a massive inefficiency in organized retail. Just that all of them are equally inefficient has ensured that all of them survive. India is a land of diverse culture where middle- and lower-middle-class people predominate. So, the concept of a department store that is an attraction to the upper-middle-class and elites of the society has a limited scope.

This is a country where every other small shop owner of whatever wares he is selling finds a niche market in an amazingly shorter time. It is very difficult for any big department store to create a niche market of the kind combining the different strengths that various small shop owners possess.

Also, the kind of personalized service that is a hallmark of all the small retail shops is visibly absent; the experience with big department stores is like dealing with a robot seller. Any concept works only on the basic expectations of the consumers, which differ from country-to-country. Being so, what works in the West need not necessarily work in countries like India.

Above all, for any new concept to be experimented with, the golden rule of the market survey has to be observed necessarily. Had Subhiksha based its exponential growth strategies on a realistic market survey at every stage, much of its misery could have been averted.

Shailesh Rajagopalan, Business Chennai, decided to close Subhiksha

1. The stores were always stocked-out for the most part of all major brands.

2. The materials available were of poor quality.

3. The management, Mr. Subramanian particularly, did a great job of hiding the true scenario, creating enough noise on the prowess of their business model and all the while drowning the feeble negative feedback.

4. All the while the company had unimaginable stock losses due to staff theft, as the salaries were never paid on time and the promised sales incentives had been perennially elusive.

The slowdown and lack of cash are creating new challenges. Of course, a few will survive. Challenge is actually what makes businesses better.

2. Trouble in Store

It was a phony game played on Indian consumers. There was a nexus between India Inc., who sought an easy road to riches, and realtors who wanted to build huge malls on borrowed money or private equity. Behind these big persons were foreign majors led by Wal-Mart. Indeed, consultants also joined the fray and predicted a huge potential for retail based on data on the growing Indian middle-class. And they referred to the role majors like Wal-Mart could play in modernizing the sector, promoting exports and lifting people out of poverty. They were unaware of the dark side of the company and its record even in its home turf. They misjudged the political context and the Indian psyche. Retail giants had grown in the West due to special circumstances. Wal-Mart could have not spread its wings without its manufacturing links with China. It was culture-specific. Soon, it was seen that Wal-Mart had to leave Germany and Korea and be shunned by the Japanese. There was deep resentment and fear over the rise of retail giants and the adverse implications for the economy, especially unemployment for about 30 million people. The left parties who were in the UPA coalition drew the attention of the government. Their concerns were ignored. Even so, the UPA government could not move ahead as the resentment over the entry of retail majors went deeper in the country. Government tried to appease the foreign majors by tinkering with FDI rules and allowing "back door" entry. These did not suit the corporate strategies of the majors. Sadly, lobbies continue to keep pressure on the government and the government seems to make futile attempts to permit entry.

3. Trouble in Store II

It was the financial turmoil that struck the last nail. The collapse of Lehman Brothers and its withdrawal of $ 20 billion in the realty market in India was a big blow. Too much investment has taken place in realty to cater to the IT and retail sectors. These projects have either been abandoned or are languishing. Empty malls and deserted stalls mark the scenario. Even at the best of times it was a niche demand confined to the growing, high-income professional class. Average citizens went into the malls more to enjoy the air-conditioning and get relief from the blistering summer heat. They drank the coffee dispensed through machines and ate in eateries. There was no retail blitz in the sense one associates with US and European malls. The economic crisis has put an end to the charade. It has dried up the salaries of overpaid IT professionals. It has dried up bank credit and put an end to debt-driven ventures. Even Indian retailers who had entered the sectors are hit. Compared to Wal-Mart they are small-town operators. Subhiksha, which seemed to have an edge as an early bird, is closing down. Vishal is another chain in distress. Reliance Retail is clearly in retreat. The story of retail even in the US is not different. As *Newsweek* wrote, "With lighter wallets and heavier burdens, Americans are rethinking their conspicuous consumption". ("Is the Mall Dead? November 12, 2008.) As another blogger put it, "Seeking Xanadu, shopping malls find purgatory instead". A record number of retailers are closing. Macy's is closing outlets or retrenching staff. There is a moral to the story. As in the banking sector, there is no universal model for retail which can be applied to all countries. Retailing is not rocket science and any entrepreneur can adopt modern IT/SAP procedures and engage in retail. Wal-Mart did not invent them. Each country, culture has to devise its own model suited to its ethos. Foreign giants in retail would do the country a service if they did not disturb the waters and left the field open to native players. Indian retail is indeed in the throes, and it may take a few years before it settles down with an appropriate model.

Entry of MNCs

The world's largest retailer by sales, Wal-Mart Stores Inc. and Sunil Mittal's Bharti Enterprises-have entered into a joint venture agreement and they are planning to open 10 to 15 cash-and-carry facilities over seven years. The first of the stores, which will sell groceries, consumer appliances and fruits and vegetables to retailers and small businesses, is slated to open in north India by the end of 2008. Carrefour, the world's second largest retailer by sales, is planning to set-up two business entities in the country one for its cash-and-carry business and the other a master franchisee which will lend its banner, technical services and know-how to an Indian company for direct-to-consumer retail.

The world's fifth largest retailer by sales, Costco Wholesale Corp (Costco) known for its warehouse club model is also interested in coming to India and waiting for the right opportunity. Opposition to the retailers' plans have argued that livelihoods of small-scale and rural vendors would be threatened. However, studies have found that only a limited number of small vendors will be affected and that the benefits of market expansion far outweigh the impact of the new stores. Tesco Plc., plans to set-up shop in India with a wholesale cash-and-carry business and will help Indian conglomerate Tata group to grow its hypermarket business.

MNC's Entry In Multi Retailing: ASSOCHAM

While The Associated Chambers of Commerce and Industry of India (ASSOCHAM) favours consistent reform-oriented approach for opening up of domestic retail to established retailers worldwide, it, however, holds that 100 per cent foreign equity in multibrand retailing shouldn't be offered to MNCs "in a single stroke" as is being proposed by Ministry of Commerce and Industry.

The Chamber has argued that organized retailing in India is just growing at a steady pace which so far gone to an extent of 12 per cent of entire retailing and until it picks up a scale of 50 per cent, 100 per cent equity in single brand retail be avoided under current FDI's regime.

Consequences for 100 per cent opening up of multibrand retail sector for MNC ought to be weighed in a calibrated manner and a cooling off period of minimum five years be provided before India is able to create a space for established retailers overseas to open up their shops for selling off items and products under the Sun without any restriction, said Dr. Swati Piramal, ASSOCHAM President.

The ASSOCHAM has, therefore, prescribed a suggestion for the government to first consult domestic industry before finalizing and announcing entry of overseas mega malls in the country. "Consultation with the domestic players is needed before any policy announcement is made'', the Chamber further stated.

In response to the ASSOCHAM questionnaire circulated to the domestic players, one of the leading retailing companies which runs value-buying chains throughout the country and is expanding very fast, wanted a period of two to three years for the domestic industry to consolidate. It has argued that the organized retail is still at a very nascent stage and forms only three per cent of the entire retail trade.

"If we open up the sector now, the country will attract small sum of foreign investments compared to what we can attract a few years later. In a few years, the share of organized retail will be significantly higher and the country will be far more attractive and ripe to attract higher levels of FDI", this firm, which is aggressively opening retail stores, share his views to the Chamber.

In support of its arguments, it wrote to the Chamber that China opened up its retail sector to FDI only after the domestic organized retail industry was large enough to face competition from the foreign players.

Many of the retail firms in the domestic sector favoured export commitments on the FDI investment; by as much as 20 times. They also wanted FDI investment in backend infrastructure like cold storage so that the supply chain becomes smooth.

As against 10,15 or may be 20 stores, the foreign players run a huge number of stores worldwide giving them the economies of scale and managing their global supply chain. The annual turnover of Wal-Mart of over 250 billion dollar is much higher than the total size of the Indian retail industry (both organized and unorganized). As against 10 or 15 large format stores, Wal-Mart has over 5,000 stores worldwide.

Besides, the domestic players suffer from the lack of infrastructure – the biggest bottleneck being the prohibitive prices of large retail spaces in the upmarket or central locations in the large Indian cities. This is primarily because the private holdings are fragmented and the impact of the Urban Land Ceiling Act. The pro-tenancy Rent Control Acts have distorted the property markets in the cities leading to exceptionally high prices.

A plethora of bureaucratic hurdles and high capital cost also place the domestic retailing firms at a disadvantage against the international players who have over the years placed efficient chains in order at a low capital cost. It is estimated that for opening a single store in the country as many as 13 licences are required.

"Absence of single window clearance, coupled with other issues like lack of property infrastructure, work as a major impediment to the growth of the retailing", ASSOCHAM said.

Notwithstanding the policy issues, the retailing has a great future in India since its total size of over 200 billion dollar comes close to being one-third of the size of the total economy. However, the share of the organized sector in the retail trade is only three per cent but it is expected to reach 10 per cent by 2010, throwing big opportunities for the prospective new players.

SPACE MANAGEMENT

The space within stores and on the stores' shelves and fixtures is scarce resource. Space management involves two decisions involving this scarce resource:

1. Allocation of store space to merchandise categories and brands, and
2. Location of departments or merchandise categories in the store.

The objective of space management is to maximize the profitability of the store, not just a particular merchandise category or department.

Store Space to Merchandise Categories: Some factors that retailers consider when deciding how much floor or shelf to allocate to merchandise categories and brands are:

The productivity of the allocated space,

The merchandise's inventory turnover,

Impact on store sales, and

The display needs for the merchandise.

When evaluating the productivity of retail space, retailers generally use sales per square foot or sales per linear foot.

Space Productivity: A simple rule of thumb for allocating space is to allocate on the basis of the merchandise's sales. For example, if artificial plants represent 15 per cent of the total expected sales for a hobby and craft retailer, then 15 per cent of the store's space is allocated to artificial plants. Retailer should allocate space to a merchandise category on the basis of its effect on the profitability of the entire store. Retailer should add more space to the artificial plant section as long as the profitability of the additional space is greater that the profitability of the category from which space was taken away. In this condition, the additional space for artificial plants will increase the profitability of the entire store. However, at some point, it will be more profitable not to take away space from other categories.

Two commonly used measures of space productivity are sales per square foot and sales per linear foot. Apparel retailers that display most of their merchandise on freestanding fixtures typically measure space productivity as sales per square foot. In supermarkets, most merchandise is displayed on shelves. Because the shelves have approximately the same width, only the length, or linear dimension, sales per linear foot, is used to assess space productivity.

A more sophisticated productivity measure such as gross margin per square foot would consider the profits generated by the merchandise, not just the sales. Thus, if salty snacks generate ₹ 40,000 in gross margin per linear foot and canned soup only generate ₹ 30,000 per linear foot, more space should be allocated to salty snacks. However, factors other than marginal productivity need to be considered when making space allocation decision.

Inventory Turnover: It affects space allocation in two ways. First, both inventory turnover and gross margin contribute to GMROI (gross margin return on inventory investment) – a measure of the retailer's return on its merchandise inventory investment. Thus, merchandise categories with higher inventory turnover merit more space than merchandise categories with lower inventory turnover. Second, the merchandise displayed on the shelf is depleted quicker for fast selling items with high inventory turnover. Thus, more space needs to be allocated to fast selling merchandise to minimize the need to frequently restock the shelf to reduce stock-outs.

Impact on Store Sales: When allocating space to merchandise categories, retailers need to consider the allocation impact on the entire store. The supermarkets 'over-allocate' space to some low productivity categories such as milk because an extensive assortment in these categories attracts customers to the store and thus positively affects the sales of categories with higher GMROIs. Retailers might also over-allocate space to categories purchased by their platinum customers, the customers with the highest lifetime value.

Display Considerations: The physical limitations of the store and its fixtures affect space allocation. For example, the store planner needs to provide enough merchandise to fill an entire fixture dedicated to a particular item. A retailer might decide that it wants to use a merchandise display as a form of promotion, as if to say, 'We have a great assortment of this merchandise.' For example, Park Avenue has a very appealing offering of its garments and suits. To emphasize this offering, it might over-allocate space for garments and present a wide range of colours. Retailers utilize various forms of atmospherics – lighting, colours, music, and scent – to influence shopping behaviour. The use of these atmospherics can create a calming environment for task-oriented shoppers or an exciting environment for recreational shoppers.

Foreign Investment in Retail Business

In the first week of September 2012, Government of India has granted permission for foreign investment in retail trade in India. In India, 51 per cent foreign direct investment in multi-brand retail trade sector is granted by our Prime Minister Dr.Manmohan Singh. The lower limit of investment is set at $ 100 million of which $ 50 million should be invested on back-end infrastructure. He says it will promote our economic growth and create employment opportunity in India. There will be no mediators, and retail companies like Wal Mart will offer products at lower prices. Walmart India president Raj Jain (also the MD of Bharati Walmart) has welcomed the Government's "calibrated and cautious approach" in opening up the country for FDI in multi-brand retail .States like Delhi, Jammu-Kashmir, Assam, Maharashtra, Andhra Pradesh, Rajasthan, Utthharkand, Haryana, and Manipur have welcomed FDI in retail business and management. On 26th September 2012, Mr.Jain opened Bharti Walmart's "Best Price Modern Wholesale Cash and Carry Store at Hyderabad". Whereas States like West Bengal, Tamil Nadu, Kerala, Bihar, Karnataka, Madhya Pradesh, Tripura and Odisha have opposed FDI in retail business and management. According to these States, it will adversely affect the people in general Indian Small retailers in particular. Indian farmers will be the worst affected people due to the entry of FDI in retail business. There was a total bandh against FDI in retail trade on 29th September, 2012.

QUESTIONS

1. What is retail strategy?
2. What is strategic planning?
3. What do you mean by situation analysis?
4. State and explain retail vision and mission.
5. Explain about sole proprietorship.
6. What do you mean by partnership?
7. Define corporation.
8. Distinguish between new business and existing business.
9. What do you mean by franchise?
10. Explain Goods-service Category.
11. Explain the steps involved in site selection/ trading area.
12. Write a note on trading area analysis..
13. Explain the various segments of a trading area.
14. Explain about delineating the trading area of an existing store as well as new store.
15. Explain Herfinal-Herschman index.
16. Explain Central Place Theory.
17. Write a brief note on "index of retail saturation".
18. Explain Relly's Law of retail gravitation.

19. Explain Huff's Law of shopper attraction with examples.
20. What are the chief factors to be considered in evaluating retail trading area?
21. What are the types of location? How would you select a particular location?
22. Write a note on: isolate store. Central business district, Unplanned-business district, Secondary business district and Neighbourhood business district. Also state their merits and demerits.
23. What do you mean by planned shopping centre?
24. Explain the evaluation criteria for the location/site selection in Retail Management.
25. What are the types of locations/sites in Retail Marketing?
26. Explain the concept of internal and external atmospherics.
27. Distinguish between mobile and immobile retailers.
28. Explain about multiple shop/chain stores.
29. Write a note on: (i) Supermarket, (ii) Box Store, (ii) Flea Market, (iv) Department Store, (v) Discount Store, (vi) Non-store retailer, (vii) Electronic retailer
30. What do you mean by positioning of retail shop?
31. Distinguish between De-positioning and Re-positioning.
32. Define positioning.
33. How to measure positioning?
34. How to succeed in re-positioning a company in the market?
35. Explain the market and retail brand positioning.
36. Define "image".
37. What do you mean by retail store image.
38. Explain "usage image".
39. What are the strategies in product positioning?
40. Explain the importance of positioning.
41. What do you mean by visual image? Point out its significance.
42. What are the errors in positioning strategies?
43. Distinguish between under, over, confuse and doubtful positioning.
44. Write a note on (i) Service Quality, (ii) Campaign Management, (ii) Gartner Study Report,
45. Define Customer Relationship Management. What are its types and implementation issues.
46. Explain Walter Christaller's Central Place Theory.
47. Explain Product Positioning Process.
48. State the Algebraic expression of Huff's Law.
49. Write short notes on: (i) Community Centres. (ii) Power Centres,
50. What are the benefits from right selection of location for retail business.
51. Explain integrate PoS System.
52. Write a note on PoS Printers.
53. Name the top four vendors in retail management.
54. What do you mean by Retail Sales Force Management?
55. What are the advantages and disadvantages of retail sales force to the manager.

56. Write a note on: (i) Nestle, (ii) Carpetright CATVU, (iii) CHOCOLATE RETAILER Thorntons,
57. Discuss the role of Supply Chain Coordinator under Channel Rebates with Sales effort effects.
58. Discuss about Retail Sales Force Management.
59. What do you mean by Sales Force Autonomous System.
60. Write a note on ACCENTURE.
61. Briefly state about Ginni System Ltd.
62. Explain GSL Business Model.
63. What do you mean by Inventory System.
64. Explain about Supply Chain and Retail Management.
65. Distinguish between Planned Supply Management, Transport and Logistic Management, Manufacturing Management, and Multi-chain Management.
66. Power centres are shopping centres that consist primarily of collections of big-box retail stores, such as discount stores, off-price stores, warehouse clubs and category specialists. Which types of locations are growing in popularity with retailers?
67. Why is store location such an important decision for retailers?
68. Pick your favourite store. Describe the merits and demerits of its current location.
69. Retailers are developing shopping centres and freestanding locations in central business districts that have suffered decay. Some people have questioned the ethical and social ramification of this process, which is known as gentrification. What are the benefits and problems associated with gentrification?
70. In many malls, fast-food retailers are located together in an area known as a food court. What are this arrangement's merits and demerits to the fast-food retailers?
71. How does the mall that you shop at frequently combine the shopping and entertainment experience?
72. Consider a big city that has invested in an urban renaissance. What components of the gentrification project attract both local residents and visiting tourists to spend time shopping, eating, and sight-seeing in this location?
73. Different brands of car dealerships are usually located near one another on the same street. What are the pros and cons of this strategy?
74. What factors do retailers consider when determining where to locate their stores?
75. What is a trade area for a store, and how do retailers determine the trade area?
76. What factors do retailers consider when deciding on a particular site?
77. How do retailers forecast sales for new store locations?
78. Where can retailers get information to evaluate potential store location?
79. What factors do retailers consider when evaluating an area of the country to locate stores? How do retailers determine the trade area for a store?
80. A hardware company plans to open a new store. Two sites are available, both in middle-income neighbourhood centres. One neighbourhood is 20 years old and has been well maintained. The other was recently built in a newly planned community. What site is preferable for a true hardware? Why?
81. Trade areas are often described as concentric emanating from the store or shopping centre. Why is this practice used? Suggest an alternative method. Which would you use if you owned a store?

82. Some specialty stores prefer to locate next to or close to an anchor store. But a pizza store-retailer typically found in strip centres, wants to be at the end of the centre away from the supermarket anchor. Why?
83. Retailers have a choice of locating on a mall's main floor or second or third level. Typically, the main floor offers the best, but most expensive location. Why would specialty stores choose the second or third floor?
84. What retail locations are best for department stores, consumer electronics category killers, specialty apparel stores, and warehouse stores? Discuss your rationale.
85. If you were considering the ownership of a franchise-store, what would you want to know about the location in terms of traffic, population, income, employment, and competition? What else would need to be researched about a potential location?
86. How do merchandise and information flow from the vendor to the retailer to consumer?
87. What is information technology?
88. How do retailers and vendors collaborate to make sure the right merchandise is available when customers are ready to buy it?
89. What are the benefits to vendors and retailers of collaborating on supply chain management?
90. Explain how an efficient supply chain system can increase a retailer's level of product availability and decrease its inventory investment.
91. Evaluate the options retailers have for dealing with returned merchandise.
92. Explain the differences between pull and push supply chains. What do you mean by delegation of authority?
93. Consumers have five key reactions to stock-outs: buy the item at another store (31 per cent), substitute a different brand (26 per cent), substitute same brand (1 (per cent), delay purchase (15 per cent), or do not purchase the item (9 per cent). Consider your own purchasing behaviour and describe how various categories of merchandise would result in different reactions to a stock-out.
94. Abandoned purchases as a result of stock-outs can mean millions of rupees a year in lost sales. How are retailers and manufacturers using technology to reduce stock-outs and improve sales?
95. In the past, manufacturers dominated the relationship between vendors and retailers. Today, retailers have more leverage, and both parties are investing in and seeing the benefits of a more trusting relationship with two-way communication. How has the emergence of mega formats, mergers and acquisitions, and technology enabled this shift to greater cooperation between retailers and manufacturers?
96. Define Retail industry. Explain Retail Supply Chain Management.
97. Write about Supply Chain Management Solution.
98. Explain the task of retail inventory management.
99. Discuss about supply chain management solution.
100. Point out the difficult task of retail inventory management.
101. Explain Quality of Service procedure.
102. Define Retail Service Quality Management.
103. What are the applications require in QoS?
104. What are the problems involved in QoS? Suggest solutions for the problems.
105. What do you mean by priority level in QoS?

106. India's largest retail store Subhiksha is closed. Why?
107. Discuss about MNC's entry in Multi Retailing in India.
108. What are the benefits and problems associated with gentrification?
109. In many malls, fast-food retailers are located together in an area known as a food court. What are this arrangement's merits and demerits to the fast-food retailers?
110. How does the mall that you shop at frequently combine the shopping and entertainment experience?
111. Consider a big city that has invested in an urban renaissance. What components of the gentrification project attract both local residents and visiting tourists to spend time shopping, eating, and sight-seeing in this location?
112. Different brands of car dealerships are usually located near one another on the same street. What are the pros and cons of this strategy?
113. Many types of locations are available for retail stores to retailers? Why?
114. What are the relative advantages of each with its own strengths and weaknesses?
115. Why are some locations to choose from: freestanding, city or town business district, or shopping centre. Retailers can also locate in a non-traditional location like an airport or within another store. particularly well suited to specific retail strategies. Why?

CHAPTER 4

Retail Shop Management

VISUAL MERCHANDISING MANAGEMENT (VMM)

Visual merchandising is the presentation of a store and its merchandise in ways that will attract the attention of potential customers. VMM deals with review of the fixtures and merchandise presentation techniques.

Fixtures: Primary purpose of fixtures is to efficiently hold and display merchandise. Fixtures help define areas of a store and encourage traffic flow. Fixtures must work in concert with other design elements, such as floor coverings and lighting, as well as the overall image of the store. Fixtures may be plastic or metal fixtures or wood mixed with metal, acrylic, or stone. Proper management of visual merchandising helps to achieve the predetermined targets/objectives. Fixtures come in an infinite variety of styles, colours, sizes, and textures, but only a few basic types are commonly used. For apparel, retailers utilize the straight rack, rounder, and four-way. The mainstay fixture for most other merchandise is the gondola. Straight racks are suitable for discount and off-price stores.

Rounder or bulk capacity fixtures are designed to hold a maximum amount of merchandise. They are suitable for apparel stores.

A four-way feature fixture holds a large amount of merchandise and allows the customer to view the entire garment. Due to their superior display properties, four-way fixtures are commonly utilized by fashion-oriented apparel retailers.

Gondolas are used in grocery and discount stores to display everything from canned foods to baseball gloves. Gondolas are also found displaying towels, sheets, and housewares in department stores. Folded apparel too can be efficiently displayed on gondolas, but because the items are folded. It is even harder for customers to view apparel on gondolas than on straight racks.

Presentation Techniques

Idea-oriented presentation

Style/Item presentation

Colour presentation

Price lining

Vertical merchandising

Tonnage merchandising

Frontal presentation

Idea-oriented presentation is a method of presenting merchandise based on a specific idea or the image of the store. Individual items are grouped to show customers how the items could be used and combined. For instance, furniture is combined in room settings to give customers an idea of how it would look in their homes.

Store or item presentation is probably the most common technique of organizing stock. Discount stores, grocery stores, hardware stores, and drug stores employ this method for nearly every category of merchandise, as do many apparel retailers. Arranging items by size is a common method of organizing many types of merchandise, from nuts and bolts to apparel.

A bold merchandising technique is by colour presentation. For example, in winter months, an apparel store may display all wool-wears together to let customer know that the store is "the place" to purchase clothing for their winter vacation.

Price lining is when retailers offer a limited number of predetermined price points and/or price categories within another classification. This approach helps customers easily find merchandise at the price they wish to pay.

In vertical merchandising, an item is presented vertically using walls and high gondolas. Customers shop much as they read a newspaper – from left to right, going down each column, top to bottom. Retailer takes advantage of this tendency in several ways. Many modern self-service grocery stores put national brands at eye level and store brands on lower shelves because customers scan from eye level down.

Tonnage merchandising is a display technique in which large quantities of merchandise are displayed together. Customers have come to equate tonnage with low price, following the retail adage "stock it high and let it fly". This technique is used to enhance and reinforce a store's price image. The retailer hopes customers will notice the merchandise and be drawn to it.

The frontal presentation is a method of displaying merchandise in which the retailer exposes as much of the product as possible to catch the customer's eye. Book retailers make use of this presentation. A similar frontal presentation can be achieved on a rack of apparel by simply turning one item out to show the merchandise.

Retailers utilize various forms of atmospheric – lighting, colours, music and scent – to influence shopping behaviour. The use of these atmospherics can create a calming environment for task-oriented shoppers or an exciting environment for recreational shoppers.

The location of merchandise categories also plays a role in how customers navigate through the store. By strategically placing impulse and demand destination merchandise throughout the store, retailers can increase the chances that customers will shop the entire and that their attention will be focused on the merchandise that the retailer is most interested in selling. In locating merchandise categories, retailers need to consider typical consumer shopping patterns.

Visual merchandising is completely different from merchandising. Visual Merchandising is the *activity of promoting the sale of goods, especially by their presentation in retail outlets.* (New Oxford Dictionary of English, 1999, Oxford University Press). This includes combining products, environments, and spaces into a stimulating and engaging display to encourage the sale of a product or service. It has become such an important element in retailing that a team effort involving the senior management, architects, merchandising managers, buyers, the visual merchandising director, designers, and staff is needed.

Visual merchandising starts with the store building itself. The management then decides on the store design to reflect the products the store is going to sell and how to create a warm, friendly, and approachable atmosphere for its potential customers.

Many elements can be used by visual merchandisers in creating displays, including colour, lighting, space, product information, sensory inputs such as smell, touch, and sound as well as technologies such as digital displays and interactive installations.

Visual merchandising is not a science; there are no absolute rules. It is more like an art in the sense that there are implicit rules but that these also exist to be broken for striking effects. The main principle of visual merchandising is that it is intended to increase sales, which is not the case with a "real" art.

Visual merchandising is one of the final stages in trying to set out a store in a way that customers will find attractive and appealing and it should follow and reflect the principles that underpin the store's image. Visual merchandising is the way one displays 'goods for sale' in the most attractive manner with the end purpose of making a sale. "If it does not sell, it is not visual merchandising."

Especially in today's challenging economy, people may avoid designers/visual merchandisers because they fear unmanageable costs. But in reality, visual merchandisers can help economize by avoiding costly mistakes. With guidance of a professional, retailer can eliminate errors, saving time and money. It is important to understand that the visual merchandiser is there, not to impose ideas, but to help clients articulate their own personal style.

Visual merchandising is the art of implementing effective design ideas to increase store traffic and sales volume. VM is an art and science of displaying merchandise to enable maximum sale. VM is a tool to achieve sales and targets, a tool to enhance merchandise on the floor, and a mechanism to communicate to a customer and influence his decision to buy. VM uses season-based displays to introduce new arrivals to customers, and thus, increase conversions through a planned and systematic approach by displaying stocks available.

Recently, visual merchandising has gained in importance as a quick and cost-effective way to revamp retail stores.

A close sister to visual merchandising is "retail experience". "Customer experience" looks at the same issues around product presentation but from the customer perspective, rather than the retailer perspective. In optimal retail environments the visual merchandising, customer experience, and store design are all in synch creating amazing environments and unbelievable sales.

Visual Merchandising (VM) is the art of presentation, which puts the merchandise in focus and in perspective too. It educates the customers, creates desire and finally augments the selling process. This is a nascent area of the Indian retail industry, therefore, a professional programme on Visual Merchandising will go a long way in addressing this gap. The success of the programme will be reflected in the better presentations, displays, indoor and outdoor communication about the stores. This course would be a niche specialization in the booming retail sector. Visual Merchandising achieves the following:

- Educates the customers about the products and services offered creatively and effectively.
- Enables a successful selling process, from browsing to buying.
- Establishes a creative medium to present merchandise in a life-like 3-D environment, thus creating a strong impact and recall value.
- Sets the context of the merchandise.
- Establishes the linkage between fashions, product design and marketing by keeping the focus on the product.
- Draws the attention of the customers and helps them match their needs with the visually merchandised product.

VISUAL MERCHANDISING IN INDIA

As the concept of large retail stores gains ground in India, the practice and concept of VM is likely to grow exponentially. In the Western countries VM receives highest priority in commercial planning of a product. As seasons change, the merchandise collections/planograms too change in a retail store. When such changes take place the store too undergoes a transformation in decor and visual presentation to appeal to the consumers while announcing new arrivals in merchandise collection. This phenomenon of transformation of visual presentations and displays of merchandise accompanied by relevant thematic props, is still very new in India. VM and Displays have a storyboard effect communicating innovatively to the customer besides being a 'Silent salesman for a retail store'.

VISUAL MERCHANDISING AT MICA

MICA in association with RAMMS India Pvt Ltd., (link to their website www.ramms.co.in) leading consultants in the retail sector, has developed a six-months professional programme in Visual Merchandising and Creative Communications (VMCC) for the first time in India.

MICA had a very successful experience with the Retail Communications Management (link to RCM page) programme, which is in its third batch of the programme currently and also the success of the first batch of Professional Programme in Visual Merchandising and Creative Communications (VMCs). Building upon MICA's capabilities in creative communications training, a combination of retail management and creative communications learning is brought about in the form of Visual Merchandising and Creative Communications programme. The programme combines the learning of the approaches currently used in the retail industry with communication expertise of MICA. The programme consists of some core modules in Retailing and Visual Merchandising, strongly supported by consumer behaviour and shopper behaviour studies, visual literacy and retail research in addition to a large number of field projects.

Visual merchandising team – members contribute to the advertising, marketing, and sales efforts of a retail location by designing, developing and taking charge of the visual look of the store and its merchandise. As a member of the in-store merchandising team, you will be executing merchandising strategies by creating and maintaining visual displays in the store windows and on the sales floor. You will also contribute to the profitability of the store with your merchandise handling, replenishment, and inventory control efforts.

The scope of your duties and responsibilities will vary depending on the size of the retail operation and the level of the visual merchandising position you hold. In general, your key responsibilities as a visual merchandising associate will include visual display, inventory management, and merchandising training.

Visual Display

You may be designing visual displays yourself, or executing the design decisions of another. In either case, you will be responsible for creating and maintaining a compelling presentation of merchandise that will engage customers and help stimulate sales activity. You will be the store's brand gatekeeper, ensuring that the image and style of the company is projected at all times. As you execute visual presentation changes, you will be moving merchandise, shelving, and fixtures. You will also be changing signs, and maintaining the cleanliness and functionality of fixtures, signage, lights, and equipment.

Window Displays

A window display is also a "**visiting card**" for the store. Windows are the most important factor within the store/shop front as they can communicate style, content, and price point. They can be seductive and exciting, based on emotional stimulus, or price-based (when they clearly emphasize value for money with easy and obvious ticketing). For the retailer, the window is among the most controllable elements in relation to image and to what is happening inside the store, and there are number of decisions to be made about a how these effects are achieved.

The best store windows can generate great excitement and talking point for an entire city. They contribute to the environment by entertaining pedestrians, while simultaneously communicating the products and services on offer.

For a retailer willing to exploit the full potential that a window gives, the image-building process can be exciting and have enormous potential. A fashion retailer, for instance, will often change a window weekly to show the latest items on offer. A glance into a shop's window by a passerby establishes the time of the year and, very likely, a timely contemporary event. It might combine seasonal and festive points of the year such as Back-to-school, Spring, Summer, Easter, Christmas, New Year approaching, Diwali, Valentine's Day, Mother's Day, etc. At other times the propping may be based on colour schemes, materials or cultural themes – the possibilities for innovative ideas around such themes are endless.

Merchandising Training

As the chief point of contact for new merchandising initiatives, you will generally be responsible for communicating key information that is vital to the success of the initiative. You will help to train the store team about design concepts, visual display standards, and the proper maintenance of the overall visual display effort. By providing on-the-job training, feedback, and recognition, you will motivate other members of the store team to actively support your visual merchandising efforts.

Prior Visual Merchandising Experience

Most retail operations will require retailers to have either retail experience or visual merchandising formal training and most will want to see marketeer's portfolio. Some larger retail organizations will probably require both education and experience.

If you have acquired on-the-job training or expertise, you may be able to obtain an entry level visual merchandising job by demonstrating a thorough understanding of marketing principles and retail merchandising fundamentals. Supervisory experience may be necessary for a visual merchandising position in a large store.

Qualifications for Visual Merchandisers

In smaller retail operations, you will likely be the one-person visual merchandising department and, therefore, you will need to be self-reliant, self-motivated, and have an ability to achieve goals and meet deadlines without supervision. In larger stores you may be executing the merchandising strategies of others, so the ability to follow both written and verbal instruction with great attention to detail is essential. You will also be expected to have effective communication skills, and demonstrate the highest level of professionalism and be a role model for outstanding customer service at all times.

Skill Requirements

Visual merchandisers are expected to have excellent organizational skills, as well as planning, project management, and time management expertise. Retailers need to possess excellent communication and interpersonal skills, as well as a strong creative flair and effective problem solving abilities. Stores will be willing to train marketing personnel with their specific systems and software, but they will want marketers to bring a basic knowledge of computer functions with the sellers into the position. A working knowledge of Microsoft Office will probably be required as well.

Physical Requirements

Because you will be responsible for creating and changing visual displays, you will need to be able to push, lift, and carry 30-50 pounds of merchandise and fixtures. The visual merchandiser position is physically demanding, and you can expect to be on your feet and walking for eight or more hours per day.

Additional Requirements

Visual display work often occurs at times when it is the least disruptive to the sales floor and the customer experience. So, visual merchandising employees should be prepared to work from early morning to late night-hours, as well as weekends and holidays.

Education Requirements

Most retailers will want you to have a high school diploma before you will be given full-time responsibility for visual merchandising. Entry level visual merchandising positions may not require additional education, but advancement will probably require additional formal education in visual merchandising, marketing, or both.

Compensation

Visual merchandising jobs are generally full-time positions which are compensated with a salary between $ 34,000 and $ 54,000 per year. The size and geographic location of the retail operation accounts for the wide salary range. The level at which you are hired and your experience and credentials will influence your compensation as well. Those working as visual merchandisers will receive the same benefits as any other store employee. Benefit packages generally include health insurance and generous discounts on store merchandise.

Retail Advertising and Promotion

Advertising is paid, non-personal communication transmitted through out-of-store mass media by an identified sponsor. Four aspects of this definition merit clarification:

Paid form: This distinguishes advertising from publicity (an element of public relations), for which no payment is made by the retailer for the time or space used to convey a message.

Non-personal presentation: A standard message is delivered to the entire audience, and it cannot be adapted to individual customers (except with the web).

Out-of-store mass media: These include newspapers, radio, TV, the web, and other channels, rather than personal contacts. In-store communications (such as display) are considered sales promotion.

Identified sponsor: The sponsor's name is clearly divulged, unlike publicity,

AIDAS Model: Implementing an advertising programme involves developing the message, choosing the specific media to convey the message, and determining the frequency and timing of the message. Ideally, the message in the ads should gain attention, hold interest, arouse desire, and elicit action and promote satisfaction. Retailer's advertising and promotional strategies are different from manufacturer's strategies. Retail promotion includes any communication by a retailer that informs, persuades, and/or reminds the target market about any aspect of that firm. Advertising, public relations, personal selling, and sales promotion are the elements of promotion. Retailers devote significant sums to promotion. For example, a typical department store spends nearly 4 per cent of their sales on ads and 8 to 10 per cent on personal selling and support services. Most department store chains invest heavily in sales promotions and use public relations to generate favourable publicity and reply to media information requests. Retailers adapt better to local needs, habits, and preferences. However, many retailers are unable to utilize national media as readily as manufacturers. Only the largest retail chains and franchises can advertise on national TV programmes. An exception is direct marketing (including the World Wide Web) because trading areas for even small firms can be geographically dispersed.

Retail ads stress immediacy. Individual items are placed for sale and advertised over short time periods. Manufacturers are often concerned with developing favourable attitudes. Many retailers stress in ads, whereas manufacturers usually emphasize key product attributes. In addition, retailers often display several different products in one ad, whereas manufacturers tend to minimize the number of products mentioned in a single ad. Media rates tend to be lower for retailers. Because of this, and the desire of many manufacturers and wholesalers for wide distribution, the costs of retail advertising are sometimes shared by manufacturers or wholesalers and their retailers. Two or more retailers may also share costs. Both of these approaches entail cooperative advertising.

Retailers get assistance in developing advertising campaigns from vendors through their coop. programmes, advertising agencies, and media companies.

Cooperative Advertising: It is a programme undertaken by a vendor. The vendor pays for part of the retailer's advertising but dictates some conditions. For example, Sony may have a coop. programme that pays for half of consumer electronics retailer's ads for Sony digital TVs, Coop. advertising enables a small retailer to associate its name with well known national brands and use attractive artwork created by the national brand. Coop. advertising programmes also are often used to support a vendor's effort to discourage retailers from discounting the vendor's products.

Agencies: Many large retailers have a department that creates advertising for sales and special events. Large retailers often use advertising agencies to develop ads for store image campaigns but develop promotional newspaper advertisements with their in-house staffs. Many small retailers use local agencies to plan and create all of their advertising. These local agencies are often more skilled in planning and executing advertising than the retailer's employees. Agencies play in other aspects of the communication programmes, such as contests, direct mail, and special promotions.

Media Companies: In addition to selling newspaper space and broadcast time, the advertising media offer services to local retailers, ranging from planning an advertising programme to actually designing the ads. Media companies also do market research on their audiences and can provide information about shopping patterns in the local area.

The media used for retail advertising are:

1. Newspapers
2. Magazines
3. Direct mail
4. Radio
5. TV
6. Outdoor billboards
7. Internet
8. Shopping guides, and
9. Yellow pages

Newspapers: Retailing and newspaper advertising grew up together over the past century. But the growth in retail newspaper advertising has slowed recently as retailers have begun using other media. Still, 16 of the nation's 25 largest newspaper advertisers are retailers.

In addition to displaying ads with their editorial content, newspapers distribute freestanding inserts. A freestanding insert, also called a preprint, is an advertisement printed at the retailer's expense and distributed as an insert in the newspaper. Because newspapers are distributed in a well-defined local market area, they are effective at targeting retail advertising. Often the local market covered by a newspaper is similar to the market served by the retailer. Newspapers offer opportunities for small retailers to target their advertising by developing editions for different areas of a city.

Magazines: Retail magazine advertising is mostly done by national retailers such as the Reliance. But magazine advertising is increasing with the growth of local magazines and regional editions of national magazines. Retailers tend to use this medium for image advertising because the reproduction quality is high.

Direct Mail: Retailers use data collected at point of sales terminals to target their advertising and sales promotion to specific customers using direct mail. Retailers can also purchase a wide variety of lists for targeting consumers with specific demographic profiles, interests, and lifestyles. Many retailers encourage their salespeople to maintain a preferred customer list and use it to mail personalized invitation and notes.

Television: TV commercials can be placed on a national network or local station. A local TV commercial is called a spot. Local retailers typically use local TV commercial which is economical.

Radio: Many retailers use radio advertising because messages can be targeted to a specific segment of the market. Some radio stations' audiences are highly loyal to their announcers. When these announcers promote a retailer, listeners are impressed. The cost of developing and broadcasting radio commercials is quite low.

Internet: Three uses of the Internet by retailers to communicate with customers are:

Banner ads and affiliate programmes to generate awareness, (These are very effective for targeting communication, but they are not cost–effective for building awareness).

Websites to provide information about merchandise and special events, and E-mail to target messages.

Outdoor Billboards: These are effective vehicles for creating awareness and providing a very limited amount of information to a narrow audience. Outdoor advertising is typically used to remind customers about the retailer or to inform people in cars of nearby retail outlets.

Shopping Guides: These are free papers delivered to all residents in a specific area. This medium is particularly useful for retailers that want to saturate a trading area. It is cost-effective and assures the local retailer of 100 per cent coverage.

Yellow Pages: They are useful for retailers because they have a long life. They are used as a reference by consumers who are definitely interested in making a purchase and seeking information.

Retail Advertising: Advertising by retailers encourage consumers to shop at a specific store, use a local service, or patronize a particular establishment. It tends to emphasize specific patronage motives such as price, hours of operation, service, atmosphere, image, or merchandise assortment. Retailers are concerned with building store traffic, so their promotions often take the form of direct action advertising designed to produce immediate store traffic and sales. Retail advertising accounts for a significant per centage of all advertising expenditures. Retailers allocate advertising expenditure to image-building campaigns designed to create and enhance favourable perceptions of their stores. Sales-oriented objectives are also used when advertising plays a dominant role in a firm's marketing programme and other factors are relatively stable.

The Effects of Retail Advertising on Shoppers: Movement from awareness to knowledge to liking to preference to conviction and finally to purchase.

Objectives of Retail Advertising

A retailer would select one or more of these goals and base advertising efforts on it (them).

- Lifting short-term sales.
- Increasing customer traffic.
- Developing and/or reinforcing a retail image.
- Informing customers about goods and services and/or company attributes.
- Easing the job for sales personnel.
- Developing demand for private brands.
- Because of the many forms and uses of advertising, it is difficult to make all-embracing generalizations. Yet the following qualities can be noted.
- Public presentation confers a kind of legitimacy on the product and also suggests a standardized offering.
- Advertising permits the retailer to repeat a message many times.
- Advertising provides opportunities for dramatizing the company and its products through the artful use of print, sound, and colour.

Advantages of Retail Advertising

- The audience is attracted.
- The cost per viewer, reader, or listener is low.
- A number of alternative media is available, so a retailer can match a medium to the target market.
- The retailer has control over message content, graphics, timing, and size (or length), so a standardized message in chosen format can be delivered to the entire audience.
- In print media, a message can be studied and restudied by the target market.
- Editorial content (a TV show, a news story, and so on) often surrounds an Ad. This may increase its credibility or the probability it will be read.
- Self-service or reduced service operations are possible since a customer becomes aware of a retailer and its offerings before shopping.

Disadvantages of Retail Advertising

- Standardized messages lack flexibility (except for the web and its interactive nature). They do not focus on the needs of individual customers.

- Some media require large investments. This may reduce the access of small firms.
- Media may reach large geographic areas, and for retailers, this may be wasteful. A small supermarket chain might find that only 40 per cent of audience resides in its trading area.
- Some media require a long lead time for placing ads. This reduces the ability to advertise fad items or to react to some current events themes.
- Some media have a high throwaway rate. Circulars may be discarded without being read.
- A 30-second TV commercial or small newspaper ad does not have many details.
- Advertising is a monologue in front of, not a dialogue with, the audience.

Retailers can choose from the media described here: Papers (dailies, weeklies, and shoppers) represent the most preferred medium for retailers, having the advantages of market coverage, short lead time, reasonable costs, flexibility, longevity, graphics and editorial associations (ads near columns or articles). Disadvantages include the possible waste (circular to a wider area than necessary), the competition among retailers, the black-and-white format, and the appeal to fewer senses than TV. To maintain a dominant position, many papers have revamped their graphics, and some run colour ads. Free-distribution shopper papers ("penny savers"), with little news content and delivery to all households in a geographic area, are popular today.

Retail Sales Promotion: A variety of short-term incentives offered by the retailer to encourage trial or purchase of a product or service may be called retail sales promotion. Although sales promotion tools – coupons, premiums, and the like – are highly diverse, they offer three distinctive benefits:

Communication: They gain attention and usually provide information that may lead the consumer to the product.

Retail space management is one of the more crucial challenges faced by retailers today with an ever-expanding volume of data to which they must refer when making decisions. Problems have emerged that are intractable using traditional means but for which interactive information visualization shows much promise. These problems or tasks are exploratory in nature and use temporal multivariate data. Department stores must maximize and optimize return on allocated retail space. Although product sales are readily available, the missing link for most retailers is a precise understanding of each store's layout in relation to its capacity and performance. This book introduces a novel approach Visual Space Management (VSM) demonstrated with a multiple-linked view application (VisMT) that explores retail data related to space performance. VisMT integrates familiar information visualization representations and a 3D interactive layout of store floor plans with retail data sources. Parallel coordinates plot serves as a multivariate visual control panel in the coordinated system. Seasonally retail data analysis is performed simultaneously in linked views through time. Visual inquiry methods are supported for conditioned temporal multivariate data.

For years, retailers, suppliers and distributors have turned to space management systems to solve one of the most critical questions in retailing: "How do I maximize space"? Personal computer-based space management systems like Pegman[R] began to penetrate the hardware industry in the late 1980s. Today, nearly 300 suppliers, retailers, distributors and wholesalers in the hardware industry use space management to optimize their retail space. "Space management allows us to put our best foot forward", says Steve Tota, merchandising presentation manager for TSC Stores, Nashville, Tenn.

Space management works by analyzing product performance data to create optimized planograms that meet financial objectives. Retailers use the programmes to allocate space for sections, categories and whole stores based on what is selling and what is not. "Our inventory is turning faster with Pegman[R]", says James Matsuda, merchandising financial director for Orchard Supply Hardware, San Jose, Calif. "In addition, space management has increased the in-store productivity quite a bit – there's less guesswork to setting the planograms."

While considerable academic attention has been devoted to the subject of shelf-space allocation, there is little research which specifically focuses on the influence of store brand in shelf-space management. This study is concerned with the space that national and private labels occupy in the shelves of stores. We aim at explaining this issue through a case study using a primary source of information: direct shelf-observation. This exploratory research allows us to conclude that the space allocated to private labels is clearly larger than that assigned to the whole of brands on average. Other aspects are also analyzed, such as assortment, prices and promotions, in order to establish their relationship with shelf-space management.

Once a retailer decides what to buy from vendors and how much of it to allocate to specific stores, someone needs to decide wherein the stores the products will sit. This is a very important step in retail since store layouts are crucial to the shopping experience. Products need to be easy to locate, near related products, and have the correct facings. Should this product be on the end cap? Should it be at eye level? Should it have eight facings or ten? Space management is about maximizing every inch of the selling floor.

Space management uses a cross-disciplinary approach to review theoretical approaches to creativity, and their relevance to the retail industry. It should subsequently assess types of retail spaces, and then moves on to compare the concept of retail design with product design and its implications for creativity and retailers.

It demonstrates the complexity of creativity as a concept, and the opportunities to create retail spaces through design-led approaches. It defines retail design and its engagement with stakeholders within and outside the organization and its impact on organizational creativity.

Research limitations/implications – Space management approach covers a number of perspectives on creativity, design and store environments. However, these are not exhaustive, and invite further discussion and scoping for future research.

Practical implications – Space management outlines ways to understand creativity in retailing, and provides guidance on how retailers can organize their organizations to engage with design projects.

Originality/value – Space management uniquely examines concepts of creativity and proposes how they might be applied to retailing. It demonstrates how creativity pervades the industry, in terms of design and the use of designed spaces. It proposes new areas for research relating to the definition of creativity in the retail industry, and the role of creativity and retailing in cultural and social contexts.

A planogram is a diagram that shows how and where specific retail products should be placed on retail shelves or displays in order to increase customer purchases. Planogramming is a skill used in merchandising and retail space planning. A person with this skill is be referred to as a planogrammer. Planograms themselves are also referred to as *PoGs*. By analyzing past and current sales patterns, a planogrammer can make successful recommendations about the number of "facings" a certain product should have on a retail display. The diagram will document how high or low on a shelf the product should display, as well as which products should surround it. The resulting planogram is printed out as a visual to be followed by the part-time help that is often hired to restock retail shelves and displays. This gives executive management of a retail store or chain more control over how products are displayed and allows them to track and improve on the success of their planograms. Planogram components are often included in large space planning and retail space management software applications. Sophisticated applications use other information about the product, such as the amount of inventory left for the product, to build the diagram.

Dig Deeper

If you look at the retail landscape as a whole, 60 per cent of retailers are using internally developed applications.

Traditionally, headquarters create a limited number of planograms (PoG) that define where products go for a particular store format. Unfortunately, not all stores are the same. Not only do their formats vary, but there's usually a degree of localization that makes them even more unique. So often the corporate PoG is treated as advice only and compliance is low. The answer is more collaboration between headquarters and the store. An increase of 10 per cent in compliance can decrease stock-outs by 1 per cent, and that leads to higher sales.

AVT's software enables leading retail companies such as Tesco, SuperValu, The Container Store and The Carphone Warehouse to plan and execute their retail floor space, including collaboration between HQ, stores, and vendors as well as compliance checking.

Incentive: They incorporate some concession, inducement, or contribution that gives value to the consumer.

Invitation: They include a distinct invitation to engage in the transaction now.

Retailers use sales-promotion tools to draw a stronger and quicker buyer response. Sales promotion can be used for short run effects such as to dramatize product offers and boost sagging sales.

Accounting

Accounting is the language of business. Accounting is a service activity. Its function is to provide quantitative information, primarily financial in nature, about economic entities that are intended to be useful in making economic decisions – in making reasoned choices among alternative courses of action. Accounting is the guide-post for retail management. A retail firm should know the financial implications of its operations. The financial score of the retail management is kept by the accounting system. It points out the problems faced or likely to be faced by the retail management. It also brings to its notice opportunities that are likely to arise.

It indicates possible action, when needed. The main objective of accounting is to provide information to the retail management to make relevant retail decisions and form retail judgement. The objectives of accounting are to provide information for the following purposes:

Making decisions concerning the use of limited resources, including the identification of crucial decision areas, and determination of objective and goals;

1. Effectively directing the controlling of retail management's human and material resources;
2. Maintaining and reporting on the custodianship of resources; and
3. Facilitating social functions and controls.
4. In providing information to users, accounting has to perform three functions:
   (a) Accumulation of information;
   (b) Measurement of information; and
   (c) Communication of information.

The accounting system identifies and gathers data. The process of data accumulation involves the recording and analysis of retailing events. The major job of accounting system is to collect and provide information. The accounting information is needed by a variety of persons involved in retail management. At each level of the retail organization, the business unit and its manager should be held accountable only for the revenues, expenses, and contribution to return on assets (RoA) that they can control. Thus, expenses that affect several levels of the organization (such as the labour and capital expenses associated with operating a corporate headquarters) shouldn't be arbitrarily assigned to lower levels. In the case of a store, for example, it may be appropriate to set performance objectives based on sales, sales associate productivity, store inventory shrinkage due to employee theft and shoplifting, and energy costs. If the buyer lowers prices to get rid of merchandise and therefore profits suffer, then it's not fair to assess a store manager's performance based on the resulting decline in store profit. Performance objectives and measures are used to pinpoint problem areas.

Retail Audit: A retail audit is one in which a retail management discovers weaknesses and undertakes a thorough study to achieve the retail target or maintain its share in the retail market. It is a comprehensive, systematic, independent, and periodic examination of a retail management's retailing environment, objectives, strategies, and activities with a view to determining problem areas and opportunities and recommending a plan of action to improve the management's retailing performance. Retail audit has the following characteristics:

1. Comprehensive: The retail audit covers all the major retailing activities of a retail business. A comprehensive retailing audit usually is more effective in locating the real source of retailing problems.

2. Systematic: The retail audit is an orderly examination of the retail management's macro and micro-retailing environment, retailing objectives and strategies, retailing systems, and specific activities. The audit indicates the most needed improvements, which are then incorporated into a corrective action plan involving both short run and long run steps to improve overall retailing effectiveness.

3. Independent: A retail audit can be conducted in six ways: self-audit, audit from across, audit from above, retail management auditing office, retail task force audit, and outsider audit. Self audits in which managers use a check-list to rate their own operations lack objectivity and independence. The best audits come from outside consultants who have the necessary objectivity, broad experience in a number of industries, some familiarity with the retail business being audited, and the undivided time and attention to give to the audit.

Periodic: Typically, retailing audits are initiated only after sales have turned down, sales force morale has fallen, and other problems have occurred. Retail management is thrown into a crisis partly because they failed to review their retailing operations during good times. A periodic retailing audit can benefit companies in good health as well as those in trouble.

A retail audit starts with a meeting between the retail management officers and the retailing auditors to workout an agreement on the audit's objectives, coverage, depth, data sources, report format, and timeframe. A detailed plan as to who is to be interviewed, the questions to be asked, the time and place of contact, and so on are prepared so that auditing time and cost are kept to a minimum. The cardinal rule in retailing auditing is: Don't rely solely on retail managers for data and opinion. Customers, dealers, and other outside groups must also be interviewed. Many retail managements do not really know-how their customers and dealers see them, nor do they fully understand customer needs and value judgements.

Situation Audit: The most critical aspect of the situation audit is for a retailer to determine its unique capabilities in terms of its strengths and weaknesses relative to the competition. After completing the situation audit, the next step is to identify opportunities for increasing retail sales.

The retail audit examines the following:

1. **Retail Environment Audit:** (i) Demographic Audit, (ii) Economic Audit, (iii) Environmental Audit, (iv) Technological Audit, (v) Political Audit, and (vi) Cultural Audit,
2. **Task Environment Audit:** (i) Audit about market, (ii) Audit about customers, (iii) Audit about competitors, (iv) Audit about distributors and dealers, (v) Audit about suppliers, (vi) Audit about facilitators and marketing firms, and (vii) Audit about publics
3. **Retail Strategy Audit:** (i) Business mission audit, (ii) Retailing objectives and goals audit, and iii) Strategy audit
4. **Retailing Organization Audit:** (i) Formal structure audit, (ii) Functional efficiency audit, and (iii) Interface efficiency audit
5. **Retailing System Audit:** (i) Retailing information system audit, (ii) Retailing planning systems audit, (iii) Retail control system audit, and (iv) Product development system audit
6. **Retailing Productivity Audit:** (i) Profitability analysis audit, and (ii) Cost-effectiveness analysis audit
7. **Retailing Function Audit:** (i) Product audit, (ii) Price audit, (iii) Distribution audit, (iv) Advertising, sales promotion, publicity, and direct retailing audit, and (v) Sales force audit.

Retail Accounting Services

SUPERVALU's Retail Accounting Services is a professional, full-service accounting firm with a retail emphasis. Retail Accounting Services supports more than 900 clients from five offices located across the US with services such as financial statement preparation, payroll processing, accounts payable processing, income tax planning and return preparation, inventory scheduling, manufacturer coupon processing and industry benchmark reporting. Retail Accounting Services provides and interprets financial information to tell clients what's going on in their business, so they can work on their business.

The focus at Retail Accounting Services is on clients and their success. All efforts are aimed at providing exceptional service at a reasonable cost and fulfilling high expectations with integrity and commitment to quality. SUPERVALU ensures that your information will be treated confidentially: we value our relationships most and your trust and confidence is the true measurement of our success.

After 45 years in business, Supervalu's Retail Accounting team stands experienced and ready to serve a variety of needs.

The Basic Format of an Income Statement for Retail Businesses

The income statement for a retail business differs in several ways from that of a service business and is illustrated in its simplest form here.

Service business		**Retail business**	
Revenue	xxxx	Sales revenue	xxxx
Less Expenses	xxx	*Less* Cost of sales	xxx
Profit	$ xxxx	Gross profit	xx
		Less Expenses	xx
		Profit	$ xx

Accounting for sales transactions including the treatment of sales returns, cash discounts, trade discounts and freight costs.

The two major transactions related to the sale of inventory are sale of goods, and sales returns and allowances. The typical journal entry for a credit sale of goods including GST is as follows (periodic inventory system):

Accounts Receivable	xxx	
Sales		xxx
GST collection		xxx

If the goods were sold for cash, the debit would be to the Cash at Bank account. If customers are dissatisfied with goods sold to them, they often return them (called a sales return) or negotiate a further discount (called a sales allowance). Both events are recorded in the account called Sales Returns and Allowances, which is a contra account to Sales Revenue. A return or allowance is recorded as follows (periodic inventory system):

Sales Returns and Allowances	xxx	
GST Collection	xxx	
Accounts receivable		xxx

If a cash refund is given, the credit entry is to the Cash at Bank account. To encourage prompt payment by customers **cash discounts** called discounts allowed, such as 2/10, n/30 (read 'two ten, net thirty'), are sometimes offered. If the invoice is paid within 10 days an amount equal to 2 per cent of the invoice amount may be deducted. If payment is not made within 10 days the full invoice amount must be paid within 30 days. To the seller, the cash discount, **discount allowed**, is a reduction of the sales price, and to the buyer, **discount received** is a reduction in the purchase price. Cash discounts are also known as *settlement discounts*. For GST-registered businesses, when customers take advantage of settlement discounts, the total GST on the original sales price needs to be reduced and the amount originally recorded in the GST Collections account has to be written back.

A **trade discount** is a discount quoted by a vendor to customers who are usually operators in the 'trade'; e.g., a hardware store quoting prices of building materials to a builder. Trade discounts are disclosed as reductions to the list price before cash discounts are considered. The cost of freight may be paid by the supplier or the customer. In 2000, a series of three-letter international commercial terms (Incoterms) was developed by the International Chamber of Commerce. Only two of these terms are used in this text. If goods are sold **EXW** (exworks) place of seller's business, freight costs incurred from the point of shipment are paid by the buyer. If goods are sold **DDP** (delivered duty paid) place of buyer's business, the seller undertakes to be responsible for paying all freight cost.

Accounting for purchases of inventory and cost of sales under both the perpetual and periodic inventory systems: A perpetual inventory system involves keeping a current and continuous record of all inventory transactions on a separate inventory card or computer record for each type of inventory held. It provides more timely information to management for use in controlling and planning for inventory. It is an expensive system because of the detailed record keeping it requires. However, computer systems have gone a long way towards overcoming the cost problems, especially through the use of optical scan cash registers which read product bar codes. Hence, it is the most common system in business use. Whenever goods are purchased, sold, returned to the supplier or returned by the customer, the inventory card or computer record is used, at the same time tracking GST collections and outlays. The cost of transporting inventory when acquiring it from a supplier is debited to a **Freight Inwards** or Transportation-in account. The purchases account is not required. Under IAS 2/AASB 102, freight inwards should be included in cost of sales and the cost of inventory. When goods are sold under the perpetual system, two entries are made — the sales entry, which records revenue at the *selling price* and GST collections, and a second entry that records the decrease in inventory (and the increase in cost of sales) at *cost*. In other words, sales of goods must be recorded at selling price and at cost price. Perpetual systems provide more timely information to management for planning and controlling inventory. However, in the absence of computer assistance they are time-consuming and costly to maintain. A perpetual inventory system must be supplemented at least once a year with a physical count to verify the accuracy of the records. Discrepancies are accounted for as

Inventory Shortage Expense. Any material discrepancies should be investigated. Businesses that sell a wide variety of items with a low cost per unit typically use the **periodic inventory system**. In this system the Inventory account is used (changed) only at the end of the accounting period when a physical count of inventory items is done. At all other times and for all transactions involving inventory during the accounting period, the Inventory account is not used. Acquisitions of inventory are recorded in a Purchases account as follows:

Purchases	xxx	
GST Outlays	xx	
Accounts Payable (or Cash at Bank)		xxx

A return of unsatisfactory goods to a supplier is recorded as:

Accounts Payable (or Cash at Bank)	xxx	
Purchases Returns and Allowances		xxx
GST Outlays		xx

Remember that all accounts used to calculate cost of sales under the periodic system will be extended to the income statement. This is because cost of sales is an expense, and expenses are found in the income statement. The accounts involved are:

(a) Inventory (beginning balance as per adjusted trial balance)
(b) Purchases
(c) Freight Inwards
(d) Purchases Returns and Allowances
(e) Discount Received
(f) Inventory (ending balance as per physical count).

The ending inventory balance is also recorded in the balance sheet columns of the worksheet, since it is the current amount of inventory on hand. In terms of closing accounts, an entity using the periodic inventory system has extra accounts to close. Purchases, Freight Inwards, Purchases Returns and Allowances, and Discount Received must all be closed to Profit and Loss Summary. The other adjusting/closing entry that must be made is to debit Profit and Loss Summary for the cost of beginning inventory and to credit Profit and Loss Summary for the ending inventory balance (as per physical count). Familiarization with the following relationships will help you to understand the characteristics of the periodic inventory system:

1. Net sales revenue = Sales revenue – Sales returns and allowances
2. Gross profit = Net sales revenue – Cost of sales
3. Cost of sales = Cost of beginning inventory + Cost of net purchases – Cost of ending inventory
4. Cost of net purchases = Cost of purchases + Freight inwards – Purchases return and allowances.

When comparing a perpetual inventory system with a periodic inventory system, two basic differences emerge. With a perpetual system, current and continuous records of all inventory transactions are maintained for each inventory item at cost excluding GST. With the periodic system, current and continuous records of inventory transactions are *not* maintained. Accurate inventory amounts can be determined only when a physical inventory count is taken. Note the two possible accounting treatments of discount received and discount allowed. Discount received can be treated as an item of income or as a deduction from cost of purchases. Discount allowed can be treated as a financial expense or as a deduction from sales revenue.

Preparing a worksheet and closing the accounts for both the perpetual and periodic inventory systems: A worksheet can be used to organize all the information needed to prepare adjusting entries, closing entries and the financial statements. A worksheet prepared for a company requires some additional accounts not found for a sole trader. Principally they are Share Capital, Retained Earnings, Provision for Dividends (dividends declared), Provision for Income Tax, and Income Tax Expense. When a perpetual inventory system is used, the account balance extended as a debit (asset) to the balance sheet columns is the balance in the inventory account. When a periodic inventory system is used, the balance in the inventory account represents the beginning inventory amount, which is extended to the income statement debit column. The ending inventory amount is entered directly as a credit to the income statement columns and a debit to the balance sheet columns. There are a number of ways to record the ending inventory amount and remove the beginning inventory balance under a periodic system. Each method produces the same cost of sales amount.

The preparation of a detailed income statement for a retail business: A company which uses a periodic inventory system reports a detailed cost of sales section in its income statement. In a perpetual inventory system, cost of sales is shown on one line. Expenses can be classified by function into various categories. Some expense items may be allocated between two or more categories based on some logical relationship.

How to perform a brief analysis of profitability in a retail business for decisionmaking purposes: Relationships between factors affecting profitability can be expressed as ratios. Comparison with the ratios of similar businesses in the industry, or industry averages, can aid in assessing performance. These common ratios are:

$$\text{Gross Profit Ratio} = \frac{\text{Gross Profit}}{\text{Net Sales}} \times 100$$

$$\text{Profit Margin} = \frac{\text{Profit after tax}}{\text{Net Sales}} \times 100$$

$$\text{Expenses to Sales} = \frac{\text{Expenses}}{\text{Net Sales}} \times 100$$

$$\text{Inventory turnover} = \frac{\text{Cost of sales}}{\text{Average Inventory}}$$

Table 29 : Registered Retailers and Shopkeepers			
Registered Retailers and Shopkeepers Across India			
North	**South**	**East**	**West**
• Delhi (812) • Indore (238) • Lucknow (224) • Ludhiana (173)	• Bengaluru (683) • Chennai (442) • Coimbatore (201) • Hyderabad (364)	• Kolkata (390)	• Ahmedabad (259) • Mumbai (581) • Nagpur (155) • Pune (222)

INTEGRATED SYSTEM AND INFORMATION TECHNOLOGY

Importance of Retail Information System

1. In India, the vast majority of retailers are mostly unorganized and operate only on guesswork with little knowledge of their actual inventory levels.
2. Organized retailing is fast becoming a reality in India and it is being made possible only with the adoption of the retailing technology borrowed from the West.

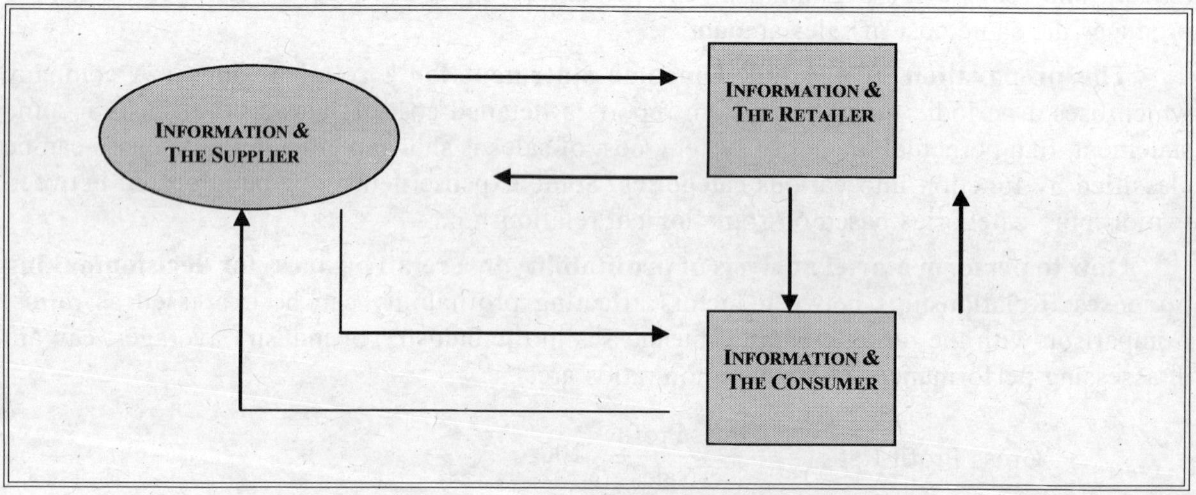

FIG. 35: INFORMATION FLOW IN RETAIL DISTRIBUTION CHANNEL

Various Information Systems

1. Merchandising systems
2. Sales and Marketing systems
3. Point of Sale systems
4. Financial Accounting systems
5. Attendance and Payroll systems
6. Administrative systems

Advantages of Computerization

1. Faster data accessibility
2. Better stock availability
3. Better choice of assortment
4. Timely distribution
5. Lesser mistakes
6. Tracking buying patterns of customers
7. Better financial controls
8. Better decision making
9. Reduction in manpower costs
10. Better return on investments

Limitation of Computerization

1. The cost factor
2. Difficulty in developing and maintaining the system
3. Confusion with extension data

Data Base Management in Retailing

1. Plan the particular data base and its component and determine the information needs.
2. Acquire the necessary information.
3. Retain the information in a usable and accessible format.
4. Update the database regularly to reflect changing demographics, recent purchases, and so forth.
5. Analyze the database to determine company strengths and weaknesses.

Choosing the Right System

Factors to Consider

1. Decide on the magnitude of retail operations that you wish to increase over a period of time, preferably at least 4-5 years.
2. Decide on the approximate number of locations that you wish to operate in and their distances.
3. Clearly define your expectations from the system, depending on the above two factors.
4. Magnitude of operations.
5. Number of locations.
6. Expectations from the system.

Emerging Trends in Systems and Communication

1. Electronic commerce (e-commerce)
2. Management Information System (MIS)

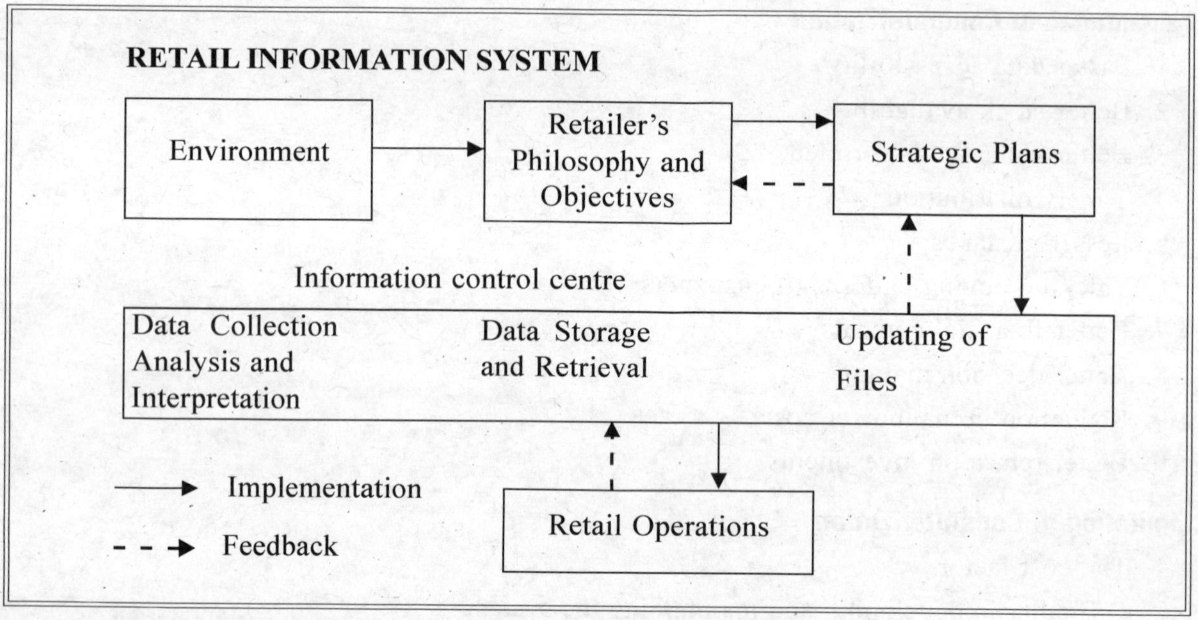

FIG. 36: RETAIL INFORMATION SYSTEM

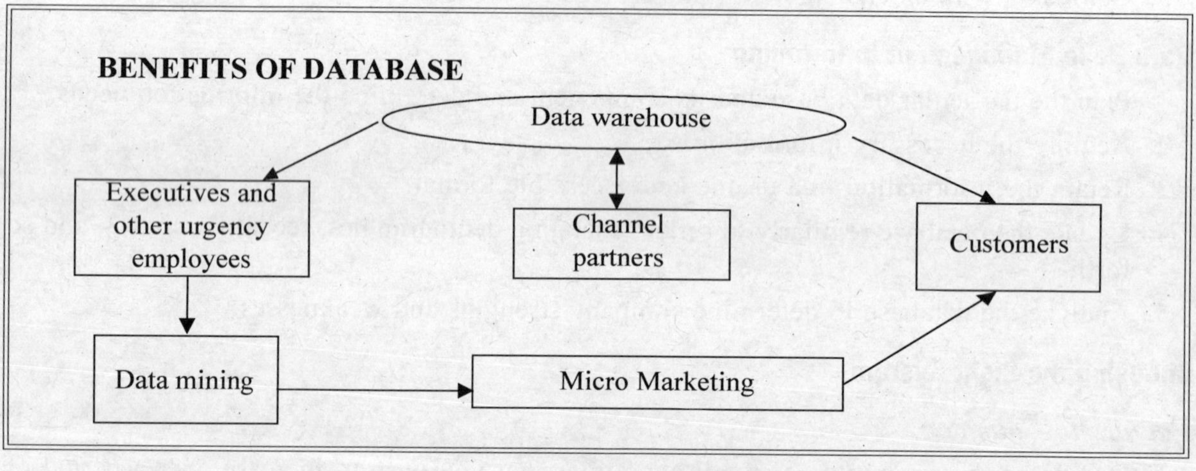

FIG. 37: BENEFITS OF DATABASE

Retail Management Information System (RMIS)

A retailer is a business that sells products and/or service to consumers for their personal or family use. The word 'Management' is used in the sense of managing the 'group of retail personnel' in an organization. Information is a datum that has been collected and processed into an organized usable form. Organized information is accurate, relevant, complete, cost-effective, verifiable, reliable and is available when needed. Information can be presented in characters, numbers, picture, image and sound. A system is a group of interrelated parts working together towards a common goal by accepting inputs and producing output in an organized transformation process. An information system is an organized combination of people involved in gathering, transforming and dissemination of information. Retail Management Information System is an organized combination of retail personnel involved in gathering and disseminating product/

service information to the present and potential customers with the ultimate aim of presenting and promoting sale of goods and services and creating delightful customers.

Retail management is a multipurpose organ that manages a retail business, manages retail manager and manages a group of inter-connected retail, retail-workers working together in the accomplishment of predetermined objectives, goals and targets. It refers to planning, organizing, staffing, directing, coordinating and controlling the efforts of retail workforce towards a specific objective. It is an art of getting things done through and with retail personnel in formally organized group. Retail management system is the art of systematically knowing what the customers want and then seeing that the customer is delighted in the best and cheapest way possible. It is the art of securing maximum results in retail management with a minimum effort so as to secure maximum prosperity and happiness for both retailer and retailee. RMIS is the systematic process of designing and maintaining of an environment in which individuals working together in groups, efficiently accomplish selected aims based on collected information in the retail market.

QUESTIONS

1. Define visual merchandise management.
2. Explain the significance of visual merchandise management.
3. Explain the role of visual merchandising management in India.
4. Write short notes on: (i) Visual display, (ii) Window display, (iii) Merchandising training.
5. What are the qualities for visual merchandisers?
6. Define retail advertising.
7. Define retail promotion.
8. Explain AIDAS formulae.
9. What are the merits and demerits of retail advertising?
10. Explain about the media used for retail advertising.
11. Write a note on internet/e-mail advertising.
12. What do you mean by yellow pages?
13. What do you mean by retail space management?
14. Define RMIS.
15. What are the benefits of database?
16. Explain the emerging trends in system and communication.
17. What do you mean by database management system?
18. Explain about various information systems.
19. State the importance of retail information system.
20. Prepare a model income statement for a retail business.
21. How to perform a brief analysis of profitability in a retail business?
22. Write a note on Worksheet.
23. Prepare a model purchase account record.
24. Write a note on: Trade discount, cash discount, different types of audit.

CHAPTER 5

Retail Shopper Behaviour

Retail Sales Force Management

Sales force management systems are information systems used in marketing and management that help automate some sales and sales force management functions. They are frequently combined with a Marketing Information System, in which case they are often called Customer Relationship Management (CRM) systems.

For many retailers, the challenges faced by increasing competition, shrinking margins, and economic slowdowns are bringing about changes in thinking and the way they do business. Some retailers are beginning to take a much more serious look at managing the top line, and are showing the benefits.

Contracts and relationships are an important part of **sales** training for the **retail** store manager and the **retail** store owner. **Sales** training has a direct and immediate influence on vendor relationships and profitability. Vendor negotiations influence profit.

Retailers large and small struggle with the same fundamental challenge: How to best match demand for their products to supply, and at the same time leave sufficient margin on the table to allow them to serve customers, compete, and grow.

Some countries have regulations that impose restrictions on the use of **sales** promotions in **retail** markets. The main motivation of these policies has been the protection of small retailers.

Although multichannel retailing has been around for over a century, the online **sales** capability brought about by the commercialization of the Internet has forever altered the retailing landscape.

Forecasting collaboration between retailers and suppliers is suggested to bring significant benefits in the form of increased efficiency and improved customer service. Yet, only few companies seem to be engaged in collaborative relationships.

A channel rebate is a payment from a manufacturer to a retailer based on retailer **sales** to end-consumers. Two common forms of channel rebates are linear rebates, in which the rebate is paid for each unit sold, and target rebates, in which the rebate is paid for each unit.

Nestle is buying Gerber from Novartis AG for $ 5.5 billion, making it the world's biggest baby food company. Nestle said today that the acquisition would give its nutrition division annual **sales** of about $ 8.21 billion, and it will boost its operating profit margin immediately.

By James Davey, London (Reuters, UK) – DSG International, DSGI, Europe's No.2 electricals retailer, reported a pick-up in **sales** in recent times, helped by store upgrades and demand for Microsoft's MSFT new Windows 7 computer operating system. DSG, which runs the Currys and PC World chains.

Definition of Buying Behaviour

The buyer behaviour may be defined as 'the decision process and physical activity of individuals engaged in evaluating, acquiring, using or disposing of goods and services. Buying Behaviour is the decision processes and acts of people involved in buying and using products. The shopper behaviour is defined as 'the behaviour that consumers display in searching for purchasing, using, evaluating and disposing of products, services and ideas that they expect will satisfy their needs. In its broadest sense, shopper behaviour is the process by which an individual decides whether, what, when, who and from whom to purchase goods and services. The retail shopper behaviour is the study of individuals, groups or organizations and the processes they use to select, secure, use and dispose of products, services, experiences or ideas to satisfy needs and the impacts that these process have on the consumer and society. The retail shopper behaviour is a complex phenomenon with several variables like marketing offer, buyer environment, buyer characteristics and purchase process, which influence the purchase and post-purchase experiences. It also analyzes shopper behaviour pattern and evaluation procedures. A marketer, who understands shopper behaviour and acts accordingly, has a great competitive advantage in the marketplace. An understanding about consumers, both present and potential, is possible through shopper research. An analysis of shopper behaviour enables marketing researcher to have an understanding of the current and future demand of different commodities and match supply with the changing pattern of demand. Demand of a product is affected by the packaging of the product, the wrapping, its attributes, its shape, the flavour, its advertisements, its availability, brand attributes, the catch words, the slogans, and the way by the agencies handling the product interact with their clients. A thorough understanding of shoppers' behaviour helps in identifying different segments and evolves suitable marketing strategies for effective penetration into defined market segments. The retail marketer who understand the shoppers' preferences, their motivation, buying processes, shopping behaviour and consumption pattern, have a great competitive advantage in the marketplace. The key to ensure shopper satisfaction lies in understanding the shoppers' likes, dislikes, buying behaviour, buying motives and buying practices. An understanding of various factors like economic, psychological, cultural, subcultural, geographical, personal and sociological factors influencing shopper behaviour is important for the survival and development of retail business in a competitive world.

Rural retail market, now, accounts for a sizable share of the total consumption for variety of shopper goods, such as package tea, washing products including detergents, toiletries of various types, bath soaps, toothpaste, toothpowder, safety razor blades, talcum powder, shampoos, hair oil and durables like electric irons, bicycles, scooters and motor cycles. In many products, rural consumption accounts for a larger share than urban. In washing soaps the rural share is over 60 per cent and bath soaps over 50 per cent. Similar is the case with packaged tea and hair oils.

Need to Understand

- Why consumers make the purchases that they make?
- What factors influence consumer purchases?
- The changing factors in our society.

Consumer buying behaviour refers to the buying behaviour of the ultimate consumer. A firm needs to analyze buying behaviour for:

- Buyers' reactions to a firm's marketing strategy has a great impact on the firm's success.
- The marketing concept stresses that a firm should create a Marketing Mix (MM) that satisfies (gives utility to) customers, therefore need to analyze the what, where, when and how consumers buy.
- Marketers can better predict how consumers will respond to marketing strategies.

Characteristics of Rural Shoppers

1. They are mostly unorganized and do not create enough pressure on traders or government to bother for their interest.
2. They suffer from the evils of illiteracy and ignorance.
3. Rigid social and religious customs, joint ownership due to joint family system, etc., influence the buying habits of the rural consumers. Other features are:
    - They have low purchasing power.
    - Most of them are least bothered about quality or standard.
    - Seasonal buying is also one of the important habits of the rural consumers because important festivals like Dushera, Diwali, Pongal (Sankranti), and Holi, etc., coincide with the crop seasons.
    - If the prices are outside the buying capacity of rural shoppers, goods will be discarded.
    - Conservatism marks the rural shoppers and they have tradition-bound lifestyles.
    - Less educated people form their brand loyalty on the basis of price, attractive packaging and easy availability in the market.

Nowadays, rural shoppers' lifestyle is going through the process of change. These changes can be attributed to factors such as:

1. Increased media reach particularly TV and radio.
2. Growth in income and change in income distribution.
3. Increasing literacy rate and awareness.

4. Growing interaction with urban consumers and marketers' efforts to reach out the rural market influence the lifestyle rural shoppers, etc.
5. Educational level of the shoppers significantly influences the formation of brand loyalty.

Customer Characteristics

Business to Consumer: The main characteristics are quite unlimited: Geographic area, age, sex, income, level of study, employment and so on. So, keep close to your benefit analysis and just list the characteristics that correspond to the benefits you offer: If you sell bathing suit, you will not care for people living in North Pole. If you sell fur clothes, do not loose your time with the characteristics of people living in Central Africa.

Business-to-Business: The main characteristics are the company size, the products or services, the level of technology, the turnover, the staff number, the location and so on.

You must describe the required customer profile according to your product or service.

Example: What's the customer profile for **fun board.**

Demographic Characteristics: 15 to 25 years old, male, healthy.

Economic Characteristics: Student or young professional, not less than $ 30,000 income coming from parents or work.

Social Characteristics: Middle and upper-middle-class.

Geographical Area: North America, Australia, Northern Europe.

Special Interests: Sport like and sea like.

You just have to think in order to define your customer profile: Of course, he is a young man. He has good money because you cannot afford to buy a fun board when you are short for your daily living. So, you can expect that he comes from developed countries. Obviously, he likes sports and sea very much.

Why do you need all these characteristics? The response is that you need the larger information to channel effectively your advertisement: For example, the fact to know where he is located will conduct you to advertise mainly in English and in sportsmen newspapers.

Changing Rural Shopper Behaviour

1. **Shopper Behaviour Undergoes Major Changes:**

The shopper behaviour of rural buyers has been undergoing a change in recent years, just as their lifestyle has been undergoing a change. In fact, the former is an offshoot of the latter to a large extent. In recent years, some convergence in aspirations seems to be taking place between the urban and rural markets. The trend seems to be stronger among the younger generation.

2. **Marketers' Efforts to Reach Out to The Rural Markets:**

Added to this, many corporates have been trying hard to develop a market for their products in the rural areas, investing substantially in these areas. This has brought about some change in the way shoppers buy different products. Developmental marketing has created discriminating buyers and hitherto, unknown demand in the market.

3. No Stereotype Rural Shopper:

The interesting position that finally emerges about the profile of the rural shopper is that one cannot proceed on the basis of a stereotype of rural shopper or of rural shopper behaviour. This signals problems as well as opportunities for the marketer. It is to be recognize that all rural shoppers do not share a common shopper behaviour. There are shoppers who can afford high-priced brands and or also willing to buy.

4. Changes in the Consumption of Rural Demand:

Rural demand has grown steadily over the years. Rural market has grown both in quantitative and qualitative terms. The composition of rural demand is also changing favourably. Many new products have entered the rural market. The shopping behaviour of upper, middle and lower segments of rural market has been changing significantly. The upper segment has started shopping and using a variety of modern shopping products.

Four types of shoppers:

(i) Economic shopper
(ii) Personalizing shopper
(iii) Apathetic shopper
(iv) Ethical shopper

Types of Consumer Buying Behaviour

Types of consumer buying behaviour are determined by:

1. Level of involvement in purchase decision. Importance and intensity of interest in a product in a particular situation.
2. Buyers' level of involvement determines why he/she is motivated to seek information about a certain product and brand but virtually ignores others.

High involvement purchases — Honda Motorbike, high priced goods, products visible to others, and the higher the risk, the higher the involvement. Types of risk:

1. Personal risk
2. Social risk
3. Economic risk

The four type of consumer buying behaviour are:

1. **Routine Response/Programmed Behaviour** — Buying low involvement frequently purchased low cost items; need very little search and decision effort; purchased almost automatically. Examples include soft drinks, snack foods, milk etc.
2. **Limited Decision Making** — Buying product occasionally. When you need to obtain information about unfamiliar brand in a familiar product category, perhaps. Requires a moderate amount of time for information gathering. Examples include Clothes, know product class but not the brand.
3. **Extensive Decision Making** — Complex high involvement, unfamiliar, expensive and/or infrequently bought products. High degree of economic/performance/psychological risk.

Examples include cars, homes, computers, education. Spends a lot of time seeking information and deciding information from the companies MM; friends and relatives, store personnel, etc. Goes through all six stages of the buying process.

4. Impulse buying, no conscious planning.

The purchase of the same product does not always elicit the same buying behaviour. Product can shift from one category to the next. For example, going out for dinner for one person may be extensive decision making (for someone that does not go out often at all), but limited decision making for someone else. The reason for the dinner, whether it is an anniversary celebration, or a meal with a couple of friends will also determine the extent of the decision making.

Buyer decision processes are the decision making processes undertaken by consumers in regard to a potential market transaction before, during, and after the purchase of a product or service.

More generally, decision making is the cognitive process of selecting a course of action from among multiple alternatives. Common examples include shopping and deciding what to eat. Decision making is said to be a psychological construct. This means that although we can never "see" a decision, we can infer from observable behaviour that a decision has been made. Therefore, we conclude that a psychological event that we call "decision making" has occurred. It is a construction that imputes commitment to action. That is, based on observable actions, we assume that people have made a commitment to effect the action.

In general there are three ways of analyzing consumer buying decisions. They are:

1. **Economic models** – These models are largely quantitative and are based on the assumptions of rationality and near perfect knowledge. The consumer is seen to maximize their utility. See consumer theory. Game theory can also be used in some circumstances.
2. **Psychological models** – These models concentrate on psychological and cognitive processes such as motivation and need recognition. They are qualitative rather than quantitative and build on sociological factors like cultural influences and family influences.
3. **Consumer behaviour models** – These are practical models used by marketers. They typically blend both economic and psychological models.

Customer buying process is not the same thing like buying a candy, a car or a real estate. We have to emphasize on the following aspects. We call it the **"DTHP process"**:

Who is the decision making person? In business-to- business, the purchaser may be a top ranking executive: The more hierarchical levels involved, the more difficult the sale.

In business-to-consumer, the buying process could imply on person or the entire family. The same observation applies: The more individuals or groups involved, the more difficult the sale.

At what time or period, does he buy? Consider frequency and regularity of the purchases. Some business follows seasoning periods such as the toys, the bathing suit. This period can be short: For example, the selling of flowers on Sunday, or the clothes during the discount periods.

How does he Buy: The buying decision includes the following process:

The customer becomes aware of a need: The need could originate from an impulse (candy) or from a recognized deficiency (such as a refrigerator).

The customer begins to explore how meeting the need: He reads newspapers, yellow pages, and so on. It is very important to know how does he explore to target advertisement channels.

According to the need and his income, the customer refines the buying criteria and defines a budget.

He narrows the field of his choice in comparing quality/price ratio. He could need physical touch or face to face interaction such as a test drive.

Finally he closes the sales. In many process, he needs to be helped by a salesman!

How does he Pay: Does he use cash, cheque, or credit card? Does he ask for times payment? Does he need a loan? If you could link some financial services to your product, such as times payments, it should give you a high advantage especially for expensive items.

The best way to get information about the buying process of your product is to talk with the retailers. You don't need a questionnaire or a customer form. **Take it easy:** Just talk with people in an informal way, have chat about the weather, and ask some short questions to collect right information.

1. Customer benefit 2. Customer profile 3. Market customer 4. Do it yourself 5. Coaching. So let's look at some of the factors that make-up the decision to buy.

Shopper Decision Process

Random utility theory and discrete choice models have been widely used to explore mechanisms underlying pedestrian shopping behaviour. However, these models tend to be mis-specified due to unrealistic assumption of utility maximizing behaviour. The bounded rationality theory may be more suitable for building models representing real shopping decision process, but existing statistical models are not able to extract information hidden in the decision process proposed by the theory. We, therefore, developed GEPAT, a computer programme using Gene Expression Programming to solve this problem with its two most significant features. The first feature is that it has an extendable multigene-section chromosome structure which allows several interrelated target functions to be estimated simultaneously. The second feature is that it uses processors, representing mental operators, as building blocks to implement simple information processing and facilitate constructing and testing complex schemes of the problem by linking the processors properly.

In order to understand the shopper behaviour, a retailer should know the process by a buyer goes through, which consists of five steps: (i) recognition of unsatisfied need, (ii) information search, (iii) evaluation of alternatives, (iv) purchase decision, and (v) post-purchase behaviour. Whenever folks make a buying decision, that decision represents the culmination of a process. It may take place almost instantaneously or stretch out over a long period of time – but it's a process, not an event.

No matter how long the process takes, the buying decision always begins when folks become aware of a need. Once they have identified that need, they begin to search for and explore possible avenues for meeting it. While gathering information, they refine and evaluate all the buying criteria that will affect the decision to purchase and narrow the field of choice to the "best few" alternatives. Once they reach a decision and choose, they take action by making a purchase. (Keep in mind those horrid shopping cart abandonment rates – making a decision to purchase is not the same thing as completing the purchase!) The final step in the process involves a reevaluation of the decision and its results.

To summarize, the steps of the buying decision process are:

- Identify
- Search
- Evaluate
- Decide
- Purchase
- Re-evaluate

Stages of the Consumer Buying Process

There are Six Stages to the Consumer Buying Decision Process (For complex decisions). Actual purchasing is only one stage of the process. Not all decision processes lead to a purchase. All consumer decisions do not always include all six stages, determined by the degree of complexity.

The six stages are:

1. Problem Recognition (awareness of need) — difference between the desired state and the actual condition. Deficit in assortment of products. Hunger — Food. Hunger stimulates your need to eat. Can be stimulated by the marketeer through product information — did not know you were deficient? i.e., see a commercial for a new pair of shoes, stimulates your recognition that you need a new pair of shoes.

Information search

- Internal search, memory.
- External search if you need more information. Friends and relatives (word-of-mouth). Marketer dominated sources; comparison shopping; public sources, etc.

A successful information search leaves a buyer with possible alternatives, the *evoked set.*

Hungry, want to go out and eat, evoked set is

- Chinese food
- Indian food
- Burger king
- Klondike kates, etc.

2. Evaluation of Alternatives — need to establish criteria for evaluation, features the buyer wants or does not want. Rank/weight alternatives or resume search may decide that you want to eat something spicy, Indian gets highest rank, etc. If not satisfied with your choice, then return to the search phase. Can you think of another restaurant? Look in the yellow pages, etc. Information from different sources may be treated differently. Marketers try to influence by "framing" alternatives.

3. Purchase decision — Choose buying alternative, includes product, package, store, method of purchase, etc.

4. Purchase — May differ from decision, time lapse between 4 and 5, product availability.

5. Post-purchase Evaluation — outcome: Satisfaction or dissatisfaction.

6. Cognitive Dissonance, have you made the right decision. This can be reduced by warranties, after sales communication etc. After eating an Indian meal, may think that really you wanted a Chinese meal instead.

Pillsbury 1-800#s

Pillsbury 1-800 #s gives the consumer a way of communicating with the marketer after purchase. This helps reduce cognitive dissonance when a marketer can answer any concerns of a new consumer.

Nutrament Debunked: Nutrament, a product marketed by Bristol–Myers Squibb originally was targeted at consumers who needed to receive additional energy from their drinks after exercise, etc., a fitness drink. It was, therefore, targeted at consumers whose needs were for either *love and belonging* or *esteem*. The product was not selling well, and was almost terminated. Upon extensive research it was determined that the product did sell well in inner-city convenience stores. It was determined that the consumers for the product were actually drug addicts who couldn't digest a regular meal. They would purchase Nutrament as a substitute for a meal. Their motivation to purchase was completely different to the motivation that BMS had originally thought. These consumers were at the *Physiological* level of the hierarchy. BMS therefore had to redesign its MM to better meet the needs of this target market. Motives often operate at a subconscious level therefore are difficult to measure.

Perception

What do you see? Perception is the process of selecting, organizing and interpreting information inputs to produce meaning, i.e., we chose what info we pay attention to, organize it and interpret it. Information inputs are the sensations received through sight, taste, hearing, smell and touch.

Selective Exposure – Select inputs to be exposed to our awareness. More likely if it is linked to an event, satisfies current needs, intensity of input changes (sharp price drop).

Selective Distortion – Changing/twisting current received information, inconsistent with beliefs.

Advertisers that use comparative advertisements (pitching one product against another), have to be very careful that consumers do not distort the facts and perceive that the advertisement was for the competitor. A current example...MCI and ATandT...do you ever get confused?

Selective Retention – Remember inputs that support beliefs, forgets those that don't. Average supermarket shopper is exposed to 17,000 products in a shopping visit lasting 30 minutes – 60 per cent of purchases are unplanned. Exposed to 1,500 advertisement per day. Can't be expected to be aware of all these inputs, and certainly will not retain many.

Interpreting information is based on what is already familiar, on knowledge that is stored in the memory.

South Africa Wine: Problems marketing wine from South Africa: Consumers have strong perceptions of the country, and hence its products.

Ability and Knowledge

Need to understand individuals' capacity to learn. Learning changes in a person's behaviour caused by information and experience. Therefore, to change consumers' behaviour about your product, retailer's need to give buyers – new information, new product, free sample after-sales service, etc.

South Africa: Open bottle of wine and pour it!! Also educate American consumers about changes in South Africa. Need to sell a whole new country.

When making buying decisions, buyers must process information. *Knowledge* is the familiarity with the product and expertise.

Inexperience buyers often use prices as an indicator of quality more than those who have knowledge of a product. Non-alcoholic beer example: consumers chose the most expensive six-pack, because they assume that the greater price indicates greater quality.

Learning is the process through which a relatively permanent change in behaviour results from the consequences of past behaviour.

Attitudes

Knowledge about the product and also positive and negative feelings about an object or activity-maybe tangible or intangible, living or non-living. Try to get correct perceptions.

Individual learns attitudes through experience and interaction with other people. Consumer attitudes toward a firm and its products greatly influence the success or failure of the firm's marketing strategy.

Oldsmobile: Oldsmobile vs. Lexus, due to consumers attitudes toward Oldsmobile (as discovered by class exercise) need to disassociate Aurora from the Oldsmobile name.

Exxon Valdez-nearly 20,000 credit cards were returned or cut-up after the tragic oil spill.

Honda "You meet the nicest people on a Honda", dispels the unsavory image of a motorbike rider, late 1950s. Changing market of the 1990s, baby boomers aging, Hondas market returning to hardcore. To change this they have a new slogan "Come ride with us".

Attitudes and attitude change are influenced by consumers personality and lifestyle.

Consumers screen information that conflicts with their attitudes. Distort information to make it consistent and selectively retain information that reinforces our attitudes, i.e., brand loyalty.

There is a difference between attitude and intention to buy (ability to buy).

Personality

All the internal traits and behaviours that make a person unique, uniqueness arrives from a person's heredity and personal experience. Examples include:

- Workaholisms
- Compulsiveness
- Self-confidence
- Friendliness
- Adaptability
- Ambitiousness
- Dogmatism
- Authoritarianism
- Introversion
- Extroversion
- Aggressiveness
- Competitiveness.

Traits affect the way people behave. Marketers try to match the store image to the perceived image of their customers.

There is a weak association between personality and Buying Behaviour, this may be due to unreliable measures. Consumers buy products that are consistent with their self-concept.

Lifestyles

Lifestyle is a person's pattern of living. It involves measuring buyer's major **AIO** dimensions: (Activities, Interests and Opinions) **Activities** (work, hobbies, shopping, sports, social events) **Interests**: (food, fashion, family, recreation), and **Opinions** (about themselves, social issues, business, products). Lifestyle captures something more than the person's social class or personality. It profiles whole pattern of acting and interacting in the world. Recent US trends in lifestyles are a shift towards personal independence and individualism and a preference for a healthy, natural lifestyle.

Lifestyles are the consistent patterns people follow in their lives. Buyers change the goods and services they buy over their lifetimes. Buying is also shaped by the stage of the family life cycle, the stage through which families might pass as they mature over-time. Retailers have to define their target markets, in terms of life cycle stage and develop appropriate products and retailing plans for each stage. Traditional family life cycle stages include young, singles and married couples with children. Today, however, retailers are increasingly catering to a growing number of alternative non-traditional stages such as unmarried couples, couples marrying in life, children couple, single parents, extended parents (those with young adult children returning home) and others.

Example: Healthy foods for a healthy lifestyle. Sun tan not considered fashionable in US until 1920s. Now there is an assault by the American Academy of Dermatology.

Social Factors

Consumer wants, learning, motives, etc., are influenced by opinion leaders, person's family, reference groups, social class and culture.

Opinion Leaders

Marketers try to attract opinion leaders. They actually use (pay) spokespeople to market their products. Michael Jordon (Nike, McDonalds, Gatorade etc.)

Roles and Family Influences

The retailers should have clear vision about their potential customers. People have many roles. Husband, father, employer/employee and individuals' role are continuing to change. Therefore, marketers must continue to update information.

Family is the most basic group a person belongs to. Marketers must understand:

- that many family decisions are made by the family unit
- consumer behaviour starts in the family unit
- family roles and preferences are the model for children's future family (can reject/alter, etc.)
- family buying decisions are a mixture of family interactions and individual decision making
- family acts an interpreter of social and cultural values for the individual.

The family life cycle: families go through stages, each stage creates different consumer demands:

- bachelor stage...
- newly married, young, no children...me
- full nest I, youngest child under 6
- full nest II, youngest child 6 or over
- full nest III, older married couples with dependent children
- empty nest I, older married couples with no children living with them, head in labor force
- empty nest II, older married couples, no children living at home, head retired
- solitary survivor, in labour force
- solitary survivor, retired
- modernized life cycle includes divorced and no children.

Two Income Marriages Are Now the Norm

Two income families are becoming more common nowadays. Hence, the decision maker in the family unit is changing. Family has less time for children, and therefore, tends to let them influence purchase decisions in order to alleviate some of the guilt. (Children influence about $ 130 billion of goods in a year). Children also have more money to spend themselves.

Reference Groups Influencing Buyer Behaviour

Individual identifies with the group to the extent that he takes on many of the values, attitudes or behaviours of the group members. The reference group influencing buyers are:

Families, friends, sororities, civic and professional organizations. Every group has a positive or negative influence on a person's attitude and behaviour. ***Membership groups*** (belong to) Affinity marketing is focused on the desires of consumers that belong to reference groups. Marketers get the groups to approve the product and communicate that approval to its members. Credit Cards, etc.!!

Aspiration groups (want to belong to) ***Disassociate groups*** (do not want to belong to) Honda, tries to disassociate from the "biker" group.

The degree to which a reference group will affect a purchase decision depends on an individual's susceptibility to reference group influence and the strength of his/her involvement with the group.

Social Class

There is an open group of individuals who have similar social rank. US is not a classless society. The buying behaviour is influence by occupation, education, income, wealth, race, ethnic groups and possessions.

Social class influences many aspects of our lives. Upper-middle-class Americans prefer luxury cars Mercedes.

- Upper Americans-upper-upper class, .3 per cent, inherited wealth, aristocratic names
- Lower-upper-class, 1.2 per cent, newer social elite, from current professionals and corporate elite
- Upper-middle-class, 12.5 per cent, college graduates, managers and professionals
- Middle Americans-middle-class, 32 per cent, average pay white collar workers and blue collar friends
- Working class, 38 per cent, average pay blue collar workers
- Lower Americans-lower class, 9 per cent, working, not on welfare
- Lower-lower class, 7 per cent, on welfare

Social class determines to some extent, the types, quality, quantity of products that a person buys or uses.

Lower class people tend to stay close to home while shopping. They do not engage in much pre-purchase information gathering. Stores project definite class images.

Family, reference groups and social classes are all social influences on consumer behaviour. All operate within a larger culture.

Culture and Subculture

Culture refers to the set of values, ideas, and attitudes that are accepted by a homogeneous group of people and transmitted to the next generation.

Culture also determines what is acceptable with product advertising. Culture determines what people wear, eat, reside and travel. Cultural values in the US are good health, education, individualism and freedom. In American culture time scarcity is a growing problem.

Culture is the most basic cause on shoppers wants and behaviour. Shopper behaviour is largely learned. Growing up in a society, a child learns basic values, perceptions, wants and behaviour from the family and other important institutions. A child normally learns or is exposed to achievement and success, activity and involvement, efficiency and practicality, progress, material comfort, individualism, freedom, humanitarianism, youthfulness, and fitness and health. Every group or society has a culture and cultural influences on buying behaviour. It may vary greatly from country-to-country. Failure to adjust these differences can result in ineffective marketing or embarrassing mistakes.

Retailers are always trying to spot shifts in order to discover new products that might be wanted. For example, the cultural shift towards greater concern about health and fitness has created a huge industry for exercise equipment and clothing, lower fat and more natural foods, and health and fitness services. The shift towards informality has resulted in more demand for casual clothing and simpler home furnishings and the increased desire for leisure time has resulted in more demand for convenience products and services, such as microwave ovens and fast food.

SubCulture: Each culture contains smaller subcultures or groups of people with shared value systems based on common life experiences and situations. Subcultures include nationalities, religions, social groups, and geographic regions. Retailers often design products and marketing programmes tailored to their needs. Examples of four such important subculture groups include Hispanic, African American, Asian, and Mature shoppers.

Will British warm up to iced tea?

No. Tea is a part of the British culture, hot with milk.

There are different societies, different levels of needs, and different cultural values.

Culture can be divided into subcultures:

- Geographic regions
- Human characteristics such as age and ethnic background.

Culture Effects – What People Buy

Understanding Consumer Buying Behaviour offers consumers greater satisfaction (Utility). We must assume that the company has adopted the Marketing Concept and are consumer-oriented. Nobel laureate **Herbert Simon** sees **economic** decision making as a **vain** attempt to be rational. He claims (in 1947 and 1957) that if a complete analysis is to be done, a decision will be immensely complex. He also says that peoples' information processing ability is very limited. The assumption of a perfectly **rational** economic actor is unrealistic. Often we are influenced by emotional and non-rational considerations. When we try to be rational we are at best only partially successful. Buying process leads to a decision to buy.

We've talked often enough about the five steps of the sales process; it's a mandatory structural element in the persuasive architecture of your site. But at the same time you're "selling", an activity you largely control, your visitors are "buying", an activity they largely control.

The trick to making your conversion rate soar is to construct your sales process so it is in tune with how folks decide to buy whatever you offer.

The Nature of the Buy

The way folks make buying decisions depends on the complexity of the problem they are trying to solve and the complexity of each step in the decision process. This will affect how you manage the sale.

If their needs and the decision making process are simple, all you need to do is make your visitors aware of you, build confidence, differentiate yourself, demonstrate value and guide them through a very simple shopping and buying process. This is why lower-end, branded products sell so well. Think of buying a book from Amazon.com.

If the needs and the decision making process are highly complex, then you need to make people aware of you, build relationships, educate them (and perhaps many different individuals or teams within the same organization), show sensitivity to the different decision makers, influencers and groups, and resolve conflicting needs, so you can custom-tailor your solutions and make the buying process as painless and positive as possible. Think of purchasing a multi-million dollar piece of equipment that needs five departments to sign off to close the deal.

It also helps if you understand and incorporate how folks think about buying what you offer. Are they going to compare similar models in different brands? Are they looking for the range offered by one manufacturer? Do they think of the purchase in terms of a hierarchy of benefits, with some more important than others? Is the best way to showcase your product or service to compare it with someone else's stuff?

Propensity to Buy

You get four types of traffic, and each group is primed with a different level of motivation and preparedness – the classic "propensity to buy". First, you've got the to-die-for perfect visitors; they are the ones who know exactly what they want and come to you looking for features, brands, and model numbers.

Then you've got the visitors who sort of know what they want. These are folks who have identified a strongly felt need, but they're still in the process of narrowing down their search criteria.

Then there are the window shoppers, folks who aren't sure they want anything, but might buy if they saw something that interested them. They have no strongly felt need in mind, but one could be suggested to them.

The fourth group is not really prospects. They're lost or there by mistake. Be happy when they go away.

You don't know where your visitors are in the process when they land on your site, so you've got to plan for each possibility. You've got to help the folks who know exactly what they want get to it quickly; make them jump through too many hoops and they're gone. You've got to help the ones still mulling it over by offering pertinent information where and when they are most likely to need it, as well as persuading them you're the logical business choice. You've got to be most engaging and appealing for the window shopper, and you've got to let the lost soul quickly figure out he doesn't belong there.

It also helps to consider that not all your visitors are prepared or even inclined to make a decision when they first visit your site – sometimes a successful conversion is the result of multiple visits. So you'd like to give folks a reason to come back.

Buying is an Emotional Decision

Folks rationalize the decision to buy based on facts, but they make the decision to buy based on feelings. The single biggest motivator in buying is emotional response. And that takes place on two levels.

In part, it's the emotional response that comes when folks imagine themselves enjoying the benefits of what you offer. Put them in the driver's seat, and they are that much closer to being able to see themselves making the decision to buy.

One should make your features available and present them as corollaries to benefits. After all, some of your visitors, particularly analytic types who will pointedly look for this stuff, feel more comfortable emotionally with facts and specifications.

And that brings me to the other aspect of emotional response. Folks buy when they feel comfortable, when they feel they can trust you, when the process feels natural and reassuring, and when they come to believe that buying will make them feel good. Ignore this, and most of your visitors will bail out. Tap into it, and watch your conversion rate climb. Because, at the end of the day, it's not a fact that convince customers to go with your company, and with its emotion.

Package Buying with Selling

The persuasive architecture of your entire site must recognize every step of the buying decision process. Each step feeds and leads to the others. Although the process ultimately is linear, there can be feedback loops within the process as folks reevaluate information. So, it's not unusual to address multiple steps on a single page.

To successfully get your visitors to take action you must be able to see the world from their "buying" point of view. So learn how to address and package the buying process within your selling process. It will make a world of difference!

Models of Buyer Decision making

In an early study of the buyer decision process literature, Frank Nicosia (Nicosia, F. 1966; pp. 9-21) identified three types of buyer decision making models. They are the univariate model (He called it the "simple scheme") in which only one behavioural determinant was allowed in a stimulus-response type of relationship; the multivariate model (He called it a "reduced form scheme".) in which numerous independent variables were assumed to determine buyer behaviour; and finally the "system of equations" model (He called it a "structural scheme" or "process scheme".) in which numerous functional relations (either univariate or multivariate) interact in a complex system of equations. He concluded that only this third type of model is capable of expressing the complexity of buyer decision processes. In chapter 7, Nicosia builds a comprehensive model involving five modules. The encoding module includes determinants like "attributes of the brand", "environmental factors", "consumer's attributes", "attributes of the organization", and "attributes of the message". Other modules in the system include, consumer decoding, search and evaluation, decision, and consumption.

General Model

A general model of the **buyer decision process** consists of the following steps:

1. Problem recognition;
2. Gathering information
3. Alternative education
4. Purchase decision
5. Post-purchase behaviour/buyer's remorse (cognitive dissonance)

There are a range of alternative models, but that of AIUAPR, which most directly links to the steps in the marketing/promotional process is often seen as the most generally useful.

1. **Awareness** – Before anything else can happen the potential customers must become aware that the product or service exists. Thus, the first task must be to gain the attention of the target audience. All the different models are, predictably, agreed on this first step. If the audience never hears the message, they will not act on it, no matter how powerful it is.

2. **Interest** – But it is not sufficient to grab their attention. The message must interest them and persuade them that the product or service is relevant to their needs. The content of the message(s) must therefore be meaningful and clearly relevant to that target audience's needs, and this is where marketing research can come into its own.

3. **Understanding** – Once an interest is established, the prospective customer must be able to appreciate how well the offering may meet his or her needs, again as revealed by the marketing research. This may be no small achievement where the advertiser has just a few words, or ten seconds, to convey their message.

4. **Attitudes** – But the message must go even further; to persuade the reader to adopt a sufficiently positive attitude towards the product or service that he or she will purchase it, albeit as a trial. There is no adequate way of describing how this may be achieved. It is simply down to the magic of the advertiser's art, or based on the strength of the product or service itself.

5. **Purchase** – All the above stages might happen in a few minutes while the reader is considering the advertisement; in the comfort of his or her favourite armchair. The final buying decision, on the other hand, may take place sometime later; perhaps weeks later, when the prospective buyer actually tries to find a shop which stocks the product.

6. **Repeat Purchase** – But in most cases this first purchase is best viewed as just a trial purchase. Only if the experience is a success for the customer will it be turned into repeat purchases. These repeats, not the single purchase which is the focus of most models, are where the vendors focus should be, for these are where the profits are generated. The earlier stages are merely a very necessary prerequisite for this.

This is a very simple model, and as such does apply quite generally. Its lessons are that you cannot obtain repeat purchasing without going through the stages of building awareness and then obtaining trial use; which has to be successful. It is a pattern which applies to all repeat purchase products and services; industrial goods just as much as baked beans. This simple theory is rarely taken any further – to look at the series of transactions which such repeat purchasing implies. The consumer's growing experience over a number of such transactions is often the determining factor in the later and future purchases. All the succeeding transactions are, thus, interdependent – and the overall decision making process may accordingly be much more complex than most models allow for.

Cognitive and Personal Biases in Decision Making

It is generally agreed that biases can creep into our decision making processes, calling into question the correctness of a decision. Below is a list of some of the more common cognitive biases.

1. **Selective search for evidence** – We tend to be willing to gather facts that support certain conclusions but disregard other facts that support different conclusions.
2. **Premature termination of search for evidence** – We tend to accept the first alternative that looks like it might work.
3. **Conservatism and inertia** – Unwillingness to change thought patterns that we have used in the past in the face of new circumstances.
4. **Experiential limitations** – Unwillingness or inability to look beyond the scope of our past experiences; rejection of the unfamiliar.
5. **Selective perception** – We actively screen-out information that we do not think is salient.
6. **Wishful thinking or optimism** – We tend to want to see things in a positive light and this can distort our perception and thinking.
7. **Regency** - We tend to place more attention on more recent information and either ignore or forget more distant information.
8. **Repetition bias** – A willingness to believe what we have been told most often and by the greatest number of different of sources.
9. **Anchoring** – Decisions are unduly influenced by initial information that shapes our view of subsequent information.
10. **Group think** – Peer pressure to conform to the opinions held by the group.
11. **Source credibility bias** – We reject something if we have a bias against the person, organization, or group to which the person belongs. We are inclined to accept a statement by someone we like.
12. **Incremental decision making and escalating commitment** – We look at a decision as a small step in a process and this tends to perpetuate a series of similar decisions. This can be contrasted with **zero-based decision making**.
13. **Inconsistency** – The unwillingness to apply the same decision criteria in similar situations.
14. **Attribution asymmetry** – We tend to attribute our success to our abilities and talents, but we attribute our failures to bad luck and external factors. We attribute others success to good luck, and their failures to their mistakes.
15. **Role fulfilment** – We conform to the decision making expectations that others have of someone in our position.
16. **Underestimating uncertainty and the illusion of control** – We tend to underestimate future uncertainty because we tend to believe we have more control over events than we really do.

17. **Faulty generalizations** – In order to simplify an extremely complex world, we tend to group things and people. These simplifying generalizations can bias decision making processes.

18. **Ascription of causality** – We tend to ascribe causation even when the evidence only suggests correlation. Just because birds fly to the equatorial regions when the trees lose their leaves, does not mean that the birds migrate *because* the trees lose their leaves.

There are five fundamental elements, *viz.,* **(i) Concept clarity** (customers want to know what retailers offer and what they stand for), **(ii) Choice**, **(iii) Clarity** (Customers do not like too much choice or too little choice. Right amount of choice is a key factor for retailers), **(iv) Control of the experience** (Retailers need to give customers control by making their stores easier to shop and by providing key information), **(v) Communications of the concept** (Customers need full information about the product), and **(vi) Closure** (Retailers have to adopt express aisles for customers. Customers do not like to waste their time while going for purchase) to create an efficient shopping experience.

The six Cs of customer in control is presented in the following diagram:

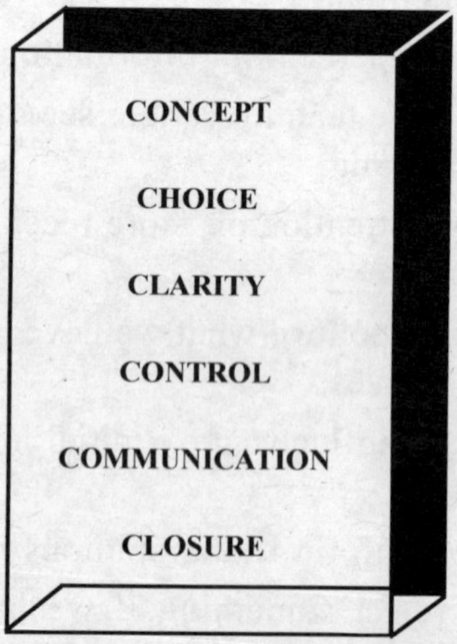

FIG. 38: SIX Cs OF CUSTOMER IN CONTROL

Profile Customers, Profiling Customers, Customer Analysis

Definition: Customer segmentation is the practice of dividing a customer base into groups of individuals that are similar in specific ways relevant to marketing, such as age, gender, interests, spending habits, and so on. Using segmentation allows companies to target groups effectively, and allocate marketing resources to best effect. Clearly, if you intend to sell fun boards, your customer profile is not those of aged persons.

Shopper Behaviour

Quantitative research was used to provide robust data, in the form of exit interviews with shoppers intending to buy. Qualitative research was used to provide deep insight; this included observation of shoppers in stores, semiotic analysis of store environment and PoS, mini-discussions with selected shoppers and face-to-face depth interviews with store managers.

Retail stores offer significant room for impact and many shoppers entering stores with an intention to buy can still be influenced, even during final stages of the purchase process. Consistent patterns of the in-store journey were observed, which led to recommendations about how to design the store around key customer moments, as this would maximize impact. Importantly, we found that the priority of critical moments differed by market and the risk of failing to deliver on these critical moments caused the customer journey to break down. Our analysis identified a number of prominent shopper typologies illustrating how different shoppers engage with stores. It was possible to redesign a retail store to accommodate all shopper types, encouraging both browser engagement and buyer sales transactions.

By working in partnership with a number of retail outlets the client was able to tailor the retail store environments of a national chain in line with customer needs. This collaboration was mutually beneficial to all parties as boosted sales volumes were observed shortly after.

Retail shopping behaviour is one of the major tenets of the retail marketing literature. The purpose of this research is to presents the empirical findings of two quantitative studies of Estonian and Canadian university students' interpretation and perceptions of retail shopping behaviour. There is a level of commonality in retail shopping perceptions, as well as non-trivial differences in how shopping practice in terms of the construct structure, and individual service drivers, should be theorized. The Canadian (Estonian retail market). Sample indicated a greater focus on retail service quality perception at the subdimension level while the Estonian sample indicated a greater focus on retail service quality at an overall or integrated level.

Retail Shopper Behaviour

The aggressive, geographic market expansion of successful retail organizations, the development of a global consumer market and the spatial diffusion of retail innovations led us to investigate the extent to which models helping managers to make strategic decisions can be generalized across time and place. To the extent that such generalization can occur, it would reduce the redundancy of research and associated costs for making decisions in major retail organizations. This article makes use of relatively recent developments in random utility theory to assess the stability over time and space of the preferences underlying retail-shopping choice. Data collected three times over four years in Canada are used to compare models of shopping centre choice based on perceived centre attributes. We hypothesize that random component variance differences are the likely source of observed differences in retailing preferences. Two waves of panel data for supermarket choice are used to assess our ability to generalize to another choice process. Data for shopping centre choice collected in Canada, USA and Norway are used to assess spatial stability. The test results support the hypothesis for the spatial consistency of preferences. The test of stability over time shows no difference at all in retailing preferences, both the random component variances and the coefficients were unchanged over the four-year period studied.

Motivations to engage in retail shopping include both utilitarian and hedonic dimensions. Business to consumer e-commerce conducted via the mechanism of web-shopping provides an expanded opportunity for companies to create a cognitively and esthetically rich shopping environment in ways not readily imitable in the non-electronic shopping world. In this article an attitudinal model is developed and empirically tested integrating constructs from technology acceptance research and constructs derived from models of web behaviour. Results of two studies from two distinct categories of the interactive shopping environment support the differential importance of immersive, hedonic aspects of the new media as well as the more traditional utilitarian motivations. In addition, navigation, convenience, and the substitutability of the electronic environment to personally examining products were found to be important predictors of online shopping attitudes. Results are discussed in terms of insights for the creation of the online shopping *webmosphere* through more effective design of interactive retail shopping environments.

Practical implications – Retail sales per capita within Estonia, and the other Baltic states, represents the fastest growing region in the European Union. Thus, there is a need for empirical and academic research that attempts to highlight the transferable (i.e., Western) and the solely domestic consumer knowledge that will allow this growth to continue. Caution needs to be taken when simply implementing best retail practices from the West as erroneous conclusions may be drawn. It may not be the practices from the West that are fuelling the retail success, and thus research such as this helps to draw attention to the need to understand the more sustainable localized nature of retail shopping behaviour.

Shopping Behaviour Explained – The 'So What' Factor

Shopping behaviour analysis combines a unique set of research tools. We compare what shoppers actually do in-store with their conscious and subconscious motivations and opinions.

Shopping behaviour analysis brings the shopper into the very heart of retail marketing, merchandising and category management. We report what happens in-store, why and what to do about it.

- How many shoppers look at your products but buy something else?
- When and where are purchase decisions really made?
- What are the purchase triggers (physiological and psychological)?
- Are there any barriers to purchase at fixture that can be easily removed?
- What information in-store actually influences shoppers and how?

Here are three reasons why you should **use us** for your next piece of shopper research.

1. We aim to meet the objectives *of the* objectives
2. We analyze what shoppers do AND how they think
3. We never lose sight of the 'So what' factor

Much fascination and speculation surrounds the impact of the World Wide Web on consumer shopping behaviour. At the same time, there is little empirical evidence underlying all this speculation. This article provides one such data set. It reports on factors that consumers found salient as they browsed through selected electronic malls on the World Wide Web. We gathered consumers' reactions via an open-ended survey using a sample of 220 shoppers. We related the reactions to the factors of product perceptions, shopping experience, customer service, and perceived consumer risk, which we had identified from the existing literature on retail patronage behaviour. This study translated these factors to the World Wide Web context and explored their relative salience. With respect to product perceptions, consumers were impressed by the breadth of stores on the World Wide Web but disappointed with the depth of a merchant's offerings. The shopping experience was reported to be generally enjoyable, but at the same time frustrating. Consumers also reported that they could perceive the potential for time savings and reduced effort compared with traditional forms of shopping, but that, at present, goal-directed shopping was difficult. Nearly everyone in the sample had something negative to say about customer service on the World Wide Web, judging that the sites were not designed to be responsive to their needs and that the presentation of goods and services seemed intangible. Risk was cited as a barrier to shopping on the World Wide Web, but was not as salient to our sample as product perceptions, shopping experience, and customer service. Overall, the results suggest that World Wide Web merchants need to think more about how they perform on the factors known to affect consumer behaviour; namely, product perceptions, shopping experience, and customer service. We offer advice for enhancing the design of World Wide Web retail sites.

Theory of Shopping

The concept of shopping can be examined according to three different dimensions in order to develop provide a holistic view of shopping and shopping behaviour: the shopping environment, the socio-cultural context and the individual motivations (Woodruffe, Eccles and Elliott, 2002).

The Shopping Environment

This refers to the landscape of shopping, changing as it did from the first departmental store to present-day malls to virtual shopping through the Internet. It has been found that shoppers behave differently depending on the type of shopping situations (Sinha and Uniyal, 2004).

The Socio-cultural Context

Culture has been defined in different ways depending on the theoretical perspective of the researcher (Smircich, 1983). Rather than define culture, we instead state the commonly accepted view of the components of culture which include values, symbols/artifacts, actions, and cognitions, emotions and meanings (Ashkanasy, Wilderom and Peterson, 2000). In our context, culture is similar to the Geertz's symbolic anthropological view by (including shopping behaviour). Which culture is defined a system of shared symbols and meanings impacting behaviour?

I. Economic Theory of Shopping

The profounder of this theory is Alfred Marshall. He was of the view that human beings are selfish and so their decision assigns due weightage to self-interest. He opined that the shoppers always try to maximize their utilities with the limited resources. It is based on the assumption that the shopper always tries to maximize his satisfaction within the limits of his financial resources; the shopper has complete knowledge of alternative for satisfying his wants and the shoppers always acts rationally.

II. Psychological Theories of Shopping

(i) Learning Theory: Leading Russian psychologist developed this learning theory. It describes about a change in the consumer behaviour, which occurs as a result of practice. The learning experiences of buying affect the shopper behaviour. This stimuli-response theory is dependent on stimulus, response and reinforcement. This theory insists on the quality of the product so as to concentrate the attention of the shoppers on a particular brand. The product features such as price, quality, brand and package, etc., and the marketing communications such as advertising and other promotional persuade the buyers to purchase the product. If the experience of shopper is satisfactory, their decision to purchase of satisfaction is repeated or reinforced. So, man is a creature who can be conditioned through repetition and reinforcement to respond in particular ways.

(ii) Psycho-analytic Theory: This theory is explained by Sigmund Freud. He contends that there are three parts of mind – the id, ego, and superego. The id houses the basic instructive drives, many of which are anti-social. The superego is our conscience, accepting moral standards and directing the instinctive drives into acceptable channels, thus avoiding guilty feelings. Sometimes, the id and ego are in conflict. The ego is the conscious, national control centre, which maintains a balance between the uninherited instincts of the id and the socially oriented superego. The basic theme of the Sigmund Freud's theory is the belief that the unsatisfied needs of a person creates tension within an individual if he is not able to satisfy all his needs within the bounds of society. This tension is to be repressed, which always is said to exist in the sub-conscious and continues to influence shopper behaviour.

(iii) Sociological Theory: Almost every society has some of social class structure. Social classes are society's relatively permanent and ordered divisions whose members share similar values, interest, and behaviours. Social class is not determined by a single factor, such as income, but is measured as combination of occupation, income, education, wealth and other variables. In some social systems, members of different classes are reared for certain roles and cannot change their social positions. Retailers are interested in social because people within a given social class tend to exhibit similar buying behaviour. Social classes show distinct product and brand preferences in areas such as dietary, clothing, home furnishings, leisure activity, and automobiles. Social class status often leads to differing forms of shopper behaviour. Shopper behaviour is influenced by social factors, such as the consumer's small groups, family, and social roles and status. In the consumer behavioural theories developed by sociologists and cultural anthropologists primary focus is on inter-personal relations and influences. The sociological theory of shopper behaviour developed by Veblen is more practical. The concept of influence of social group in shopper behaviour is also supported by the research of early Gastals psychologists like Wertheimen, Kohler, and Koffka. This theory explains the influences of social forces such as social classes, reference groups, culture, lifestyle, etc. It also says that the buyer's behaviour is motivated by need for prestige. The marketeer should identify those social forces, which influence the demand for his product. His hypothesis is that much of economic consumption is motivated by the intrinsic need or satisfaction so much as by prestige seeking.

III. Est Theory Model

The Est theory for retail success was first presented by Norm McMillan in the early 1990s, at an international food industry trade show in France. The Est theory derives from the word *best,* and it essentially says that a retailer must be best at one proposition that's important to a specific group of customers. Est is not simply a 'marketing thing', a way to position a company in advertising and external communications. This theory played well in Paris and in Peoria. Retailers must strive for a specific positioning to a specific set of customers rather than attempting to be great at everything to everybody. To accomplish this might mean targeting a specific customer at the exclusion of others, giving up on merchandise categories that today might still be yielding profitable sales, or forgoing short-term growth and profits with an eye toward long-term success. These ideas were heretical for most retailers at the time and are concepts that most struggle with even today. Winning retailers are identified by sales growth and profitability. The shoppers have less time to shop. They are more knowledgeable about the products they want to buy and the stores that sell them. They have more choices of where to shop than ever before. The Est retailers had devoted their organizations from top to bottom to becoming the best in one particular area. Est theory was the driving force of their businesses.

Cheap Est Defined: It means consistently having lower prices than the competition on the products that a retailer sells. It is an easily understood proposition in the USA. The Cheap Est retailers in America have the opportunity for huge sales volumes. Wal-Mart, the quintessential Cheap Est retailer, is now the world's largest company – bigger than conglomerates like Exxon and General Electric.

Shoppers frequently go to mediocre stores because of historic attachment- that is where their parents always shopped. Shoppers are also influenced by sales promotion. Consumer research indicates that shoppers are attracted by the location of the store. Pretty good stores cannot satisfy increasingly demanding customers. Pretty good stores also cannot compete with today's sharpest retail chains. Stores like Wal-Mart, Target, and Kohl's have raised customer expectations. Falling short of expectations means not satisfying customers, and that is the most direct path to the Black Hole. The buzzword today is *branding.* Est retailers devote themselves with laser like focus to their core shopper proposition. It is known as *Est position.* They commit employees from the top to the bottom of their organization to that position. They communicate that positioning to their customers and execute it relentlessly at the store level. Est retailers also base strategic and day to day operational decisions on their positioning. An Est positioning is not simply the marketing message *du jour* – it is a way of life for successful retailers.

Winning Retail

1. Well defined customer proposition and product positioning
2. New concepts and formats
3. Give customers more of what they want and less of what they don't want
4. Honest and straightforward approach (Retailers have neither the time nor the inclination to digest euphemisms and sugar-coated remedies)

Black Hole: It is the place where retail companies that are no longer relevant to customers go to die. Kmart (US), the nation's third-largest discount store chain, was closed in January 2002. Less than a decade ago, Kmart was the nation's second-largest retailer. Other large retail chains that may seem a long way from the brink are also in peril. That's because stores like

Kmart are adrift in a place that we call the Sea of Mediocrity. These stores aren't best at anything, and they don't have a distinct or sharply defined customer proposition.

The Individual Motivations

A fairly extensive amount of research examining individual shopping orientations indicates that orientations impact shopping behaviour including store choice based on several factors such as consumer demographics and Hui, 2002; Darden and Ashton, 1974; Hansen and Deutscher, 1977 psychographics (Cheung, Yee-Man), usage situation (Moye and Kincade, 2002); price sensitivity (Magi, 2003); social referents (Evans, Christiansen and Gill, 1996), involvement (Williams, Nicholas and Painter, 1978), and need.

Shopping Behaviour Xplained Ltd., is one of the world's leading specialist shopper research agencies. We offer both qualitative and quantitative research services via a number of unique and bespoke research methodologies. We compare what shoppers actually do in-store with their conscious and subconscious motivations and opinions.

Our ongoing success means that we are expanding and therefore we are looking to grow our specialist team by adding a further very specialist field based engineer. An exciting new role now exists for a person who can set up and configure wireless networks. You will have good inter-personal skills and a keen eye for detail. In addition, the following key attributes are essential:

The ability to set up temporary wireless networks of cameras in order to create CCTV systems in-store.

Be able to discuss with store managers the needs of the CCTV and what that entails in terms of impacting in store operations.

A skilled engineer is happy to work around UK, Europe and The Far East, staying away for two or three nights at a time.

If one is able to also input Excel spreadsheet data that would be a definite advantage.

One will need to have experience of travelling and be able to be self-sufficient whilst 'on the road', although all expenses will be reimbursed.

A keen interest in understanding people's behaviour is a definite advantage.

Competitive salary and benefits are offered for this permanent role. If you think that you could add value to our team and that the role would inspire and excite you, then please send your CV to Phillip Adcock: pa@sbxl.com.

Shopping Behaviour Xplained Ltd., is expanding by appointing specialist team and by adding business development professionals. The successful candidates will have excellent communications skills, be genuinely self-motivated and have a proven track record of new business development. In addition, the following key attributes are essential:

Experts of shopping behaviour Xplained Ltd., examine shopping behaviour combined with a unique 3-way study of interview data which provide much more reliable understanding and insight to make key decisions.

One needs ability to build relationships with some of the top retail professionals in UK.

Tips to Retailers

Be able to identify, pitch for and WIN new shopper research business.

A skilful presenter can engage prospects by way of an informative manner.

Have a good working knowledge of Microsoft Office is a necessity.

Possess a full (preferably clean) driving licence.

A keen interest in understanding the human mind and people's behaviour is a definite advantage.

The ability to analyze data to uncover real insights is much needed.

One will need to have a good understanding of Excel and PowerPoint.

The customer profile is deduced from the customer benefit. It includes also the customer buying process.

Definition: The customer profile describes the characteristics of the customer who could really benefit from the product or service of retailers.

Shopper Profile Analysis

Shoppers' Stop Profile – Presentation Transcript

1. Introduction About Retail Sector: Retailing in India is up for change. It has broken the eggshell and ready to grow into a giant that will match the retailing practices of the West. There are two types of retailing first – organized and another is unorganized, in India there is unorganized retailing. In India the share of organized retailing is less than 10 per cent and only 8 per cent people are engaged in organized retailing. Delhi has maximum space which can be utilized as Retail space.

2. Next, Gurgaon has the Maximum Space: India is being seen as a potential goldmine for retail investors from over the world and latest research has rated India as the top destination for retailers for an attractive emerging retail market. India's vast middle-class and its almost untouched retail industry are key attractions for global retail giants wanting to enter newer markets. Even though India has well over five million retail outlets, the country deeply lacks anything that can resemble a retailing industry in the modern sense of the term. This presents international retailing specialists with a great opportunity. The organized retail sector is expected to grow stronger than GDP growth in the next five years driven by changing lifestyles, growing income and favourable demographic outline. About Shoppers' Stop is a chain of retail stores in India owned by K Raheja Corp. It was started in 1991, for its first store in Andheri in Mumbai near Vishnu Baug Colony in S.V. Road. Currently it operates stores in Bengaluru, Hyderabad, Lucknow, Gaziabad, Jaipur, Delhi, Chennai, Mumbai, Pune, Gurgaon and Kolkata.

3. Shoppers' Stop is a mixture of the leading international and national brands in clothing for men, women, and kids; accessories, fragrances, cosmetics, footwear; home furnishing and decoration products, their employees taim to provide shoppers a truly international shopping destination in local areas. In April 2008, Shoppers' Stop changed its logo and adopted the mantra "\Start Something New\". Around the same year it was awarded as the Emerging Retailer of the Year by the World Retail Congress (WRC). Its Managing Director Mr. B.S. Nagesh who is incidentally the first employee of the company has been inducted into the Retail Hall of Fame at the WRC. Shoppers' Stop started off as a department store in the early nineties. Subsequently, it has diversified into Specialty business represented by Crossword Book Stores, Brio (Coffee Chain), Desi Cafe (Indian Fast Food), Mother Care (Franchisee of the UK brand for mothers and kids) and MAC (Make-up Artist Cosmetics). Shoppers' Stop the department store runs one of India's most effective loyalty programmes called First Citizen which has over one million members. Over 65 per cent of Shoppers' Stop revenues come from these First Citizens members. Actually these First Citizen members are their loyal customers mean they are the main customers who come again and again for shopping. Shoppers' Stop is recognized by the Indian Retail industry as pioneer in the use of technology. Organized retailing; supported by world-class systems and practices; and a talented group of people with a shared passion for making every shopper visit a memorable one, has helped Shoppers Stop to grow from a single store in 1991, to the largest chain of Department Stores in India today.

4. Vision of the Shoppers' Stop: "To be a Global Retailer in India and Maintain No.1 position in the Indian Market in the Department Store Category". This statement was described by the employees and he says as you all know that we are king in our sector so we want to maintain that position in the market and they are thinking of opening more stores because of increasing competition. But if we analyze current trend then we have to use wait and watch policy. He added that, "they are looking festive season as opportunity for their business". India – 2000 and Beyond... Expanding its operations to Bangalore, Hyderabad, Jaipur, Delhi, Chennai, Mumbai, Pune, Gurgaon and Kolkata, Shoppers' Stop is today recognized as India's premier shopping destination. Their employees told us that around 1,000 customers visit there on daily basis out of which many are for window shopping but they are planning for making those customers to buy something and currently they are dealing with over 250 brands of garments and accessories. Shoppers' Stop has clearly become a one-stop shop for all customers. Customer profile Shoppers' Stop customers fall between the age group of 16 years to 35 years, the majority of them being families and young couples with a monthly household income above ₹ 20,000 and an annual spend of ₹ 15,000. A large number of Non-resident Indians visit the shop for cultural clothes in the international environment they are used to which means people from abroad are also interested in shopping in Shoppers' stop. Their target customers are upper-middle class and upper class. Customer Rewards – The First Citizen Shoppers' Stop customer loyalty programme is called The First Citizen. The programme offers its members an opportunity to collect points and avail of special benefits. Currently, Shoppers' Stop has a database of over 2.5 lakh members who contribute to nearly 65 per cent of the total sales of Shoppers' Stop.

5. International Affiliations to Shoppers' Stop is the only retailer from India to become a member of the prestigious Intercontinental Group of Departmental Stores (IGDS). The IGDS consists of 29 experienced retailers from all over the world, which include established stores like Selfridges (England), Karstadt (Germany), Shanghai No. 1 (China), Matahari (Indonesia), Takashimaya (Japan), C K Tang (Singapore), Manor (Switzerland) and Lamcy Plaza (Dubai). This membership is restricted to one member organization per country/region. The IT Backbone Shoppers' Stop was the first few retailers to use scanners and barcodes and completely computerize its operations. Today, it is one of the few stores in India to have retail ERP (Enterprise Resource Planning) in place, which is the best retail planning system in the world. With the help of the ERP, they are able to open new stores faster and get information about merchandise and customers online, which reduces the time in taking quick decision.

Objectives of Shoppers' Stop: Its main objective is to make its customers delightful and then profit through sales. Afterall, every organization works to earn money which is possible through good sales and if the customers are not satisfied then it will be difficult for the retailers. So retailers have to put their efforts on retaining their customer because retaining old customers are more profitable than making new customers. And if we analyze this statement then we come to know that 65 per cent of the customers are first citizen customers. Today, people go for variety and Shoppers' Stop is doing that, they offer in toto 250 brands to their customers which act as their strength and help them retaining as well as making new customers. They believe in producing quality so they offer quality products basically international brands like Louis Phillip, Black Berry, Police, DKNY, Ferrari, etc.

Shoppers' Stop aims to position itself as a global retailer. The company intends to bring the world's best retail technology, retail practices and sales to India. Currently, they are adding four to five new stores every year. Type of Retail Outlet Shoppers' Stop is known as multi-brand retail out let because of their variety of products. They offer various products like Apparels, Accessories, Toys, Fragrances, Beauty Products, Travelling products, Home Appliances, etc. It will be easier to understand with Merchandise Hierarchy which Shoppers' Stop offers to his/her customers

Retailers offer various products like Apparels, Fragrance and Beauty, Home and Travel, Gift ideas. Under this they have different categories, brands and styles to offer customers. They have many other showrooms of Shoppers' Stop in Delhi.

Popular retailers have long chain of retail outlets. They also offer online purchasing which means that they are using new technology to increase their sales.

Controllable and Uncontrollable Factors: Controllable and Uncontrollable factors are those which are directly or indirectly affect the retail outlet. The difference between these two factors is that one can be controlled by the retailer and another cannot be controlled. The variables which are controllable can be changed according to the retailers but if we talk about uncontrollable factors then the retailer have to change him/her according to those factors. There are various controllable and uncontrollable factors. When we asked about these factors to the employees of Shoppers' Stop, he told us that Controllable Factors of Shoppers' Stop 1. Pricing 2. Store Location 3. Managing a business/workforce pricing. He told us that setting price of a product is in our hands. This is our decision that how much profit we want to make by selling our products. Sometimes we have to set our prices according to the competition.

Store Location: Selecting the location for the store is in the hands of retailers because before selecting the location they have to check many factors like walking, traffic, competitor, parking, infrastructure, etc. The retailers also have to decide whether they want to buy the site or take it on rent. So, after deciding all these things, they reach to the final decision relating to managing a business/workforce. Managing the workforce means a lot to the retailer, because they have to decide about what type of people they need, what type of training for the employees needed, and what will be the salary of the employees. All these things can be controlled by the retailers. Uncontrollable factors of Shoppers' Stop 1. Government Policies, 2. Seasons, 3. Inflation Rate, 4. Technology, 5. Infrastructure, 6. Supply Chain etc.

Government policies or legal restriction cannot be controlled and the big example of this is "sealing of illegal shops". The taxes and duties which retailers have to pay to the government. Seasons. Natural climates cannot be controlled. Retailers have to change their theme and products according to seasonal change. Sometimes, season plays a negative role like in rainy season and their sales goes down. So, these things cannot be controlled and they can only launch new marketing strategies to attract the customers.

Inflation Rate: Retail inflation, based on the Consumer Price Index, rose to 8.83 per cent in February 2012 against 7.65 per cent in January 2012. The increase in February has been attributed to higher prices of protein-based items and edible oil products. Only vegetable prices saw a decline of 4.73 per cent over the February 2011 level. According to data released by the Central Statistics office on 19-3-12 combined retail inflation, calculated on base 2010 = 100, for rural and urban areas stood at 8.36 per cent and 9.45 per cent in February 2012 against 7.28 per cent and 8.25 per cent, respectively, in January 2012. The prices of egg, meat and fish went up by 10.62 per cent. Milk and its products, too, turned costlier by 15.76 per cent, year-on-year. Cereals and products saw a moderate rise in prices at 2.40 per cent in February 2012, while pulses and products increased by 4.17 per cent. There was a 12.76 per cent rise in inflation in the oil and fat category. Condiment spices were costlier by 8.68 per cent. Higher CPI inflation suggests that retail prices have not fallen as much as wholesale prices. February CPI inflation is largely due to food related base effects. Inflation in the oil and fat category shot up by 12.76 per cent and condiment spices became costly by 8.68 per cent on an annual basis.

Now inflation rate is more that 12 per cent. So, it is creating more problems for the retailers because due to this people are getting more awareness of saving money and due to which sales is also affected. If we analyze the global market then we will see that every sector is going down except one or two. And retail sector is also not doing well these days. Against this we can't do anything, we can only wait.

Technology: Day by day the technology is upgrading and the problem is that the new competitor comes with new technology because of which the retailers also have to upgrade their technology which results more expenditure, and which is not good for any business.

Infrastructure includes the roads, surroundings, etc. All these things are governed by the allotted authorities like DDA, NDMC, HUDA. So, it can't be controlled.

Supply Chain: It means understanding the importance of distribution and logistics in ensuring that merchandise is available on the shop floors. It has led Shoppers' Stop to streamline its supply chain. The company has developed process manuals for each part of the logistics chain. These modules include vendor management, purchase order management, stock receiving systems, purchase verification and inventory build-up, fixing of price and store tags, dispatch of stocks to the retail floor and forwarding of bills for payment. If we talk about various brands, then the answer is that they have a direct tie-ups with different companies and companies deliver all the needed products to their doorstep. But there are some companies which do not provide them these services so for those they have their own carrier.

Situational Analysis: Situational analysis includes current organizational mission, current ownership and management alternatives, and current goods/services category.

The SWOT Analysis of Shoppers' Stop:

Strength • Variety • Range • Different Brands. **Weakness** • Very high rates: Retailers provide international brands due to which their prices are very high. • **Less Schemes:** They do not offer so many schemes, they offer schemes only on special occasions like Diwali, Independence Day, etc. • **Less Discounts:** Retailers offer less discount in their schemes, they basically offer 10 per cent to 20 per cent discount **Threats** • Government policies • Entrance of New Players **Opportunities** • Awareness About the Brands • Quality • Youngsters

Recommendations

1. The retailers should introduce more schemes, discounts, sales to increase the sales.
2. The retailers should introduce low rate brands which will attract the middle-class customers also or brands for masses.

MARKET CUSTOMER

Retailers do not intend to sell to only one person. So knowing the customer profile, the retailers have now to group all the customers sharing the same profile: It is their market customer.

Definition: A market is a group of customers (or prospects) sharing the characteristics which cope with the benefits offered by retailers product or service.

Example:

- There is a group of customers eager to travel: This is the tourist market.
- There is a group of customers who use car. This is the car market.

Then the retailers have to separate undifferentiated markets and market segments.

Undifferentiated Market

If retailers product brings benefits to everyone, the retailer can treat the market as a whole. For example, anybody whatever his age, sex or revenue drinks soda. Nevertheless, you have to take notice of the geographical area. For a retailer, the soda market is around his shop. For Coca-Cola, that is the entire world.

Market Segments

In most cases, inside a broad market, the marketeers have to differentiate segments. It means that the **market segmentation is one of the most basic concept in marketing.**

Definition: The market segmentation is the process of splitting customers within a market customer into different groups sharing some specific characteristics.

The important word is the adjective **"specific"**. Among the common characteristics of market customer, the retailer has to focus on some **"specific characteristics".**

Examples:

If your project is to manage a hotel, the tourist market is your customer market but it is not very useful. The tourist market includes cruisers, hotels, tour trip, trekking and so on. Within the tourist market, you have to study the hotel market and inside this broad segment the specific one which corresponds to the benefit that your hotel will offer (Is it a five-star or a two-star hotel? is it located on seashore or in the rocky mountains?)

With a segment the retailer can execute his/her advertising activities to yield his/her business targets. Without a segment, the retailer has to face the risk of wasting his/her money.

Once again, three major variables are used:

Geographic segmentations divide the market by country, region and city: It is often a good starting point to begin with a single geographical territory. Once you have completed the segmentation for it, you can test the applicability to other and larger areas.

Demographic segmentations divide the population on measurable variables such as age, sex, income, educational level and so on.

Psychological segmentation is often quite difficult and needs costly surveys.

Anyway, each segment must be:

Homogeneous: It's the first quality required for a segment. It means that a segment must be clearly different to others segments in the same broad market. For example, a segment having people income ranking from $ 20,000 to $ 2,00,000 is not homogeneous and worthless for a marketing strategy.

Consistent: If your segment counts only three prospects, and expects you to sell nuclear plant, it's not enough to develop sales and profits. A segment must count a large number of prospects.

The factors which can influence the size of the segment are the increase in population, the situation of employment and the changes in income, the supply of resources, the evolution of laws, the consumer tastes and preferences and notably the fads.

Profitable: A segment must generate profit. It means that the prospects in the segment have a sufficient income with regard of the product price. If you sell luxurious car, it's not very smart to isolate a segment which only contains deprived peoples.

Executable: It means that you (i.e., the retailers) can reach the segment through advertising, sales force, distribution. It is worthless to isolate a segment if you are unable to join the people who are inside it. For example, there is certainly a consistent segment for fun board in China but if you do not speak Chinese, you will never make a dollar with it.

From a practical point of view, **your first task is to evaluate the size of the segment.** Easy to say but it's a real hurdle, because you have to calculate the entire sales volumes of all the suppliers in the segment. It means that you should add all the turnovers of the competitors existing in this segment. **How could you manage that in the specific case of our fun boards?**

Down-earth Advice

With chambers of commerce, producer associations, and so on, you can know how many cars, how many tons of cotton, rice, crude oil and so on, have been produced and imported in the US, and consequently consumed. By the same way, you can know the global amount in $ of the sport sales in the USA by year 2012.

Let's suppose that retailer's own segment is in Arizona. First the retailer must do the following calculations:

Total sales in the USA, Arizona population/ US population and then calculating sales in Arizona.

If the retailer is interested to evaluate the average price of a fun board he has to (just visit a lot of shops and quote the prices) and divide the sales volume by the average price:

The key elements stimulating throughout the shopping experience are depicted in the following diagram.

Brand Shoppability during Shopping Experience

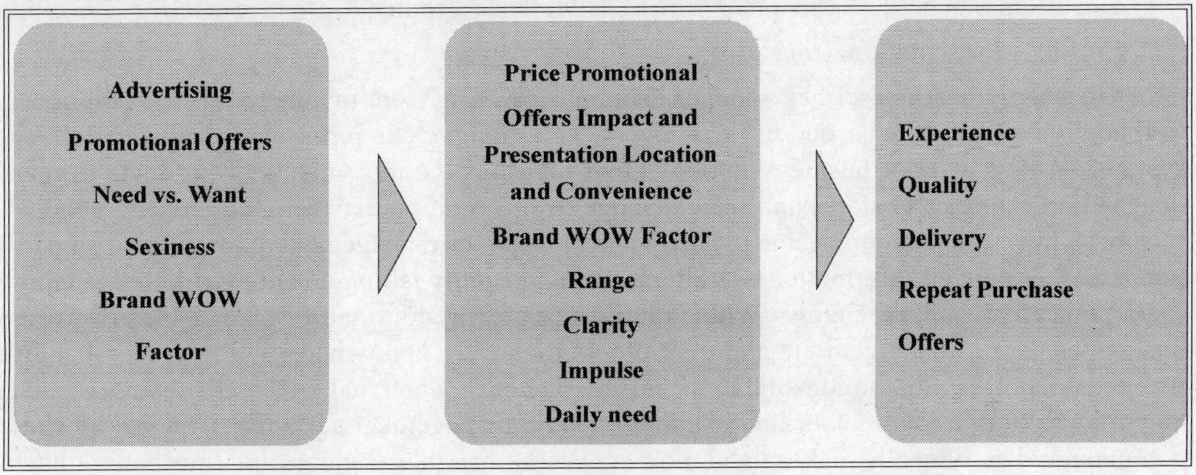

FIG. 39: KEY STIMULI THROUGHOUT THE SHOPPING EXPERIENCE

Real Life Example

Once, an European consulting group decided to study the world milk market. Most of the top executives were convinced that the market was made up with crude milk in bottle and concentrated milk in can. At this time, the Europeans were not familiar with powder milk.

The import and export statistics of about 120 countries were collected. It was discovered that the world market was made-up of powder milk by 80 per cent

The executives who had trust their intuition were quite astonished by these results. Intuition appears often to be wrong in assessing retail marketing.

When you get a homogeneous, consistent, profitable and executable segment, it means that you have a marketable product.

Cluster Analysis

To target one's customers, retailer can split the segment into little groups according to a multi-criteria approach:

Example: Customer market can be split in **clusters,** according to new criteria: (i) People who focus on price, (ii) People who had subscribed life insurance, and (iii) People who only buy from well known brand.

As data do not give answers about such characteristics, **you can create a sample**. It's a little group of persons that represent all the characteristics of a larger population. It may be created with friends, relations, chambers of commerce and so on. You must be sure that it is really representative of your whole segment.

In short, the advanced marketing segmentation looks like the precision guided munitions. It needs complex computer software, pool opinions, sample analysis and high fees charged by consulting groups. It's good for big corporates that can afford it.

Market segmentation is a compulsory step to define a marketable product. Keep also in mind that only marketable products make money. This point must be underlined.

1. Customer benefit, 2. Customer profile, 3. Market customer, 4. Do it yourself, 5. Coaching Profile – Presentation Transcript.

The supply chain describes a longer channel stretching from raw materials to components to final products that are carried to final buyers. The supply chain represents a value to delivery system. SCM is a set of business activities that manages the movements of products to retail distribution centres and stores and the exchange of information between retailers and vendors. It is the delivery of economic value to customers through the management of the flow of physical goods and associated information. Retailers are increasingly taking a leading role in managing their respective supply chains. When retailers were predominantly small, family-owned businesses, larger manufacturers and distributors dictated when, where, and how merchandise was delivered. But with the consolidation and emergence of larger, national retail chains, retailers now play an active role in coordinating supply chain management activities. The size of these national retailers typically makes them more powerful than their vendors and thus better able to control their supply chains. In addition, retailers are more knowledgeable about their customers. They are in the unique position to collect purchase information customer-by-customer, transaction by-transaction. This information is being shared with suppliers to plan production, promotion, deliveries, assortments, and inventory levels.

Efficient supply chain management provides two benefits to customers:

Reduced stock-outs, and

High involvement purchases — Honda Motorbike, high priced goods, products visible to others, and the higher the risk the higher the involvement.

Types of Risk

- Personal risk
- Social risk
- Economic risk

Quantitative research was used to provide robust data, in the form of exit interviews with shoppers intending to buy. Qualitative research was used to provide deep insight; this included observation of shoppers in stores, semiotic analysis of store environment and PoS, mini-discussions with selected shoppers and face to face depth interviews with store managers.

Retail stores offer significant room for impact and many shoppers entering stores with an intention to buy can still be influenced, even during final stages of the purchase process. Consistent patterns of the in-store journey were observed, which led to recommendations about how to design the store around key customer moments, as this would maximize impact. Importantly, we found that the priority of critical moments differed by market and the risk of failing to deliver on these critical moments caused the customer journey to break down. Our analysis identified a number of prominent shopper typologies illustrating how different shoppers engage with stores. It was possible to redesign a retail store to accommodate all shopper types, encouraging both browser engagement and buyer sales transactions.

By working in partnership with a number of retail outlets the client was able to tailor the retail store environments of a national chain in line with customer needs. This collaboration was mutually beneficial to all parties as boosted sales volumes were observed shortly after.

Retail shopping behaviour is one of the major tenets of the retail marketing literature. The purpose of this research is to presents the empirical findings of two quantitative studies of Estonian and Canadian university students' interpretation and perceptions of retail shopping behaviour.

There is a level of commonality in retail shopping perceptions, as well as non-trivial differences in how shopping practice in terms of the construct structure, and individual service drivers, should be theorized. The retail market sample indicates a greater focus on retail service quality perception at the sub-dimension level and also a greater focus on retail service quality at an overall or integrated level.

Retail Sector at Risk Through Lack of Engagement

WAYNE, Pa. (Feb. 21, 2012) – Employee engagement in the U.S. retail sector has sunk to its lowest levels since 2009, according to a new study which claims that engagement is directly linked to customer satisfaction, staff retention and financial performance.

The **Kenexa High Performance Institute** – a division of **Kenexa** (NYSE: KNXA), a global provider of business solutions for human resources – has conducted global, evidence-based research into employee engagement for more than 25 years. Its latest report – "The World of Retail: How Employee Engagement Can Help the Registers Ring" – examines employee engagement trends in the retail sector since 2007 in six nations: the US, Brazil, China, Germany, India and the United Kingdom. The results show a marked drop in employee engagement in all six nations in 2011. Retail engagement scores in the US trail only the UK and Germany. "The economic downturn has hit retailers everywhere hard, as costs have been cut, plans have been put on hold and brands have gone out of business", said Rena Rasch, research manager of the Kenexa High Performance Institute. "The sector has also seen an increase in employee theft and shoplifting, which has been attributed to low pay, poor benefits and a perception among employees that their companies don't care about them". The new study reveals that employee engagement has a direct correlation with customer satisfaction and organizational performance. "The simple truth is that engaged employees make a difference, particularly those in customer-facing positions", Rasch said. "When engagement is low, customer satisfaction and organizational performance tend to be low. But when engagement levels rise, these factors also improve because employees are more motivated to contribute to the organization's success and more willing to put in extra effort to accomplish tasks that are central to the goals of the organization. In other words, by improving employee engagement, retailers can enhance customer satisfaction and increase sales volume". According to the study, a low level of employee engagement also results in higher staff turnover. More than 50 per cent of unengaged retail employees plan to leave their employer in the coming year, compared to only about 10 percent of highly engaged workers.

"Employees who are not engaged are much more likely to consider leaving their organization", Rasch said. "As the global economy slowly emerges from the recession, opportunities for employees will open up elsewhere and retailers could find themselves competing for talent. This could prove costly for those with a less engaged workforce".

The study also reveals that, out of six industry sectors surveyed globally, retail has the lowest level of employee engagement. The other sectors include high tech manufacturing, health care, banking and financial services and the public sector. "The retail sector has faced a perennial struggle with employee engagement, partly because it employs many part-time, low skilled and seasonal workers", Rasch said. "However, retailers are at risk if leaders and HR practitioners don't act to bolster employee engagement in their organizations".

The Kenexa High Performance Institute's report includes four recommendations to help retailers improve employee engagement:

- *Develop effective leaders*: Leaders need to inspire confidence in their employees through their actions and their demeanor. They must be trustworthy, honest and caring.
- *Help employees to balance their work and life priorities:* Retailers should provide practical support, such as flexible work schedules, as well as emotional support and understanding.
- *Ensure compensation levels are fair:* More than the amount of compensation, what matters most is each employee's perception of pay fairness. Explain how their pay was determined and show the link between their pay and their performance.
- *Foster a climate of innovation:* Employees want exciting work. They like trying new things, sharing their ideas and being listened to. The chance to be innovative challenges and motivates them to perform at their best.

"Offering employees fair compensation, exciting work and flexibility are proven approaches for improving employee engagement", Rasch said "However the most effective way to enhance employee engagement is to improve your leadership and management. Our research shows that employees who believe that their leaders and managers are effective have an engagement level that is three-to-five times higher than those who feel their leaders and managers are ineffective. Anyone in a position of authority should look in the mirror, evaluate their own practices and develop their leadership skills and competencies".

A shop is a building or part of a building where goods are shown and sold retail. A person who is shopping is called shopper. A shopper is the person or group of persons, who decide what to buy, when to buy and what not to buy. In competitive environment one cannot thrust a product on shopper. The retailer shop has to supply what is demanded or what can be demanded. The retail seller has to study shopper behaviour to find out what can be sold and what goods or services are likely to be rejected. Through the study he is motivated to buy or not to buy particular product. The retail seller has to understand how sales can be pushed of existing products, what changes are required in existing products, what changes are required to get the targeted sales figure.

Shopper behaviour is seen to involve a mental decision process as well as physical activity. The actual act of purchase is just one stage in a series of mental and physical activities that occur during a period of time. Suppose a photographer who regularly purchases one brand of film suddenly switches to a competing brand even though there has been no change in either the films or their prices. What has caused this shift in loyalty? Just noting that the individual's purchase behaviour has changed does little to help our understanding of the situation. Perhaps the competing film received a strong recommendation by a friend, or possibly the photographer switched because he believed the competing brand best captures the colours of some subject matter of interest. On the other hand, his decision may have been caused either by general dissatisfaction with results from his regular film or from recent exposure to an advertisement for the competing brand.

Shoppers avoid those supermarkets where they are surrounded by many unfamiliar products and indecent neighbour. They shop at department stores where discounts and gifts are offered by the retailer when they make heavy purchases. They expect cordial welcome and good treatment from the retailers. Price and quality are their primary motivation in choosing a store.

Teenagers often spend more hours in shopping, especially on weekends. They spend more money in stores they patronize. Youth often have a great deal of authority in store-selection decisions, which means that stores must reach them with an effective appeal. Although the popular belief is that young people buy products impulsively and are less rational than the market as a whole, surveys indicate that most respondent aged 14 to 25 compare prices and brands before buying. Research on adolescent shopping behaviour has produced the following tentative conclusions:

The retail shopper behaviour is dependent on a number of factors which may be economic or non-economic factors and are dependent upon economic factors such as income, price, psychology, sociology, anthropology, culture, and climate, etc. Therefore, the study is dependent upon all these factors and retail shopper behaviour analysts study it through shopper-survey and they believe that behaviour can be influenced which has been proved by actual sales promotion of a large number of products. However, there is dispute whether shopper should be influenced or not and what methods should be applied to influence him. In certain cases, objectionable or wrong statements are made to influence the shopper. For instance, producers of certain face creams advertise that with the usage of their creams complexion will become fair but actually it does not happen. There are ads for removing baldness by certain oils or creams. In many countries several Acts are passed and actions are taken against erring shops in order to safeguard the interest of shoppers. In India, there is Consumer Protection Act (1986) to safeguard shoppers' interest.

Retail shopper behaviour can well be understood by throwing light on:

- The personality of the shopper
- Motivation and involvement
- Learning and memory and
- Self-concept
- Information processing
- Attitudes

Adolescents tend to rely on personal sources for information on products of high socio-economic and performance risk, and on most media for information on products perceived as low for such risk. At the product-evaluation stage of the decision process, price and brand name are perceived as the most important evaluative criteria, with a relatively low social influence coming from parents and peers. As teenagers mature, they use more sources of consumer information prior to decision making, rely more on friends and less on parents for information and advice in buying and prefer to purchase products without parental supervision.

Table 30 : Shopper Behaviour Roles

Role	Description
Initiator	The individual who determines that some need or want is not being met and authorizes a purchase to rectify the situation.
Influencer	A person who by some intentional or unintentional word or action influences the purchase decision, the actual purchase, and/or the use of the product or service.
Buyer	The individual who actually makes the purchase transaction.
User	The person most directly involved in the consumption or use of the purchase

Source: Gerald Zaltman and Philip C.Burger, Marketing: *Fundamentals and Dynamics,* 1975.

Factors affecting individuals in their daily lives also influence their purchase activities.

The following are the main factors that influence the shopper behaviour:

I. Economic Factors

Economic environment of retail business comprises the totality of external factors over which a retail shop has no control. Economics is the study of people's production, exchange, and consumption of goods and services. Economic factors include the monetary and fiscal policy, industrial licensing, price policy, foreign trade policy, development of banking and financial institutions, level of economic development, strategy of economic planning, rate of capital formation, research and development, mode of production, size of market, factor environment, infrastructural facilities, division of labour etc., Shopper behaviour forms part of economics. According to economic theory with rise in income, the quantity demanded should go up. But for inferior products the demand declines with increasing income. The shopping behaviour of elite customers with high income is to buy prestigious goods even at high price and they care for the quality of the product.

Price: The price theory is based on shopping behaviour that is as more quantity will be offered the price will come down, the utility of additional unit will be less than the previous one and therefore, rate of increase in demand will fall with the satisfaction of demand. The economic theory further states that with the fall in price, demand should rise and with rise in prices demand should fall. However, the retail shop owners feel that with change in shopping behaviour this is not always true. If the product is for show, prestige, many people will buy high priced goods. If a product is cheap, it is considered to be of poor quality and may not be in demand. Even in India, the demand for motorbike which is double the price of scooter, and is rising faster than that of scooter because of change in shopping behaviour. For many products, shoppers show high concern for prices. In fact, many retailers have noticed that the more a watch costs, the better it seems to sell. The 'expensive' market comprises who want to tell the world something about themselves – and their financial situation.

Pricing decision in a foreign market may also be affected by the nature of the culture. Consumer price perceptions may vary from country-to-country, affecting the appropriate price charged. For instance, in the competitive West European market, American products may be perceived as roughly equivalent to domestic products there, and so must be similarly priced. However, in developing countries, American products may be perceived as superior and should be priced at a sufficiently high level, because consumers may be suspicious about the quality of merchandise when prices appear to be unbelievably cheap.

In markets where price controls exist on important products, government approval is required to increase prices, often through a lengthy process. When price increase requests are announced in advance, consumers may rush to stock up in order to beat the price rise, thereby distorting sales patterns.

Place: The place variable involves consideration of where and how to offer products and services for sale. It also is concerned with the mechanisms for transferring goods and their ownership to shoppers. Decisions influenced by shopper behaviour include:

What type of retail outlet should sell the firm's offering?

Where should they be located, and how many should there be?

What arrangements are needed to distribute products to retailers?

To what extent is it necessary for the company to own or maintain tight control over activities of firms to the channel of distribution?

What image and clientele should the retail seek to cultivate?

Some retail companies offer a great many products to shoppers. What is to be considered here is that a given product must be offered through existing outlets. For instance, Sears is a massive retailer with a vast number of customers. Sears has formed the Sears Financial Network. This network is comprised of All State Insurance, the Dean Witter investment group (stocks, bonds, and so on) and Coldwell Banker, which deals in real estate. The promotion of a given product depends on the goals and methods of communicating the offerings to target shoppers. The Shopper-related decisions include:

What methods of promotion are best for each specific situation?

What are the most effective means for gaining consumers' attention?

What methods best convey the intended message?

How often should a given advertisement be repeated?

It is interesting to know that the management of Sun Cloud decided on a rather novel advertisement for their sunglasses. The advertisement was a dog wearing sunglass with the title "HOT DOGS, COOL CLOUDS".

Income: The national income, the per capita income, and the disposable income also influence the shopper behaviour in the retail market. The per capita spending index differs markedly for a variety of consumption categories among high, middle and low income peoples.

Distribution of Income: If there is disparity in income distribution, the rich will become richer and the poor will become poorer. The shopper behaviour between the poor (who are majority in number) and the rich (who are minority in number) will widely differ. The rich will demand costlier products and the poor will demand cheaper products.

Competition with Substitutes

Utility: Utility refers to the satisfaction derived from the product purchased by the customer/consumer/buyer. It is a mental phenomenon. The shopper gives more consideration to the utility of the product. Quality product gives the expected satisfaction to the shopper. Quality is defined as the totality of features and characteristics of a product or service that bear on its ability to satisfy stated or implied needs. Quality is measured by the cost of quality which is the expense of non-conformance- the cost of doing things wrong. Quality performance standard is zero defeats. Present day shopper is better informed and enlightened. He is no longer prepared to accept things on their face value or to take things for granted, thanks to the spread of general education and awareness, mass media, TV, Radio and other marketing and publicity techniques. The shopper wants genuine return for the money he/she is prepared to part with. The quality expectation is referred as its 'fitness for use', 'fitness for purpose', 'shopper satisfaction' or conformity to requirements of the shopper. Defined needs of the shopper include the following:

1. Size, weight, colour, texture and taste
2. Functional reliability
3. Affordability
4. Safety in use
5. Durability
6. Secured packaging, labelling
7. Delivery time
8. Payment facilities
9. Prompt after–sales services
10. Response times to failures, etc.

Retailer management should improve upon the shoppers' response management by improving the complaints handling process. The shoppers must be delighted by the product purchased by them. Shopper delight means doing something that feels special to the shopper – exceeding his/her expectations.

Consumer Preferences

Demography: It refers to the vital and measurable statistics of a population. It relates to total population of a country, state, region, town or villages. In shopping behaviour, literacy and level of education plays an important role.

Social Class: Social classes in India are based on two different criteria and there are two types of social classes. First based on the level of income and the other on castes, religion, etc., Social class refers to upper-class, middle-class – rural, urban, tribes, professionals, etc. In India on the basis of income there are four classes. First, below the poverty line who are not able to consume minimum requirement and therefore, they are not able to buy most of the things. They depend on public distribution system. They wait for long hours of time by standing in the queue in front of the ration shop to get their quota products at subsidized rate. Their shopping behaviour needs patience and even ready to wait for many days to get their basic goods. Second is low income group who are above the poverty line but are able to meet their minimum products like TV, coolers, refrigerators and ordinary furniture. They wait for special offer period to buy such goods. The last one is high income group. In this group there is further division of very high income group who account for nearly 10 per cent of country's population and are able to consume anything they want. They never bother about price but quality of the product. The second social class is based on community, castes, religion, etc. These groupings are not only in places of their origin but also in places where they move. A South Indian or Bengali in metropolitan cities of Kolkata, New Delhi, Chennai or Mumbai like to consume some food items for which they are accustomed. Even when they go abroad and become NRI they want food of their liking. As a result there are exports of Gujarati, Punjabi, and South Indian food products to places of their concentration abroad. The food habits die very rarely and therefore, these classes will have to be catered wherever they settle or cluster. Certain shopping behaviours are also based on community basis and they like certain products or services. The food and dress habits of Sikhs, Muslims, Jains, Hindus are well settled and for this purpose they are social class. Their shopping behaviour differ especially on the occasion of marriages, festivals, and religious functions. Shopping behaviour also differs based on rural-urban base. People of rural area even in the same region and of same religion have different demands than their urban brothers. In India there are socially and economically backward people. The behaviour of these people differ in needs, expectations, inspirations and preferences which should be properly studied by retail management personnel in order to offer those goods and services which would satisfy their needs.

There are non-users, light users, medium users, heavy users and very heavy users of certain products like cigarettes, panmasala, gutkas, and alcohols, cosmetics to mention a few. Of course government policy also alters the shopping behaviour of people. For instance, smoking in a public place is banned in Tamil Nadu and Kerala. The government is trying to shape the behaviour of the people keeping in view their health condition and their special needs.

Shopper behaviour varies from place-to-place, from one religion to another religion, and from one society to another society. This may be attributable to socialization processes that operate differently among the above listed factors. For example, Black shoppers spend more per shopping centre trip than their Hispanic or white counterparts. The special appeal to shoppers in TV, Radio, magazines, and newspapers change their shopping behaviour.

Culture: The concept of culture has been characterized as 'that complex whole that includes knowledge, belief, art, morals, law, custom, and any other capabilities and habits acquired by man as a member of society. The beliefs and values, customs and tradition, tastes and preferences, education are all the basic factors that shape shopper behaviour. Subcultures distinguished on the basis of age and ethnic dimensions receive particular attention in the study of shoppers' behaviour. To understand the behaviour of the shopper, the retail management must know about anthropology. Anthropology is the study of people in relation to their culture. The culture of different regions is different. Bengali culture is quite different than that of Punjabi or South Indian culture. There are differences not only in speech but also in dress, fashions, thinking, expectations and behaviour based on the region. The liking of music is also much different than in South or North. The festival of Kerala, Tamil Nadu and other states are not same, nor their food preferences are similar. The taste of people also differ widely from region-to-region. Punjabis like gaudy, bright colour clothes, milk and lassi, maize bread and sarso ka sag and paratha. South prefers tea and coffee, idli, dosa. Actually in India there are so many cultures, habits, preferences that without in-depth study of them one cannot optimize sales. Therefore, in-depth study of regional differences is essential for research of shopping behaviour, within the state also a many times it is required to describe upon differences in their behaviours.

The values and beliefs associated with colour varies significantly between different cultures. Blue considered feminine and warm in Holland, is seen as masculine and cold in Sweden. Green is favourite colour in the Muslim world but in Malaysia it is associated with illness. White indicates death and mourning in China and Korea but in some countries it expresses happiness and is the colour of the wedding dress of the bride. Red is a popular colour in the communist countries but many African countries have a national distaste for red colour. Reliance company in India has red colour in its retail business.

Cultures are gradually and continuously changing. Several information services are available to track the changing cultural pattern of values, attitudes, and lifestyles. Hence, shopper behaviour can be changed by following an appropriate marketing strategy in conformity with changing culture. For example, .major corporations like Coca-Cola, Hoover, IBM, Pfizer and Gillette, receive over half of their earnings from foreign operations either by creating new cultural values or by adopting to changing cultural values. Since there is no common culture of management, the retail management must take into account cultural differences among international markets and of their influence on consumer behaviour. When a company is marketing products internationally, a thorough understanding of cultural practices is useful in determining whether a single strategy can be effective in different national environments, or whether several strategies must be adopted, with each geared to the distinctive cultural setting.

A study of Canadian women revealed two broad groups – those who focus on home life and those who focus on work involvement – but five types of beaviour:

1. **Contented Striving:** In this category women aged above 40 who are home-makers come. They are contented with that role. They believe it is unwise to buy on credit (other than house and car). They read advertisements and use coupons.
2. **Independent Self-confident:** This is the youngest segment. With an average age of 32, she thinks she is a leader, is ambitious, and has initiative. She doesn't spend a lot of time talking with friends about brands or products. She is not one to save and redeem coupons, shop by catalogue, or take advantage of special offers on packages. She is not overly price-conscious or likely to buy brands on sale.
3. **Insure:** This is the third-largest segment, with an average age of 35. She is not satisfied with herself or her role in life and tends to feel lonely and inadequate. She believes generics are as good as nationally advertised brands, and is not brand-loyal. She values price over convenience and quality.
4. **Traditional:** This segment, predominant in Quebec and rural areas, has an average age of 42. She believes the best values are from the past; she is strongly committed to the belief

that a man should head the family and women in the home. She's comparison shopper but seeks quality and convenience over price. She is loyal to stores and brands, and reluctant to buy new brands unless recommended by someone. She prefers paying cash and shops on the basis of a budget.

5. **Career-oriented:** This segment, with an average age of 39, is similar to independents but more committed to work and opinionated about role. She prefers doing things other than shopping. She views brands as homogeneous, pays cash, is not price-conscious, and will pay more for convenience.

Shopper behaviour can be attributed more to cultural differences than to economic differences.

Religion: In a country of the size of India with different religions, shopping behaviour differs according to his faith and religion. If Hindus do not eat cow's meat, muslims do not eat pig meat. Mostly the male Sikhs wear turban but it is not compulsory in any other religion. In Jainism non-vegetarian food is strictly prohibited but Christians and Muslims have no inhibition. In Hindus there are both veg. and non-veg. population. Jains, specially, elderly people do not eat many vegetables specially those produced underground. The dress for worship and articles used for worship have been prescribed in Jainism and Hinduism, but Christians and Sikhs have not prescribed dresses for worship, but in most of the religious head should be covered while worshiping by turban, dhoti, cap or handkerchief, dupatta. Worship of festival occasions also have difference at the time of festival affecting consumption and creating demand of certain products in festival times. For example, during certain festivals demand of fruits and vegetables goes up because during this period many devotees do not take foodgrains. Similarly at the time of most festivals demand of sweets go up. All these factors have impact on shopping behaviour and so on the demand of various products.

Attitude of Society

Social Values: Sociology is the study of the collective behaviour of people in groups. An individual's shopping behaviour is influenced by the collective behaviour of people in group. Social psychology is the study of how individuals influence and are influenced by groups. Shopper behaviour forms part of social psychology. In retail market based on individual choice, shoppers strongly influence what will be produced, for whom it will be produced, and what resources will be used to produce it. Consequently, the collective behaviour of shoppers has a significant influence on the quality and level of our standard of living. The societal forces strongly influence individual and group shopping behaviour.

Lifestyle: Lifestyle can be viewed as a unique pattern of living which influences and is reflected by one's consumption behaviour. Lifestyles reflect a person's activities, interests and opinion. It can be defined as patterns in which people live and spend time and money. It can also be defined as a mode of living that is identified by how people spend their time (activities), what they consider important in their environment (interest) and what they think of themselves and the world around them (opinions). It is one of the most popular concepts in retail management for understanding shopper behaviour. Retailers try to relate the product to lifestyle, often through advertising, to the everyday experiences of the target market. Lifestyles change more rapidly and hence shoppers' behaviour. Retail management takes into account the track trends and changes in lifestyles and makes changes in advertisements accordingly. Some marketeers have committed fatal bloopers in their zeal simply to export intact their product's brand name or advertising themes to a foreign market or to attempt direct translation of such words. Coca-Cola's first attempt to translate its trademark into Chinese characters resulted in something that sounded like 'Coca-Cola' but meant 'bite the wax tadpole'. It was later changed to 'happiness in the mouth'. "Body by Fisher' became 'Corpse by Fisher' in Flemish. Colgate-Palmolive's 'Cue' toothpaste is a pornographic word in French. Standard Oil's Enco brand meant 'stalled car' in Japanese – a good reason for changing to Exxon, which is meaningless in any language.

Table 31 : Lifestyle Dimensions

Activities	Interests	Opinions	Demographics
Work	Family	Themselves	Age
Hobbies	Home	Social issues	Education
Social events	Job	Politics	Income
Vocation	Community	Business	Occupation
Entertainment	Recreation	Economics	Family size
Club membership	Fashion	Education	Dwelling
Community	Food	Products	Geography
Shopping	Media	Future	City size
Sports	Achievements	Culture	Stage in life cycle

Source: Joseph T. Plummer, "The Concept and Application of Lifestyle Segmentation", *Journal of Marketing,* 38:34, January 1974 published by the American Marketing Association.

The shopper behaviour may be approached from the following angles:

(i) Brand-user segmentation

(ii) Product-user segmentation

(iii) Loyalty segmentation

(iv) Situation segmentation

Personality: By personality, we mean distinguishing psychological characteristics that lead to relatively consistent and enduring responses to environment. Personality is usually described in terms of such traits as self-confidence, dominance, autonomy, deference, sociability, defensiveness, and adaptability. Personality can be a useful variable in analyzing shopper behaviour, provided that personality types can be classified accurately and that strong correlations exist between certain personality types and product or brand choices. For example, a computer company might discover that many prospects show high self-confidence, dominance, and autonomy. This suggests designing computer advertisements to appeal to these traits.

1. Size of family
2. Education

3. Health standards
4. Group decision

Anthropology: Climate, region, history all affect shopping behaviour. In hot countries like India, certain products which keep us cool like squashes, and sarbatas are demanded but they have no demand in cold regions. The dress and culture **are also influenced by climate along with other factors.**

Geographical and Ecological Factors: In a big country like India, China, the USA ,etc., the location is very important factors in determining the shopper behaviour of people, their needs, and their consumption pattern. Weather, topographical factors, locational aspects influence the shopper behaviour. For example, in hilly areas with difficult terrain, jeeps may be in greater demand than cars. The difference in behaviour is not only due to climate but also due to wide differences in languages. There are 18 languages which are spoken in one or more states. All these language differences have impact on producers, sellers and advertisers. Shopper behaviour is very much influenced by the words and the style of the language.

Physiological Factor: It relates to the service of the properties and functioning of human beings in normal conditions. Shopping behaviour differs based on phases like babies, child, adults and elderly people, men and women. Shopping behaviour differs widely depending upon the nature of their occupation, physical development, etc.

Technology: In the case of purchase of equipments, tools, machinery, utensils, and even semi-durable and perishable goods, the shopping behaviour is much influenced by technological innovations and features. Innovations and introduction of new product also depends upon technological developments. The sale of television, for example, i.e., is limited by the extent of the coverage of the broadcasting. Similarly, the demand for refrigerators, air-conditioners and other electrical appliances is affected by the extent of electrification and reliability of power supply.

Political Factors: The ideology of the state has considerable influence over the shopper behaviour. In a capitalistic system, the government interferes too little, whereas in a socialistic economy all activities are directed by the state. Under communism, the political policy may have various restrictions on the growth of business houses.

Government Services and Decision: The government must make a variety of decisions, including where to locate highways, what areas to consider for future commercial growth, and the type of public services to offer. The effectiveness of these decisions will be influenced by the extent to which they are based on an adequate understanding of shoppers. This requires knowledge of people's attitudes, beliefs, perceptions, and habits as well as how they tend to behave under a variety of circumstances. The economic policy of the government, needless to say, has a very great impact on the shopper behaviour. Shopper behaviour is affected by government decisions, laws, distribution policies, production policies, etc. Shoppers have freedom to buy the product of their choice under LPG policy.

Psychology: Psychology is the study of the behaviour and mental processes of individuals. It decides the personality, taste, attitudes of individuals or groups, lifestyles, preferences especially on special occasions. The demonstration effect also influence the shopping behaviour of consumers.

Shopping behaviour depends on the personality, taste, attitudes of individuals and groups, lifestyle, preferences especially on occasions like marriage. There are different types of shopping behaviour based on their age, sex, income level, education, their rural or urban background, etc. For instance, a person living in Mumbai or New Delhi behaves differently than person living in remote rural area of Chhattisgarh, Jharkhand, Bihar, or Odisha. Their thinking about product and services are different and their needs and perceptions are different than urban elite. The study of their psychology helps the retail management to segment the market and produce goods according to their requirement rather than thrusting same product on all. For instance, psychology of rural population of older generation is to wear only dhoti, they will not buy trousers whatever efforts are made. Similarly, large per centage of them do not wear shoes or chappals.

In India, the study on shopper behaviour is seldom conducted. Only a few big companies and MNCs especially after 1990s have started to pay attention on the shopping behaviour of the consumers/customers. For example, Hindustan Motors continued to produce the same car for decades till Maruti appeared on the arena. The emerging competition in the retail market both at the national and international level resulted in the study of shopper behaviour of consumers. The establishment of over 1,000 management institutions is also helping greater use of the tool of shopper behaviour for retail business.

Physical Factors: It is the responsibility of the retail management to calculate the social cost and social benefits of the retail business. The retail has to take into account the influence of physical factors on the retail business such as water pollution, availability of land, etc.

Retail Shopper Behaviour

The aggressive, geographic market expansion of successful retail organizations, the development of a global consumer market and the spatial diffusion of retail innovations led us to investigate the extent to which models helping managers to make strategic decisions can be generalized across time and place. To the extent that such generalization can occur, it would reduce the redundancy of research and associated costs for making decisions in major retail organizations. This article makes use of relatively recent developments in random utility theory to assess the stability over time and space of the preferences underlying retail-shopping choice. Data collected three times over four years in Canada are used to compare models of shopping centre choice based on perceived centre attributes. We hypothesize that random component variance differences are the likely source of observed differences in retailing preferences. Two waves of panel data for supermarket choice are used to assess our ability to generalize to another choice process. Data for shopping center choice collected in Canada, USA and Norway are used to assess spatial stability. The test results support the hypothesis for the spatial consistency of preferences. The test of stability over time shows no difference at all in retailing preferences, both the random component variances and the coefficients were unchanged over the four-year period studied.

Motivations to engage in retail shopping include both utilitarian and hedonic dimensions. Business to consumer e-commerce conducted via the mechanism of web-shopping provides an expanded opportunity for companies to create a cognitively and esthetically rich shopping environment in ways not readily imitable in the non-electronic shopping world. In this article an attitudinal model is developed and empirically tested integrating constructs from technology acceptance research and constructs derived from models of web behaviour. Results of two studies from two distinct categories of the interactive shopping environment support the differential importance of immersive, hedonic aspects of the new media as well as the more traditional utilitarian motivations. In addition, navigation, convenience, and the substitutability of the electronic environment to personally examining products were found to be important predictors of online shopping attitudes. Results are discussed in terms of insights for the creation of the online shopping *webmosphere* through more effective design of interactive retail shopping environments.

The ten tactical measures that can improve shopper efficiency:

1. Be open on days and times when your shopper want to shop..
2. Be in stock everyday, especially on important, high-volume items.
3. Provide plenty of self-help information for customers.
4. Make sure prices on all items and services are clear and current.
5. Keep checkout times to less than two minutes.
6. Handle exceptions away from the normal checkout areas (or use single snaking-type lines to minimize the inequities in shopper waiting).
7. Review and simply phone-handling processes, procedures, and systems (checkout your own voice-mail system once in a while).
8. Develop consistency in customer policies and handling processes across channels.
9. Ensure that employees are well-trained on products and processes.
10. Review your equipment and computer systems. Make sure they are current, operative, easy to use, and informative.

Much fascination and speculation surrounds the impact of the World Wide Web on consumer shopping behaviour. At the same time, there is little empirical evidence underlying all this speculation. This article provides one such data set. It reports on factors that consumers found salient as they browsed through selected electronic malls on the World Wide Web. Consumers' reactions via an open-ended survey using a sample of 220 shoppers were gathered. It related the reactions to the factors of product perceptions, shopping experience, customer service, and perceived consumer risk, which were identified from the existing literature on retail patronage behaviour. This study translated these factors to the World Wide Web context and explored their relative salience with respect to product perceptions. Consumers were impressed by the breadth of stores on the World Wide Web but disappointed with the depth of a merchant's offerings. The shopping experience was reported to be generally enjoyable, but at the same time frustrating. Consumers also reported that they could perceive the potential for time savings and reduced effort compared with traditional forms of shopping, but that, at present, goal-directed shopping was difficult. Nearly everyone in the sample had something negative to say about customer service on the World Wide Web, judging that the sites were not designed to be responsive to their needs and that the presentation of goods and services seemed intangible. Risk was cited as a barrier to shopping on the World Wide Web, but was not as salient to our sample as product perceptions, shopping experience, and customer service. Overall, the results suggest that World Wide Web merchants need to think more about how they perform on the factors known to affect consumer behaviour; namely, product perceptions, shopping experience, and customer service.

A successful information search leaves a buyer with possible alternatives, the *evoked set*.

Hungry, want to go out and eat, evoked set is

- Chinese food
- Indian food
- Burger king
- Klondike kates, etc.

1. ***Evaluation of Alternatives*** — Need to establish criteria for evaluation, features the buyer wants or does not want. Rank/weight alternatives or resume search. May decide that you want to eat something spicy, Indian gets highest rank, etc. If not satisfied with your choice then return to the search phase. Can you think of another restaurant? Look in the yellow pages, etc. Information from different sources may be treated differently. Marketeers try to influence by "framing" alternatives.
2. ***Purchase Decision*** — Choose buying alternative, includes product, package, store, method of purchase etc.
3. ***Purchase*** — May differ from decision, time lapse between 4 and 5, product availability.
4. ***Post-Purchase Evaluation*** — Outcome: Satisfaction or Dissatisfaction. ***Cognitive Dissonance***, have you made the right decision. This can be reduced by warranties, after sales communication, etc. After eating an Indian meal, may think that really you wanted a Chinese meal instead.

Complaints Management

1. Complaints are an indicator of areas of the business that are not operating satisfactorily for customers. Senior management should therefore ensure that their firm has a philosophy that understands and acts on the basis that effective management of complaints is a key part of treating customers fairly.
2. Smaller firms that experience low numbers of complaints may also be able to benefit by considering these findings and conclusions.
3. Complaints should not be viewed negatively, but as a source of rich customer feedback and an opportunity to identify how to improve performance. The FSA recognises that a short-term increase in the volume of complaints does not necessarily indicate non-TCF behaviour – it may mean a firm is becoming more effective at capturing complaints and expressions of dissatisfaction.
4. Handling complaints fairly is not just about processes and time limits. It is also about the culture within a firm and the behaviours and attitudes of staff when receiving complaints and deciding what actions to take.

5. TCP does not mean that all complaints should be upheld. It is about having fair, consistent and prompt investigation, decision making, and redress which should be embedded in well documented procedures.
6. Effective and prompt analysis of the root causes of complaints, and a commitment to remedying such causes, can help ensure fairer treatment to current and future customers.

Efforts needed to Handle Complaints

1. Some firms are working towards a step change in their handling of complaints. This effort is mainly driven by commercial considerations and strategic focus on customer satisfaction and retention.
2. A new mindset in these firms means complaints are understood as a valuable opportunity to enhance the customer relationship. This has required management to work to overcome views that complaints are an irritant, best ignored.
3. While we have seen some encouraging progress, it is not consistent across the industry and there is still considerable improvement required by many firms if the industry is to consistently treat fairly all customers who complain.
4. Where improvement is still required, it generally needs to address one or more of the following;
   - Spreading a progressive vision for complaints handling across the organisation;
   - Changing organisational models to manage and respond to complaints better;
   - Improving the ability to capture complaints;
   - Improving the ability of staff to make fair decisions in response to complaints;
   - Improving communication with customers;
   - Gathering and using management information;
   - Analysing the root causes of complaints and addressing those causes.

Customer complaint management has become an integral part of business, both from a regulatory perspective and a customer service standpoint. Regulatory bodies have established specific requirements for capturing, investigating, resolving and reporting customer complaints. Simply stated, complaint management is the formal process of recording and resolving a customer complaint. Complaints are expensive, both in direct and indirect costs. But for this price, companies can extract priceless knowledge, because complaints contain the direct voice of the customer. If complaints are transformed into knowledge about customers, they can provide a valuable amount of capital for enterprises. To exploit this capital, companies must design, build, operate and continuously upgrade systems for managing complaints. These systems are called "customer complaint management systems" (CCMS). Complaint management is just one initiative under a broader compliance management strategy.

Best Practices

The following paragraphs highlight four best practices for automated, complaint customer compliant management processes:

1. Classify customer complaints
2. Analyze and report trends
3. Take management action
4. Continuous improvement of the complaint process

Classify customer complaints – As individual complaints are recorded, the nature of the complaint, along with the product or service the complaint is about, requires classification. In the banking sector, for instance, complaints that violate federal laws, or internal bank policies and procedures should be classified separately from other customer service issues.

Analyze and report trends – Once complaints are classified, the data should be analyzed and reported on a regular basis. The goal of analysis is to identify themes or trends that occur with front-line service delivery. This is done with an eye towards both regulatory matters, and those that help improve customer experiences. Given that many bank Ombudsmen report to their chief executive and board of directors on a semi-annual basis. This ensures complaint management activities receive senior executive attention and accountability.

Take management action – With issues identified, actions must be taken to improve front-line service delivery. This may include updating customer service standards, improving communications, or providing additional training to staff on products/services. Actions should remedy systemic issues. Changes should be monitored closely to ensure actions result in fewer customer complaints.

Continuous improvement of the complaint process – Although a complaints management process may exist, it is important to know how well it is working. Ask key questions to customers who use the system, including whether or not they view the process as accessible, easy to use, and fair. This will identify areas for improvement. Since research indicates that complaints handled professionally and in a timely manner result in customers continuing to do business with a company, it is essential that customers who complain are satisfied with the complaint management process. This will not only help retain business, but will also reduce the damage that negative "word-of-mouth" has with existing or potential customers.

There are examples of firms improving how they identify, capture and assess complaints...

1. Decision making policy set by a committee comprising strategy, compliance, legal, and senior management.
2. Piloting new decision making approach on a number of test cases before adopting them more widely
3. Gap analysis completed on decision making procedures, in light of recent FSA enforcement decisions on complaint handling
4. Procedural changes communicated though company intranet, which staff have to read before being able to start work that day.
5. Senior management review a sample of decision letters each month to check appropriateness and consistency.
6. Risk-based QA samples complaint decision focused on new approaches, technical issues and weak handlers

7. New central FOS liaison team tracks and applies them to cash flow
8. All handlers have to pass training tests as new decision making policies are implemented

But some firms fail to encourage or capture complaints well and do not assess complaints fairly. This includes:

1. Aggressive and negative internal culture predisposed to view complaints as mainly unjustified.
2. Applying a rigid or tick-box decision making approach with too narrow an interpretation of the issue as expressed by the customer.
3. Inconsistent decision making particularly between more and less valuable customers.
4. Failing to investigate the issues diligently or clarify ambiguous issues or achieve a fair reconstruction.
5. Failing to consider relevant guidance published by the FSA or FOS.
6. Avoiding significant potential by offering smaller ex-gratia payments to encourage the complainant to settle.
7. Incorrect and inappropriate use of time barring or of mitigation.
8. Inconsistent decision making, reflecting excessive subjectivity by case handlers or lack of guidance.

Effective Complaints and Feedback Management Solutions

Our customer service solutions let organizations manage, collate and analyze customer complaints and feedback positively to improve customer service efficiency, customer experience and increase business profitability. Managing customer feedback effectively improves customer confidence and converts dissatisfaction to loyalty.

With customer service recognized as a key business performance differentiator, Charter's award winning software – Charter Continuum, provides dedicated complaints management expertise across all organization's departments and customer touch points.

With Charter Continuum installed, the retailers can maximize their customer service staff productivity, provide comprehensive case reporting and documentation, manage outstanding work loads, deliver best practice, ensure consistency of customer interaction, improve customer satisfaction ratings and produce powerful management information reports on every part of retail business's performance. With Charter's Call Logging Software the retailer can closely monitor the progress of business initiatives, delivering the power to capture and act on key content from every customer contact.

How companies react to their customers' complaints and feedback is what makes the difference between mediocre organizations and market leaders. Charters heritage is complaints management, and its successful products for complaints handling provide long-term customer satisfaction. That is charter continunous customers include UK's leading retail, travel, food, manufacturing, leisure, utility and financial service brands as well as local government and not-for-profit organizations.

Businesses who invest in Charter understand that their success relies on satisfying their customers.

The Federal Trade Commission, together with other members of the Organization for Economic Cooperation and Development (OECD), today adopted a Recommendation on Consumer Dispute Resolution and Redress. The OECD recommendation offers a framework for governments and businesses to help consumers resolve disputes and settle claims, both for individual consumers and groups of consumers, and offers mechanisms for getting money back for wronged consumers. It recommends that national consumer protection agencies have legal authority to obtain and facilitate redress on behalf of consumer victims. The OECD is a 30-nation forum that promotes economic growth, trade, and development.

The OECD recommendation offers principles for domestic and cross-border disputes, and addresses both real world and online commerce. It also contains specific principles for member countries to make cross-border dispute resolution and redress more effective, including participating in international and regional consumer complaint, advice, and referral networks; expanding the awareness of justice system participants, including the judiciary, law enforcement officials, and other government officials, as to the needs of foreign consumers who have been harmed by domestic wrongdoers; encouraging greater use of technology to facilitate resolution of cross-border disputes; taking steps to minimize legal barriers to consumer dispute resolution and redress mechanisms outside the consumer's country; and developing multi- and bi-lateral arrangements to improve international judicial cooperation in the recovery of foreign assets and the enforcement of judgements in appropriate cross border cases. The recommendation also calls for the private sector to work cooperatively in developing consumer dispute resolution and redress mechanisms.

The recommendation is one of several OECD recommendations aimed at protecting consumers in the evolving global marketplace. It builds on the OECD's 1999 Guidelines for Consumer Protection in the Context of Electronic Commerce, and the OECD's 2003 Guidelines for Protecting Consumers from Fraudulent and Deceptive Practices Across Borders. The earlier two recommendations recognized the importance of effective dispute resolution and redress mechanisms and called for the development of effective cross-border redress systems. The FTC hosted a workshop on this topic in 2005.

The FTC works for the consumer to prevent fraudulent, deceptive, and unfair business practices and to provide information to help spot, stop, and avoid them. To file a complaint in English or Spanish, click http://www.ftc.gov/ftc/complaint.shtm or call 1-877-382-4357. The FTC enters internet, telemarketing, identity theft, and other fraud-related complaints into Consumer Sentinel, a secure, online database available to more than 1,600 civil and criminal law enforcement agencies in the US and abroad.

United States of America - Gross Domestic Product 15,094.03 (US dollars, billions) in 2011

Gross Domestic Product (GDP) is the value of all goods and services produced in the US GDP is used to measure economic output. The growth rate in GDP is closely evaluated by the Federal Reserve to determine whether the economy is growing too slowly, or too quickly. Recessions are often defined as two consecutive quarters of contraction in GDP.

Table 32 : Export Explore Embed

Date	Value (US $ billions)	Change, per cent
2011	15,094.03	3.91 per cent
2010	14,526.55	4.22 per cent
2009	13,938.93	–2.47 per cent
2008	14,291.55	1.87 per cent
2007	14,028.68	4.87 per cent
2006	13,377.20	5.98 per cent
2005	12,622.95	6.49 per cent
2004	11,853.25	6.38 per cent
2003	11,142.23	4.70 per cent
2002	10,642.30	3.46 per cent
2001	10,286.18	3.36 per cent
2000	9,951.48	–0.323 per cent

Source: World Economic Outlook, April 2012

Indian Retail Market

The Indian retail market, which is the fifth largest retail destination globally, has been ranked as the most attractive emerging market for investment in the retail sector by AT Kearney's eighth annual Global Retail Development Index (GRDI), in 2009. As per a study conducted by the Indian Council for Research on International Economic Relations (ICRIER), the retail sector is expected to contribute to 22 per cent of India's GDP by 2010. With rising consumer demand and greater disposable income, the US $ 400 billion Indian retail sector is clocking an annual growth rate of 30 per cent. It is projected to grow to US $ 700 billion by 2010, according to a report by global consultancy Northbridge Capital. The organised business is expected to be 20 per cent of the total market by then. In 2008, the share of organised retail was 7.5 per cent or US $ 300 million of the total retail market.

Tier II cities like Noida, Amritsar, Kochi and Gurgaon, are emerging as the favoured destinations for the retail sector with their huge growth potential.

Moreover, many new apparel brands such as Zara, the fashion label owned by Inditex SA of Spain, UK garment chain Topshop, the Marc Ecko clothing line promoted by the US entrepreneur of the same name and the Japanese casual wear brand Uniqlo are preparing to open outlets in India. Buoyed by improved consumer spending, sales of listed retailers increased by 12 per cent in the September 2009 quarter compared with the same period in 2008. Australia's Retail Food Group is planning to enter the Indian market in 2010. It has ambitious investment plans which aim to clock revenue of US $ 87 million from the country within five years from start of operations. British retail major Marks and Spencer (M&S) is looking at scaling up its India operations and plans to open at least 50 more outlets in the country over the next few years. Koutons Retail India plans to open 200 stores in FY11 in addition to its existing 1,400. Of the 200 stores, 100 would be family concept stores, which would include women and children's wear. Reliance Footprint, part of Reliance retail, plans to spend US $ 86.62 million to add 100 outlets across the country in two years to sell branded footwear. It currently has 16 outlets. Retail chain Suvidhaa Infoserve plans to open 1,000-1,200 new outlets every month across the country and is eyeing a 1,00,000 strong network in the next two to three years. At present, the Mumbai-based firm has 18,000 convenient neighbourhood stores called 'Suvidhaa Point' across the country in over 20 states and over 400 cities. Lifestyle International, part of the Dubai-based US $ 1.5 billion Landmark Group, plans to have over 50 stores across India by 2012–13. These will include 35 Lifestyle stores for retailing apparel, cosmetics and footwear, besides 15 Home Centres that sell home furnishing goods. Watch maker, Timex India, is looking at increasing its presence in the country by adding another 52 stores by March, 2011 at an investment of US $ 1.3 million taking its total store count to 120. Wills Lifestyle plans to expand its operations by opening 100 new stores in the next three years. It also plans to concentrate on online buyers. Pantaloon Retail India (PRIL) is planning to invest US $ 77.88 million this fiscal to add up to 2.4 million sq. ft. retail space at its existing operations. Pantaloon Retail is also looking to hive off its value retail chain, Big Bazaar, into a separate subsidiary, which may eventually go for an initial public offer (IPO). PRIL proposes to open 155 Big Bazaar stores by 2014, increasing its total network to 275 stores.

POLICY INITIATIVES

100 per cent FDI is allowed in cash-and-carry wholesale formats. Franchisee arrangements are also permitted in retail trade. 51 per cent FDI is allowed in single-brand retailing.

ROAD AHEAD

According to a new market research report by RNCOS titled, 'Booming Retail Sector in India', organised retail market in India is expected to reach US $ 50 billion by 2011. Number of shopping malls is expected to increase at a CAGR of more than 18.9 per cent from 2007 to 2015. Rural market is projected to dominate the retail industry landscape in India by 2012 with total market share of above 50 per cent. Organised retailing of mobile handset and accessories is expected to reach close to US $ 990 million by 2010. Driven by the expanding retail market, the third party logistics market is forecasted to reach US $ 20 billion by 2011.

INDIAN ORGANISED RETAIL - RISE AND SHINE

Retailing in India is gradually inching its way toward becoming the next boom industry. The whole concept of shopping has altered in terms of format and consumer buying behavior, ushering in a revolution in shopping in India. Modern retail has entered India as seen in sprawling shopping centres, multi-storeyed malls and huge complexes offer shopping, entertainment and food all under one roof. The Indian retailing sector is at an inflexion point is going to take a higher growth trajectory. The Indian population is witnessing a significant change in its demographics. A large young working population with median age of 24 years, nuclear families in urban areas, along with increasing working-women population and emerging opportunities in the services sector are going to be the key growth drivers of the organized retail sector in India.

It was argued that the best period for Retail in India will be between 2009-13, when the Retail industry will expand and consolidation would set in with most of the top global retailers having a presence in India. Also argued that the Indian market is unlike the US where the market is already saturated. Hence, if Retailers play their cards right, they can get customers, make profits and all concerned in the entire value chain can grow by leaps and bounds. Industry experts also highlighted that organised retail in India is booming and is set to grow at 42 per cent to touch US $ 70 bn by 2011, which means that organised retail would be twice as big as the size of the Mobile Telecom industry in India. Currently, India is the fourth largest economy and is all set to become the third largest by 2013, leaving Japan behind. It is estimated that there would be around 300 million middle class consumers in India by 2013, and organised retail market share would reach 10 per cent, which would reach 24 per cent by 2025. The game has just begun for organised retail in India. Though the global economy is witnessing a slowdown, the Indian economy is set to grow at 7.5 per cent p.a., driving higher consumption and consequently, the Retail industry. Total retail sales in India are estimated to grow at a CAGR of 10 per cent to $ 680 bn by the end of 2011 increasing from to $ 511 bn at the end of 2008. The $ 25.44 bn Indian organised retail sector is still at a nascent stage with barely 5 per cent share in the total retail market, the lowest compared to peers in the BRIC countries viz., Brazil (36 per cent), Russia (33 per cent) and China (20 per cent). On a global platform, organised retail captures about 52 per cent of total retail sales with developed nations like the US, UK, Germany and France constituting 80 per cent or more of total Retail sales. The organised retail is set to grow at 40 per cent hereon to touch US $ 70 bn and capture around 10.3 per cent of the total Indian Retail industry market share by the end of 2011. Thus, there is lot of room for the Indian organised Retail segment to grow. Moreover, the presence of the global players will not impact the domestic players too much as size of the Retail industry is set to grow.

GLIMPSES FROM INDIA RETAIL REPORT

As per the Images F and R Research estimates for India Retail Report the Indian Retail market stood at ₹ 1,330,000 crore in 2007 with annual growth of about 10.8 per cent. Of this, the share of organised Retail in 2007 was estimated to be only 5.9 per cent, which was ₹ 78,300 crore. But this modern retail segment grew at the rate of 42.4 per cent in 2007, and is expected to maintain a faster growth rate over the next three years, especially in view of the fact that major global players and Indian corporate houses are seen entering the fray in a big way. Even at the going rate, organised retail is expected to touch ₹ 2,30,000 crore (at constant prices) by 2010, constituting roughly 13 per cent of the total retail market. The consumer spending is ultimately pushing the economy into a growth-and-liberalisation mode. The Indian market is becoming bolder by the day, with the economy now expected to maintain its growth at over 8 to 9 per cent and average salaries being hiked by about 15 per cent, there will be lot more consumption. In the overall retail pie food and grocery was the dominant category with 59.5 per cent share, valued at ₹ 7,92,000 crore, followed by clothing and accessories with a 9.9 per cent share at ₹ 1,31,300 crore. Interestingly, out-of-home food (catering) services (₹ 71,300 crore) has overtaken jewellery (₹ 69,400 crore) to become the third largest retail category, with a 5.4 per cent market share – this largely reflects the massive employment opportunities to youngsters in the services sector and accompanying changes in consumer lifestyles. Consumer durables (₹ 57,500 crore) is the fifth largest retail category followed by health and pharmaceuticals (₹ 48,800 crore), entertainment (₹ 45,600 crore), furniture, furnishings and kitchenware

(₹ 45,500 crore), mobiles and accessories (₹ 27,200 crore), leisure retail (₹ 16,400 crore), footwear (₹16,000 crore), health and beauty care services (₹ 4,600 crore) and timewear and eyewear (₹ 4,400 crore) in the order. In the organised retail segment, the picture is different altogether. Apparel and fashion accessories is the largest category with 38.1 per cent of the market share, valued at ₹ 29,800 crore, followed by food and grocery accounting for 11.5 per cent of the organised retail market at ₹ 9,000 crore , footwear with 9.9 per cent of the organised retail market share at ₹ 7,750 crore, consumer durables with 9.1 per cent market share at the fourth place (₹ 7,100 crore), and out-of-home food (catering) services and furniture, furnishings and Kitchenware retail in the order. Timewear (48.9 per cent) and footwear (48.4 per cent) are the most organised of all retail categories. Apparel and fashion accessories retail comes next with the organised segment controlling 22.7 per cent of the market.The mobile and accessories retail market has shown fastest growth in 2007 (25.6 per cent) over the previous year, the other two prominent categories being out-of-home food (catering) services where growth was 25.1 per cent and books, music and gifts leisure category which achieved 23.3 per cent growth. In the organised retail segment, however, the fastest growth was recorded in the tiny heath and beauty care services category (₹ 660 crore), which grew at the rate of 65 per cent in 2007 over the previous year – again a reflection of rise in services sector employment that demands proper grooming. The second fastest growing organised retail category is that of entertainment (53.8 per cent), followed by the mobile phones and accessories and the food and grocery retail categories, both of which achieved 55.2 per cent growth in 2007. Much of the stupendous growth opportunity in catering services (25.1 per cent) and leisure retail (23.3 per cent) categories was utilised by the unorganised retailers because organised players could not keep up to the desired growth momentum. A closer study of the retail growth story at constant prices shows that in both these categories growth of organised retail was higher in 2006 (41.7 per cent and 26.1 per cent respectively) as compared to 2007 (37 per cent and 25 per cent). At constant prices, growth in the fashion and accessories retail category, both in the overall market and the organised retail segment, have been consistently positive since 2004: while the overall market grew 12.8 per cent in 2007, the organised segment grew 35.5 per cent.In jewellery retail, the overall market growth was higher in 2007 (9.6 per cent) as compared to the previous year (9.2 per cent) but growth in organised retail was slightly at a lower pace in 2007 (31 per cent) as compared to the previous year. The overall market growth in the timewear category has declined from 10.7 per cent in 2005 to 9.7 per cent in 2006 and further down to 8.9 per cent in 2007. However, growth in organised retail was higher in 2007 (16.6 per cent) as compared to 2006 (14.8 per cent). Popularity of mobile phones is to a large extent responsible for the dampening of the overall market growth in this category while the renewed enthusiasm in the organised segment is on account of the fillip from luxury brands and offerings that are positioned more as a hi-end lifestyle statement than on the functionality aspect of the product. Footwear retail, the overall market as well as its organised segment, has grown faster year after year but growth in 2007 was especially remarkable: the overall market grew 12 per cent in 2007 as against a 9.2 per cent growth in 2006 while the organised segment grew 42.3 per cent and 36.4 per cent respectively for the two years. The global brands have actually turned the heat on, and the domestic brands too appear to have accepted the challenge in the true spirit. Growth in the health and beauty care category has been remarkable in 2007, though the organised segment growth in 2007 (57.5 per cent) was slightly lower as compared to 2006 (59.1 per cent). The demand is stupendous but organised players have hardly much to boast of in terms of innovative concepts and global standards when it comes to providing the customers with an experience that is superior and radically different from what the unorganised segment offers. This category needs to be positioned as a "wellness" category that provides individualised services to customers with synergies of health and beauty care, pharmaceuticals and specialised clinical services – all at one place. Another category that merits special mention is furnishings and furniture retail, where the overall market grew at seven per cent in 2007 as compared to just 3.2 per cent in 2006 – thanks to the housing sector boom. The organised segment also grew faster at 29.7 per cent in 2007 as compared to 23.1 per cent in the previous year, but this ₹ 45,500 crore category calls for better attention from organised players. Consumer durables and the mobile phone and accessories categories have both grown faster in 2007 as compared to 2006. At constant prices, the overall food and grocery retail market grew slightly higher at 2.3 per cent in 2007 as compared to a 2.2 per cent annual growth in the previous two years. But the organised retail segment in this category is simmering in the true sense – a 50 per cent growth in 2007 as compared to 42.9 per cent in 2006, and lot more fireworks can be expected this year and the years ahead. Valued at ₹ 9,000 crore, this organised market constitutes barely 1.1 per cent of the total food and grocery retail market.

KEY PLAYERS IN INDIAN RETAIL SECTOR

AV Birla Group has a strong presence in apparel retail and owns renowned brands like Allen Solly, Louis Phillipe, Trouser Town, Van Heusen and Peter England. The company has investment plans to the tune of ₹ 8,000 – 9,000 crore till 2010. Trent is a subsidiary of the Tata group; it operates lifestyle retail chain, book and music retail chain, consumer electronic chain etc. Westside, the lifestyle retail chain registered a turnover of ₹ 3.58 mn in 2006 Landmark Group invested ₹ 300 crores to expand Max chain, and ₹ 100 crores on Citymax 3 star hotel chain. Lifestyle International is their international brand business. K. Raheja Corp Group has a turnover of ₹ 6.75 billion which is expected to cross US $ 100 million mark by 2010. Segments include books, music and gifts, apparel, entertainment etc. Reliance has more than 300 Reliance Fresh stores; they have multiple formats and their sale is expected to be ₹ 90,000 crores ($ 20 billion) by 2009-10. Pantaloon Retail has 450 stores across the country and revenue of over ₹ 20 billion and is expected to touch 30 million by 2010. Segments include Food and grocery, e-tailing, home solutions, consumer electronics, entertainment, shoes, books, music and gifts, health and beauty care services.

RETAIL IN INDIA - A CHALLENGE

The retail industry in India is growing at a significant pace. However, there are several problems faced by the industry. The major challenges for the organized sector include:

Taxation laws that favor small retailers.

Different structure of sales tax in different states.

Multi-point octroi collection.

Lack of trained workforce.

Problems of supply chain and logistics.

High cost of real estate.

Limited land available at prime locations.

According to analysts, for this industry to thrive, Indian retailers need to emulate worldwide retail practices such as accuracy in financial reporting, increased levels of corporate governance and greater accountability among employees. Retailers need to use the latest techniques to enhance the consumer's shopping experience.

INDIA, CHINA - NEW ARCH RIVALS?

The Indian organized retail segment is currently growing faster than the retail revolution in China. If retail growth is compared in the two countries, undoubtedly, China is moving faster but the marginal increase of the total effect in India is more than the marginal increase in China at this point of time. India was compared with its arch rival China on the Four P's - 'politics' which is hampering the growth of retail industry due to inept policies, cost of retention and hiring of good talented 'people', development issues of 'property' and supply of 'products'. India needs to circumvent challenges that come in form of these 4Ps that China was able to do, which led to higher profits and better standards of living in China. Industry experts also discussed whether central and state governments could be more flexible in easing the taxes imposed on the retailers, and revise policies pertaining to FDI, in order to aid growth of the Retail industry in India. India has long been:

SECTOR KEY PLAYERS

1. Binayak Tex Processors Limited
2. Store One Retail India Limited
3. Shoppers' Stop Limited
4. Pantaloon Retail (India) Limited
5. Trent Limited
6. Vishal Retail Limited
7. Brandhouse Retails Limited
8. REI Six Ten Retail Limited

Compared with China on almost every aspect of the growth story: Key takeaways from China included opening up the Retail sector, modernizing the supply chain and increasing product categories. But, it should be borne in mind that the path to retail growth in India and China is different. India believes in inclusive growth by simultaneously developing smaller towns along with big cities. In China, retail growth was led by the big cities and coastal areas while interiors are still devoid of it. Another important factor aiding growth of Indian organised Retail when compared to China is that Indian consumers benefit from a sizable market for consumer credit. In India, non-mortgage consumer debt is roughly 5 per cent of GDP compared to 2 per cent in China. India's private financial sector is better developed than in China and more geared towards meeting the needs of consumers than China's industry-oriented banking system. We believe that India is currently at a crossroad similar to where China was during 1992-96.

From there, it took China 16 years to increase the share of organised Retail to 20 per cent . It is firmly believed that if China can manage such growth, India definitely has the potential to grow faster. Lastly, the situation would improve as and when the sector reforms are ushered in and India gradually lifts FDI restrictions on the sector.

RETAIL AND RECESSION

The global economic slump has had its impact on the India retail sector. One of the earliest players in the Indian retail scenario Subhiksha's operations came to a near standstill and required liquidity injection. Vishal Retail secured corporate debt restructuring (CDR) plan from its lenders while other players like the Reliance Retail run by Mukesh Ambani and Pantaloon led Kishore Biyani by went slow on expansion plans and even scaled down operations. However, during the last quarter a bit of confidence was restored as the economy showed signs of growth.

FUTURE TRENDS

Lifestyle International, a division of Landmark Group, plans to have more than 50 stores across India by 2012–13. Shoppers Stop has plans to invest ₹ 250 crore to open 15 new supermarkets in the coming three years. Pantaloon Retail India (PRIL) plans to invest US $ 77.88 million this fiscal to add up to existing 2.4 million sq ft retail space. PRIL intends to set up 155 Big Bazaar stores by 2014, raising its total network to 275 stores. Timex India will open another 52 stores by March 2011 at an investment of US $ 1.3 million taking its total store count to 120. In the first six months of the current fiscal ending September 30, 2009, the company has recorded a net profit of US $ 1.2 million. Australia's Retail Food Group is planning to enter the Indian market in 2010. It has plans to clock US $ 87 million revenue in five years. In 20 years they expect the India operations to be larger than the Australia operations.

THE ROAD AHEAD

Industry experts predict that the next phase of growth in the retail sector will emerge from the rural markets. By 2012 the rural retail market is projected to have a total of more than 50 per cent market share. The total number of shopping malls is expected to expand at a compound annual growth rate of over 18.9 per cent by 2015. Recently, the government decided to allow 51 per cent FDI in single-brand retailing which, has been welcomed by the industry. However, most are of the view that its impact will be largely limited to attracting more luxury brands. The limited foreign direct investment allowed by the government in the retail industry will not have much impact on the Big Bazaars and Shopper's Stops but it will allow luxury brands like Marks and Spencer, Louis Vuitton or Versace - which are currently taking the franchisee route - to open more stores in the country.

Table 33 : Ranking of Retailers in France, Sector: Fashion and Clothing

Rank	Company name	Banners/Brands	Turnover in million	Number of outlets
1	H and M	H and M	866	136
2	Kiabi	Kiabi	833	308
3	Camaieu	Camaieu	765	580
4	Vetit	Gemo		

Retail-Index is the most comprehensive, updated and user-friendly database about national and international retailers in all major retail-sectors: food, fashion, consumer electronics, DIY and gardening, furniture and decoration, home-ware, footwear and leather, personal care, baby-ware, sport and leisure, toys gamesand music, books and magazines, jewellery and watches, optical, pet-care, telecom and petrol.

This practical and unique source of information displays clear rankings and profiles with key data on national and international retail chains in any European country and several major countries outside Europe. The retailer profiles feature the name and headquarter address as well as contact details, management (CEO), turnover development, banners, number of stores, website, webstore etc. The retailer rankings per country provide a clear overview of the retailers based on recent turnover data and numbers of shops.

QUESTIONS

1. Define RMIS.
2. What are the benefits of database?
3. Explain the emerging trends in system and communication.
4. Explain the various information systems.
5. Define DBM retailing.
6. What are the advantages of computerization?
7. Explain the importance of RIS.
8. Prepare a model income statement for a Retail Business Unit.
9. Give a brief analyze of profitability in a retail business.
10. Write short notes on Worksheet, Purchase Account Record, Trade Discount and Cash Discount.
11. What is the basic format of an income statement for retail business?
12. Write about retail accounting statement.
13. What do you mean by situation audit?
14. What do you mean by retail sales force management?
15. Define buyer behaviour.
16. What are the characteristics of rural shoppers?
17. What are the four types of shoppers?
18. Explain the stages of consumer buying process.
    (b) "Nutrament Debunked" Discuss
19. What do you mean by "Lifestyles"?
20. What are the types of reference groups?
21. Explain the factors that influence buyer behaviour.
22. What are the characteristics of various types of social classes?
23. Define Culture and subculture.
24. "Culture affects what people buy" – Do you agree?

25. Explain buying decision process.
26. Explain customer buying process.
27. What do you mean by propensity to buy?
28. What are the models of buyer decision making?
29. What is the impact of cognitive and personal biases in decision making?
30. Explain shopper decision process.
31. What are the 5Cs of customer in control?
32. Explain shopper behaviour.
33. Explain retail shopper behaviour.
34. Discuss retail shopper behaviour and the "so what" factor.
35. What are the types of shopping?
36. Explain shopping environment in the given socio-economic context.
37. Discuss briefly the various theories of shopping.
38. Explain economic theory of shopping.
39. Explain psychological theory of shopping.
40. Explain learning theory of shopping
42. Explain EST Theory.
43. Define Cheap Est.
44. Explain psycho-analytic theory and sociological theory of shopping.
45. How to win in retail?
46. What do you mean by Black Hole?
47. Who is a Market Customer?
48. What do you mean by Market segment?
49. What are the different market segments in retail business?
50. What do you mean by brand shoppability?
51. Point out the key stimuli that prevails throughout real life experience.
52. What do you mean by cluster analysis?
53. Explain strategic profile model.
54. What are Pull and Push in supply chain?
55. What do you mean by shopper profile analysis?
56. What are the objectives of Shoppers' Stop?
57. What do retailers do?
58. Why is retailing important in our society?
59. What career and entrepreneurial opportunities does retailing offer?
60. What type of decisions do retail managers make?
61. How do retailers differ in terms of how they meet the needs of their customers?
62. How do services retailers differ from merchandise retailers?

63. What are the types of ownership for retail firms?
64. Who is your favourite retailer? Why do you like this retailer? What would a competitive retailer have to do to get your patronage?
65. From your perspective, what are the benefits and limitations of purchasing a garment directly from a garment-manufacturer rather than from a retailer?
66. What trends are shaping today's retailers?
67. What are the different types of retailers?
68. Explain the micro and macro-environments the influence retail management?
69. Choose any two retailers and explain how the companies started and how they have changed over time.
70. How can small, independent retailers compete against large national chains?
71. What do off-price retailers need to do to compete against other format in the future?
72. Compare and contrast the retail mixes of convenience stores, traditional supermarkets, super centres, malls. Can all of these retail institutions survive over the long run? How? Why?
73. Which type of the store-based retail formats is most vulnerable to competition? Why? Which is least vulnerable? Why?
74. Many experts believe that customer service is one of retailing's most important issues. How can retailers that emphasize price (such as discount stores, category specialists, and off-price retailers) improve customer service without increasing costs and thus, prices?
75. What are the unique customer benefits offered by the retail stores?
76. How might technology affect the future shopping experience?
77. How do customers make decisions?
78. What social and personal factors affect customer purchase decisions?
79. How can retailers get customers to visit their stores frequently and buy more merchandise during each visit?
80. Does the customer buying process end when a customer buys some merchandise? Explain your answer.
81. Using the steps in the consumer buying process, describe how you used this process to select your college. When you were deciding on which college to attend, what objective and subjective criteria did you use in the alternative evaluation portion of the consumer buying process?
82. Why is geo-demographic segmentation used by retailers to locate stores?
83. Any retailer's goal is to get a customer in its store to stop searching and buy a product at its outlet. How can a garment retailer ensure that the customer buys garments at its outlet?
84. How would you expect the buying decision process to differ when shopping on the Internet compared with shopping in a store?
85. Choose a retailer and describe how it has developed a competitive strategic advantage.
86. Identify a store or service provider that you believe has an effective loyalty programme. Explain why it is effective.
87. How is retail strategy reflected in retailers?
88. Why do retailers need to evaluate their performance?

89. What is the strategic profit model, and how is it used?
90. What measures do retailers use to assess their performance?
91. Buyers' performance is often measured by their gross margin per centage. Why is this measure more appropriate than net profit per centage?
92. How does the strategic profit model assist retailers in planning and evaluating their marketing and financial strategies?

CASE STUDY

Introduction

A retail chain differs from other industries by nature of its number of locations. A conventional manufacturing industry has a production at a limited number of locations and sales being handled from a few more. However, a retail industry has sales from a large number of locations. If it is in the food and beverage business, you could say that its production is also being done at all locations. This means that material handling, production, sales and distribution as well as finance transactions are being conducted at all their stores. Each store requires an inventory control system, a point of sales system and an accounting system (may be also a production system).

Major procurement is conducted at the HO, material receipt is done at the stores and bill passing and bank payments conducted at the HO, Some extent of local procurement is also sometimes being done at the stores, sales is an activity which is being done completely at the stores. Most of these activities are handled through a PoS system. However, while a PoS system handles sales satisfactorily, it is generally not geared up to manage inventory, consumption or requisitions for material.

Contrary to popular belief (even within the organisation), the problem for a retail organisation is not the PoS system. The problem is integration and accurate information flow and the issue goes beyond just the consolidation of sales figures, A PoS was meant for entering sales tickets and printing them, which it does without too many problems. It was then extended to contain some inventory information at each location. It is not capable of becoming an inventory, sales and procurement management solution, which is what a lot of PoS solutions attempted to do.

Retail Client

The client is a food and beverage retail chain. Beverages are made at each store using a combination of ingredients while the food items are traded items, which are procured from a third party. The client is a very fast expanding chain with over 100 stores. The stores are spread over a vast geographical location. Four regional offices manage stores within their area and four warehouses manage supplies of consumables and capital items to the stores. All of these report to one centralised HO. For every region there is a regional office which manages the stores within its territory and one warehouse to supply consumables (non perishables or raw material) to the stores within a territory.

Problems

1. Procurement is a centralised activity at the HO. Prices are negotiated with vendors for consumables and perishables, which are meant to be directly delivered to the stores. On confirmation from the stores the vendor bills are cleared. The confirmation of items and their quantity received at the stores was a very irregular activity. The HO did not want to depend only on the receipt document given by the vendor, HO also wanted details of items rejected due to quality problems. Often the vendor would deliver items to the stores, which were not ordered for and in quantities greater or lesser than specified. For Bill passing, the vendor would submit his delivery notes, which could be different than the original purchase order. Stores normally sent their MRN by normal Post or informally communicated through e-mail. If all the stores did not send the MRN, vendor payment would get delayed.
2. Changes in confirmed purchase orders was a regular activity. At the time of Bill passing finding the reference of the purchase order was very difficult, since PQ's were primarily a manual process.
3. Requisition of material from stores was done through verbal communication or through e-mail. There was really no proper procedure of either estimating requirements or of raising the requisitions. As a result, stores would get stocked out of key ingredients.
4. Daily sales figures from the stores were received through SMS or by verbal communication or by e-mail. Without a proper procedure, the sales figures were being received in a random manner. HO was unable to receive the sales figures from all stores in any single day. Some stores would send their figures twice. Some stores would send it after two days and some would not send the sales figures at all HO was never able to get proper and timely sales figures which was a major constraint in planning and MIS. Also only the consolidated sales figures were being received, so there was no way to do a timely sales break-up by products.
5. Stores would deposit the daily sales collections in a local branch of the organisation's main bank. They would then inform the HO of the deposited amount again through verbal communication or by e-mail. The HO could view details of the amount deposited by each store through the Bank's EDI interface. The problem was that the amount deposited and the collection figures of the store would rarely, if ever, match. There were valid reasons for this. The stores would require to pay cash for local expenses which they would pay from the daily sales collections. However, there was no way of informing the HO on a daily basis of these expenses.
6. Recording of consumption in each store was simply not feasible. The PoS would be able to keep details of opening stock of material. At the end of the day, a physical check of the material would be done and the closing stock entered. For the kind of raw material that the organisation used, the inaccuracy of this physical verification was high since the UOM of the material could be a bottle while the consumption was a few millilitres. They were unable to track the amount of raw material consumed against each sales product sold in the case of beverages. The discrepancies in the stock consumption between the stores were substantial even if their daily sales figures were roughly the same.

7. Price changes and promotional schemes were decided by the HO and the information was sent to the Stores. However, some stores would incorporate these changes immediately, some would do it a day later and some would end up not having received this information at all. Some stores would also express helplessness at being able to reprogram the PoS system. In addition, the HO would sometimes send a revised price list with only product codes marked. However, the same item in one store would have a different code from another store. A related problem to this was also that if the items had different codes for the same products, they could never be automatically consolidated in a single report as was required by the HO.

SOLUTION

Overview

Reckoner ERP, eReckoner retail was provided to the client. Reckoner would be used by the HO while eReckoner retail was to be used by the stores, warehouses and the regional offices. We would like to mention that there is a fundamental difference between the eReckoner retail as compared to other eReckoner modules. A local database at any of the remote locations is never provided for any other eReckoner module. The kiosks and the application were meant to use the internet for all transactions so that the information viewed by everybody would be online and no consolidation would be required. However, with eReckoner retail, a local database was provided to each location. The reason for this was that the internet connections at all the locations was not always reliable. If the connection went down, the eReckoner retail would not be able to connect to the main server, which would stop all local invoicing. This would simply not be acceptable. Also, even if the connection was reliable, the cost of remaining connected to the internet for 18 hours a day did not appear justifiable. For eReckoner, which is used by the regional offices, a local database was not required.

Operations

The stores would conduct daily transaction in eReckoner retail using the in built PoS system. (Initially, we used their existing PoS systems and built an interface with Reckoner to upload the sales data from the PoS. However, it was not Possible to remotely program the PoS for any price change or addition of new products,) The Reckoner PoS system was an easy to use simple interface, At the end of the shift, the stores would connect to the internet and subsequently to the main server at the HO. The data from the local database would be automatically uploaded to the main server. The server would have checks built in to prevent the same data from being uploaded twice. A consolidated sales invoice would be generated for each store. Using the BOM definition in the system, eReckoner would also generate the consumption vouchers, and would also calculate the consumption of raw material at each store. This would also automatically update the stock at the stores for them "to know their current stock availability". The total sales figure would be available and could be reconciled with the amount deposited in the bank. HO would also now receive sales details break-up for each product.

To enter material receipt notes, the stores would require to connect to the main server, select the vendor or the PO and enter details of their receipt. Vendor deliveries were now automatically available to the HO for bill passing.

The same process would be used by the stores to enter requisition for material. The requisition would be authorised by the regional offices or HO, which would allow the warehouses to despatch the items requested for.

Any price changes or promotional schemes decided by the HO would be entered in eReckoner. Whenever the stores connected to the HO server, the database at the stores would be automatically updated.

The stores could enter all expense and other financial transactions online in eReckoner. These transactions would be available to the HO so that they could reconcile the cash collection and expense figures for each store.

Regional office used eReckoner for financial entries and Purchase orders. There were a lot of local purchases being done for the stores for perishable items. The regional offices would enter the PO in eReckoner, HO would authorise them and transfer the required amount to the regional offices for payment to the vendors.

Note:

This case study is meant to given an overview of the main problems for the organisation and how the implementation of Reckoner and eReckoner solved them. We have not mentioned the detailed analysis of each problem in this document.

CASE STUDY-1

Akashganga

This case study is about a product and service named Akashganga sold by a small, entrepreneurial business named Shree Kamadhenu Electronics Private Ltd., [SKEPL]. Akashganga is for dairy farmers and it is intended to enable to them to increase their efficiency and productivity. The Indian dairy industry is plagued by several problems, the major ones being low quality caused by manual handling, corruption and mismanagement, and, of course, endemic dilution of milk with water. Akashganga attempts to alleviate some of these issues. Akashganga is a computerized system. When a farmer gets milk into the collection point, it's weighed and the amount of fat measured and immediately an entry is made on the farmer's swipe card. The money can be collected immediately. This is marked contrast to the previous system where the financial calculation was done later to avoid holding up the queue of farmers ready for milking; the calculation was done by hand and was some what complicated. With the new system, calculation is done automatically which makes it possible to pay the farmer on the spot rather than having him wait for a couple of days. Also the potential for cheating is reduced. An entry is made electronically on the farmer's swipe card.

When SKEPL wanted to market this service, it ran up against the skepticism of the Indian rural people against unproven technology. This is the classic catch-22 situation as the farmer does not trust the tool till he tries it, and is reluctant to try it till he trusts it. SKEPL got around this problem by offering free trials and delayed payment schemes stretching up to several months. The company also provided responsive and efficient after-sales service. It established a service network covering the rural areas, and typically would attend to a compliant within a few hours of receiving it.

It's important to note that the company's local presence whether for marketing, sales or service helped tremendously, since the villagers would not be disposed to make a journey to a town or city to learn about their products. The company also used a name Akashganga a that Indian villagers can relate to. This was a very important factor that helped the farmers relate to and trust the company.

Of course, the company had a solution that was superior in terms of time, transparency, fairness, etc., and that played a big role in their success.

As a result of these factors, SKEPL gained a threshold in this large market and earned respect among farmers.

CASE STUDY-2

ITC e-Choupal

About ITC- IBD

ITC is one of India's foremost private sector companies with a market capitalization of over US $ 14 billion and a turnover of US $ 3 billion. ITC has a diversified presence in Cigarettes, Hotels, Paper Boards and Specialty Papers, Packaging, Agri-Business, Packaged Foods and Confectionery, Branded Apparel, Greeting Cards and other FMCG products. Its International Business Division [ITC IBD] was created in 1990 as an agriculture trading company; it now generates US $ 150 million in revenues annually.

Initially, the agricultural commodity trading business was small compared to international players. By 1996, the opening up of the Indian market had brought in international competition. Large international companies had better margin-to-risk ratios because of wider options for risk management and arbitrage. For an Indian company to replicate the operating model of such multinational corporations would have required a massive horizontal and vertical expansion. In 1998, after competition forced ITC to explore the options of sale, merger, and closure of IBD, ITC to retain the business. The ITC-IBD taken the challengers to use information technology to change the rules of the game and create a competitive business that did not need a large asset base. Today, IBD is a US $ 150 million company that trades in commodities such as feed ingredients, food-grains, coffee, black pepper, edible nuts, marine products, and processed fruits.

ITC e-Choupal and the Strategy

ITC followed a different media/communication strategy which is more elaborate and extensive in rural marketing so far, which benefits both the farmers and the organization. The strategy is to use the information technology and bridge the information and service gap in rural INDIA which gives an edge to market its production like seeds, fertiliser, and pesticides and other products like consumer goods. With this strategy it can also enhance its competitiveness in global market for agri-exports.

A pure trading modal does not require much capital investment. The e-Choupal model, in contrast, has required that ITC make significant investments to create and maintains its own IT network in rural India and to identify and train a local farmer to manage each e-Choupal.

The company has initiated an e-Choupal efforts that place computers with Internet access in rural farming villages; the e-Choupals serve as both a social gathering place for exchange of information [Choupal means gathering place in Hindi] and an e-commerce hub. The computer, typically housed in the farmer's house, is linked to the Internet via phone lines or, increasingly, by a VSAT connection, and serves an average of 600 farmers in ten surrounding villages within about a five kilometre radius. Each e-Choupal costs between US $ 3,000 and $ 6,000 to set-up and about US $ 100 per year to maintain. Using the system costs farmers nothing, but the host farmer, called a sanchalak, incurs some operating costs and is obligated by a public oath to serve the entire community; the sanchalak benefits from increased prestige and a commission paid him for all e-Choupal transactions. The farmers can use the computer to access daily closing prices on local mandis [government-mandated markets], as well as to track global price or find information about new farming techniques either directly or, because many farmers are illiterate, via the sandialah (the village farmer who runs the e-Choupal and acts as ITC's representative in the village). In addition they can also know about weather forecast [local] and best practices in the world from e-Choupal website. They also use the e-Choupal to order seed, fertiliser, and other products such as consumer good from ITC or its partners, at prices lower than those available from village traders; the sanchalak typically aggregates the village demand for these products and transmits the order to an ITC representative. At harvest time, ITC offers to buy the crop directly from any farmer at the previous days closing price; the farmer then transports his crop to an ITC processing centre, where the crop is weighed electronically and assessed for quality. The farmer is then paid for the crop and a transport fee.

Launched in June 2000, 'e-Choupal', has already become the largest initiative among all internet-based interventions in rural India. 'e-Choupal' services today reach out to more than 3.5 million farmers growing a range of crops – soyabean, coffee, wheat, rice, pulses, shrimp – in over 31,000 villages through 5,200 kiosks across six states (Madhya Pradesh, Karnataka, Andhra Pradesh, Uttar Pradesh, Maharashtra and Rajasthan).

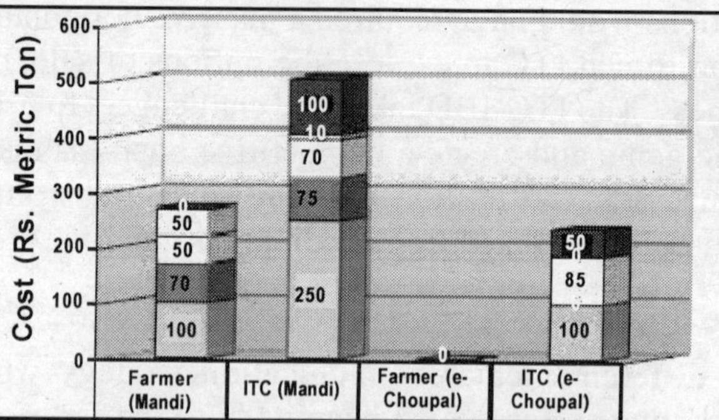

	Farmer (Mandi)	ITC (Mandi)	Farmer (e-Choupal)	ITC (e-Choupal)
Commission	0	100	0	50
Handling and Transit Losses	50	10	0	0
Labor Costs	50	70	0	85
Bagging and Weighing	70	75	0	0
Transportation	100	250	0	100

Transportation Bagging and Weighing Labor Costs
Handling and Transit Losses Commission

FIG. 40: TRANSACTIONAL COST UNDER MANDI AND E-CHOUPAL SYSTEM

Table 34 : Operational Cost and Comparison with Mandis					
Fixed Cost of Equipment at e-Choupal (in ₹)					
	Printer	**Power related**	**VSAT**	**PC**	**Total**
2001-02	7,000	19,000	90,000	39,000	1,55,000
2002-03	7,000	15,000	70,000	30,000	1,22,000
2003-04	7,000	15,000	70,000	30,000	1,22,000
2004-05	6,000	14,000	60,000	27,000	1,07,000
2005-06	6,000	12,000	50,000	24,000	92,000

Vision and Planning e-Choupal

Implementing and managing e-Choupals is a significant departure from commodities trading. Through its tobacco business, ITC has worked in Indian agriculture for decades, from research to procurement to distribution. ITCs translation of the tactical and strategic challenges it faced and its social commitment into a business model demonstrates a deep understanding of both agrarian systems and modern management. The principles followed in implementing the e-Choupals are:

1. **Re-engineer, Not Reconstruct:**

   Present mandi system have some success factors in it. ITC decided to build e-Choupal on existing system. Already ITC has trading agents in local mandis for its tobocco business. It retained the efficient providers and created roles for inefficient people. It recruites and engages members of landscape thereby making their expertise available to ITC. With this principle ITC can avoid the reinventing the system in areas where it can add no value with its presence, i.e., in areas where efficient agents are there.

2. **Address the Whole, Not Just One Part:**

   The farmers various activities range from procuring inputs to selling produce. Currently, the village trader service the spectrum of farmers needs. He is a centralized provider of cash, seed, fertiliser, pesticides, and also the only marketing channel. As a result, the trader enjoys two competitive benefits. First, his intimate knowledge of the farmer and village dynamics allow him to accurately assess and manage risk. Second, he reduces overall cost by aggregating services. The linked transactions reduce the farmers overall cost in the short term, but create a cycle of exploitative dependency in the long-term.

   Rural development efforts thus far have focused only on individual pieces rather than what the entire community needs. Cooperatives have tried to provide agriculture inputs, rural banks have tried to provide credit, and mandis have tried to create a better marketing channel. These efforts cannot compete against the traders bundled offer. Functioning as a viable procurement alternative, therefore, must eventually address a range of needs, not just the marketing channel.

   ITC e-Choupal provide service as a bundle what the entire agricultural community needs.

3. **An IT-Driven Solution:**

   Delivery of real-time information independent of the transaction. In the mandi system, delivery, pricing, and sales happen simultaneously, thus binding the farmer to an agent. E-Choupal was seen as a medium of delivery critical market information of the mandi, thus allowing the farmer an empowered choice of where and when to sell his crop.

4. **Risk Analysis and Challenges**

   - Radical shifts in computing access will break community-based business models.
   - The sanchalaks are ITCs partners in the community, and as their power and numbers increase, there is a threat of unionization and rent extraction.
   - The scope of the operation; the diversity of activities required of every operative and the speed of expansion create real threats to efficient management.
   - If ITC fails to fulfil the aspiration of farmers, they will look elsewhere for satisfaction.

Strategies to be Followed

1. Adopt the ability to determine the grades of the crop (grains) in the field which commands the price premium for the crop. e.g., wheat.
2. Build the concept of traceability into the supply chain which will allow to address the food safely concerns, e.g., for perishables such as shrimps, which decays quickly within short period of time, it need to define standards of production and product quality.
3. Provide the service as marketplace for commodities where ITC is not a sole buyer. It will reduce the operational cost of e-Choupal such as IT infrastructure and transaction costs, e.g., coffee grains.
4. Marketing value added products and services to rural India , in addition to marketing agri inputs, though e-Choupal system.
5. Source IT-enabled services from rural India. Telemedicine, ecotourism, traditional medicine and traditional crafts are some of the service that can be sourced from rural INDIA.

Conclusion

ITC e-Choupal, an innovative strategy which is elaborative and extensive in rural markets so far. Critical factors in the apparent success of the venture are ITCs extensive knowledge of agriculture, the effort ITC has made to retain many aspects of the existing production system, including retaining the integral importance of local partners, the company's commitment to transparency, and the respect and fairness with which both farmers and local partners are treated.

CASE STUDY- 3 : WAL-MART

Wal-Mart training programmes teach new (and existing) personnel how best to perform their jobs or how to improve themselves. Training can range from one-day sessions on operating a computerized cash register, personal selling techniques, or compliance with affirmative action programs to two-year programs for executive trainees on all aspects of the retailer and its operations:

- A Wal-Mart (www.walmart.com) assistant store manager trainee gets 20 weeks of instruction in merchandising, people development, and operations. Part of the training is computerized and part is with a management sponsor. After completing the program, the trainee becomes an assistant store manager and oversees a section of a store, known as a "store-within-a-store" – with fiscal, merchandising, and human resource responsibility for it.
- Sears University (www.sears.com) offers retail education courses plus self-study options. Annually, several thousand managers enroll in hands-on programs ranging from one day to one week. Some programs involve buying, merchandising, and human resource management. Others involve strategic leadership. Courses are taught by seasoned managers, training and development experts, and university faculty consultants.

CASE STUDY- 4: CUSTOMER PSYCHOLOGY

Economic, H1N1 Worries will Impact Holiday Shopping Behaviour

The H1N1 flu virus is expected to impact retail sales on Black Friday and throughout thanksgiving weekend, but perhaps the bigger concern for retailers is that most consumers likely will spend less money this holiday shopping season.

According to the most recent Morpace Omnibus study, nearly half of all consumers are expecting to spend less money during this holiday shopping season than they did last year. Forty-six per cent of all respondents anticipated spending less on gifts than they did 12 months ago. Those groups who are even more likely to spend less include women (50 per cent), consumers aged 35-54 (53 per cent), and individuals earning less than $ 50,000 per year (52 per cent).

Just 5 per cent of all respondents indicated that are expecting to spend more this holiday shopping season than in 2008.

These results suggest that retailers should consider ways to specifically attract consumers to their stores and websites, said Morpace vice-president of retail services Kirsten Denyes.

"Retailers may be competing for a smaller piece of the holiday spending pie", Denyes said. "It will be more important than ever for retailers to draw the attention of consumers once they walk in a store or logon to their website because the competition will be extremely fierce for disposable income."

During this highly competitive holiday shopping season consumers may respond favourably to promotions focusing on value and the practical utility of the items being marketed, Denyes said. This is a difficult environment for products that appear to be frivolous and/or expensive, she added.

The H1N1 flu virus remains a concern for retailers as well given that women and individuals aged 55 and over are more likely than other consumers to avoid retail stores during busy days like Black Friday, according to the Morpace Omnibus Study.

Overall 15 per cent of all respondents said that they will avoid busy holiday shopping days and large crowds because of the flu virus. Additionally, 19 per cent of all women and 26 per cent of respondents aged 55 and over plan to avoid the busiest shopping days such as Black Friday.

"These results are very consistent with what we saw from respondents who answered a similar question about H1N1 last month", said Morpace vice-president of retail services Tom McGoldrick. "The main trend we see is that the economy and H1N1 could both adversely impact retail sales this holiday season".

CASE STUDY- 5: " MILKMAN OF INDIA " IS NO MORE

Verghese Kurien, father of "White Revolution" and founder of the cooperative dairy movement in India, died at the age of 90 in a hospital at Nadiad early on Sunday the 9th September 2012. He made Anand, the small town in central Gujarat as "the milk capital of India." Born in Kozhikode, Kerala, on November 26, 1921, Dr. Kurien, a mechanical engineer with dairy engineering as a minor subject, came to Anand in 1949 at the behest of the then Union Home Minister, Sardar Vallabhbhai Patel, to solve some problems of the local farmers. The problems were resolved, but he could not leave Anand. From one milk project to a larger one, Mr.Kurien saw India emerge from a milk-deficient country into the largest milk producer in the world, overtaking even the once milk-abundant Netherlands. It is because of Dr. Kurien that India today contributes about 17 per cent of the total milk production in the world. Amul, with a turnover of over ₹ 13,000 crore, is Asia's top milk producing brand and is counted, with one of the best recall values, among the world's leading brands in any sector. He transformed a small-scale household activity into the world's largest milk producing enterprise. First, soon after his return from Michigan State University, he rightly concentrated on the processing, pricing and marketing aspects of milk production. He knew that if dairying became profitable, farm women and men would automatically care for the animals and look after breeding and nutrition. He also knew that in our country, only a decentralised production of milk, done by women, supported by key centralised services in the fields of animal nutrition, health care and processing would help to ensure both the income security of rural families and the production of the necessary quantities of milk for the country. He developed a 'one stop' method of meeting the needs of over 75 million women engaged in milk production. Thus, the Amul cooperative units not only purchased milk but also provided breeding health care and nutrition support for the animals, to the great benefit of the milk suppliers. He introduced Amul Products and milk products for babies.

Table 35 : Honours, Awards and International Recognition for "MILKMAN OF INDIA"

Year	Name of Award or Honor	Awarding Organization
1999	Padma Vibhushan	Government of India
1993	International Person of the Year Award	World Dairy Expo
1989	World Food Prize	World Food Prize, USA
1986	Wateler Peace Prize Award	Carnegie Foundation, The Netherlands
1986	Krushi Ratna Award	Government of India
1966	Padma Bhushan	Government of India.
1965	Padma Shri	Government of India.
1963	Ramon Magsaysay Award	Ramon Magsaysay Award Foundation

REFERENCES

1. Arussy, Lior (2005). "Understanding the Fatal Mistakes". *Passionate and Profitable: Why Customer Strategies Fail and 10 Steps to Do Them Right*. John Wiley & Sons, Inc., p. 151.
2. Paul H. Selden (April/May 1996). "SFA Myths Abound". *Sales and Marketing Strategies and News* **6** (3): pp. 51 and 53.
3. Paul H. Selden (November 2000). "The Power of Quality Thinking in Sales and Management". *Quality Progress*: pp. 58-64.
4. Strativity Group (2009), 2009 Global Customer Experience Management Benchmark Study, Strativity Group, Inc., http://strativity.com/products/2009-Experience-Management-Benchmark-Study.aspx.
5. Edwards, John (2007-11-29). "Get It Together with Collaborative CRM". *insideCRM*. Tippit. http://www.insidecrm.com/features/collaborative-crm-112907/. Retrieved 2008-02-01.
6. Bligh, Philip; Douglas Turk (2004). *CRM unplugged – releasing CRM's strategic value*. Hoboken: John Wiley & Sons. ISBN 0-471-48304-4.
7. Paul H. Selden (1997). *Sales Process Engineering: A Personal Workshop*. Milwaukee, WI: ASQ Quality Press. p. 23.
8. Gartner, Inc. (2008-09-12). "Gartner Says Worldwide Customer Relationship Management Market Grew 23 Per cent in 2007". Press release. http://www.gartner.com/it/page.jsp?id=715308. Retrieved 2008-08-15.
9. Gartner, Inc. (2009-06-15). http://www.gartner.com/it/page.jsp?id=1074615. Retrieved 2009-10-27.
10. *Urban Geography: A Global Perspective* Michael Pacione, (Routledge, Informa UK Ltd. 2001) ISBN 9780415191951.
11. "The Arcade, Providence RI". Brightridge.com. http://www.brightridge.com/pages/arcade.html. Retrieved 2009-07-17.
12. "Shoppers Throng to Opening of Bergen Mall in Jersey". *New York Times*. November 15, 1957 http://select.nytimes.com/gst abstract.html?res=F00B12FC355A177B93C7A8178AD95F438585F9. Retrieved 2007-06-07. "Paramus, New Jersey, November 14, 1957. The $ 40,000,000 Bergen Mall Regional Shopping Centre opened here this morning."
13. "10 Shopping Centres Scheduled for Allied Stores Within 3 Years; Chain's Chairman Gives Details of Biggest, 7 Miles From George Washington Span, Where Stern Will Open Branch by '57: Store Chain Plans Retail Centres", *The New York Times*, January 13, 1955. p. 37.
14. "The Super Centres". *Time (magazine)*. January 24, 1955. http://www.time.com/time/magazine/article/0,9171,861189,00.html. Retrieved 2008-06-25. Eastern Connecticut State University (January 2007). "World's Largest Shopping Malls". http://www.easternct.edu/depts/amerst/MallsWorld.htm. Retrieved 2008-07-29.
15. International Council of Shopping Centres Shopping Centre Definitions: information Accurate as of 1999.
16. Tony O'Donahue, *The Tale of a City: Re-engineering the Urban Environment* (Toronto: Dundurn Press Ltd., 2005), p. 43.

17. Bernard J. Frieden and Lynne B. Sagalyn, Downtown, Inc.: *How America Rebuilds Cities* (Cambridge, MA: MIT Press, 1989), p. 233.

18. Judd, Dennis R. (1995) "The Rise of the New Walled Cities" in Liggett, Helen and Perr, David C. (eds.), *Spatial Practices*, Sage, Thousand Oaks, pp. 144-168.

19. Carlyn, Marcia. "An Assessment of the Myers-Briggs Type Indicator.", *Journal of Personality Assessment,* 41.5 (1977): pp. 461-73.

20. Cheng, Many M., Peter F. Luckett, and Axel K. Schulz. "The Effects of Cognitive Style Diversity on Decision Making Dyads: An Empirical Analysis in the Context of a Complex Task." *Behavioural Research in Accounting*. 15 (2003): pp. 39-62.

21. Gardner, William L., and Mark J. Martinko. "Using the Myers-Briggs Type Indicator to Study Managers: A Literature Review and Research Agenda." *Journal of Management.* 22.1 (1996): pp. 45-83.

22. Henderson, John C., and Paul C. Nutt. "Influence of Decision Style on Decision Making Behaviour." *Management Science*. 26.4 (1980): pp. 371-386.

23. Kennedy, Bryan R., and Ashley D. Kennedy. "Using the Myers-Briggs Type Indicator in Career Counselling." *Journal of Employment Counselling*. 41.1 (2004): pp. 38-44.

24. Myers, I. (1962) Introduction to Type: A description of the theory and applications of the Myers-Briggs Type Indicator, *Consulting Psychologists Press*, Palo Alto Ca., 1962.

25. Nicosia, F. (1966) *Consumer Decision Processes*, Prentice-Hall, Englewood Cliffs, 1966.

26. Simon, H. (1947) *Administrative Behaviour*, Macmillan, New York, 1947, (also 2nd edition 1957).

27. Volkema, Roger J., and Ronald H. Gorman. "The Influence of Cognitive-Based Group Composition on Decision-Making Process and Outcome". *Journal of Management Studies*. 35.1 (1998): pp. 105-121.

28. Rigby, Darrell K.; Frederick F. Reichheld, Phil Schefter (2002). "Avoid the Four Perils of CRM". *Harvard Business Review* 80 (2): 101–109. doi:10.1225/8946.

29. *Urban Geography: A Global Perspective* Michael Pacione, (Routledge, Informa UK Ltd. 2001) ISBN 9780415191951.

30. *The New York Times,* January 13, 1955. p. 37.

31. "The Super Centers". *Time* (magazine). January 24, 1955.

32. Danny Chung, Reach for the sky, *The Standard*, December 09, 2005.

33. An Annotated Bibliography, Communications of AIS, 7(8) pp. 2-54.

34. "Retail reality." *The Economist*, 7 November, 2007.

35. "ICRIER Begins Survey of Indian Retail Sector." 19 March, 2007.

36. "Retailing in India Unshackling the chain stores". *The Economist*. 2008. "India again tops global retail index." 22 June, 2007.

37. "Economic and financial indicators" 3 July, 2008.

38. *I Too Had A Dream*, co-authored with Gouri Salvi, ISBN-13: 978-8174364074.

39. *The Hindu* dated 27th September, 2012, Madurai Edition.

40. *The Hindu* dated 28th September, 2012, Madurai Edition

SUBJECT INDEX